"To Be a Christian
is To Be a Revolutionary"
—PADRE J. GUADALUPE CARNEY

TO BE A REVOLU-TIONARY

AN AUTOBIOGRAPHY

Padre J. Guadalupe Carney

1817

Harper & Row, Publishers, San Francisco
Cambridge, Hagerstown, New York, Philadelphia
London, Mexico City, São Paulo, Singapore, Sydney

The prayer by Charles de Foucauld on page 94 appears in Carlo Caretto, *Summoned by Love*. Maryknoll, NY: Orbis Books, 1978. Reprinted by permission.

TO BE A REVOLUTIONARY. Text copyright © 1985 by Padre J. Guadalupe Carney Fund, Communication Center #1. Prologue and Epilogue copyright © 1985 by Padre J. Guadalupe Carney Fund, Communication Center #1. All rights reserved. Printed in the United States of America. No part of this book may be used or reproduced in any manner whatsoever without written permission except in the case of brief quotations embodied in critical articles and reviews. For information address Harper & Row, Publishers, Inc., 10 East 53rd Street, New York, NY 10022. Published simultaneously in Canada by Fitzhenry & Whiteside, Limited, Toronto.

FIRST EDITION

Library of Congress Cataloging in Publication Data

Carney, J. Guadalupe
  To be a revolutionary.

  Includes index.
  1. Carney, J. Guadalupe   2. Jesuits—United States—Biography.   3. Jesuits—Honduras—Biography.   4. Social reformers—Honduras—Biography.   5. Honduras—Social conditions.   6. Honduras—Economic conditions—1918–
  I. Connolly, Joseph.   II. Connolly, Eileen.   III. Title.
  BX4705.C3144A37   1985   271′.53′024 [B]   84-42844
  ISBN 0-06-061319-X

85 86 87 88 89   HC   10 9 8 7 6 5 4 3 2 1

This book is dedicated to the
poor people of the world

The spirit of the Lord has been given to me,
    for he has anointed me.
He has sent me to bring the good news to the poor,
    to proclaim liberty to captives
    and to the blind new sight,
    to set the downtrodden free,
    to proclaim the Lord's year of favour.

                    —LUKE 4:18–19

I love the poor of Honduras, especially the campesino.
    I want to live their life as fully as possible.

                    —PADRE GUADALUPE CARNEY

Contents

Prologue

He showed up at the airport the same way he did every three years—in a short-sleeved cotton shirt, khaki work pants, black work shoes with white socks, and a small nine-by-fifteen-inch canvas suitcase that contained all his possessions. He had his usual smile, a strong embrace, and thanks for meeting him. (He did not take kindness for granted, even from his family.) He never had an ounce of extra weight on his browned six-foot frame.

"Why did they throw you out?" was my first remark. (A brother-in-law can be blunt.)

"You're lucky to be alive!" was Eileen's, as she hugged her brother.

Jim's first words were, "I've got to get back to Honduras!"

This was Father Jim Carney, S.J., as he arrived in Saint Louis on November 21, 1979, after having been tracked down by the Honduran military and intelligence, and, left unprotected by the U.S. embassy, locked up—first in jail, and then, handcuffed, inside an airport broom closet—and finally shipped involuntarily out of Honduras and away from the *campesinos,* the poor peasants, whom he had loved and served for twenty years. His battle for land and human rights for the landless, rights-less campesinos could no longer be tolerated by the rich, the powerful, the "haves."

As always, Jim did not stay long in Saint Louis. He was just "touching base" with his Carney and Jesuit families. His home was now Honduras; his family, the Honduran campesinos. Before the end of the year he was as close to Honduras as he could get, working in the little villages of Nicaragua along the Honduran border.

For three years (1980–83) he walked the borders, serving Nicaraguan campesinos struggling to better their lives after fifty years of slavery under the fascist dictator Somoza. He comforted Nicaraguan families whose sons, daughters, and spouses had been tortured and killed in the gruesome "contra" war and terrorism backed by the American CIA. He gathered together Honduran refugees, set up a Honduran information center, and planned for his return to Honduras, where the revolution of the poor had not yet taken place. And here, in a little shack a mile from the tiny, remote village of Limay, by candlelight on sleepless nights, he wrote this autobiography. His solitary, candlelight vigil was long and demanding, since Padre Lupe wrote two editions of his book: one for the peasant campesinos; one for the more literate, educated reader. He wrote each edition in both Spanish and English.

To Be a Revolutionary is the personal history of fifty-eight years in Father Jim Carney's life, 1924–1983:

- his conservative Catholic upbringing and education in the thirties;
- his soldiering across Europe and his adjustment to home and work as an ex-GI in the forties; and
- his search for God and formation as a Jesuit priest in the fifties and sixties.

To Be a Revolutionary is the story of a revolution in the soul of this man in the decades of the sixties, seventies, and eighties. During these decades as an American Catholic priest he fell in love with the poor people of Honduras and decided to do something about their poverty. The poor people he served were Hondurans but could have been Haitians, Salvadorans, or Guatemalans or Africans, Indians, Asians, or poor white North Americans. This is the story of how his love for the poor campesino transformed a priest into a revolutionary.

To Be a Revolutionary is the history, odyssey, chronicle, of how this priest awakened a revolution in the souls of these landless campesinos in a tiny third world "banana republic" so that they began to see again, feel again, judge again, act again, and become human beings again after centuries of poverty and oppression. It is the story of how he fought for peasants against their exploitation by big business, big labor, big government, and big landowners. Jim was a brother to the campesinos in this "revolution of the poor."

To Be a Revolutionary is, finally, a call to revolution in you the reader—in your thinking, in your feeling, in your life. You might feel uneasy with the challenge to become a revolutionary. Even the words *revolution* and *revolutionary* sound subversive to many people. This uneasiness with revolutionary change is a commentary on our memory as a people; we are, after all, a country born out of the courage of citizens who joined a revolutionary movement fighting a "legitimate" government in a revolutionary war.

Before concluding this prologue, it is important for us to say explicitly that this autobiography is solely and only the product of Father Jim Carney and that we do not necessarily agree with all of his conclusions. We do admit that his life and words have caused us to deeply rethink some of our own personal and national priorities and we appreciate the courage and commitment it took for him to speak as he did. He has more than earned the right to address the peoples of North, South and Central America. We hope you will give him a fair hearing and we offer three suggestions that have helped us better understand this Christian Revolutionary.

First, keep in mind the stark reality of the third world poor as you read this book. Living comfortably here in North America, most of us do not feel the agonizing hunger or paralyzing fear felt by the poor in the third world. In "living the good life" we seldom question the benefits or morality of our capitalistic system, our free enterprise, the U.S. military, political, and economic domination of the third world. But Father Jim Carney bluntly questions his fellow Americans, on behalf of the poor of the third world:

- Do we North Americans eat well because the poor in the third world do not eat at all?
- Are we North Americans powerful, because we help keep the poor in the third world weak?
- Are we North Americans free, because we help keep the poor in the third world oppressed?

It will be impossible to understand the full significance of these questions or to understand Father Jim Carney, the revolutionary, without trying to see the world as he did, through the eyes of the third world poor.

Our second suggestion is to keep in mind that Father Jim

Carney took the Gospel seriously and decided to live it. Thus, his life is a clear, radical challenge to the human conscience. The problem is that we humans have a history of killing our prophets rather than listening to them and reforming our lives.

Our third suggestion for helping you understand this revolutionary is to ask you to keep in mind that the perfect human society of brotherhood and sisterhood of which Father Jim Carney dreamed and for which he worked, and that is described in this book, certainly goes beyond the capitalist and communist systems of government that the human family has so far developed. Time alone will judge how real and how practical his vision was.

When Jim finished writing, he did a simple thing, as he often did. He simply phoned Saint Louis and asked if Eileen and I could come down to Nicaragua and pick up his manuscripts. He knew his time was at hand, his days numbered, for he would soon be returning to Honduras, where he was liable to be killed.

We went to see Jim for the last time. He gave us his manuscripts and told us to use the profits from his books for the Honduran poor. A few months later, Jim slipped across the Honduran border, and disappeared. The epilogue will tell of the search for his body and his fate. But this book is about his life. It is a privilege to share it with you.

In conclusion, we want to acknowledge some of the people who have made this book possible. First of all, we want to thank Jim's sisters, Virginia Carney Smith and Maureen Carney, and Jim's brother, John Patrick Carney, who have worked with us almost daily for two years to uncover the facts regarding Jim's disappearance.

We want to thank the thousands of individuals and hundreds of organizations throughout the world who have offered prayers and help in searching for this missing priest, and encouraged the publication of his autobiography.

Our special love and affection go to Jim's many friends in Honduras who helped us search for the truth at risk to their own lives. As one example of this courage, during our visit to Honduras, a small, fragile, elderly nun, who had seen rape and torture first-hand, whispered to us her commitment to seeking the truth. "As long as you are breathing," she said, "you cannot be passive."

We would like to thank various individuals who reviewed the manuscript. Many times they (and we) wished we could consult the author for clarification regarding the text but this was impossible.

A very special debt of thanks is due to Clayton Carlson, John Loudon, Richard Lucas, Tom Dorsaneo, and various staff people at Harper & Row. Their personal warmth, enthusiasm for the book, and practical help and advice were indispensable.

Lastly, we would like to thank Audra Browne for her many hours of typing and dedicated service in the publication of this book.

JOSEPH AND EILEEN CONNOLLY
Family members of Padre Guadalupe

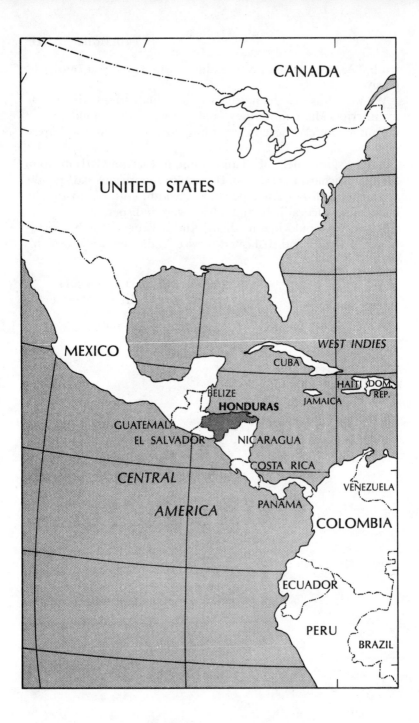

CANADA

UNITED STATES

MEXICO

WEST INDIES

CUBA

BELIZE

HONDURAS

HAITI DOM.
REP.

JAMAICA

GUATEMALA

EL SALVADOR

NICARAGUA

COSTA RICA

CENTRAL

VENEZUELA

AMERICA

PANAMA

COLOMBIA

ECUADOR

PERU

BRAZIL

An Open Letter

In 1971, at almost the midway mark of his twenty years of struggle for the poor in Central America, Padre Guadalupe visited his family and friends in the United States. Upon returning to his parish among the poor Indian tribes of the Honduran mountains, he wrote the following letter explaining himself, "a strange fellow," to his American friends. This letter is placed at the beginning of this book knowing that only the autobiography itself can fully explain this remarkable, saintly human being to the American public.

My dear American friends, Jesuits and non-Jesuits:

I love all of you, and I think you're wonderful loving persons, but I can't stand living with any of you. I was raised like all of you, as a middle-class, Catholic white American. But right from high school age on, I've had a deep conviction that most middle-class Catholics are phony Christians, just as materialistic and self-seeking, and as liable to go along with others, as any non-Christian, and often more so. But immediately I soften my judgment of my peers by saying that it isn't really your fault, and, all in all, you are probably much holier than I am. By holy I mean sincerely loving God and your neighbor, sincerely following your own conscience and convictions. For my greatest suffering and only unhappiness in life is that I often don't really and sincerely live up to my conscience and convictions. But I've been trying. When I got away from home and on my own in the Army, I began my life of a nonconformist, trying to follow my convictions and the heck with what others think or do. I was always in trouble in the Army and later in the Society of Jesus for being a nonconformist, and worst of all, I never could really be "one of the boys" and be everyone's friend. I was and still am always rebelling. I'm still rebelling in Honduras against many things, but I've found my vocation and my happiness. I have a deep peace of soul that I think no trouble or sickness could take from me. I have God in my soul! Even though I have no exterior peace, because I'm a rebel.

I'm really a lover, even though I often don't act like it. I love people, all kinds of people. Also I'm a contemplative. My greatest joy is to contemplate what God's loving Providence does in this world, especially in people I meet or read about and in my own life. I think I sincerely love the poor, not only out of pity for what they are forced to suffer and out of rebellion against the system that forces them to be poor, but as lovable persons in themselves, as bits of God, of Christ. With Charles de Foucauld, I say that I don't know about others, but as for me, I can't conceive of true love that doesn't want to share the life of the beloved. To love Christ really is to try to live as he lived. If I love the poor as Christ did, I, too, freely choose to become one with them, live with them, share their lives, besides trying to use my talents to help and teach them. To live as bourgeois, comfortable, well-dressed white people, and then try to help the poor is okay, I guess, but it's not my kind of love, and it's not what Christ did. He freely chose to become one of the masses of poor people of the world, of the eighty percent of the world who "have not," rejecting the comfortable life of the twenty percent who "have" (even though he loved them too). And he tore into the system and those that held the masses in the bondage of ignorance and poverty. He cursed them, and said, "Woe to you hypocrites, you priests, and to you rich, and to you who are honored and accepted by the world." And he was killed for it. To be killed for my following of Christ would be my greatest joy too.

I love Christ and the poor so much that I have to be celibate. I could never do the traveling missionary work and the social apostolate work, with its risks, if I had to worry about a wife and kids. It would also be very hard to be a nonconformist, which I feel I have to be to call myself a Christian. I probably could never find a woman who would share the kind of life I *have* to lead in order to be true to myself, nor have I yet found a man, not even among the Jesuits, who shares my ideas fully, and who wants to share my kind of life with me. But I am never really lonely; Christ and people are enough for me, and if I were ever laid out in a prison or a hospital with no chance for activity, Christ-God would be enough for me. With my life integrated like this, I feel so completely free. Little by little I'm freeing myself of all kinds of slavery or bondage. With all this, I'm one happy priest.

But besides this great driving force of love that has led me to Sulaco in Honduras, I have to recognize in myself two other great driving forces. One is a kind of pride that makes me want to signalize myself in the service of my King, to seek adventure and never rest in the fight. This driving force can be good if I can keep it under the helm of love and work at being humble. The other great driving force in my life is hate. I hate injustice, and I hate hypocrisy. I hate doing something, or dressing, or acting, or talking in any way just because most other people do it that way. I hate the bourgeois, American way of life, keeping up with the Joneses, the sophisticated, cocktail party, Playboy Club, comfort-seeking "Great Society." I hate the way blacks, Indians, dark-skinned foreigners are treated and kept marginated. I hate the way the United States tries to control all the countries of the world, and world trade, for its own benefit, trying to export our materialistic way of life to other countries. I hate and resent the way the rich and middle-class Americans *and* Hondurans can live in big, comfortable houses, have cars, land, and education, while my brothers and sisters, the poor, are forced to live as they do. I've seen too much of poverty starting from my days in France in the army when the poor refugees came to beg for our mess-hall garbage. I don't hate the "haves," but I hate the system that not only allows but forces society to be made up of the "haves" and the "have-nots." I hate injustice and hypocrisy and materialism. This hatred, as I said, is a driving force in my life that *makes* me do many things that I do, like go live in another country, by myself, risk my life, be looked down upon, misunderstood, considered kind of crazy. But what can I do? I feel moved by the Holy Spirit in all the important decisions I make. I have to follow Him. And I'm happy, very happy with my life, with life in general. I love the world and love to watch its evolution toward Christ. I want to participate in this evolution. For me the closest following of Christ, or the evangelical counsels, are poverty, chastity and nonviolence. For me, bourgeois living is at best halfway Christianity. After what I've seen of worldwide reality, I have to rebel against that.

I have to write this because my last visit to you all in the States xviii / TO BE A REVOLUTIONARY

has again made me rethink and embrace my vocation with more gusto, and I always leave with the idea that you all must think I'm a strange fellow, so I wanted to explain myself a little to you, since we are close friends. I'm sorry if this hurts you, but I hope you can now understand a little better why I say I love you all very much and it's nice to visit you, but I can't stand living with you in your way of life.

Love, in Christ,

Jim

FATHER JIM CARNEY, S.J.

INTRODUCTION

If I am going to write about some of my memories, it will be in order to make known the wonderful ways of God's mercy, working to form one of his servants into an instrument for the liberation of the oppressed in Central America and for the formation of his Kingdom in this world. Who would imagine that a middle-class, bourgeois North American could become a Honduran revolutionary fighting for human rights and against exploitation as one of the advisers and leaders of the masses of Honduran peasants (campesinos) and workers? Only as a miracle of the grace of the Holy Spirit who works within all of us can this phenomenon be explained. Surely each one of you who reads these memories of mine could relate the wonderful work of the Holy Spirit in your own soul.

I am convinced that it is by means of the Spirit of Jesus working in the souls of all men and women that God, little by little, moves the universe in its dialectical evolution toward his Kingdom, that is, toward "the new heaven and the new earth," the new universe transformed, where all good men and women of all times are going to rise from the dead to live with God in a paradise, the Kingdom of God, a society of perfect brotherhood and sisterhood and equality, a classless society.

When we say that this evolution that is directed by the Spirit of Jesus is dialectical, that means that it is conflictive, that it advances toward the truth by means of a series of struggles between people of contradictory ideologies. Many times there are steps backward in the history of humanity, but analyzing the march of history as a whole, from the beginning, we can notice a definite advancment toward greater humanization of society and control of the universe by human beings. It is obvious that there has to be an Intelligence with a plan for the universe behind all this. There exists a personal God, intelligent and loving, who handed this universe over to men and women, gifted with intelligence and freedom, and he is continually "inspiring" all human beings, from within, to fight for truth, justice, liberty, equality—for, in one word, brotherhood, for all men and women. The contemplation of this action of the Spirit of Jesus in myself and in other human beings is the great joy of my life. I am a contemplative. Carrying out these inspirations of the Spirit of Jesus that are moving me to participate in the revolutionary struggle to advance his Kingdom of love in this world is my whole aim in life. Thus I am a "contemplative in action." I am a disciple of Saint Ignatius of Loyola.

I get angry when I read the documents of the popes and Catholic bishops. Eighty percent of the adults in the world have not finished grade school; yet the bishops write their teachings in language only a university graduate could understand. That is why I am going to try to write these pages of my memories in simple, conversational language, directing them especially to my thousands of Latin American *campesino* (peasant) friends. Still, I do not exclude the possibility that some members of the middle and upper classes might also read this book and re-examine their own ideologies.

The new society has to include all people. Therefore, the revolution to transform this world into the "brotherhood and sisterhoood of all humanity" has to be a double revolution: the economic-social-political revolution of society, and the cultural-spiritual revolution to change the selfish mentality of each person. Even as the Spirit of Jesus has transformed me into a revolutionary through a process that I call a metamorphosis, I hope that these pages will serve the Spirit of Jesus as an instrument in the metamorphosis of other revolutionaries.*

Metamorphosis is what scientists call the transformation of some animals at different stages of their life from one kind of an animal to another. The example I am thinking of when I speak of my metamorphosis is that of a beautiful butterfly, which passes the first half of its life as a worm. All butterflies are born from eggs as ugly worms, and they develop into full grown caterpillars. Then they wrap themselves into a cocoon and remain immobile, for a long time, as if asleep, while their metamorphosis

---

*Padre Guadalupe entitled his manuscript *The Metamorphosis of a Revolutionary.* This theme of metamorphosis is developed throughout the book.

takes place: their transformation into a butterfly, developing wings with lovely colors. At last they are reborn, breaking out of the cocoon that has held them imprisoned, and they take off flying for a new life with complete liberty and great splendor of colors, which gives delight to all who observe them.

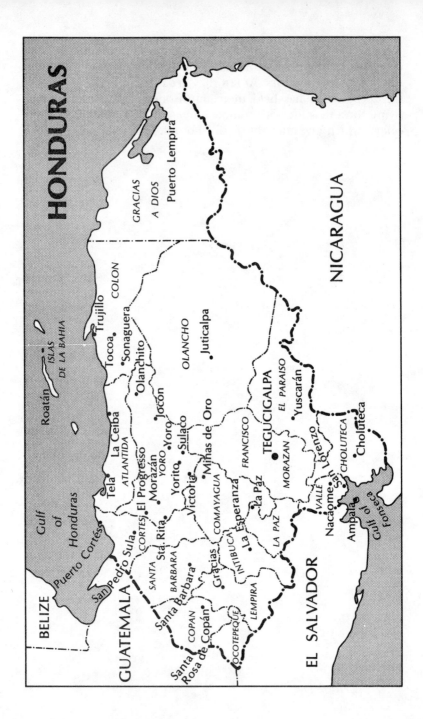

PART I. MY FORMATION AS A NORTH AMERICAN

1. Growing up: 1924–1942

I was born in Chicago, Illinois, then the second largest city in the United States, on October 28, 1924. My parents were very good Catholics, both from Milwaukee, Wisconsin. Both had immigrant grandparents; their grandmothers (my great grandmothers) had come from Germany and their grandfathers (my great grandfathers) from Ireland. My mother, Catherine Hanley, was a graduate of the School of Music of Marquette University in Milwaukee and was the star soloist of the musical opera company of that city when she fell in love with my father, Joseph Carney, who sang in the chorus.

After my father joined the army during the First World War, he got a furlough from Fort Custer, Michigan, in order to marry Catherine in Milwaukee. After the war, Joseph returned to work as a salesman for Burroughs Adding Machine Company, where he had worked before the war. He worked for this same company for forty-three years, until his death. He never realized that he was practically owned by this company. His company sent him to a number of different cities in the Midwest, which was the reason we children had to break with our friends every three or four years to move with our family to another city.

We are seven brothers and sisters, all still alive. My older sister Virginia and her husband, Ken Smith, a professor of aeronautical engineering at the University of Detroit, have twelve children. My other older sister lives in Ohio and has four children. I was the third child, and after me came my only brother, John Patrick, a year and a half later. You can imagine the very close friendship Pat and I developed! Pat lives in Minneapolis now, is happily married and the father of three children. I miss him, but we keep in touch regularly.

I have three younger sisters. Eileen lives in Saint Louis. She and her husband, Joe Connolly, have doctorates in psychology and travel throughout the United States giving skill development workshops for religious and community leaders. My youngest sister, Maureen, is also a psychologist and lives in Los Angeles. My other sister has five children and lives in Massachusetts.

As I said, I was born in Chicago, where the family lived on the northwest side of the city. I was baptized James Francis, and was always called Jim. The only incident I recall from the first six years of my life is a little friend, Bobby Applebaum, teaching me how to tie my shoes.

From my sixth until my thirteenth year we lived in Dayton, Ohio. I spent seven years in the parish grade school run by very strict nuns. I do recall a few things about this period of my development. I remember that every evening, right after supper, the whole family had to kneel down around the table to pray the rosary, led by my father. We also had to finish and show to our father our homework for school the next day. Only then could any of us go outside to play, until eight or nine at night.

After my First Holy Communion, when I was eight years old, I enjoyed walking to the parish church with my father every morning at 6:00 A.M. for mass and communion. Afterward we would eat breakfast, and then my father would leave for his office in his car. I was also a server at mass from the time I was eight years old.

I was a great sports fan. As soon as I could walk, I started to play baseball, basketball, and football. I had a lot of talent for sports and played on all the school teams. It seemed as though sports were the biggest interest of nearly all the boys, and every minute of my free time and every school vacation were spent practicing. I also learned to be pretty good at swimming, boxing, wrestling, tennis, golf, ping-pong, volleyball, and track.

Since my father was the oldest of thirteen children and from childhood had had to work to help his family, he knew a bit of everything, carpentry, plumbing, electrical work, and so on. Thus he taught his sons to enjoy doing all the jobs around the house, like cleaning, painting, and repairing the house and the car. I am grateful to him for the fine training he gave us. To this day I enjoy and prefer to do such things as wash my own clothes, fix things in the house, cut the grass with a machete knife the way Latin American peasants do, and chop wood.

We never had a servant or any household help at home,

though, after the end of the Great Depression of 1929, we enjoyed a middle-class standard of living. North Americans, in general, have this good quality of enjoying manual labor, even though they may be rich. Of course, the very rich do have servants to do all these tasks.

Along this same line, our father encouraged us to get jobs in order to earn a few dollars in the afternoons after school, on weekends, and during school vacations. At the age of nine I was a newspaper boy for the *Dayton Daily News,* which I distributed every afternoon to the houses in our neighborhood that had subscriptions. I had about forty regular customers who paid me on Saturdays.

For five years I had this paper route. With my earnings I bought my first bicycle, and also balls, gloves, and other sports equipment that I wanted, besides paying for all my own books and other school material and all my own clothes. Since my father played a lot of golf, he helped me get a job as a caddy at his golf club during school vacation in the summers. My sisters also got small jobs, like baby-sitting for the neighbors, to earn enough for their clothes.

Americans learn from their childhood how to be good, efficient, docile, obedient employees or workers. It becomes very natural for them to enter into the capitalist system of competition and of seeking personal gain, because in school and in sports children learn to compete with each other to see who wins the prize or the highest marks. Those who win are praised and honored, and those who lose or lag behind are often looked down on. This prepares them for competing later on in the economic world of capitalism. It is very deep and penetrating teaching of individualism and selfishness. It is also a subtle teaching of violence, to live according to the law of the strongest. Instead of teaching children to share things with others, to seek equality and brotherhood, to serve the community (which are Christian ideals), they are taught to seek their own advancement, their own development and betterment. Sad to say, Catholic grade schools, high schools and universities participate in this type of education.

My inseparable friend during these years that we lived in Dayton was Jack Early who was a year older than I. At this moment there comes to mind the memory of his teaching me how to fish in the Miami River, which passes through Dayton. You can imagine how very hard it was for me and for my brother and sisters to separate ourselves from our friends in Dayton when the Burroughs Adding Machine Company transferred my father to Toledo, Ohio, in 1937.

At the time of the move, I only needed one more year to graduate from grade school. It was especially hard for me to leave the sports teams, because this last year in grade school would have been my best year in sports. To go to a new school in a new town, to start from scratch making friends among the eighth-graders, who had already formed their close friendship ties with classmates of the last seven years, to try to win a place on the sports teams already formed—all this caused in me feelings of resentment against my parents.

But nothing could be done about it, and we all moved to Toledo, which in those days was slightly larger than Dayton, about 300,000 inhabitants. Within a few months I was quite happy with my new parish school (of the Cathedral in Toledo), with my new teachers (nuns), with my new friends. Right away I made the different teams of the interschool sports competition, got a job selling *The Toledo Blade,* bought a new bike, and, as I recall, even had my first crush—on a classmate named Dorothy.

After I graduated from grade school, my parents enrolled me at Central Catholic High School, where my older sister was studying. This was a marvelous new world for me. I remember that the nuns who ran this diocesan high school were very friendly and understood young people. Once, when I did something wrong (I do not remember what it was), my teacher instead of punishing me, began to cry (because I was her favorite), and I could not help crying also, even though I was very ashamed to do so in front of all my classmates. This was a coeducational school, with boys and girls together in all the classes except religion.

I used to ride to Central High every day on my bike, taking a big sack of sandwiches for lunch, and always stayed after school to practice with the different high school teams. From my second year, I was on the first team in football, basketball, baseball, track, and tennis. Our teams played in well-organized leagues with all the other high schools in town, and each high school had its stadium and gymnasium. Football was, and still is, the most important sport, with the most ferocious competition among the high schools and universities of the United States, and it has always been my favorite sport.

I remember Russell, the fellow who lived next door to us in Toledo and attended the biggest public high school in town. He was the star of their football team and, thus, a big hero, not only for me, but for all the people in the city. Well, it was he who taught me how to throw and catch the football correctly. Russell played with my brother and me for hundreds of hours in the street in front of our houses.

I have often thought about the advantages and disadvantages of these sports for young people, because in the new society that we want to form in Central America we want to take advantage of whatever is good in the old society and get rid of whatever is bad. Sports are really important for the development of both boys and girls, especially team sports. Besides being good recreation, they foster friendships, help in physical development, and teach coordinated and planned teamwork, subordinating the individual's desires to those of the team.

We have to figure out how to retain these advantages while eliminating the very bad tendencies that sports often instill: the spirit or mentality of violence, of domination, of conquest or winning over the other, the spirit of standing out, of seeking honors and glory, of pride, of selfishness, and the danger of making sports a god, a principal interest in life. Perhaps we Christian revolutionaries can contribute a bit to solving this problem in the new society.

All these disadvantages of sports that I mention had been manifested in me, especially the pride and the seeking of vain glory. I really think that sports were the false god that I most adored during my whole childhood and youth, even though, not only out of custom, but more and more from personal conviction, I continued with daily mass, communion, and family rosary, and served mass as an acolyte in the cathedral.

I was very sincere in trying to keep the sixth and ninth commandments with regard to sex and purity. During all this time in Toledo I had plenty of girlfriends and went to many dances and parties. In spite of having a lot of young friends from the sports teams who had as their false god the seeking of sexual pleasure, who adored this above all things, I could not be compromised in this area. Really palpable to me was the force for resisting temptations that daily prayer and the sacraments gave me. I had a great fear of sin, not so much out of fear of hell as fear of offending God, who so clearly loved me and helped me succeed in sports and in my studies.

Now, however, I recognize that this fear I had of offending God was out of fear of losing his help. I thought that God rewards those who carry out his commandments with success in this life, and punishes or denies his help to sinners. These are primitive ideas about God.

Now that I know better the only true God revealed in Jesus Christ, the God crucified for seeking justice and the liberation of the poor, I know that God rewards those closest to him with trials and sufferings in order to sanctify them. God is a loving Father who treats us as adult and free sons and daughters. God never punishes anyone; he does not send anyone to hell. We ourselves, with our sins, and the "situation of sin" (as it was called by the Latin American bishops at Medellín) in which we live, are the cause of the punishments we suffer: from poverty, from corruption, from war, from the exploitation of one person by another. We cannot blame God for that. If I get sick or if there is an earthquake, God is not sending these things; it is just the nature of the world that God handed over to us to dominate and control. Little by little the spirit of truth is illuminating scientists on how to control different diseases, the flooding of the rivers, and other things. We are evolving little by little toward the humanization of this world, toward human control over the universe.

The idea of asking eveything from God is very deeply ingrained in Catholics, and it is true that Christ taught us to ask our Heavenly Father, "Give us this day our daily bread." But it seems ridiculous and alienating to me to ask God to cure me when I have a cold, or a cut on my foot, or a headache, or to ask him to send rain for the crops, or give us nice weather for a picnic. I remember that the whole student body went to mass on the days of our big football games to ask God for a nice day without rain and for victory in the game. Immediately before starting a game, when we were out in the stadium, all the players would go into a huddle with the coaches to say Hail Marys, asking her to help us to win.

It was not until I was in the novitiate of the Society of Jesus that the Holy Spirit enlightened me to rebel against the custom in the novitiate of asking the Virgin Mary for a nice day without rain for our hike in the country. I thought, "The farmers are undoubtedly asking God for rain for their crops, and we Jesuits are begging him not to let it rain." I remember in high school playing against LaSalle High School; the Salesian Brothers who run it were praying three Hail Marys with all *their* players and students for a victory against *us*. Across the field, our faculty & students of Central Catholic were praying against them. And later, in 1969 in the short war between Honduras and El Salvador, there appeared in the newspapers a photo of a Salvadoran bishop blessing the pilots and their planes before they took off to bomb Honduran cities. At the same time all the people in Honduras were asking God to give them victory over the Salvadorans.

We all want God to intervene to solve our problems for us. That is what (in many cases) I call ridiculous: as if God had to choose between those he was going to favor, the Honduran Catholics or the Salvadoran Catholics, those of Central Catholic High or those of LaSalle, the farmers who need rain or the Jesuits who want to go to a picnic. That is what in every case I call alienating —expecting God to solve the problems that we ourselves should solve.

This kind of religion is what Marx called the "opium of the people." Opium is a tranquilizing drug that puts one to sleep. This "religion" teaches people that it is God who sends or takes away disease, rain, flood, war, and plagues that destroy crops, that it is the will of God for some people to be rich and others poor, for some to be owners and others their workers. This kind of religion is like opium, it tranquilizes the people, makes them conform themselves to the unjust systems of exploitation. Thus it is clear that the custom of many Catholics to ask God for everything, thinking that everything that happens comes from God or is God's will, prepares them to react to life passively, resigning themselves to unjust social class distinctions.

The Catholic church has been, and in some of the teachings of many bishops, priests, and nuns still is, alienating—that is, it makes human beings less human, less free. Instead of helping people develop themselves, it impedes them. All kinds of slavery, ignorance, vice, and superstition are alienating. They take away from people the responsibility to "dominate the earth," to use science to solve problems of sickness, of floods, and so on, and to form a society of real brothers and sisters. For example, when Guatemala suffered the terrible earthquake about ten years ago that killed thousands of poor families and children, Cardinal Casariego of Guatemala told the people in his sermons that it was God punishing them for their sins. What kind of a God is this who kills little children?

These are all ideas taken from a literal, narrow understanding of the Old Testament of three thousand years ago. These people knew nothing of modern science and explained everything mysterious to them in nature—the coming of rain, for example—as direct acts of God. (God opens a few doors of the heavenly dome covered by water so that some water can fall on the earth.) Even in the time of Christ, about two thousand years ago, everyone, including the Evangelists, called miracles or direct interventions of God whatever phenomenon they could not explain—the curing of a sick person, victory in a war, and so forth. For some examples, just read the psalms: King David is continually asking God to destroy the Egyptians, to punish his enemies—as if the Egyptians were not God's sons and daughters also! Today when Catholics ask God to cure sickness, to send rain for the crops, or to protect them against earthquakes, what they are really asking for is a miracle, an extraordinary intervention of God to change or suspend the regular course of the material nature of the world.

I do not believe that God works material miracles very often. He certainly could; and some of the events in the life of Jesus, like the Resurrection, without a doubt were miraculous suspensions of the laws of physical nature to show us that God indeed rules the universe. But *I do believe that God continually intervenes directly in history in human souls, spiritually, by means of what we call his actual grace.* The Spirit of God that all of us—Catholics, Buddhists, or even atheists—have in our souls, is continually trying to illuminate our minds and move our free decisions toward the Truth and toward love. That is the way the Spirit of Jesus is moving the evolution of the world and its history toward the formation of his Kingdom, the society of perfect brotherhood and sisterhood.

Well, then, instead of asking God for material miracles to solve our material problems, we should carry out this Spanish refrain: *"a Dios regando con el maza dando"* ("asking God for it, but with the hammer doing it"). Or we should follow the advice of Saint Ignatius of Loyola: "asking God as if everything depended on him, but doing it myself as if everything depended on me." What we definitely should ask God for is his spiritual help to understand things and the courage to act as we should.

If I was upset when our family had to move from Dayton to Toledo, leaving my friends and teams in my last year of grade school, you can imagine how I felt when, just as I was finishing my third year of high school, the same thing happened! Burroughs transferred our father to their office in Saint Louis, Missouri. I only needed one more year to graduate from Central Catholic High School. I was even more involved in Toledo than I had been in Dayton with my friends, my special girlfriend, and with the big interschool sports leagues. I was in rebellion; I did not want to go with the family. I looked for alternative ways to stay at least one more year to finish high school in Toledo.

The coaches of our school teams talked with my parents. They had found me a good place to live and a job during vacation so that I could be economically independent of my family. But it was all in vain! My father insisted that I could not separate myself from the family. I did not want to disobey him; I loved my parents too much.

It was in 1941, during school vacation in June, that I had to say good-bye to everything that was most important to me in life, to go and start all over again looking for friends and trying out for a place on new ball teams. In Saint Louis this was much more difficult. As a matter of fact, I never really became as deeply involved with sports and friends in Saint Louis; it was a big city, with about 1.5 million inhabitants in the metropolitan area and it was harder for a new family to make friends with their neighbors.

My father became friendly with a certain Father Dieter of Saint Louis University High School (SLUH), run by the Jesuits, where he was trying to get me a scholarship to play on the school's football and basketball teams. But the Saint Louis high school leagues had a rule that a player had to be a student at the school for at least a year before he could take part in league games. The reason was that some high schools "bought" good players who were students in other high schools, and they wanted to avoid this.

I tell you that sports, especially football, are like a god, an idol, for many persons in the United States. Besides, they are good business. Often, having a good football team brings more fame and attracts more students and money to a high school or university than their scholastic record does. Because of the league's rule, I could not play in any of the league games, but the head coach at SLUH, Jack Reilly, became my friend and insisted that I practice every day with the football team anyway. He also promised to get me a scholarship to St. Louis University to play football there the following year.

Jesuit schools in the United States are rather expensive, and many families cannot pay their monthly fee. They give some scholarships to a few poor kids and a few blacks as an effort toward racial and social integration, but the majority of their students are from the upper middle or upper classes. They say they want to give a Christian formation to the future leaders of the United States. Father Dieter arranged with our father for a special lower monthly fee for Pat and me. This is how Divine Providence got us involved with the Jesuits.

Jesuit high schools in the United States do not admit women, only men. Until recently this was true of their universities also. A good many of the teachers in their high schools are Jesuit scholastics, that is, seminarians preparing for the priesthood. These young men are usually around twenty-five years old and have just received their university degrees, bachelor of philosophy. They now need, as part of their training, these three years of teaching experience before entering their theological studies.

These young Jesuit scholastics are the teachers closest to the students and have a big influence on getting vocations for the Jesuits. In those days about ten young men used to enter the Jesuit novitiate each year as soon as they graduated from SLUH. I do not know what Pat was thinking, but I did not have the slightest idea of becoming a priest. I just wanted to get to know the world and to play sports.

There is no doubt that these Jesuit high schools for boys of good Catholic families of the middle and upper classes, selected after passing a difficult entrance exam, with their strict, almost military, discipline, maintain a level of intellectual scholarship superior to that of most other Catholic high schools and public high schools. Public schools have to admit any young boy or girl, because secondary school education is obligatory for everyone in the United States. SLUH was directly designed to prepare young men to go on to the university with a broad general background. For example, we all had to study Latin and a good deal more literature than in the public schools, which gave a more practical kind of education that prepared their students to go out and get a job after graduating.

In Saint Louis our family lived on Waterman Avenue about four blocks from the biggest park in Saint Louis. Forest Park is about four square miles of forests, lakes, and sports fields right in the middle of the city. We young people practically lived in Forest Park when we were not in school. SLUH is on the opposite side of the park from where we lived. I used to walk these seven miles to school every day. I did not have a bicycle, or a job, so, besides wanting the exercise, I wanted to save the bus fare.

From the time I was a little kid I had the habit of getting up at 5:30 in the morning to go to mass and communion every day. But at SLUH the whole school had mass at 7:30 A.M., before starting classes. I used to leave the house at six after making my own breakfast and preparing a dozen peanut butter and jelly sandwiches to take to school with me for lunch. I was seventeen then and really ate a lot. I am fifty-six now, when I am writing this, and a meal of two sandwiches is plenty.

As I said, I never really sank roots in Saint Louis during high school and college. I had some friends, especially among my sports companions. But since we were a boys' school, we met girls only at the ball games or at school dances. As a matter of fact, in all my time in Saint Louis I never had a really close boy or girl friend, as I had had in Dayton and Toledo—except for my brother, Pat, who was and always has been one of my most faithful friends.

As promised, Jack Reilly got me a full scholarship to play football at Saint Louis University (SLU), also run by the Jesuits. "Dukes" Duford, the head coach of SLU, came out to the high school a number of times to observe us during football practice, and five of us who were going to graduate in June received football scholarships that covered all the expenses of matriculating: monthly fees, books, and everything. Besides, Dukes got us full-time jobs for the two months of school vacation in June and July, and part-time jobs after classes in December through June, after football season.

In June of 1942, I graduated from SLUH with high grades on my report card. This "graduation thing" bothered me. There were big expenses; just in order to go along with the rest, you had to buy an expensive graduation ring and a new suit for the big "graduation ball," which lasted all night in one of the best hotels in the city.

There was much pressure to belong to "high society." Many of my classmates were showing off new cars that their parents had given them as graduation presents. For the dance we were supposed to buy a formal "tuxedo" to wear. I managed to rent one from a pawn shop; I knew that this would be the first and last time I would ever use one. I did not buy the graduation ring, either. I was already forming a little bit of class consciousness. I resisted the silly hollowness of "high society" and of some of my rich friends.

In my opinion, there was (and still is) a lot of pressure in U.S. high schools to learn the customs of the rich. Parents and even some Jesuits encourage these customs of the "high society" in the students. In my time I do not recall any campaign by the Jesuits to promote social consciousness in their students, to get them to know a poor neighborhood of the city, to at least visit some poor families at Christmas to give them a gift basket of food, as the Jesuits at SLUH do nowadays. Even now there remains a lot to be done in the area of social service. I was in the United States in 1979, after I was expelled from Honduras, and I again noted a tendency toward self-centeredness in many young Jesuits, in many of their students, and in young people in general in the United States. It seems as though they lack social consciousness.

What is happening in the rest of the world does not seem of major interest to them.

I have the notion that the selfishness, or self-centeredness, in American youth today is worse than it was in my time, and that it is because the propaganda of the consumer society is worse today. Today much of education, propaganda and stimulation in the capitalistic system is designed to form self-centered individualists who seek their own development and comfort rather than to form youth that will take as a goal in life the service of others.

What a difference there is between education in the United States and in Nicaragua where I am writing this two years after the triumph of the Sandinista revolution! A big part of the youth of Nicaragua fought in the armed insurrection with the Sandinista Front for National Liberation, and thousands of them gave their lives for the liberation of their people from the long Somoza dictatorship, which was always supported by U.S. governments. In 1980 practically all the high school and university students, voluntarily and without pay, went out to remote mountain villages to live with poor campesino families during the five months of the great literacy crusade. In the towns and cities the young workers and housewives who knew how to read taught those who did not. Ninety thousand taught four hundred thousand how to read and write in five months!

The sixty thousand young students (including the sons and daughters of the rich) in this small country of 2.5 million shared the life of the poorest campesinos, enduring hunger and a complete lack of the comforts of modern life. The young students lived and worked where there are no roads, no electric lights, no piped-in water, no schools, no medical clinics, no bathrooms. They lived the way 60 percent of the Nicaraguans and more than 60 percent of all humanity live.

The majority of North Americans cannot even imagine how this two-thirds of humanity in the third world live. And at present, just about all the Nicaraguan students are voluntarily out working in the fields and mountains helping to pick cotton and coffee during their school vacations. The socialist system of education combines study and work. These kinds of experiences open the eyes of the middle and upper class youth and make them feel compassion for their poorer brothers and sisters. They forget themselves when they see that their brothers and sisters are lacking even the most essential food that is needed for good health. This is the educational system needed to form the new man and the new woman that Saint Paul talks about in his epistles. In a socialist society it is harder to be selfish. I do not mean to say that socialists are not selfish (this is the original sin that we all have), but the socialist society and socialist system of education try to form men and women who are not selfish, who sacrifice themselves for others, for the community.

I am grateful to my father for teaching me to like manual labor from the time I was a small child, even though the motivation that he gave me was to make money for myself to satisfy my desires. I mentioned that Coach Dukes Duford of SLU got me a full-time job during the summer after I graduated from high school in 1942. I was a helper on a truck that went around all the poor neighborhoods selling ice. I had to carry up to a hundred pounds of ice on my shoulder from the truck into the houses. Dukes always looked for jobs that required hard manual labor for his players, for their physical development, and that is the kind of work I have always liked. With the money I earned in June and July, I bought my first car, a secondhand white Chevrolet, for a thousand dollars and drove to the university every day.

The war with Japan broke out in December of 1941, and in 1942 the United States entered the war against Hitler and Mussolini—the Second World War. Almost all the young men, one by one, were drafted into the armed forces.

When I became eighteen on October 28, 1942, I too had to sign up for the draft; however, in my physical exam I came out 4–F, the classification for those who were not physically fit for the army. It was because I am so myopic; I had worn ugly glasses ever since childhood. I was frustrated. I had a great desire to know the world. I wanted to be with my friends who went into the army.

In August of 1942 we started full-time football practice, a month before classes began at SLU. The university students closest to graduation were exempt from military conscription, so the football teams and the university leagues continued playing until

1944, when all the students were drafted. But since many of the veteran players had been drafted, even we new first-year players were put on the main team. Ordinarily the freshmen had a special team and a special intercollegiate freshmen league, which served as a training ground for young players. This year there was no freshman league, and I got to play in some of the games of the big Missouri Conference, but only when we were winning easily.

What I did get out of that football season was a ruined left knee. With the continual blows, a piece of cartilage in the joint broke off. At times it would get stuck in the very socket, and I would not be able to bend my knee. By pulling on my leg another person could help free my knee, but it would swell up and I would not be able to run on it for a few days.

This happened to me about five times that year, not only playing football but also while playing on the university basketball team. Dukes Duford talked about sending me to the hospital for an operation, but he never did; in my second year at SLU he took away my scholarship, because it was obvious that I would not be able to play much football with my weak knee.

I had decided to study civil engineering, for the simple reason that I liked to work in the open air surrounded by nature, and a civil engineer builds highways and bridges. The first two years of university are general studies, with an emphasis on the physical sciences and mathematics, but I also took courses in philosophy each semester because that interested me. A course in Catholic doctrine was obligatory each year for the approximately ten thousand students at SLU. Almost the only contact we students had with the Jesuits who ran the university was in these religion classes, contrary to the way it was in High School, where almost all our teachers were Jesuits. I never became a close friend of any of these Jesuits, either at SLUH or SLU, even though I admired them for their intelligence.

I always preserved a great love for our Catholic religion, and I continued to receive Holy Communion almost daily during my university years. During the first nineteen years of my life I lived always in a Catholic environment and did not really have much knowledge of people of other religions or of no religion. Of course, I had contacts with many non-Catholics through my jobs and sports, but since I had always lived with my family, I was quite protected from outside influences. That is why it made such an impact on me to leave my family and join the army, and to have to live with people, the majority of whom had no real faith. (I will talk more about this later on.)

My first year of university studies went well, and during the three months' vacation I worked for a construction company repairing highways close to Saint Louis. It was easy to get a job then because so many men were in military service. I had to earn and save enough to pay for all my university expenses in 1943 because I no longer had the scholarship. Just the yearly fee for studies was eight hundred dollars in this private Jesuit university, and to buy all the required textbooks was also very expensive. Many of the big state universities in the United States were free as far as school fees go, but my parents insisted that I should continue with the Jesuits. I myself wanted to continue at SLU, especially for the Catholic philosophy courses. As I did not dare play any more football with my bad knee, I got a full-time job as night watchman at a factory after classes at the university.

In October 1943, when I received in the mail my call to report for induction into the U.S. armed forces, I recall that I felt a great joy. It is not that I had any desire to fight the Nazis or to defend the "democratic free world." I only half believed all the propaganda in the United States about how horrible the Germans and the "Japs" (Japanese) were. In that period I had no real political ideology. It did not interest me. I was too selfish, worried only about my own life and desires.

The only political formation that I remember that impressed me in my youth and made me read a little was in the thirties. My parents were great fans of Father Charles Coughlin, who lived in Royal Oak, Michigan and had a radio program on a nationwide network. Every Sunday for more than fifteen years he analyzed and commented on world events and explained the social encyclicals of the popes. He also had a newspaper, wrote many popular pamphlets, and had a great influence on the political formation of millions of Catholics.

Father Coughlin was quite liberal and, with his propaganda, helped a lot in the election of Franklin D. Roosevelt as president of the United States in 1932. But, following the line of the papal encyclicals, he was very anticommunist. In the forties he became so anti-Semitic that many people started to call him a "Nazi." His bishop finally ordered him to retire from public life and not to publish any more books or papers. It is to his credit that he obeyed and continued as pastor of the parish in Royal Oak.

The joy that I felt about entering the army was not for ideological reasons, but because of my shame at being 4–F when my friends were already in the service. I also dreamed of getting away from my family and getting to know the world. It was not that I did not like my family, but rather that I felt too protected, too much controlled. I wanted more freedom, especially freedom to know other countries, other ways of thinking. I believe that this desire came from the Holy Spirit in me. I wanted to define my ideals now and decide my vocation in life. I felt that living with my family in their closed Catholic atmosphere was like living in a ghetto. I felt isolated from the world, not knowing if, perhaps, there were other worthwhile ideals in life besides those that my parents and the Catholic university gave me or that were imposed upon me from above or from outside, not born from within me from my own experiences of life.

This book is about my metamorphosis into a revolutionary, the history of an American reared and educated to be a Catholic, bourgeois "gringo," but who little by little was transformed by the Spirit of Jesus, using the experiences of his soul in contact with the world around him. I think it is important, therefore, to understand that this desire of mine—or inspiration of the Holy Spirit—to free myself from my family and their closed environment was a qualitative leap in my metamorphosis.

Without formulating it in words, I believe that I suspected even then what I now am convinced of: that many of us Catholics were victims of a closed system of Catholic propaganda, giving prejudiced, stereotyped ideas about Jews, blacks, Protestants, communists. Everything that was not Catholic, North-American, bourgeois was (without doubt, subconsciously) considered and treated as an enemy.

My parents and my brother and sisters were, and in some respects still are, ideologically naive, the same as the majority of North Americans, including many Catholic bishops and priests. They do not have a true critical conscience. Many of us were, or still are, victims of a system of education and daily propaganda from the mass communication media—radio, television, movies, newspapers, and so on. We do not even realize that we are victims of this. It is especially sad that the Catholic church in the United States often (consciously or unconsciously) plays a part in this un-Christian system of ideological education. Thus, it should come as no surprise that, when I was nineteen, I was quite deformed by prejudice. But, thanks be to God, with my entrance into the army and liberation from my closed world, the Holy Spirit could start in me a long, slow process of transformation.

PART II. JOURNEYING, DOUBTS, MY VOCATION

2. The War Years: 1943–1946

On the day assigned in November 1943, with real pleasure, I reported to Jefferson Barracks on the outskirts of Saint Louis along with hundreds of other young men who were also called to the army for that day. We submitted to complete physical, psychological, and intellectual exams that lasted all day. Those with the best physical and mental capacities were selected for the Marine Corps. Since I am terribly nearsighted and have had to wear glasses ever since childhood, I could not be a marine. I chose the army instead of the navy because I feared being cooped up on a ship for weeks or months at a time. The disadvantage of the army, which we were all aware of, was that up to 50 percent of us might never return; we would be cannon fodder. The marines and the soldiers have a much higher percentage of casualties in a war than the sailors or air force personnel.

We army men were sent to Fort Benning, Georgia, for the three months of basic military training that all soldiers receive. Since the war in 1943 was going badly for the United States and the Allies, more troops were urgently needed for the battlefronts in Africa against the Germans and Italians and in the Philippines and other islands of the Pacific against the Japanese. That is why basic training, which usually lasted six months, was accelerated to three months. After this, each soldier was assigned to a company of one of the many corps of the army: infantry, cavalry (tanks and armored cars), artillery, engineering, medical, communications, administrative, and so on.

Right from the beginning there were many aspects of army life that I liked, and others that I did not. The disciplined regimen for every moment of the day from 5:00 A.M., when we got up at the sound of a trumpet, until lights out at 9:00 P.M. was easy and interesting for me. I have always loved physical exercise and outdoor life, which we had plenty of during basic training, so I was happy.

But for many fellows who had never lived a disciplined life, all this was hell. It was a complete change in their rhythm of life, especially for some of the university students who had spent their days in classes or in their rooms and their nights in bars or movies. These companions spent all their time in basic training griping and criticizing. It really cost them, but after three months just about all had adapted to their new army life.

What I in no way liked in the army was the way the officers and the sergeants treated us: as though we were dogs, with insulting, obscene language, with degrading punishments for the slightest infractions of the rules. I remember that a group of us recruits arrived a little late for a class one day, and during the hour for sports in the afternoon the sergeant made us scrub down the wooden barracks floor on our hands and knees, using toothbrushes. He stood over us the whole time, insulting us with obscene words and even kicking us if we stopped for a minute to rest.

The reason they put the most violent and merciless sergeants and lieutenants in charge of basic training was to "make men" out of the recruits, or rather, to make brutes out of us. They mistreated us like that with the idea that a man has to learn to be violent and merciless in order to be a good soldier, so that he can kill an enemy without thinking twice about it. Also, to be a good soldier, they said, one has to learn to obey any order of one's sergeant or lieutenant without thinking, as an automatic reflex, without questioning or discussing it. That way, in battle soldiers will kill without worrying about it, obeying automatically. We all have heard of cases of atrocities and torture that our soldiers have perpetrated against the enemy, even women or children in a captured town, "obeying orders" of their superior officers.

Right from our first day in Fort Benning, after giving us our uniforms and our beds in the dormitories, they started our political indoctrination with movies and talks about history and about the war. It was all designed to develop in us reactions of love and admiration for the United States, its armed forces, its leaders, its "pure" ideals, its "spotless" record in international relations, and so on, and at the same time, to foster in us a blind hatred of the "enemies of mankind": the "Japs," the Germans, the Italians, and the other allies of the "imperialist Fascist Axis." Every day in many different forms, during all the classes and activities, they filled us with these ideas.

The government tried to instill these same political ideas and these same sentiments of love for everything North American and for our allies, and profound hatred for our enemies, in the civilian population also. Almost all the movies, newspapers, and radio programs, and even the popular songs and commercials, promoted these ideas and sentiments. They painted the Japanese as primitive little monkeys, the Germans as big-headed brutes who drank the blood of women and children, and the Italians as ridiculous clowns. These were the stereotyped images with which they filled the minds of Americans during the Second World War. In a similar way, the western movies used to depict the American Indians, the "Redskins," as evil brutes and the white cowboys as pure and good.

All of what I have just described is the modern system of propaganda and ideological struggle to control and dominate the people of a country, filling their minds with stereotyped ideas that cause prejudices and automatic sentiments of fear and hatred on thinking of these "enemies." It is the same system, but intensified, that is used today in the capitalist countries, especially the United States, to instill fear and hatred of communism and, even worse, of "communists," our fellow human beings. Religious ideas and sentiments are used to fortify prejudices and reactions of hatred against other people we do not even know; this is un-Christian.

The traditional social doctrine of the Catholic church had helped to instill this fear and hatred of whatever might be against the "natural right of private property." The traditional teaching against socialism and "atheistic" communism has instilled prejudice in almost all the Christians of the world against "communists" and "socialists." Naturally, the capitalists who control the United States and other countries use this Catholic propaganda to defend and justify their system of exploitation of the workers and the dependent countries of the third world.

You only have to call a person a "communist" enough times and everybody will be afraid of him or her. Here in Latin America, where I am, if a priest causes trouble for the capitalists, criticizing their injustices, they call him a communist in their newspapers and over the radio, and even the Catholics who are poor campesinos and workers will be afraid of him. In the United States, there is "freedom" of thought and of speech, and the Communist Party is legal, but someone who is pointed to as a "communist," even though falsely, will often have difficulty getting a job. Everyone will be afraid of such a person, especially if he or she is a teacher or a labor leader. A neighbor or a job foreman can sometimes ruin someone's life simply by labeling that person a "communist" or a "Marxist" enough times.

Setting up a negative stereotype to represent a group so that all who belong to the group are to be feared or condemned: this is the same mechanism that the Protestant majority in certain regions of the United States used to use against "Catholics," that the whites use even today against blacks and against "Latins," and that Christians use against "the Jews who killed Christ." There are still laws in many cities of the United States that indirectly impede blacks or "undesirables" from buying houses in certain neighborhoods, or attending certain schools, or belonging to certain clubs. All this is completely anti-Christian and the opposite of the "liberty, equality, and fraternity" that was proclaimed as the principal ideal both of the French Revolution and of the American Revolution in the Declaration of Independence.

During the Second World War the propaganda against the Germans and "the Japs" in the U.S. armed forces was terrible, as I have explained. Nevertheless, I never accepted all of this, principally because of my reflections on the gospel: that all of us are brothers.

I was beginning to be rebellious, different from the majority. Right from the start in the army I also rebelled against the system of segregation and privileges for the officers. It was practically forbidden for us simple soldiers to have a friendship with an officer, with our lieutenant or captain. They lived apart in better houses, ate much better food in the officers' mess, recreated in the officers' club. It was forbidden for us even to enter the exclusive section of the camp reserved for officers. Even during battles at the front they tried to follow this system of segregation and special privileges, as though the officers were better than we were. The theory behind this is that it is necessary to put the officers on a level superior to the troops in order to assure discipline and obedience.

They were like our owners, and we their slaves, completely at their bidding in everything. On passing an officer in the street, we had to give him the military salute, with the extended right hand touching the right eyebrow. After a year in the army thinking about this inequality and lack of brotherhood, I started to deny them the military salute, pretending I did not see them, and a few times they stopped me to demand that I salute. In France I had the reputation of being an enemy of the officers because I was denying them the salute. At last a captain gave me punishment, three days in jail; the jail was just a house set aside in the camp with military police guarding the locked doors.

Since I had completed a year and a half of pre-engineering at the university, on three different occasions my superior officers called me into their offices to offer me the opportunity of going to officers' school, where in four months I would become a lieutenant. The first time was in the States after I had spent about four months in the army; the second was in England; and the third was in France after I had been in the army for about a year and a half. Each time I told them no, that I preferred to be one of the troops. The real reason I did not accept being an officer was what I have already explained: that right from the start in the army I rebelled against the system of segregation and privileges for the officers.

The last time they offered this to me I told our battalion colonel what I really thought. I told him that it was just like the Japanese system, in which the soldiers had to adore Emperor Hirohito as a god, and the army officers as his high priests. The Japanese soldiers had to kneel down before them and touch their foreheads to the ground in adoration. The propaganda movies against the "Japs" that they put on for us in the army showed us all this. The colonel become very angry with me when I told him that the system in the American army was the same.

All this, without a doubt, was entered on my dossier or personal record together with the list of my punishments, so they did not make me any further offers to become an officer. I only reached the rank of corporal, the second in command of a squad of twelve men under a sergeant, before finishing my training in the States and going to England with our infantry division. Even though a corporal in those days only received $120 a month, I remember that I used to send $90 of that to my father each month to deposit in a savings bank for me.

Speaking of my experiences as a rebel and a nonconformist, which started in the army, reminds me of the system they had to control the high rate of venereal disease among the troops. Every month they marched us to the theater to see very realistic movies about venereal disease. We all wound up experts in this particular branch of modern medicine. Every month, also, all the soldiers had to strip naked and fall in the long line to be examined by the medics. From the beginning I rebelled against this presumption of the officers that all the troops went to see prostitutes every time they got a pass for a day's leave in town. But I was never able to avoid these films and medical checks.

What I did manage to get around was another rule they had that required every soldier who left camp with a pass to show the contraceptive condoms that they gave to us. I refused to accept them. I told them it was against my religion to use contraceptives or even possess them. I went to see the captain of our company, a Catholic named Dwyer. He insisted that I should take the condom along in my pocket and not cause problems. I went to see him a second time and told him I was going to denounce this to the bishop so that he would complain to Washington about this anti-Catholic practice in the army. With that, he gave me special written permission to leave on pass without taking contraceptives.

But actually, these practices in the army to control venereal disease were very necessary and very wise. It is a fact that, at least in my outfit, many of the soldiers who left camp for a day or two of leave went to the whore houses or wound up sinning with one of the thousands of street prostitutes who abounded around every military camp in the United States, Europe, Africa, and Asia, wherever there were troops. These prostitutes were impossible to control or eliminate, and many of them had some type of venereal disease.

I remember that the films they forced us to see about this always started with a good-looking girl flirting with some soldiers. One soldier always tells his buddy to be careful, and the buddy always answers that there is no worry, that this girl is obviously "as clean as a whistle." Of course, this soldier winds up a few days later suffering the effects of one of the many venereal diseases. That is why it was a standing joke among soldiers in every part of the world to comment about any woman who passed them on the street, even a nun, that "she's as clean as a whistle."

After a short time in the army, I really became confused at seeing young Catholic soldiers behaving no differently from the others who openly said that they did not believe in "those religious superstitions." At least as far as the sins of drunkenness and fornication went, Catholics happily went to the houses of prostitution right along with Protestants, Jews, and atheists. Very few of them went to the masses that the chaplains assigned to each battalion celebrated every Sunday.

There were always some soldiers from the strict Protestant sects and some independently sincere Catholics who tried to avoid these sins; these were the fellows with whom I preferred to make friends. I would go out with them to walk around the closest town whenever we got passes. In that way I became close to a good Protestant from Alhambra (near Los Angeles, California) who was in my infantry platoon. For more than a year we were together in the United States, England, and France, and we became inseparable buddies. His name is Don Cogswell. Don also was trying to be pure and chaste. He was deeply in love with his girlfriend, Cindy, whom he had left in Alhambra, and he did not want to be unfaithful to her.

Don was another sports fanatic like me; he had been the star of his high school football team and had a college scholarship waiting when he got out of the army. We always took advantage of whatever free time we had to play some sport together. Because of this friendly competition, after about five months in the army and while still in the States, I hurt my bad knee while running the obstacle course. I had to go to the hospital to recuperate, but they still did not operate on my knee.

As I said, I became really confused in the army, as my eyes were opened to what was religious reality for Americans. At nineteen I naively imagined that almost everyone really believed in God and tried to keep his commandments, and that only a few were corrupt and perverse. So it was a shock to me to realize it was just the opposite and that even Catholics, who were married in the church and went to mass once in a while, were not faithful to their wives while they were in the army.

Little by little I have come to realize that most people follow the customs of the group they belong to, without critical reflection. The environment in which they live is what most determines the attitudes and actions of almost all men and women. Only a very few have enough moral courage to go against the stream, to be different, to live according to moral principles, even though others make fun of them for it. This is what most "gets to" a young man or woman: being laughed at by his or her companions. That is why so many young people, while they live at home with their families, try to keep the commandments, but when they are with a group, as I was in the army, they are afraid to be different. They start to use the same obscene language as the rest, tell the same dirty jokes, and commit the same sexual sins as their companions.

Don and I were the object of many dirty jokes by our companions for not participating in their drunken parties or their obscene conversations. But since he and I were probably the strongest of all of them physically, and since we had proven on a couple of occasions that we could handle five or six of them in a fight, they respected us a little.

During all my time in the army I tried to carry out my daily prayers, read the Bible or some other religious or philosophical book, and attend mass and receive communion at least every Sunday. It was hard, as I said, to be a good Christian in the army, in an atmosphere where one is made fun of for any sign of religiousness. But such trials are very important for the formation of a true Christian. People who practice their religion in an environment where everybody is doing it do not do it so much from personal conviction as from custom. In the army I had to exercise my personal freedom, firmly judge and decide for myself, and overcome the fear of being laughed at. It was a period of great spiritual growth for me. In an atmosphere where, at least in practice, the existence of God was denied, I had to meditate a lot about his existence.

For the first time in my life I was living with people who openly claimed to be atheists or agnostics. I had many conversations with them about God and religion and was astonished to find so many fellows who openly admitted during a discussion that they did not know if God existed or not—"no one has ever seen him." In the United States there are relatively few who will say that there is no God, who are declared atheists, and in the army I ran into only about ten of them.

After leaving the army I found an almanac with religious statistics on the United States, which helped me to understand what had so astonished me in the army: very approximately (from what I can recall), 25 percent of Americans declare themselves Catholics; another 25 percent are Protestants, but divided into about five hundred different churches or sects (the largest being the Southern Baptist church); a small percentage are Jewish or Muslims, or belong to one of the Asian religions; another small percentage declare themselves atheists; and almost 40 percent are agnostics.

Agnostics are those who say that they do not know whether or not God exists. Since they do not know whether God exists or not, in practice they can live without worrying about God's design for the world, about avoiding sin, about scruples of conscience.

However, it would be unjust to throw all the blame for the evils in the United States on the agnostics. Some agnostics are more generous in sharing what they have with others than many Catholics are. The truth is that the capitalist idea of using the selfish tendency in human beings as the base of the economic system was not born among atheists and agnostics, but among Christians, mostly Protestants, in England, Germany, and France. And this capitalist system goes on transforming Christians into materialists, into agnostics, in practice if not in theory, who in their daily lives do not take God and his commandments into account.

This is what disappointed me with regard to religion while I was in the army. The Catholics and Protestants, in general, did not try to keep the commandments any more than the atheists and agnostics. Only a very few of us took our religion seriously. I really started to have doubts about God's existence.

The real philosophy of more and more people is that the world goes on functioning without God. We human beings are the ones who have to control the world by means of science and technology. We do not need God. We are discovering the laws of the functioning of the universe, and it makes little difference whether there is a God who made the world with these laws, or if the world is eternally evolving without some God, as the Marxists say. For science and technology, what role does God really play in the universe? The universe functions without God. As some philosophers say: "For modern people, God is dead!"

But the arguments against the existence of God that caused the greatest doubts in me were these: first, most of the people in the world live and die as if God did not exist, and second, there is so much injustice and misery in the world that it is hard to believe that there is a God, a good Father who loves us, who controls this world.

While I was in the army in France, this second argument hit me in the face with all its force. That was where my eyes were opened to the misery and poverty in which the majority of humanity lives. There was awakened in me a conciousness of the great injustice and inequality among human beings. I could say that there, for the first time in my life, was the awakening in me of a social consciousness.

I could not stand it in France! I wanted to vomit when I saw hundreds of French children, women, old people, refugees from the war, fighting with each other to get a bit of the garbage that we soldiers threw out after each meal. The people of France were dying of hunger, while we ate well.

But it was in southern France that I first began to realize that most people do not live the way we do in the United States, England, or even wartime France. It was my first contact with the third world, where the masses who form the majority of humanity live in a poverty and misery that is inhuman and frightening. Close to our army camp on the outskirts of Marseilles was a huge refugee camp for Arabs from North Africa. Many times I went to see them. They lived like animals: practically naked, sleeping on the bare ground without blankets, eating whatever garbage they could get. The kids were all naked, with their bellies swollen. All of them were sick, dirty, doing their physical necessities behind any tree, fornicating behind any tree. This truly gave me doubts that there exists a good Father-God.

In the beginning, while I was still in the army, these doubts pushed me closer to God. I read many Catholic philosophical works, Saint Augustine and Saint Thomas Aquinas, that treated of God's existence. I made great efforts to go to daily mass and communion, walking far to find a church with an early morning mass. It was not until I was out of the army that these doubts about God's existence caused a crisis in my life, the crisis that saved me, that transformed me.

Before talking any more about my transformation, I will describe my life in the army more fully. In basic training, besides a lot of physical exercise and week-long hiking with eighty pounds of equipment and ammunition on our backs to prepare us for living out on the battlefield, we learned to fire our M–1 rifles, also carbines, pistols, bazookas, rockets, grenades, and the .30-caliber and .50-caliber machine guns. We learned to dismantle all these weapons blindfolded in the dark to be able to repair any defect in them. We practiced man-to-man fighting with our rifle butts and with bayonets on our rifles. We learned all about land mines and booby traps and other types of explosives and had classes on every imaginable detail of modern warfare. Basic training gave us only an introduction to all of this, and throughout our army life we continued this training.

When we finished our three months at Fort Benning, we were each assigned to one of the many branches of the army and sent to different parts of the States to be incorporated into already existing battalions. A good number of us were sent to Fort Chaffee, Arkansas, the base of the 100th Infantry Division that was being formed and prepared for the invasion of France. This was in February of 1944, and, of course, no one told us anything about these plans for our division.

The 100th Infantry Division existed for only about eight months. The biggest part of its twelve thousand members, officers and "men" (as the troops were called to distinguish them from the officers), were new recruits. Each company had a few officers, sergeants, and soldiers who belonged to the regular army, that is, who were professional soldiers with a number of years of experience. Many of these professional soldiers had already served in the war in Africa and been sent back to the United States to rest and to help train us new recruits.

After three more months of training at Fort Chaffee, our division received secret orders to move everything to New York to board ships to England. By that time I was a corporal and instructor in the M–1 rifle and bayonet fighting. We were all given two weeks of vacation to visit our families, after which we were to report back to Fort Chaffee. Our veteran companions predicted that this vacation meant we were going overseas.

And so we were. As soon as we got back from vacation, the whole division of twelve thousand men (and a few women) packed all the equipment—vehicles, weapons, and personal belongings—on a number of special trains that took us in three days nonstop to the Port of New York. From the trains we passed directly aboard a number of "Liberty" ships, especially remodeled to transport troops. We did not see anything of New York City.

After a few days on our ships, waiting until everything that belonged to our division was loaded, at last the fleet of some twenty ships, accompanied by several destroyers and antisubmarine warships, slipped slowly out to the great Atlantic Ocean. Passing the Statue of Liberty, we headed for sea without knowing where we were going. But everybody guessed, with the help of the veterans who knew more about these things, that we were going to England to invade France. Some of those in our battalion really became afraid because of these rumors; a few had managed to desert in New York while we were loading, for fear of going to the front. I was not tempted to desert; for me this was a most interesting adventure.

This voyage on the troop ship across the Atlantic, however, was one adventure I would gladly have escaped. I vividly recall that Liberty ship. Its crew of sailors and one thousand soldiers were packed like sardines in the holds, which had been converted into dormitories—tiers of five iron bunk beds one on top of the other, the foot of one bed touching the head of another. Hundreds of us slept in each hold below sea level with hardly any ventilation. The thousand men would not all fit on the decks of the ship; we could go up in the fresh air only by turns. With this, and with the continuous, day-and-night rocking and rolling of the ship on the waves of the ocean, it is no wonder that within a few days most of us were seasick. Once seasick, one could not get out of bed or keep down any food.

Most of the sick stayed in their bunks, vomiting into their steel helmets. But with the violent movements of the ship, little stayed in the helmets. The floor of each dormitory and the beds on the lower tier were covered with vomit, which the rolling of the ship sent sloshing from one side of the hold to the other. It was a nightmare trying to sleep in those dormitories. I practically never went down to the hold. I slept up on deck in the fresh air even when the temperature in the North Atlantic was below freezing. I think that is why I was one of the very few who were not sick for a single day.

The officers insisted that the healthy ones work in the kitchen and dining room, because those who were seasick could not; the mere smell of food turned their stomachs. If the dormitories were ugly with vomit, the dining hall was worse. The sick did not eat a thing for a few days, but then they finally had to eat something. Imagine a dining hall filled with two hundred men eating when one of them started to vomit. As in a chain, the sight of the soldier vomiting caused an immediate reaction in those closest to him. In a few minutes all two hundred were throwing up on the floor of the dining hall. With the rolling of the ship, these pools soon formed a lake of vomit that moved around with the motion of the ship.

We healthy ones had to clean up these lakes in the dining hall. But it was only possible to work about ten minutes before going up on deck for ten minutes of fresh air, then you had to return for another ten minutes of hell. I learned to breathe through my mouth.

During a big storm, the sea was like a volcano for two days and nights. Huge waves came up over the ship, and it was forbidden to go up on deck. Waves threw our ship up in the air and back down; it was like a little cork on the ocean.

One of our troop ships was lost; no one knows whether the weather sank it, or something else. The fleet went close to the Arctic Ocean to avoid the German submarines that infested the waters along the ordinary Atlantic routes. If most of the men were seasick before, they were really seasick during the storm. But luckily I still was not.

Ordinarily, crossing the Atlantic in a good ship takes eight days at the most. It took us fifteen days to cross the Atlantic from New York to Liverpool because of the zigzag route the fleet took through the North Atlantic. There were many rumors of submarine attacks against us, but on our ship we never felt or saw a thing.

What joy filled all the men and our officers (who also were on the ship with us, but in private staterooms) when we heard the shout of the sailor in the loft, "Land ho!" There was a priest chaplain on board with us on the trip, and he told me that almost all the Catholics had gone to confession for fear of dying on that hellish voyage.

The only thing I remember about Liverpool is that our battalion slept on the floor in a big warehouse in the port for a couple of weeks while we awaited our destination. Afterward, the 100th Infantry Division was stationed in a huge camp near Liverpool for many months; some were transferred from our infantry company to a company of combat engineers belonging to the 100th Division. Our company of engineers was sent to London to help construct prefabricated houses for the families of the city who had lost their homes in German bombardments.

I enjoyed life in London for about six months. We lived by squads in rented houses right in the city, and worked six hours a day putting up "Quonset huts." We went all over the city in trucks, hauling materials, loading and unloading sacks of cement, and I got to know the city quite well. I remember that we used to go dancing every Saturday in the Hammersmith section of London, traveling there on the subway. There I met a nice English girl and used to visit her home frequently to take her to the movies or to a dance. This gringo was still quite unconscious of the great suffering around him. I just thought about enjoying myself and getting to know more of the world.

Along with the new interest in dancing that I acquired in London, I became an expert on the popular music of the big dance bands. I spent hours listening to the records of Glenn Miller, Harry James, Benny Goodman, Tommy Dorsey, Artie Shaw, Louie Armstrong, and all the others. I knew by heart all the words of the love songs and jazz tunes. Dixieland music was my favorite. Even today I enjoy the music of that era, which continues to have some popularity everywhere in the world.

But now I am ashamed to have to admit that music and dancing were my biggest interest in life, while millions of human beings were being sacrificed to the gods of war, of power, and of the oligarchies who wanted to dominate the world. Right around me the English people were suffering terribly—while I danced—and while I went to daily mass and communion! How self-centered can one be?

Hitler had conquered all of Europe by 1944. He had placed in concentration camps or murdered and incinerated more than six million Jews. He was trying to conquer Russia, burning Leningrad even as he had burned Warsaw. He was planning the invasion of England. Every day his planes came over the island, bombing cities, leaving hundreds of dead and wounded among the English civilian population.

In 1944 Hitler brought out his secret weapons, the V–1 and V–2 rocket bombs that were launched from France especially against London. There were no airplanes or antiaircraft weapons that could stop these rockets. Every day a number of them fell on London while I was there. The worst of it was that the radar could not detect them in time to warn the people so that they could rush into bomb shelters, as they did during the airplane bombing raids.

There was hardly a family in London, a city then of some 5 million, who had not suffered some loss in those bombings that had been going on for a year. You can imagine the state of nervousness in which the population lived, just waiting to hear the whistle of one of those V–2 rocket bombs that could end their lives or leave them crippled.

I recall once when we had just turned over to the British government fourteen new houses made in a semicircle around a small square, the next day (thanks be to God, before anyone occupied them) a V–2 fell directly in the square, completely destroying all of them. I went to see them and was astounded that just one of these bombs could cause so much destruction.

But in my seven months in England, even though I was in many bombardments by the Nazi planes and heard hundreds of those whistles of death from the V–2s, I was never even close to where a bomb fell. Whenever bombers came toward London, the radar picked them up from far away, and loud sirens were sounded in the whole city. Everybody immediately rushed into a bomb shelter, the principal ones being the underground subway stations. It was said that if you heard the whistle of a V–2 rocket, you did not have to worry. It was the bomb that you did not hear that would fall on you. During my first weeks in London I certainly did feel scared, seeing the fear in all the people. But one gets used to everything after a time; and for me it became just a bit of excitement every time we heard the planes or the V–2s.

With reason, Prime Minister Churchill of England insisted that they had to invade France as soon as possible. In 1944 the U.S. and the British air forces were already fighting off a lot of German bombers and even began bombing some of the towns and German camps in France. But they had no way of stopping the V–2 rockets. D day for the invasion of Normandy was in June of 1944, while I was peacefully playing around in London. Our 100th Infantry Division remained in England in reserve for a couple of months more. Only when the battle fronts were well within France and the V–2s no longer fell on England were we all sent to France, with our engineering company reincorporated into our division. I kissed my girlfriend good-bye and eagerly looked forward to getting to know France and new adventures.

Close to the Port of Le Havre, France, our division made a big city of tents, dispersed and camouflaged because of the danger from German bombers. Our company of combat engineers had more work there than the infantry, who were simply awaiting the call to go up to the combat zone which was already close to Paris. Meanwhile, we engineers were repairing roads and bridges in this whole sector of France that had been reoccupied.

We were called combat engineers because we went up to the front with the infantry. We were always equipped with our weapons to fight side by side with the infantry if it became necessary. But our special mission at the front was to go out ahead of the infantry, opening roads and making bridges for them, cleaning out the mines from the roads and fields ahead of them, and so on. After a territory was conquered, other companies of noncombatant engineers from the rear guard would fix up the roads, bridges, and houses, in a more permanent fashion. I enjoyed being with the combat engineers much more than being with the infantry, who, ever since we had left the United States, were just left waiting for their call to go and fight. We, on the contrary, went out to work every day in the fields and roads doing the kind of physical labor I have always enjoyed.

From our time near Le Havre I recall an adventure that my friend Don Cogswell and I had. We went for a swim in the Rhône, which passes through the city before emptying into the sea. What we did not know was that the daily tide from the sea entered well up the river. We had left our clothes and shoes on the bank and were swimming and horsing around in the middle of this wide river, when all of a sudden a big wave came upstream, and then another, and then another. We took off swimming like mad for the bank, but before we got there, we watched our clothes and everything go floating rapidly down the river, which had risen a couple of feet within five minutes.

There we were, Don and I, in our undershorts on the bank of the river, amazed at the sudden rising of the river, and lamenting the loss not only of our clothes, but of our glasses, money, and personal documents. Don lamented most the loss of the photo of his sweetheart, Cindy, in his billfold which was undoubtedly by now entering the sea. Without my glasses I cannot see anything, which was the loss that most bothered me.

We stood there a long time laughing and joking about how funny we looked with just our wet underwear and the "dog tags" around our necks. It was strictly forbidden ever to take off these "dog tags," even while bathing. They were for identifying us in case of accident or being wounded or killed in combat, and had our name, army serial number, and blood type on them.

There was nothing to do but start walking barefoot along the highway that went back to our camp, about five miles away. We walked and tried hitchhiking. When a green jeep or car of our army came along, we hid, because we had left camp without permission. We waited until it was getting dark before we entered camp, but to no avail. Some of our buddies spotted us, and soon our whole platoon was out on the street waiting for us and making fun of us. Our lieutenant punished us for leaving camp without permission.

Our company began to specialize in the construction, or rather the putting together, of "Bailey" bridges. They were named after the engineer who designed these prefabricated steel bridges whose pieces could be packed on a truck. They were a type of suspension bridge for rivers that were not very wide, or for connecting sections of a bigger bridge of which one section had been destroyed. The pieces were connected with steel pins, and the structure of the bridge was built up on the bank of the river and pushed over rollers on the bank out in the air and over the water. We gradually added more and more pieces on the bank until it reached all the way across.

As our company became expert in putting up and taking down these bridges, they used to call us to work in many different parts of France. This was around October of 1944, and I remember working almost continually in the rain and in the mud on the banks of the rivers, close to, but always behind, the battlefronts. After about three months at this we became expert at making strong cement approaches to a bridge that were deeply sunk below the mud on the banks of the river. Since they carried all the weight of the bridge and also of all the truck traffic and even of big tanks, it was essential that these bases have a deep, strong foundation.

One day they changed our lieutenant, who got along very well with us, for a new lieutenant, a recently graduated civil engineer. He knew only in theory how to construct bridges and had never made one in the rain and deep mud. I fought with him constantly, correcting him almost every time he gave an order about how to do this or that. The bridges never would have lasted a week in the mud doing things as he ordered. We saved one bridge by disobeying him and doing it finally as I suggested.

He threatened to transfer me to another company, so my companions told me that we should make the next bridge exactly as he directed. Well, that we did. The base of the approach was not sunk far enough in the solid earth below the mud. With the third truck that hit the approach to cross this bridge, the whole base moved to one side and half the bridge with another truck on it fell into the river. We all stood there laughing.

The lieutenant was furious. Two days later I had orders from our battalion colonel transferring me from my company of combat engineers, and from the 100th Infantry Division, to a military police company in Marseilles, in the extreme south of France.

Many of my buddies and I tried to talk with the colonel to protest against this injustice, but he did not give us the chance.

I had been very happy with this hard work of putting up Bailey bridges. What most bothered me was to have to leave Don Cogswell and other good friends in my company. But I was now a marked man in the army. Three times already I had refused to go to officers' school to become a lieutenant, and I had been sent to jail for refusing to salute some officers on the street in Rouen. All this was on file in my service record, and it was easy for the new lieutenant, who hated me, to convince the colonel that I was trying to ruin his work and cause a division between the officers and the men.

It is interesting to analyze the class struggle in the U.S. Army. I have already explained the antidemocratic system of segregation and privileges and blind obedience to the officers that put them on a superior plane to the troops, not just like bosses and their workers, but more like owners and their slaves. The officers who demanded the fulfillment of this system were hated by the men, especially the lieutenants and captains, who were in more immediate contact with the troops because they commanded the platoons and companies in their daily activities. We heard of a few cases in our own division of lieutenants who fell overboard into the ocean while crossing the Atlantic during a dark, stormy night when no one could see or hear anything. There were also many cases of lieutenants and captains who died in battle with .30-caliber bullets from an M–1 rifle in their backs.

Well, nothing could be done about it. I had to say good-bye to my buddies, catch a train, and report to the captain of a camp close to Marseilles. Only on arriving there did I find out that it was one of our containment camps with thousands of German prisoners inside a high barbed-wire fence with many towers for guards with machine guns. I did not like this at all. But what could I do?

After showing my orders to the guard at the gate, I was taken to the captain who was in command of the camp and of the full company of military police. I cannot remember either the name of the company or the captain, but only that all this was still part of the Third Army under General Patton, as my 100th Infantry

Division was. I told the captain that I preferred to go to the front to fight against the Nazis instead of being here guarding those who were already prisoners. I offered myself as a volunteer for the infantry. The captain only laughed and said maybe later, but that right now he had orders to put me to work guarding the prisoners of war.

It was a big lie that I wanted to kill the Nazis. On the contrary, in England I had promised Jesus Christ that I would never kill anyone, not even to defend myself. I had thought that our division was going to be in the first waves of the Normandy invasion, and I had to think of what I would do in combat. I theoretically decided to fire in the air and let myself be killed instead of killing, if I found myself face to face with an enemy. I reasoned that I was living in God's grace and would go to heaven, whereas the Germans probably were like the majority of the American soldiers, living in mortal sin. I would send them to hell if I killed them.

It is true; that was my pious way of reasoning. During all these subsequent years I have reflected a good deal about pacifism and nonviolence. Thanks be to God that up to now I have never had to really make that decision in a concrete case of killing or being killed. (I will explain later how my ideas about fighting have changed after eighteen years in Latin America.) What I was really thinking and wanting when I told the captain that I preferred to be on the battlefront rather than guarding prisoners was that I preferred to be risking my life in interesting adventures than tranquilly sitting around bored, guarding prisoners.

Those six months in the military police were the darkest period of my three years in the army. I really felt alone in this new company of soldiers made policemen. The living was very easy and comfortable. I principally had to watch over groups of prisoners while they worked on different projects both within and outside the concentration camp. We had a lot of free time to go to Marseilles, which was only a half hour by bus from the camp.

What was bad was that I did not have a close friendship with any of my new companions. They had already been together for a long time and had their closed groups of friends. I spent a lot of time out walking alone in Marseilles, and more and more in the desert mountains close to our concentration camp. I would take long hikes through rocky mountains uninhabited except for a few poor herders who took care of goats. I read many books, especially philosophy, and made long meditations in the solitude of these barren mountains. I also spent whole days walking along the sandy shore of the Mediterranean Sea.

As I mentioned earlier, it was during this time around Marseilles that I first encountered people from the third world. It was in a camp of Arab refugees who had fled from the war in North Africa. Many times I went just to see them, just to look at them. Their living like animals impressed me so much that there started to awaken in me something of a social consciousness. I first began to recognize the great injustice in the world, the great inequality of opportunity between the people of the poor countries, who are the majority in the world, and those of "civilized," developed countries.

I have also mentioned my doubts about the existence of God when I saw this poverty and misery for the first time in my life. I did not go too close to these Arabs, not even to the kids; I just watched them. I was afraid of them, as though they were beings from some other planet. But all this, and long days alone in the mountains or on the seashore, without a doubt played a big part in forming my contemplative character. This was a tough period in my life, but very important and profitable. I started to look for God in all seriousness. It was this beginning in me of a preoccupation with my neighbor, with those who suffer, that moved me toward a search for God.

My contact with the German prisoners also helped me in this sense. We had heard only bad things about the Germans. All the American propaganda filled us with the idea that they were inhuman, cruel, cold brutes. I had studied one semester of German at the university before joining the army; here I had the opportunity to practice my German with the prisoners. Besides, I was very curious to ask them if all this we had heard and read about Hitler and the Nazis were true.

I started to make friends with some of the younger prisoners. We would secretly talk together just about every day, even though it was strictly forbidden to fraternize, that is, to show friendship or sympathy for the Germans. They taught me many German words, and we were able to understand each other well enough for them to explain many things to me. They explained how they had been forcibly drafted into the army; how they too were filled with propaganda against the English, the Americans, the Jews, and against everyone who was not of their pure German, Aryan race. Little by little we realized, they and I, that we had been equally duped, that we were brothers. We became good friends. One of them was only fourteen years old.

I had read some of the life of Adolf Hitler and parts of his famous book, *Mein Kampf (My Struggle)*, which contained his Nazi philosophy. Hitler taught that the German race (the white, blond, blue-eyed, pure Aryans, without any mixture of "foreign" blood) was a super-race, the master-race destined to dominate and perfect the world. Germany was left so devastated and poor after the First World War that the Germans longed for a savior, and hoping that Hitler was just that, they adored him. Only after consolidating all the power of the government and of the armed forces of Germany in his hands did Hitler reveal his insane idea of wiping out all the Jews (who, more than anyone, so he claimed, had corrupted the Aryan blood) and to conquer all the countries of the world under the "Third Reich" ("Third Kingdom").

My German prisoner friends, when we talked about this, admitted that Hitler was insane; that he had big concentration camps for all his enemies and for all the Jews. These prisoners asked me if it were true that the German aviators had completely destroyed New York City. When I explained to them that it was a lie, and that the German armies, on the contrary, were in complete rout on the Russian front and had already been pushed out of France back into Germany, they admitted that the German people had been fools to believe and follow such a madman.

My sergeant caught me talking with the prisoners a couple of times. He warned me that it was forbidden and that, if I continued to do it, he would have to report me to the captain, who would punish me. Well, naturally, I went right on talking in secret with my new friends, "my brothers," as I called them. The captain found out, and after two warnings, he finally punished me with three days in jail. After getting out of jail, I continued to look for my German "brothers," but now more secretly. However, the captain found out once more, and (thanks be to God) he no longer wanted to have me in his company of military police.

It was in April of 1945 that I received written orders transferring me to the Fifth Army, whose headquarters were in Fontainebleau, near Paris, where I was to report for further orders. The Third Army was now fighting inside Germany. I heard reports that my 100th Infantry Division had been in the famous Battle of the Bulge, the last desperate offensive attack of the Germans before they retreated from France and Belgium. Ninety percent of the troops of the three infantry battalions of my old division were killed or wounded in this battle. My old combat engineer company had fewer casualties. Don Cogswell came out unscratched and wrote to me about it while I was still in Marseilles. I thought gratefully that it was the Providence of God that had saved me from that horrible battle!

To get to Fontainebleau, I took a train to Paris. This change was like a resurrection for me; I felt a great new joy, a strong sentiment and desire for adventure. Fontainebleau is about twenty miles from Paris. I remember that it was springtime and there were flowers and birds everywhere, making Fontainebleau seem the most beautiful place on earth. The little town was like a park, and in the center was a large palace, former residence of French kings.

In the main headquarters of the Fifth Army at a luxurious house in Fontainebleau, they told me that I would stay with them to wait for further orders. Meanwhile, I was given some small jobs like cleaning the kitchen and the buildings of the soldiers who were assigned to headquarters. We lived very comfortably in some confiscated houses that now served as a military camp.

I immediately struck up a friendship with a sergeant who was secretary to one of the colonels in charge of personnel. His name was Adam Kaplan, a small, thin, young, very religious, Jewish soldier from New York. We were roommates, and every time we were free, we would go together into Paris.

I was happy. Every Saturday we would go to the dance at the USO (United Service Organization) in the Fontainebleau palace. The USO was a private American organization of the parents with sons in the service that provided decent recreation and economic, legal, and psychological help to soldiers and marines.

Every big military camp in the United States and overseas had a USO house where any soldier could go to read in the library, play ping-pong or cards, eat free donuts with coffee, or just talk with the receptionists, who were young local women volunteers.

In Fontainebleau every Saturday, practically all the young women of the town, married or single, used to come to the palace to dance with the soldiers. I soon found a pretty French girlfriend. I could not speak French, and she could not speak English, but both of us were studying German, and this language was our common link. I remember that she was a very devout Catholic and that we used to often go together to mass. If I had stayed more than four months in Fontainebleau, I could easily have fallen in love with and married this fine girl, whose name I cannot even recall now.

Adam and I loved to walk through the streets and parks of Paris, which was the most beautiful city we had ever seen. Every two or three blocks in this big city there was some kind of park with big, beautiful trees and flowers. The great pastime of the citizens in good weather was to go with the whole family to one of these parks or to sit in one of the many open-air sidewalk cafes drinking wine. We visited all the famous museums, the Cathedral of Notre Dame, the Eiffel Tower, and so on.

The war had passed through, or around, Paris without destroying it and was now in Germany, where the Americans and the British were bombing daily and completely destroying many cities. In Paris we selfishly enjoyed life as though the war did not exist. I had already forgotten all about the inequalities—and the poor Arab refugees. I was a selfish young man enjoying the new adventure of getting to know my French girlfriend and Paris. Since Adam was a great fan of classical music, I used to go with him to concerts and operas and began to like this music, but I still preferred the popular music of the big-name bands of the United States that we heard at the USO dances and over every radio.

That is the way I spent the whole beautiful summer of 1945, while the war was drawing to a close in Europe. As soon as the Germans surrendered in Berlin (although the war continued against Japan), the headquarters of the Fifth Army, with all its personnel, was transferred to Heidelberg, Germany. Adam and I went, too, and were put in charge of a new service. We organized excursions to famous places in Europe for the troops of the Fifth Army, who were now given a vacation periodically.

Since I was always looking for new experiences, new adventures, I rejoiced at the transfer to Heidelberg. The only sad part was saying good-bye to my madamoiselle, who was lovely spiritually as well as physically. However, after a month of being in Heidelberg I had a German girlfriend and soon forgot the French one.

Adam and I shared a room at the University of Heidelberg. The university had been picked by the general of the Fifth Army as an ideal place for his headquarters during the occupation of Germany after the war, and that is why Heidelberg was preserved and is practically the only city in Germany that was not destroyed by bombs. It is a beautiful little city, and I spent my last six months in the army there very happily. During this time I took advantage of our excursion service to go on one to Rome.

We saw Pope Pius XII at mass in Saint Peter's Cathedral and in an audience in the famous Sistine Chapel, and we all sent rosaries and medals blessed by the pope to our families. The guided tour through the Roman catacombs, where the first Christians hid out and secretly taught their revolutionary doctrine, was the part of the trip that most impressed me. These great tunnels run many miles underneath the city. The persecuted early Christians buried their martyrs there and met for secret masses; it was a crime against the state to be a Christian and deny adoration to the Roman emperor.

The early Christians were relatively few and persecuted; thus they were Christians by conviction. They were revolutionaries; they wanted to change the world; they were a light for the world. "The blood of martyrs was the seed of Christians." The more Christians the government killed, the more persons who were serious became Christians. But after A.D. 300, when the emperor Constantine was converted to Catholicism and even gave away palaces and lands to the bishops and priests, everyone in the Roman Empire, which included practically all of Europe and North Africa, had to accept the Catholic religion. Then, the biggest number were Christians, not from personal conviction, but for convenience, and later on, out of custom.

I was amazed at the riches of the Vatican palace and museum, and at the medieval pomp of the pope entering Saint Peter's Cathedral like a king seated on his throne. He was carried on the shoulders of eight of his soldiers, with their medieval uniforms, swords, and lances. But as I did not have much critical social consciousness, I accepted all this, and even defended it against the criticisms of some of my soldier companions who were not as piously naive as I.

Now, in 1981, when I am, at last, a revolutionary, you can imagine how much I hate all this counter-Christianity that is in our Catholic church. Jesus and his first pope, Peter, went around without shoes, as poor workers, without a home and without any political power. And look how their successors live! Everything about the Vatican's pomp and wealth now fills me with disgust. I want to help make the revolution within the Catholic church. What ruined the Church was receiving riches, possessions, and power; what will make the Church the "light of the world" again will be poverty, loss of all its possessions, and persecution. But in 1946 on vacation in Rome I did not think like that at all.

My German girlfriend was very intelligent and very religious. As a matter of fact, I met her in the chapel of the University of Heidelberg, where both she and I assisted at daily mass. She was a student of English literature at the university and asked me for help with her homework. Well, she taught me German and I helped her with her English. What I did not like was that after a few months she already considered me her private possession. She clearly wanted to marry me and return to the United States with me. I started to react against our exclusive friendship, and I offended her several times by dancing with other girls and telling her I had not made any commitment to be exclusively hers.

When I finally received my orders to return to the United States to leave the army, she told me right out that she wanted to marry me, that I should take her with me. I told her no, I was not ready to get married to anyone. I have always considered myself a fellow who could not be easily fooled or dominated by women, because after growing up with five sisters, I thought I understood them quite well. I was also thinking that I would have preferred marrying either my mademoiselle from Fontainbleau or my friend in London.

These are my memories of my almost three years of military service. I liked the experience of seeing the world and these years forced me to develop my own conscience and to stand up for my own Christian beliefs. I recommend a couple of years away from home to all graduates of the Catholic high schools staffed by the Jesuits, Christian Brothers, Salesians, Marists, and others in order to break with the closed Catholic environment of family and school and to learn to decide for themselves which moral principles they are going to follow in life. It would be a help for their personal liberation and the development of their characters. I especially recommend to all young Americans that they go to see with their own eyes how most of the people in the rest of the world live, not in Europe, but in Africa, Asia, and Latin America. It is incredible how ignorant Americans are, in general, about life in the third world.

3. Postwar GI: 1946–1948

I had had enough of military life and I was glad to return to the U.S. and leave the army. The government gave us all a big bonus check upon discharging us from the service, and Congress passed the "G.I. Bill," giving us scholarships with all expenses paid to study in any school or university in the country for the same number of years that we had served in the armed forces.

It was May of 1946 when I returned home to my family in Saint Louis dressed as a civilian again. It had been about two years since I had visited my family, before I went to England. You can imagine the joy of my parents and sisters on seeing me back from the war safe and sound, and then shortly afterward to also welcome my brother, Pat, back from the navy. Pat had been drafted a few months after I was and had chosen the navy. He had been a sailor on different ships and got to see all the principal ports of the Pacific Ocean, of the islands as well as mainland Asia. Being confined so many months aboard ship, he, like many sailors in World War II, became an expert gambler. He won and lost thousands of dollars playing poker in his years at sea and returned home after the war without a cent in savings.

Pat and I wanted to take advantage of the G.I. Bill to continue our university studies. He wanted to be a lawyer and matriculated at Saint Louis University (SLU) so that he could live at home. I wanted to be a civil engineer, but they did not have that branch of engineering at SLU immediately after the war. I stayed at SLU with our family for the fall semester to complete the credits I lacked in general pre-engineering studies before looking for another university.

A good friend of my brother's, Gus Schlafly, invited Pat and me to go to Minnesota with him to work on the construction of a new highway for two months before starting classes in September at SLU. He had the promise of a job and said that they were looking for more workers. I wanted to go to California to visit my buddy from the army, Don Cogswell, so I invited Pat and Gus to accompany me first to California in June and then go to Minnesota in July.

So it was that the three of us put ourselves on Route 66, which goes from Chicago, Illinois, to Los Angeles, California, passing through Saint Louis. From Saint Louis to L.A. is about twenty-five hundred miles. Our idea was not to spend a cent for traveling since we could hitchhike all the way, or for sleeping, which we would do in parks or anywhere, but only for food. It was an adventure, and we enjoyed the whole trip, which took us about ten days.

I cannot recall all the details of the trip, but I do remember that the first night we were sitting in the comfortable soft chairs in the lobby of the best hotel in Columbia, Missouri, listening to music on a jukebox. Finally, at ten o'clock I lay down on one of the big sofas there in the lobby. The hotel manager tried to wake me up and throw us out of there, but we told him we were waiting for one of his guests to come. We stayed there sleeping comfortably all night long.

The next night in a town in Oklahoma we tried to do the same in a fancy hotel, but when we were all sleeping, after midnight, a policeman came and took us to jail. There in the jail we slept in a cell on cots with dirty mattresses, and the next day the police sergeant told us to leave town right away. We thanked him and went out to the highway to continue on our way, saying that it was not bad sleeping in jail.

The following night in a small town in Texas we went directly to the jailhouse to ask the policeman to lock us up for the night so we could sleep there. We explained to him that if he did not we would sleep in the lobby of a hotel, and they would call him at midnight to throw us in jail. If he jailed us now we would lose no sleep and neither would he, and the next day we would hit the road again for California. That night, I recall, the whole town heard about the three students sleeping in their jail, and a crowd of young people sat around outside our window listening to me play my harmonica. I had practiced since I was a little kid, and I played quite well the harmonica I had bought in Belgium while I was in the army.

Every day brought some interesting adventure. I remember that in Las Vegas, Nevada, Gus (who had been in the navy during the war and, like Pat, was a great cardplayer) and Pat wanted to stay in that city, which had the most famous gambling houses in the country. What hurt us was that in the first club we entered, in the first pinball machine Pat put a silver dollar in, he hit the jackpot. This was one of the machines with an "arm" the player pulls down that makes dials spin. When they stop, one either wins something or loses the dollar. This animal spat out of its mouth into our hands, and all over the floor, 150 silver dollars.

With this, Pat and Gus went crazy; for two days they played these machines and also the card games with the professional gamblers in the clubs. Sometimes they won a little, but on the night of the second day Pat and Gus had lost, not only the $150, but every last cent they had. They begged and begged me to lend them some money to recover their losses; they would not let me sleep (we stayed those nights on the grass of the big park in Las Vegas) until at last I lent them one silver dollar to see if God wanted to give them the jackpot again from one of those machines. They soon returned to the park, saying that now they knew why those machines are called "one-armed bandits."

Route 66 passes through the Mojave Desert, 150 miles of just sand without a single tree or creek, before reaching the California mountains. In all this stretch there were no towns and only two or three gas stations, which sell water, but at the same price as beer. The heat there is terrific; no animal can last more than two days without water in this desert. After spending quite a while trying to hitch a ride in the gas station at the beginning of the desert, at last we got into the back of a little pickup truck. The people in the cabin of the pickup advised us that it would be better to wait for another car, because we would not be able to stand the noonday sun in the open back. But we did not want to lose any more time, so we went with them.

On finally reaching the hills of California, we stayed in a hotel in a small town, not only completely toasted and burned by the sun, but also plenty sick, all three of us. It was the only night we paid for sleeping; or rather, I had to pay for all of us. The following day, with another ride, we went into Los Angeles, a huge city of over four million inhabitants (one third of them of Mexican heritage). There we had to pay bus fare to get to Alhambra on the outskirts, where Don Cogswell lived.

We stayed a week with Don and his family, going to the beautiful Pacific Ocean beaches for a swim just about every day. Don had a car and took us all around. It was a great pleasure to get to know his family and his friends. As it was now the end of June and we had to go to Minnesota to work on the highway, Don lent us money, and we returned to Saint Louis on the Greyhound bus.

To go to Minnesota from Saint Louis we used the same system of hitchhiking and sleeping in hotel lobbies, parks, and sometimes jails. (In Des Moines, Iowa, I recall, the police denied us hospitality.) In the United States all the jails have metal cots with mattresses, and the only inconvenience of sleeping in prison cells is that at any hour of the night the police are liable to throw into the same cell a couple of drunks who will not let you sleep. Besides hitchhiking, on the trip to and from Minnesota, especially traveling from one town to another in Minnesota, we hopped freight trains, hiding away in empty boxcars.

The first time was from Des Moines, Iowa, to Saint Paul, Minnesota. We met a man in the park where we were going to sleep who was also going to Saint Paul, and he invited us to hop a train with him. Since he knew all the routes, we only had to hide ourselves away with him to sleep in an empty boxcar on a train that would pull out at 3:00 A.M. for Saint Paul. So it was that we woke up in the railroad yards of Saint Paul.

I remember that once we were going to hop a freight train already in motion when it was passing a highway where we had not been able to hitch a ride. We threw our suitcases into a boxcar that passed with its doors open. We had to run and run to reach and climb onto the last car of the train and go up on the roof. Since we had seen that there were some men in that open boxcar when we threw our suitcases in, we were worried about them stealing all our belongings. But no, on reaching the town where the train stopped, some nice young guys brought us our suitcases. There was a great spirit of comradeship among those who hitchhiked and hopped trains. After World War II there were many decent young fellows and girls who, like us, went all over looking for adventure.

You have probably already guessed that I enjoyed this vagabond kind of life so much that I would gladly have gone on this way for a few more years. I will finish this part of my story by explaining that, as it turned out, all this information about the job on the new highway was false. They told Gus that he was not on the list and that they did not need any more workers. We did find a job in Red Lake Falls, Minnesota, digging with shovels to make a basement underneath a wooden house that was elevated above the ground and temporarily sitting on pillars under its four corners.

All the kids in the neighborhood used to come to play in this big hole where we were digging. My brother Pat loves kids so much that he hardly did any work, but only played with the kids. This, and the fact that when it rained our hole would fill with water, made our shoveling in the mud very difficult and held up our progress so much that the owner finally got mad and fired us.

Another job we got in a little town near Bimidji was with the railroad gang, changing rotted ties on the line. This was another really hard job using pick and shovel, carrying those big, heavy wooden ties, or pounding in huge railroad spikes with a sledge hammer for hours on end. I was enjoying the work, but after being there about three weeks Pat came into the little room we rented to tell us that we might as well pack up and leave because he had just told the boss that the three of us no longer wanted to work.

After traveling some more around Minnesota and spending everything we had earned, we hitchhiked and hopped trains back to Saint Louis at the end of August. In September the three of us started classes at SLU.

I could not even think of playing football on the university team because my knee was so weak. I always played other sports, though, like basketball, on teams in nonschool leagues. I wanted to live away from my family, to feel more independent. With my savings and bonus check from the army I bought a secondhand car and felt free driving along the highways wherever I wanted to go.

As I indicated earlier, one of my sisters, Virginia, and her husband, Ken Smith, lived in Detroit. One weekend before Christmas I drove up to see them and also to investigate the civil engineering course at the University of Detroit (U. of D.). I liked their system: three months' study and three months' work in a civil engineering job that the university would get for the students with some construction company, thus alternating study and work for three years.

When I finished the semester at SLU and the required courses for pre-engineering, I matriculated at U. of D., and in January of 1947 I went there to live in one of the dorms. They were five-story buildings that housed two students to a room. We paid so much a month for the room and meals in the cafeteria on the first floor of the building. I roomed with an army veteran named Bob who was from Chicago and in my same class. We became great friends. After classes we worked for four hours each night at a dry cleaner's. Every Saturday we went dancing.

I decided to be a civil engineer simply because I liked physical labor in the open air making bridges and highways. As yet, the thought of being a priest had never even crossed my mind. On the contrary, in Detroit I had a group of atheist friends, communists, who lent me Marxist books showing that religion was an ideological superstition used by the dominating class to subjugate the masses.

Bob and I went around a lot with these Marxists when we started work in the big assembly plant for Ford trucks in Detroit. They were our companions at work and at play. After the first three months of study, the university got us the job with Ford because there were no jobs available in construction. On reading these atheist books and enjoying the friendship of these atheist companions, there arose in me again, but now more seriously, doubts about God's existence.

I have already mentioned that, even though I was studying engineering, I always took some philosophy courses. And, especially during this period in Detroit, I read more and more books of Saint Thomas Aquinas and his commentators, with their proofs for the existence of God. This theme became the principal interest of my life! I read and discussed with my friends both theses, the pros and the cons, for the existence of God.

I remember that a book about the history of religions impressed me very much. I think it was written by Engels. It explained how the ideas of a "son of God" becoming man, being born of a virgin, being savior of the world, working many miracles, and rising from the dead were not ideas original with Christianity. He cited texts from religious books of Mesopotamia and India that were much older than the New Testament, and included all these same ideas.

This book claimed that the Christian religion would have disappeared if the Roman emperors after A.D. 300 had not used this new religion as the ideology to control, domesticate, and unify the peoples of the different countries of the empire. Also, it explained how the popes, bishops, and priests used this religion in the feudal age to amass riches and power for themselves, teaching the masses to resign themselves to being slaves and to patiently wait for their liberation in the next world. These last arguments did not impress me much then, because I did not understand them yet. But now that I am recalling them, I recognize that they contain a lot of truth.

I want to explain about working in the Ford factory, because there are a lot of people, especially in third world countries, who cannot even imagine what it is like working on an assembly line as a great number of workers in the industrialized countries do. I worked in one of the biggest factories in the world for two periods of three months each, and I belonged to one of the biggest labor unions in the world, the United Auto Workers (UAW). In this factory in Detroit Ford produced and assembled various types of trucks: dump trucks, freight trucks, semitrailers, and others.

I worked on the assembly line for dump trucks, where the slow-moving transmission belt brought past me, one by one, a steady stream of already assembled chassis and cabs without doors. Each worker added a piece to each truck as it passed; for instance, a bulb in the headlights, some screws in the seat, part of the horn. I had to put in and tighten one screw in the dashboard of every truck. All day long I had to stand in my place in line, stick the screw in and tighten it with a screwdriver, all in half a minute. Within a minute the next chassis was passing me, and I repeated the operation. Then another one, then another one, then another one came by without rest for four hours; after a half hour for lunch, there were three and a half hours more of the same.

Try to imagine how many men and women worked on this assembly line. How many screws and other pieces are there in a big truck, including its motor, its brakes, gears, electrical system? Well, there are one or more workers for each piece, and there are thousands of screws and other pieces; before they are brought to the assembly line, many workers are involved in making each screw, each piece of the motor and the chassis.

Not all the parts were made in this same factory, but the majority of them were. The big battery for the truck was made in a Delco Corporation factory. The tires came from Firestone Company. The big steel beams for the chassis were not made at Ford, but at Bethlehem Steel Corporation.

Just about all the parts of the motor were made in our factory. A whole big department had electric lathes, saws, drills, and other big machines to make the pistons, the valves, the motor case, and so on. The steel and other materials, of course, were brought in from other factories. Nowadays, a good deal of this machine work is electronic, automatic; for example, bolts can be stamped out at the push of a button.

Ours was not the only factory of the Ford Motor Company. In Detroit alone they had at least three big plants; ours for big trucks, one for pickup trucks, and the biggest one for the various models of Ford cars, including the cheapest and best-selling family car in the United States. Their luxury limousine, the Lincoln, was made at a plant in another part of the country, if I remember correctly, as were their farm tractors. In California, in the South, and on the Atlantic coast they had smaller plants just for the assembly of the most popular Ford cars; the parts were shipped in from the Detroit factory. In the same way, Ford has assembly plants for its popular cars, trucks, and tractors in a number of different countries of the world.

How many hundreds of thousands of workers did Ford have just in the United States? Our labor union, the UAW, represented not only Ford workers but also the hundreds of thousands of workers at Ford's biggest competitor, General Motors, at Chrysler Corporation, at Allis Chalmers, at John Deere, at International Harvester, at Kaiser Corporation, and others. The UAW had about two million members. It was one of the most powerful organizations in the country, and one of the richest. Think of the income just from the monthly fees, five dollars from every member: about $10 million a month. Besides this, the UAW and other big labor unions had many of their millions invested in their own enterprises and in other corporations, which gave them big profits. No wonder the leaders of these unions defend the capitalist system; they are an integral part of it.

Labor unionism is one of the biggest businesses in the United States. It is easy to understand why the criminal Mafia tries to control the unions and take out their share. It is also easy to understand why the big capitalists, military officers, and politicians in the United States try to buy and dominate labor leaders. Imagine the power that just the UAW has in case of a strike at Ford. How many trucks were turned out of just my factory in Detroit each day? How much is each truck worth? If the UAW closes all the plants of all the automotive companies, with their millions of workers, what happens to the U.S. economy?

Practically all the unions in the States were affiliated with the American Federation of Labor (AFL) or with the Congress of Industrial Organizations (CIO). In 1947 when I was working at Ford, they were fighting among themselves, but for many years now they have joined together in the AFL–CIO, under one governing committee. Until 1980, the AFL–CIO was directed by George Meany, who was thus one of the most powerful men in U.S. politics, because the AFL–CIO controlled about 20 million workers plus their families and relatives. Traditionally, almost all of them backed the Democratic Party, because it was liberal on social reforms in the United States, legislating more benefits and more protection for the working class than the Republican Party, which always has been more conservative and favors the capitalist, banking, and commercial interests.

With regard to the foreign policy of the United States, the AFL–CIO and the Democrats are just about as conservative, imperialist, and anticommunist as the Republicans. It often seems that the foreign policy of the United States is to dominate, if possible, the entire world for the benefit of its big business interests, to assure the raw materials it needs for its industries. Its transnational companies try to dominate the world economy and bring all these riches to the United States. The United States has about 6 percent of the world's population, but uses and consumes about half of all the world's riches and natural resources.

George Meany and the other main labor leaders, in connivance with the industrial-military oligarchy who control the power in the United States, have kept the American working class dormant and deceived. Against the economic interests of their own workers, the AFL–CIO supports and promotes the foreign policy in favor of the transnational companies. Why does the Ford Motor Company, for example, put a big assembly plant in Argentina (or South Africa, Mexico, etc.) instead of putting up another plant in Detroit? It is simply because labor is so cheap in Argentina that the company makes much more profit from a plant in Argentina than from its plant in Detroit. What they save in salaries and other social benefits for the workers abroad is much more than it costs them to send all those parts and the whole factory all the way to Argentina.

With these policies of the transnational companies, there is at times considerable unemployment in the United States. There are fewer automobile workers now, in 1981, than there were in 1947, and there is more unemployment in the States now. At the same time, the workers in Argentina are being terribly exploited by Ford. The minimum salary in the United States in 1980 was $3.00 an hour, or $24 for an eight-hour day. The minimum salary in Honduras is $1.50 a day, about 19 cents an hour. In Argentina the minimum salary is undoubtedly much more than in Honduras, maybe $4.00 a day, or 50 cents an hour.

Although Ford might pay workers in its Argentina plant up to $1.00 an hour (which would be double the minimum wage that the law demands), by having its plant in Argentina instead of in the United States, where they would have to pay at least $4.00 an hour (and probably more), they save $3.00 an hour—$24 a day, or about $500 a month—for each worker. If they have twenty thousand workers, this comes to $10 million a month, or $120 million a year, at the very least, that they would save on labor *in just one plant.* Also, without doubt, Argentina charges Ford less in taxes than the U.S. government does.

The workers in Argentina and in other countries of the third world who work for transnational companies that pay them two or three times the minimum wage are quite satisfied with these companies and even defend them against anticapitalist revolutionaries. The AFL–CIO helps all this with their big international program called the American Institute for Free Labor Development (AIFLD) directed by known agents of the CIA (U.S. Central Intelligence Agency). For all this, they spend millions from their own funds, and other millions of dollars from the government and from big business in the United States, to help form "free and democratic" labor unions in other countries according to the AFL–CIO model, that is, unions that tranquilize workers, satisfying them with small economic gains so that they do not recognize that they are exploited. I will explain all this in more detail later on when I write about life in Honduras.

To return to my boring job of putting the same screw in each truck that passed on the assembly line, I could hardly stand this day after day. The good part was that I earned more than $4.00 an hour. How could my companions do this inhuman kind of work for five, ten, or more years? Every three or four months the foreman of a section of the line changed a few workers from one job to another so that they would not go crazy and so that they would not fall asleep doing these few automatic movements, repeated all day long, every day, without need to think or to decide anything. The union demanded this periodic rotation on the assembly line.

It seems to me that this kind of inhuman, automatic work that millions and millions of men and women do in the industrialized world tends to make robots out of them, nonthinking conformists. They work just for their salary without any interest in what they are doing. It makes no difference to them whether they are helping produce trucks or war tanks, milk bottles for babies or atomic bombs to kill babies. What does interest them and what they will fight to get is a good salary and what they can buy with it. They often become selfish materialists.

This is a big problem, not only for the capitalist countries, but also for the socialist countries, which claim that their aim is "production to serve people" and not "people to serve production." How can we have industrialization without making robots out of workers?

After my experience on the assembly line at Ford, I wanted more than ever to become a civil engineer and work in the open air constructing highways and bridges. Looking back now, it seems to me that the most interesting jobs are those that involve dealing personally with others to help them with their needs, like being a teacher, nurse, doctor, priest, nun, social worker, lawyer, politician, even police officer, but it depends on whether one is consciously doing it to serve one's neighbor and community. It seems that many of these professionals, after a number of years, also lose interest in helping others and do their jobs principally to earn money. Many of them even wind up dominating and exploiting their neighbor in need.

Nonetheless, there are always exceptions to these social laws. There are some lawyers, doctors, teachers, and so on who do exercise their profession to help the poor, even sacrificing a better salary to do so. But they are rare.

This same phenomenon impressed me in the Ford plant and made me look for friendship among the only ones who rebelled against the slavery on the assembly line, the communists. They were not robots; they were not just looking for money or doing their work without thinking. They were always thinking, and trying to make their fellow workers see that they were being enslaved, exploited by the rich owners of the company.

They had little success, however. They did not even convince *me* that the capitalist system was exploiting us. We had no idea who the owners of our factory were. If it was the Ford family, well, they had earned their millions after many years of hard work, or so we thought. But we were not even interested in thinking about this, when we were receiving better salaries than most of the workers in other companies. And since one was, and still is, considered practically a criminal in the United States if one is a communist, it was dangerous for us workers to be seen speaking much with communists—the company could fire us.

During the Second World War there was not much propaganda against communism in the United States, so as not to offend our ally, the Soviet Union, but as soon as the war ended, there was unleashed a huge anti-Soviet, anticommunist campaign. Now it was Stalin and the communists who were the enemies ambitious to conquer the world and against whom we had to fight to defend ourselves. The famous Catholic, Senator McCarthy, and his Committee on Un-American Activities sought to detect and jail all suspected communist spies who had infiltrated the labor unions, the universities, and the political parties. Together with the FBI (Federal Bureau of Investigation), McCarthy created the phobia, the psychopathic fear of communism still present in almost all Americans today.

Before and during the Second World War the communists had plenty of influence in the labor movement in the United States and completely controlled some labor union federations. But after the war, with all the anticommunist propaganda, it was dangerous even to have a Marxist book or magazine or to be friends with a known Marxist. If someone should denounce you, you could go to jail, or at least lose your job. To be an elected leader of a labor union, you had to be fanatically anticommunist. Many opportunists used, and still use, this banner to go up the ladder of power in the unions, in the two main political parties, and, in general, in any business or other activity in the United States, including public education and the Catholic church.

I, as a young man, did not read the newspapers much or hear the news on radio, but listened only to popular music; I had no interest in politics. I paid almost no attention to the political propaganda. I was very anticommunist, however, because of what I read in papal encyclicals and pronouncements of bishops about the persecution of the Church in communist countries, and what I read in books by priests who had been in concentration camps in Russia or China. I read mostly Catholic newspapers and magazines. I especially liked the *Maryknoll* missionary magazine and *Jesuit Missions,* which were in the lobby of our dormitory at U. of D. Since I had been overseas, I was interested in the photographs of the people of other countries.

For me it was like an adventure to have a friendship with my "dangerous" communist fellow workers. Since my principal interest in life more and more was the problem of God's existence, I wanted to read and listen to all the arguments against his existence. At the same time I was reading more and more books of the Greek philosophers and of modern Catholic philosophers that set forth the proofs for his existence.

After a month of putting those screws in the dashboard of each truck, I asked the foreman to give me a harder job with more physical exercise, because I could not stand that boring job any longer. He told me that he could not, because the harder jobs paid better and he could only pass a worker with more job seniority to a position of higher pay. I was in agreement with this policy of the labor unions of giving priority to those who had spent more time working for the company, but I told him that I would do it for the same, or even less, pay than I had, because I could not stand that boring job. The foreman got me a change to another department farther along on the assembly line putting the big windshield into each truck, working with a companion. I was still paid my original salary. This job was not very hard either, but at least we were always moving our bodies, bringing over and putting in these big windshields.

I continued with this job until my three months were up and I had to return to classes at the university for three months. After this, when I returned to the same Ford plant for my next three-month period, I asked that they give me the hardest job in the factory that did not require a skilled workman. They told me that the hardest job on the assembly line was putting the new tires on the wheels, but that there was no vacancy at the moment. They gave me another somewhat heavy job working with a companion putting on the big metal hoods that covered the motor. There were three pairs of us doing this because it took us a few minutes to go and get the hood, put it in place on the truck, and put in and tighten three screws on each side.

In order to be closer to the factory when I first began to work at Ford in May 1947, I had left the U. of D. dorm and my roommate, Bob, who was still my best friend, and rented a small room in a private home. The owner was a very devout Catholic widow who lived there with her three daughters. Two of the girls were children, and Colleen, who was twenty, worked as a secretary to help support the family. Colleen was shy and timid and, in the beginning, never talked to me. She was very beautiful, Irish-looking, with black hair and green eyes, and I was eager to get to know her. We would sometimes chance to meet in the parlor of the house, and little by little we started to converse. She had never had a special boyfriend; her mother was extremely strict. But since I went to mass and communion daily with her mother, she liked me very much and agreed to let Colleen go out alone with me to movies, for walks in the park, to play tennis, or go to dances.

Almost right away, the two of us fell in love. For me the most beautiful part of Colleen was her soul. She was a completely innocent girl, not yet corrupted by the consumer society. As she only saw movies, books, and magazines that were approved by her mother, her mind was still clean. With regard to sex, she was completely ignorant. I wanted to kiss her, but she allowed me to kiss her only on the cheek. After being frustrated like this a few times, I got mad one day and asked her why she would not let me kiss her on the lips. I almost could not believe it when she told me that she could not allow that until we were married; her mother had told her that if a man kissed her on the lips, she would become pregnant and have a baby.

I insisted that she read some Catholic books and pamphlets about sex and human biology. After a few months I obtained her consent to kiss her on the lips, but that is as far as our sexual activity went. I was twenty-three years old and certainly wanted to enjoy full sexual pleasure, but especially with Colleen, who was so pure, I would not give myself the pleasure of even thinking of sinning with her. Both of us, indeed, were thinking about marriage; we were deeply in love. Nevertheless, when I was in my second three-month period of work at Ford, around February 1948, I had to tell her frankly that I could not promise to marry her: I was then in the great crisis over my vocation.

I had to decide what God (if he existed) wanted me to do with my life. Being a civil engineer no longer attracted me much, and working as a robot on an assembly line, much less. I just felt like studying more philosophy and traveling more extensively around the world, perhaps to India, to look for God, to find out if he exists.

I was deeply impressed by a movie called *Lost Horizons* about an English soldier who, after a number of tragedies, decided to dedicate himself to look for "the Truth." He went to work in the depths of the mines in France to see if the miners knew God. He concluded that, even though they said they did, they did not really take him into account in their lives; they did not truly believe in God. He tried other things: a university in Germany, the business world in the United States, and he always concluded the same: no one really believes in God; they talk about him, but do not live as though he exists. The picture ends with the former soldier entering a Buddhist monastery in Nepal to dedicate his life with them to look for God.

I identified so much with this character that I, too, seriously considered going around the world looking for God in my neighbor, in the poor. More and more I remembered my experiences with the poor in France during the war and the thousands of starving Arabs who, saddest of all, were Muslims and did not even know Christ. More and more I was thinking about using my life for something more important than constructing highways and bridges or assembling trucks. I wanted to serve the poor— like Christ and like those missionaries that I saw in the Catholic magazines. If God exists, I have to take him into account in my life. If he exists, he is more important than this whole world, more important than I am, or Colleen. If I could be sure that God exists, I would dedicate my life to him, to serve Him.

For the first time I got the idea of being a priest—if I could be sure that God exists—of dedicating my life to him and to the poor, of converting people in some distant country like China. But I was no longer sure that God exists. How can one be sure? Who has seen God? How could I dedicate my life to God as a priest if I was not sure he exists? And how could I leave Colleen, whom God had sent into my life? Of her, yes, I was sure, but of God, no. I spent more and more time alone, in reflection, in prayer, studying again the arguments of Saint Thomas and his commentators proving the existence of God. They did not satisfy me. I had doubts. I wanted to get married.

But I did not really want to get married; I wanted to wander through the world looking for God, helping the poor. I was afraid of getting married and losing my freedom to go around the world having new adventures. If I married, I thought, I would have to be an engineer to take care of Colleen and the twelve kids we would undoubtedly have. I did not want to be an engineer; it appeared to me now as slavery, like being in a prison, working every day for a salary. I had to go around looking for God, getting to know other parts of the world.

In February of 1948 I expressed all this to Colleen. It hurt her terribly; she just cried and cried. I told her that I loved her, but that it was better that we were not engaged, that we were free. I had to decide my vocation. I could not deceive her by promising to marry her; I had never made that promise. It was better that we did not see each other so often. She did not understand; she just cried. Her mother was very angry with me; for a long time she had been planning for me to be the perfect husband for Colleen.

I decided to finish the following three months of classes at the university and then, in May, go to Europe or to Rio de Janeiro in order to be more free to decide my vocation. I was thinking of that summer when I had felt so liberated, hitchhiking from Saint Louis to California, and afterwards to Minnesota with my brother and Gus, but in these months there was deepening in me the idea of being a missionary priest. Since U. of D. was a Jesuit school, I quietly asked around about the formation and the studies that the Jesuits pursued. I knew that they studied more than any other priests; almost all of them had a doctorate or a master's degree.

It was during one night, when I woke up after midnight and lay in bed thinking and thinking without being able to get back to sleep, that I suddenly received the great enlightenment that left me tranquil and decided about what I should do. If I wanted to look for God and study more about his existence, why not become a Jesuit? They study these things more than anyone. If I become assured that God exists, well, all the more firmly would I have to dedicate my life to his service, and if I decided, after studying it thoroughly, that God does not exist, I would immediately leave the Jesuits and look for a wife. I would lose Colleen; she should not wait for me, but God is more important than Colleen.

This idea, or enlightenment from the Holy Spirit, stayed with me almost continuously during the following weeks. It was now practically a firm decision: I would join the Society of Jesus to find out if God exists or not. Besides, the idea of being a missionary to help the poor in China attracted me more and more. In the university library I now read all the back issues of *Jesuit Missions*. Until then I had only known Jesuit high school or university teachers. None of them attracted me much as a hero whom I would want to imitate, but these missionaries who appeared in *Jesuit Missions* definitely inspired my admiration. I wanted to be like them, not like the Jesuit professors. I read that the Jesuits were the religious order with the most missionaries in the world.

Until then I had not consulted with anyone about my vocation. I told my sister Virginia that I no longer wanted to be an engineer, that I wanted to be free and travel around the world. She told me that I was crazy, because I only needed one more year of studies to get my civil engineering degree, and that I should finish that. I told her that being an engineer was repulsive to me now, so I would wind up my studies in May.

It was in March of 1948 that I received the great enlightenment that made me decide to become a Jesuit. A few weeks later, I went to the Jesuit residence at U. of D. and asked for any Jesuit to whom I could speak about applying for entrance to the Society of Jesus. After a year and a half of attending U. of D., I had not made friends with a single Jesuit. A Father Crane spoke with me and explained that I would have to be interviewed by several Jesuit examiners to see if I really had a vocation. I told him that I wanted to be a Jesuit to be a missionary in China.

On my following visit to Father Crane, he informed me that he had telephoned to California, which was the province of the Jesuits that had missions in China, and they had answered that it was impossible to go to communist China now as a missionary. On the contrary, all the foreign missionaries were in prison or had been expelled. With another inspiration of the Holy Spirit, I immediately told him that if I could not go to China, I wanted to be a missionary in Yoro, Honduras, in Central America. This was the other mission that had most caught my attention in *Jesuit Missions,* with the photographs of missionaries mounted on horses in the jungle, or embracing very poor, emaciated children. I have always felt great tenderness for all children. I would have to enter the Missouri Province of the Jesuits, which had that mission, not the Detroit Province, he told me. I would have to go to Saint Louis with a letter from Father Crane to talk to the Jesuits there.

So it was that in May I was accepted to enter the novitiate of the Society of Jesus, in August, at Saint Stanislaus Seminary in Florissant, Missouri. I had to take an intensive course in Latin at SLU from June until August, because in those days all the studies in the seminaries were still in Latin. Thank God that they no longer follow that Latin foolishness nowadays.

It was after I was accepted for the novitiate that I told my family in Saint Louis what I was going to do. That was a pleasant surprise for my father and for the whole family; but a few days later our surprise was greater, especially for me, when my brother, Pat, announced to everyone that he too had just been accepted to enter the Jesuit novitiate with me in August. I had had no idea that Pat, who was studying law at SLU, had been thinking about this; neither did he imagine that I in Detroit had applied for admission to the Jesuits.

To say good-bye to Colleen in May was very hard for both of us. We really loved each other very much and would have married. Thanks be to God for the crisis that he sent me, the doubts about his existence that made me consider him, God, the most important thing in the world—which is exactly what he is. If I had married Colleen, I would not be writing this history of mine; there would have been no metamorphosis into a revolutionary. I would most likely have remained a bourgeois gringo, quite family-centered, taken up with my wife and kids, with my job to earn enough money to fix up our home and to send our children to the best private schools, and with sports. God and the poor would have stayed on a lower plane in my life, even though I would have continued to go to daily mass and to talk a lot about religion, and to help the poor with monthly checks to the social agencies or the missions.

PART III. ENTRY INTO THE SOCIETY OF JESUS (1948–1962)

4. The Formation of a Jesuit - I

When my father, with great pride, along with my mother and all five of my sisters, took Pat and me to Florissant to the novitiate on that eighth of August 1948, a new chapter was started in my life and a new process began in my metamorphosis.

In that period after the war there was a big increase in religious vocations all over the world. Saint Stanislaus Seminary was the novitiate and juniorate for the Jesuits of the two provinces of Missouri and of Wisconsin. Before the war about forty new candidates used to enter each year; in 1981, after the big crisis of religious and priestly life in the Church, only about twenty entered for the two provinces.

On arriving at Florissant in 1948, we met a big crowd of sixty new candidates and their families. Everyone was very happy getting to know each other and the master of novices.

S.J. stands for *Societas Jesu* in Latin, Society of Jesus in English. (But the students of the Jesuit high schools in the United States say that S.J. stands for "soft job.") "Jesuit" is a nickname that the people have used for the members of the Society of Jesus since its foundation by Saint Ignatius of Loyola (in Spain) in the sixteenth century. In Latin *"Jesu-ita"* means "like Jesus."

I said that it was a joyful day for all these families of the new candidates getting to know Saint Stanislaus Seminary. But with one single blow everyone became very sad. All of a sudden, just as mass was over and before we said good-bye to our families, the master of novices announced two of the novitiate rules: first, no novice could leave the novitiate grounds; and second, only the immediate family could come to visit us for one day twice a year.

This was no problem for me since I was accustomed to army restrictions and being away from home; but most of the sixty new novices were seventeen or eighteen years old who had just graduated from high school and had never lived away from their families. There were, however, a good number of war veterans, like Pat and me: Jim Short had been a captain in the air force; Harold Bradley, a sergeant in command of a Sherman tank in several battles in Africa and Italy; Dick Spillane, a captain in the marines; Dick Lundstrom, a corporal, like me, in the infantry; and others.

Other things that were hard for the younger men to adapt themselves to in the novitiate life were sleeping on cots close together in a big dormitory; jumping up at 5:00 A.M. at the sound of the big seminary bell to make an hour's meditation together in a classroom (in absolute silence); having every minute of the day scheduled according to a program put on the bulletin board the night before; having to break off immediately, at the sound of a bell, whatever one was doing to go to the next activity; having to limit oneself to very little wash water, drawn from a well with a hand pump, and with only one bath a week; having to ask permission for everything—for paper, soap, another shirt, a pill, an extra bath during the week, and so on.

This was all so similar to life in the army that it caused no problem for me or for the other vets. But for those young men, whom I call bourgeois because they were almost all from the upper middle class and accustomed to life with their families (in big, comfortable houses, getting up and going to bed late, and doing what they wanted all day long), the novitiate regimen was hard—but necessary.

What was really difficult for all of us, the younger men and vets alike, was the rule of silence. Most of us had made 3-day retreats in silence with the Jesuits before entering the novitiate, but to keep silence every day of the year, even during meals, was almost impossible. Nevertheless, it was strictly forbidden to talk except during the hour of recreation at night after supper, in classes to answer the professor, at confession, or a few other times. If out of necessity we had to say something to a companion, like, "Pass the salt," or, "You start sweeping there, and I will start here," or, "Lend me the dictionary," it was required to say it in a low voice and in Latin, with no jokes.

Our novice master used to watch us like a hawk, and jump on us worse than a sergeant in boot camp. But as you can imagine, the sixty young fellows of first-year and the fifty of second-year novitiate with whom we lived, all between seventeen and twenty-seven, made plenty of secret jokes and did a lot of "talking" through hand signs or notes.

I especially remember the two big jokers, Jack Valenta and Marty Whelan, who did not let anything go by without a whispered joke or some kind of horseplay. They would use the filthiest words in order to scandalize our most pious and scrupulous fellow novices. Jack Valenta invented a substitute word "shrat" (instead of "shit"), which became quite popular among all the ten thousand Jesuits in the United States.

When one enters the novitiate, the first week, called First Probation, is to get to know the novitiate and its rules and to make a 5-day retreat to see if you are serious in your vocation. After this week, you put on a cassock (a full-length black robe over your shirt and pants, held together by a belt), which from that day until your death you were supposed to wear all day long, every day, except when going to bed or bathing, or playing sports or doing some kinds of manual labor. Haven't you seen pictures of priests riding motorcycles or horses with their robes tucked up around their waists?

Nowadays, thank God, they have eliminated much of these medieval practices, but in my day we could not leave the dormitory without the cassock and the biretta, the ecclesiastical cap with three peaks sticking up. You were only supposed to take the biretta off by grabbing the middle peak between the second and third fingers of your right hand. For all this, we continually repeated in whispers, "Shrat!"

This five-day retreat in First Probation was just made for me; it was exactly what I needed. Father Joseph Fisher, the young "socius" (assistant) to the master of novices gave the first week of the spiritual exercises of Saint Ignatius, with the idea that each young man should make a general confession of his life and start his novitiate with a cleansed and tranquil conscience. It was not the general confession that helped me so much, but the first meditations about the existence of God.

I entered the Society of Jesus to resolve my doubts about God's existence. (Of course, I did not mention this to my examiners as one of my reasons.) Well, the Holy Spirit, through the assistant master of novices, began immediately to resolve this big problem I had. In this retreat he enlightened me, not with the metaphysical arguments of Saint Thomas, which I had already studied and which did not satisfy me, but with an argument that Father Fisher taught us, which was so simple and so convincing that I have repeated it almost daily in my soul ever since.

Even today, in 1981, I use this same proof that Father Fisher proposed to us in 1948 in the retreats I give to others. It is actually an adaptation of one of Saint Thomas's five famous proofs, but in a language and with examples that are so simple that unlettered peasants in Honduras understand it perfectly. The argument goes: "Where there is order, there has to be an intelligence that put the things in such an order for an end he had in mind."

Let me try to explain this principle with simple examples: Who could deny that it was some intelligent person who put together the different parts of my watch with such an order and organization for telling the time? If a watch exists, there had to be a watchmaker. Or who could doubt that there had to be an intelligence who planned the ordering of all the different parts of an automobile—the motor, the wheels, the seats, the steering wheel —in such a way for the purpose he had in mind, namely, transporting the people seated in the car? If there is great order in a watch and an even more complicated order in an automobile that demand an intelligence who designed them, how much more does this world need an intelligence who put all its parts in such marvelous order!

How many stars are there in the universe? Our earth is a relatively small planet (a million earths could fit in the sun). It is moving at great velocity, 66,600 miles an hour (faster than a bullet fired from a gun, though the earth is so balanced that we do not feel this motion), in an enormous orbit around the sun. The sun itself is just one of the thousands of millions of stars of our galaxy, the Milky Way, which is just one of the hundreds of millions of galaxies that we have discovered so far.

If the earth were just a little bit closer to the sun, everything would burn up. If we were a little farther away from the sun, everything would turn to ice. That is why, according to our present knowledge, only on our planet do plant, animal, and human life exist.

A complete turn of the earth on its own axis takes twenty-four hours. This is the basis for the watch. The complete orbit of the earth around the sun is exactly 365.25 days. This is the basis for the calendar.

What a marvelous order! It follows infallible laws of nature. But how can there be laws (order) without a lawmaker (an intelligence)? This intelligence is what we call God. If God has intelligence, he is a personal God and is a person.

You could also meditate about the great order in the human eye, alive and organized for the purpose of seeing this world in motion and in color. The system of animal and human reproduction has always fascinated me and made me think of God, who designed it all. A flower, a tree, a fly that lands on my table, or my finger that moves when I want it to move, who can doubt that they are more marvelously ordered than a watch, and that they require a truly marvelous intelligence who designed them for purposes he had in mind?

To try to explain this marvelous order in the universe by saying that matter in motion has existed from eternity and that it develops through evolution does not explain anything. Rather, evolution demands that there be an intelligence that organized matter in such a way that it would evolve toward the order of the universe that we have and toward a future end that he has in mind.

It is true that this is not an argument that proves everything about God, for instance, that he is eternal and immortal, infinite, unchangeable, pure spirit, and so on. Nonetheless, at least for me, it gives a rational basis for belief in God, to not doubt his existence. What God is like, his nature—that God is love, is our Father, is three persons, Father, Son, and Holy Spirit—was all revealed by Jesus Christ, and one can believe everything that is in the New Testament once intellectually sure that God exists.

This retreat in First Probation gave me a peace of soul about God's existence that I had not had during the five previous years. However, it was not until the month-long spiritual exercises that the last traces of doubt about God were wiped out for good. It is not that I had never read or thought about this famous proof from order in the universe before entering the novitiate. I had used it since childhood in one way or another every time I admired the sky or the flowers. But it was not until this retreat that the Holy Spirit enlightened me with assurance down to the depths of my being that there has to exist this Intelligence, this personal God. This enlightenment and assurance in my soul about God was one of the most important events in my life, so that all that "shrat" in the novitiate was secondary, without importance, easy to endure.

I am not exaggerating when I explain the great psychological or nervous tension under which most of us 110 novices lived because of the novitiate training and regimen as practiced in those two years. Two novices had mental breakdowns. Quite a few suffered some damage to their nervous system. In my second year of novitiate I started to have tremendous headaches. Trying to concentrate on my studies, or meditations, or on the rule of silence, or on the rule of recalling God's presence every five minutes with a short prayer and, believe it or not, marking it down in a notebook to see how many times a day I carried out this rule—all this only gave me more headaches.

In our novitiate training almost everything was a sin: to waste a minute of time was a sin; to entertain yourself by thinking, not of sexual things, but simply of idle or useless things from your past, about your family or a party, was a sin; to sit with your legs crossed was a sin; to allow the cuff of your pants to rise up so that one could see a part of your bare leg was a sin; not to control distractions during meditation or study was a sin; to fall asleep during the meditation from 5:30 to 6:30 in the morning was a sin; to break the rule of silence and talk to a fellow novice or comment on something that happened was a sin; to speak in English instead of Latin, not only in times of silence, but even during recreation period after supper, was a sin; to come a minute late for meditation, or a meal, or study was a sin; and so on, and so on, and so on.

These examples will give you some idea of the great psychological pressure many of us felt during the two years, trying to dominate our natural instincts by sheer force of will, trying to control our every thought by sheer force of will. Something had to give. Some, indeed, seemed to have steel nerves. As for me, my head could not take it, nor my brain; even today, thirty years later, I get a severe headache if I concentrate too hard.

For me the saddest part of it was to see my closest friends, the most serious and rebellious young novices, leave the novitiate and return home because they could not take the regimen. Most of them also had headaches that they could not get rid of, and it was feared they also might have breakdowns. The regimen did not weed out the weakest, it ruined the best. I had special permission during my second year to leave meditation or classes when I had a severe headache and go outside to walk around or chop firewood on the extensive novitiate grounds. If I had not been able to do this, I also, without a doubt, would have been sent home.

There was another thing I did not like. When a classmate had to leave the Jesuits, a novitiate policy forbade him to tell any of us, and we would not know it until he was already gone. Then the novice-master would tell us about it in one of his daily classes, speaking of the former novice as though he were a failure, as though he were a traitor. From the beginning he gave us the idea that the most dishonorable thing one could do was to "put your hand to the plow and then look back." To leave the Jesuits was to abandon Jesus, to betray Jesus.

It was this atmosphere of fear that spoiled the asceticism and the spirituality of our novitiate and that caused this nervous tension, at least in me. I wanted to be a Jesuit missionary; that was the only thing that I wanted in life now. I did not want to fail, to turn back on Jesus.

In my second year of novitiate this great fear took hold of me. If I could not get rid of these headaches, I would not be able to continue the long studies for the priesthood and would have to leave, or worse, the master of novices would send me home. Naturally, this fear increased a thousand times the nervous tension in me and was one of the causes of my headaches.

Only at the end of this second year, a few months before taking vows, did the Holy Spirit give me a real enlightenment that left me quite tranquil and conformed. He made me understand that if I was now sure that God exists and has his plan for this world and for me, then the only thing important in life is to do his will. I had entered the Society of Jesus convinced that this was the will of God for me, but now, though I had a great desire to be a Jesuit, if through my Jesuit superiors God said that I could not be a Jesuit, I would have to do God's will and leave. This would not be a betrayal but rather a fulfillment of my vocation.

I no longer accepted some of the teachings of the novitiate. It was wrong to give us this horror of leaving the Society of Jesus. God gave me the opportunity and the privilege of being a Jesuit, and if God takes that away from me, if God no longer wants me to continue as a Jesuit, well, "Blessed be God," as Job said. To try to do God's will is the only way to love God. "Not my will, but yours be done, Lord," said Jesus in his agony.

I have to be honest and cannot put all the blame on the novitiate training for my nervous tension. Why was it that more than half of the novices did not suffer this tension, at least not as much as I? I recognize that the root cause of my tension came from my great pride. This is really the capital sin, or vice, that had me, and still partially has me, enslaved, not free. It is because I thought I was the best. I had to carry out and could carry out all the demands of the novitiate, to have complete control of myself, to perfect myself, and to stand out in all this better than the rest. I did it all in a spirit of competition and as in sports, I wanted to win, to stand out as superior. This is pride, a sin.

At least it seems to me that this partly explains why I felt more tension and pressure to perfect myself than some others did. Many novices did not make such strenuous efforts to carry out all the rules and suggestions. They were more humble, recognizing their limits. They were content with laughing at themselves and saying, "Ah, shrat!" when they failed in something. They did not take it all so seriously.

Another thing that takes a great deal of blame from our particular novice master was that he was simply a product of the training of the older Jesuits before him. He had learned in the three volumes of *The Practice of Christian Perfection*, written by a certain Alfonso Rodriguez, S.J., in the eighteenth century, that all those things were sins that he told us were sins. All of us novices had to read these volumes three times. The novice master tried to imitate his great hero, Willy Doyle, S.J., who used to take the discipline, that is, beat himself with a whip until he could no longer stand up, and who carved in his chest with a knife the name "Jesus." All the novices also had to read the biography of Willy Doyle. Looking back now I question how wise it was for his superiors to assign him as master of novices for twenty-two straight years. This long tenure would give him, or anyone else, a somewhat narrow vision of the world.

There were only four months to go to finish the second year of novitiate and take our vows, when the novice master fell into a new water well that was being dug, broke his hip, and had to remain in the hospital for several months of recuperation. Father Fisher, the young assistant to the master of novices took over. We began to have recreation and sports four afternoons a week instead of two, and some of us novices, who loved sports, immediately felt a great lifting of psychological tension.

The older man never returned to be novice master. He afterwards worked in the retreat movement for laypeople, and then as a parish priest in Saint Louis. I met him there about six years ago, and you should see what a lovable old man he had become! He was no longer like Willy Doyle, but like Jesus Christ!

I have talked too much about the negative side of the novitiate. It was really a tremendously positive experience. Even the headaches helped (and still do help) to make me more humble, to make me feel limited, to show me that I cannot win out over others by my own will power, that I am not better than the rest. However, the really qualitative leap in my spiritual evolution was during the complete thirty-day Spiritual Exercises that all the novices make a few months after entering the novitiate.

This month of Spiritual Exercises in silence with God is the basic experience that forms a Jesuit; it is the epitome of the Jesuit spirituality that our founder, Saint Ignatius of Loyola, left us. The novice master directed our Exercises, and they made such an impression on me that I can state in all truth that the sentiments of the great meditations (or "exercises") really became a part of my being. These are still the most basic motivating forces in my life.

I am not going to explain all the Exercises; it would take too long. Besides, in order to understand them one has to make them, not the whole thirty days, but at least for eight days, as we Jesuits do every year. I am continually giving these same Exercises of Saint Ignatius to campesino, labor union, and political leaders, although in an abbreviated three-day form. Later on, in the course of my explanation of the basic options for my priestly life, it will be seen that the roots of these options are in the Exercises of Saint Ignatius.

One of the experiences during the first week of the month of the Exercises I consider a miracle of grace, a true intervention of God in my life was with regard to my former doubts about God's existence. Not only did the Holy Spirit enlighten me more clearly than ever that there has to be an Intelligence that ordered this beautiful world in such a way for an end he has in mind, but I really experienced the presence of God. I felt God. He touched me spiritually; he spoke to me spiritually. I felt the Holy Spirit enlightening me, helping me to understand myself, to understand him, and to understand the world.

It was this very personal experience of God, the actual feeling of his presence, which invaded me during this month of the Exercises and which deepens itself in me more and more every day, that took away once and for all every doubt about God's existence. My spiritual life is founded on the solid rock of being sure that God exists, not only because I know that this great Architect of the universe has to exist, but because I have experienced and almost continuously feel the presence in me of my Father who loves me and of the Spirit of Jesus who directs my life.

We novices came out of the long retreat of the Exercises sitting on a cloud, and all that "shrat" of the rules of the novitiate was much easier to carry out. But after a few weeks the nervous tension in the novitiate was felt again. As a reaction against this and in order to relax, you should have seen the extreme fanaticism with which we threw ourselves into sports on Thursday and Sunday afternoons. Also, once a month we had an entire day to go walking in groups of three along the highways of the rural area where we lived near Florissant, or in summer time to walk the eight miles to the Jesuit villa on the Missouri River, called Charbonierre, for a swim in the pool there.

We had a competition going among the novices to see which group could go the farthest and return in the six hours we had for these walks. John Schauz (who is now a missionary priest near Salta, Argentina), my brother, Pat, and I were the champions. Pat once separated himself from his group and was running at full speed through the streets of the little town of Florissant when the police arrested him on suspicion.

For this he received the penance of publicly confessing his fault, kneeling before the priests' table during supper, and kissing the shoes of each priest. This punishment we called the *pin culpa* because there was a big diaper pin that the last novice to receive this penance, or *culpa,* wore on his cassock as a reminder. We were told by the novice master that if a novice received this *pin culpa* three times, he would be automatically expelled from the novitiate.

That, however, was not so, because in my two years of novitiate I received it six times. Although the novice master threatened each time that he would give me just one more chance, I believe that he cared for me because only a few novices besides myself really wanted to be foreign missionaries and so he did not want to expel me. He was the one who gave me the special permission to leave classes to relax when I had a headache.

My first *pin culpa* was shared with two others, John Schauz and John Schak because we got back fifteen minutes late from one of those marathon walks. We had walked and run forty-eight miles, well into the city of Saint Louis, in the six hours and fifteen minutes.

Another of my *pin culpas* was shared with a classmate named Tom. On the way to "Charb" (Charbonierre, the villa) Tom and I were wrestling, which is definitely against Rule 32, which forbids Jesuits to touch anyone (to avoid homosexuality, I suppose). It turned out that we were tossing and rolling each other around on the ground right in a bunch of poison ivy without realizing it. Later, on reaching the pool and taking a swim, this poison was spread all over Tom's body. Thank God nothing happened to me. The next day Tom had to go to a hospital and nearly died. The doctors had never seen such a severe case of ivy poisoning.

I do not recall what the other three *pin culpas* were for, but my sixth and last was just one week before taking vows. Father Fisher, who was now in charge of us, was so angry with me that he was going to throw me out of the Society. However, since I already had the provincial superior's permission to take my vows, he had to call the provincial, who told him that he should pardon me. The fact was that there were three of us in the group, but I was to be the only one expelled, for being the "intellectual author" and the leader of the adventure.

It was a wonderful adventure, a lot like what happened to Don Cogswell and me in the Rhône in France during the war. John Schak and I had talked for months about doing it, and at last we had our chance when all of the novices had a day of rest at Charb. Jack Lemoine also wanted to go with us, so the three of us slipped away early in the morning from Charb in just our bathing suits and went down the hill to the Missouri River. We chose a big fallen tree trunk, which the three of us pulled down to the bank and into the river, and we lay on top of it with our legs in the water to direct it a little.

Charb was about twenty-five miles from the mouth of the Missouri River, where it empties into one of the largest rivers in the world, the Mississippi. The Missouri River at this point just below Charb was about a quarter of a mile wide and had a very swift current. It was forbidden, not only for novices, but for all citizens, to swim in this dangerous river, but a few of us had already gone swimming a number of times. This day our plan was to float with the swift current about five miles downstream to where a small back road comes down to the river and there get out and walk back secretly to Charb in time for lunch. When we did not get back for lunch at Charb, or for supper at the novitiate, a fellow classmate who knew our plan told Father Fisher and he, at about six in the evening, went out with the police to look for us.

At seven, we three entered the novitiate in our bathing suits— to be welcomed back with joy by our classmates and to be bawled out by all the priests. What happened was that the river current had been so strong that it took us close to the opposite bank of the river and we could not get out at the small road as we had planned. We decided to go on downstream to the bridge of a major highway that passes over the river very close to its mouth and return to Florissant by hitchhiking. That is what we did. We got out of the water at the bridge about five miles on the other side of the river, walked across the bridge, and got a ride, first to the crossroads, and then to Florissant and the novitiate.

For me it was a nice adventure "to prepare the three of us to be missionaries." After so much bawling out, I became a little angry and told the fathers that if they were going to punish me and expel me that they should do it for my big sins, my mortal sin of pride, and not for an interesting adventure that at the most was only a venial sin of disobedience. The fact is that the threats of being expelled from the Society of Jesus no longer scared me; the Holy Spirit had enlightened me that if God wanted me to be a missionary, I would be one, and if it was not God's will, then I could not insist on it.

Of the sixty who entered the novitiate in August of 1948 (if I remember correctly) in August of 1950 about forty from the two provinces of Missouri and Wisconsin were left to take our perpetual vows of poverty, chastity, and obedience until death in the Society of Jesus. Ever since my meditations about the life of Jesus in the thirty-day Spiritual Exercises, the vow of poverty was for me the most important of the vows. We promised to be poor like Jesus.

For some religious, the vow of poverty means "spiritual poverty," being indifferent, not attached, to material possessions. A religious and a religious congregation can be owners and live in big houses with many bourgeois comforts, can have cars, television, tape decks, expensive cameras, and so on, as long as all this is "necessary" for the apostolate or for needed rest and recreation. Ever since the novitiate, since our long retreat, I have had hundreds of discussions with other religious men and women about this.

For me, the life of Jesus as seen in the Gospels demonstrates his identification with the poor and their problems, his personal life of material poverty, the fact that he, the Lord God, chose to become one of the masses of poor who make up the majority of humanity. All of this makes obvious Jesus' meaning when he said that if anyone wants to follow him, he has to sell whatever he has, give it to the poor, and follow the Son of man who does not have a place to lie down, though the birds have their nests and the foxes their caves. I concluded right from the novitiate that "spiritual poverty," not being attached to material things, is the obligation of every Christian who wants to save him- or herself and not sin. The "evangelical counsel" to follow Jesus, the poor campesino from Nazareth, imitating him, is to voluntarily be poor, identify yourself with the poor, live with and like the poor—the materially poor, the masses of poor men and women in the world who have no material security in life, no savings in the bank. It was the memory of those poor Arab refugees in Marseilles that left me no doubt about what the word poor meant.

That is what I wanted to do, that is what I promised to do by my vow of poverty. That is also why, more than when I entered to be a missionary to save souls, when I finished the novitiate I wanted to be a missionary in Honduras to live with and like the poor, like Jesus. During these days, I read a lot about the Jesuit priest-workers in Europe, about the lives of Saint Francis Xavier in India and of Saint Isaac Jogues with the North American Indians, and about all the Jesuit martyr saints, almost all of whom were missionaries.

It is not that I already had an ideology of class in those days, or that we had been taught something about the struggle "for the liberation of the poor and oppressed." Even though I had been a labor union member, I had almost no interest in "the class struggle" until I began to live with the poor, with the campesinos in Honduras. The spirituality of the novitiate was "Jesus and I," to seek our own personal perfection: an individualism in the spiritual life. There was very little emphasis on the great injustices in the world.

We never heard news reports on radio or television, and it was even forbidden in the novitiate to read a newspaper. Before going further, I want to point out that Jesuit novitiate training in the U.S. has changed since my time. Also I do not mean that all the Jesuits do not love the poor. I have never met a Jesuit who does not help the poor in some way. But thanks be to God there are some provinces in the Society of Jesus, like the Central American Province, where the novices are, right from their entrance, made conscious of the theory and the practice of identifying themselves with the poor in their struggles for liberation.

Just to give one example: the novices of the novitiate in Panama went to Nicaragua after the triumph of the Sandinista revolution to help in the big national campaign to teach a half million poor adults who never had the opportunity to go to school. Each one lived for five months with a poor campesino family in the mountains of the department of Boaco. Another experience of these novices is to spend a month harvesting coffee—or cotton or sugar cane—living during this time just like the poor live every day of the year, sleeping on wooden boards without a mattress and eating rice, beans, tortillas, and coffee three times a day every day. These future priests feel in their own flesh the exploitation of the poor, of the unlettered, of the majority of humanity, and they rebel against these injustices. If we want to further develop the Society of Jesus in the United States, the novices there should also experience in their own flesh what it means "to live like the poor." I wish they would all spend one or two months in Central America picking coffee with the poor campesinos before taking their vow of poverty!

Here is a good place to share a few of my present concerns about religious obedience. I believe that good, balanced spiritual training should strive to develop a critical conscience in novices rather than an automatic, military blind obedience that encourages conformity. In the United States the Jesuits learn that obedience is the most important vow, but I do not find anything in the New Testament about religious obedience (that is, obedience to a religious superior) as an "evangelical counsel." Jesus did not belong to any religious congregation under obedience to any superiors, nor did any of the first Christians. During the first centuries all Christians strived to live "the spiritual life," "the life of perfection." For me, the three evangelical counsels are poverty, chastity, and nonviolence.

Before closing this chapter on my spiritual development in the novitiate, I want to share a favorite meditation on Rule 11 of the Summary of the Constitutions of the Society of Jesus, written by Saint Ignatius in the sixteenth century. In synopsis form it says:

> To advance in the spiritual life we should love and embrace with all our strength whatever Jesus loved and embraced. And just as worldly men love and seek honors and fame and a good reputation, we should follow Jesus and desire just the opposite, that is, insults, calumnies, and even to be called crazy for trying to be like Jesus.

During all my years since the novitiate, whenever I have been considered crazy in my efforts to live the gospel fully, "for trying to be like Jesus," I have always drawn great strength and support from these words of Saint Ignatius.

5. The Formation of a Jesuit - II

After taking vows, we passed on to the juniorate, which simply meant going to live in another one of the big buildings at the same Saint Stanislaus Seminary. There was a different regimen in the juniorate, a bit more human, with new superiors and new Jesuit priest professors. Each one of us now lived in a small private room, a cell separated from the neighboring one by a partition that did not reach the ceiling. The schedule was usually classes and study and prayer, with two hours of recreation with sports every afternoon.

The juniorate was basically the first two years of university studies (credits were recognized by Saint Louis University), with emphasis on the classics: we studied Latin, Greek, Hebrew, English, French, history, and so on. I hated these studies. For me this was worse "shrat" than the novitiate regimen. My headaches naturally grew worse when I had to concentrate on something repugnant and useless (for me) like Latin, Greek, or Hebrew.

I still had permission to leave class or study when my headache was too bad, and this saved my vocation as a Jesuit. Without escaping for a while each day to cut down trees and chop them up for firewood while my companions were studying, I would surely have had to leave the Society in the juniorate. Several times I talked about this with the superior.

This was the worst period, the most unhappy time of all my Jesuit life and a great trial of my vocation. More than ever I wanted to be a missionary in Honduras. I even started to study some Spanish on the side. In the juniorate Tom Quiery, who was one year ahead of me, became my best friend; he too had decided that he wanted to be a missionary in Honduras.

Most of us "juniors" threw ourselves like mad into sports each afternoon in order to relax, while a few preferred to listen to classical music. I started to practice the guitar using a booklet that showed a simple method for learning it. Singing cowboy music to myself was a big help for relaxing and enduring the juniorate.

Several times in games I hurt my bad knee. Finally I had to go to the hospital in Saint Louis for an operation to remove the broken piece of cartilage that would slip into the joint. It was four rough months before I could run and play sports again, but the operation turned out well. Nevertheless, even today if I walk or run too much, my knee swells up and hurts.

Since I had four years of university before entering the Society, I could have gone to study philosophy in Saint Louis after one year of juniorate, as did the others who had more than one year of university before entering. But, imagine it, the superiors decided that I had to make a second year of juniorate "because I had not acquired a love of classical studies, which all Jesuits should have."

I suppose you have guessed it; instead of learning to love more the classical literature of ancient Rome and Greece, and Shakespeare, Byron, and Keats, I finished the juniorate with a complete antipathy for these studies. Since most of the Jesuits in the United States are going to spend their whole lives as priests teaching in one of our high schools or universities, which in those days demanded that all the students take Latin and Greek, the preparation of United States Jesuits is designed to form professors.

Ever since the juniorate I have resented this and have often expressed my resentment. Practically all our great Jesuit heroes, our saints and martyrs, have been missionary priests in foreign countries, or in their own country with workers or Indians or blacks, or prisoners, like Father Dismas Clark of our own Missouri Province. I resented it that they would not let me study and prepare myself for this kind of priestly work. I assured them that I did not want to be a priest-professor. They were quite right when they said that I "did not have the spirit of the juniorate."

Thanks be to God, everything in this life is passing. I finally finished the juniorate and my imprisonment in the seminary outside of Florissant and went to live in the big city of Saint Louis in the philosophate at Saint Louis University. It was like a brand-new life, like rising from the dead after being crucified and buried in a tomb. Even the studies were more interesting: three years of philosophy and in third year, at least, they let me take some Spanish courses.

Our way of living really changed. Back in 1952 we philosophers lived in one of the old original buildings of the university, as part of the same community as the priest-professors at SLU. The hundred of us students lived apart from the nearly one hundred priests, but we ate together in the same dining hall, and thus we had a lot of contact with them, which helped broaden the vision of us young philosophers. Also, we had certain classes with the lay students in the university.

Now that I had resolved once and for all my doubts about the existence of God, I no longer had the same interest in the study of philosophy as before entering the Society. All the textbooks and classes were in Latin, and I had to repeat many of the same courses that I had had before. My superiors decided that I would make a good university religion teacher because I had so much previous experience in the world. Therefore I was supposed to get a master's degree in philosophy, which would require a fourth year of philosophy studies.

They assigned to me as a personal counselor and spiritual director a big intellectual, a professor of philosophy who had written several books. He was also a man who became angry very easily. Well, he insisted that I had to be a priest-professor of religion. "Being a missionary is for those who don't have many brains, the same as being a policeman," he said. With that, I never again spoke to my "counselor."

Thanks be to God, in my third year, instead of getting a "B", as was demanded for continuing on with postgraduate studies for a master's, I received a "C" from Dr. Collins in his course, "The History of Medieval Philosophy." With this I could only get a bachelor's and a licentiate degree in philosophy and could not go on for my master's. The big joke is that before entering the Society I took this very same course from the same Dr. Collins, using the same textbook that he had written, and had received a "B." How I rejoiced when our superior gave me the "sad" news that I could not go on for my master's in philosophy!

I have always had problems with my superiors, in the army and in all my time in the Society of Jesus. Only now in Nicaragua, in exile, where I am writing this, I have no problem with any superior. One superior with whom I had lots of problems was our rector during the time when we passed to the new philosophate, "Fusz Memorial," to form a separate community from the priest-professors of SLU. He was a strict disciplinarian. For example, he used to go smelling with his nose up against the doors of our little rooms to find out if one of the philosophers was smoking, which was strictly forbidden.

On entering the philosophate, I got permission along with others to help teach catechism to the children of the parish grade school connected with the university, Saint Francis Xavier, run by the Sisters of the Blessed Virgin Mary. With this excuse for getting out of our philosophate house, I used to visit the families of these children and try to help them with their problems, especially the older children who had delinquency problems. Most of the families of the parish and of the neighborhood around the university were black and very poor.

I used to visit the juvenile courts, and there I met the famous chaplain of the prisoners, Father Dismas Clark, S.J. He took me along several times to visit the jails with him and quickly became my hero. When my superior learned that I was going around with Father Clark, he forbade me ever to see this rebel priest "who used dirty language." The fact is that some of the priests at SLU felt very uncomfortable with Father Clark because he publicly criticized the rich benefactors of the university for exploiting the poor in Saint Louis.

I admit that I disobeyed this order several times, and also the other order of the superior not to have an apostolate, not with the children, the university students, or anyone. He ordered me to dedicate myself exclusively to my studies. I had clashes with some of our priest-professors from the time we moved into Fusz Memorial. I criticized in class and in Jesuit meetings the bourgeois, middle-class style of life in our "palace." From our back windows we could see the poor, dirty, ramshackle apartment buildings of the black families, and the contrast was too much for me. I just could not keep quiet.

A few of the philosophers agreed with me. We often discussed the huge problem of racial discrimination in the United States. Even though since 1954 there have been laws forbidding segregation, the fact is that blacks and whites in the United States often live in two worlds, apart. Blacks are about 17 percent of the population in the United States, but in some southern states and in many of the cities in the north they are around half of the population. Over the past 20 years, many of the whites in these cities moved to the wealthy suburbs where blacks were neither represented nor welcomed. However, the blacks, in general (and also the Puerto Ricans, the Mexicans, and the other Latins), stayed in the centers of the cities, often in neighborhoods of poor, crowded housing and tenements. Lately, some whites are moving back into the cities, upgrading the neighborhoods, and causing some poor people to move again.

Even today, in 1981, after the big campaigns organized by black Christians (like Martin Luther King who was assassinated), to gain some of their civil equal rights, there is still a lot of de facto segregation. There are churches, theaters, schools, shops, clubs, parks, swimming pools, and so on, where, de facto, only whites enter, or only blacks enter. Thanks to the nonviolent resistance campaigns of the black masses there is much more integration than before, but there is still a long way to go before we can say that there is no discrimination against blacks (or against Latin Americans, or other groups) in the United States.

I got the idea that the principal way to end segregation would be by intermarriage of black and white, but it could be furthered also by whites going to live in black neighborhoods, going to their schools, theaters, churches, rest rooms, and so on. In the philosophate I started telling everyone that I was partly black, that my great-grandmother had been a black woman. It was not true, but who can prove one's ancestry? Later on when I had the opportunity, it was interesting to go into the places reserved for blacks, to sit in their parts of the Greyhound bus stations, to use their public rest rooms, but in the philosophate my superior forbade me to visit or even talk to these poor black families who lived behind our residence. I often did it anyway; it was like forbidding me to fraternize with the German prisoners during the war.

I want to relate a beautiful experience I had during these years of philosophy. I fell in love with a nun, one of the teachers of the children where I went to teach catechism. After sending the kids home, she and I used to sit around talking. I started coaching the grade school basketball team, and this also gave me the opportunity to see and talk with my friend.

Our conversations were very intellectual and very spiritual, but little by little we both admitted to each other that we were falling in love. We decided not to see or speak to each other any more. By then the superior had already forbidden me to have any apostolate, and so I had to give up teaching catechism and coaching at the school anyway. I still remember the love that I felt for this religious sister, a pure and beautiful love. After leaving the philosophate, I never saw her again, and I do not know where she is now.

Other memories that I have of these years include that of the Dixieland band we formed with Ed Lavin of the New York Province on trumpet, Bill Quiery, Tom's brother, on the piano, me on the trombone, which I was trying to learn to play, and three others. It was great fun. I also remember the summer vacations at the big Jesuit villa on the lakes at Waupaca, Wisconsin. I practiced every day there for a big ten-mile swimming race held every year through the chain of lakes. One year I won the race; I was still a big sports fanatic. I still had my problem with headaches when I studied too much, but with all these diversions in the philosophate, I was learning how to control them.

After finishing the three years of philosophy and graduating from SLU, we Jesuits were to receive the four minor orders as steps toward the priesthood, which we would receive after our third year of theology. But the superior was so angry with me that he wanted to expel me from the Society of Jesus. Our other priest-teachers convinced him that, instead of expelling me, he should hold off my minor orders for a few years to see if I could "learn to behave better." He informed me that I could not receive minor orders and that I had to go to talk with the father provincial, who lived in a different Jesuit house in the city. In the Society of Jesus the highest authority after the Father General in Rome is the provincial.

The Missouri provincial, Father Daniel Conway (called "Cowboy Dan" because that is what he had been before in Colorado), was a very open and understanding man. He told me that he had been just like me when he was in philosophy; that he only wanted the active apostolate; that he too had often escaped from the philosophate without permission to wander around in the city visiting the jails and hospitals. He said he was going to tell the superior to pardon me and allow me to receive minor orders with my classmates. As the most wonderful surprise, he told me that I would go to the Belize Mission to teach at Saint John's College for my three years of regency. I almost kissed him, I was so grateful.

With regard to my development or evolution in the spiritual life during this period of philosophy, I had three books I read and reread and used in my hours of daily meditation. They are the only books that I have bought in all my years of study in the Society of Jesus and the only ones that I took with me to reread when I changed houses or jobs in the following years. They are *Abandonment to Divine Providence* by de Caussade, *In the Heart of the Masses* by Charles de Foucauld, and *My Experiments With Truth* by Mahatma Gandhi.

De Caussade wrote his famous book and letters of spiritual direction in the eighteenth century. He helped me a lot to understand, not only that God is in everything, but also how it is that God can control the evolution of the world using human beings who are free to collaborate with his plan or to ruin it. The Holy Spirit enlightened me in my meditations on this book in regard to "actual grace" and the famous fight (which we studied in philosophy) between the Jesuits and the Dominicans who were trying to reconcile human free will with the control that God has over everything that happens in this world.

Here is my understanding of actual grace. Every time we are going to make a free choice, the Holy Spirit in us enlightens us by means of actual grace to know which choice would be the better one, and with another kind of actual grace stimulates our free will to decide for the better one. "Actual" grace means to move us "to act" (freely) in the line of love of neighbor and against selfishness (or love of self). It is true that most people and even most religious, when they are going to make some decision, are not conscious of these movements of the Holy Spirit, pay no heed to them, and make their decisions according to their natural instincts and following the habits they have formed since childhood.

De Caussade explains that the spiritual life, our sanctification, implies being docile to these movements of the Holy Spirit in our soul. More and more I have to learn to recognize the actual grace enlightening me in every choice I have and more and more forget myself and my desires and instincts in order to choose God's will, to love. I have to be very recollected and contemplative to listen to the inspirations and feel the movement of the Holy Spirit.

I should abandon myself into God's hands like the poor who have no other security than their trust that God will take care of them. I should also abandon myself into God's hands as an instrument for him to use as he wants, to help in the salvation of the world. That is what Saint Ignatius teaches also: that God should direct my life and all my decisions. He knows best. Only he knows which action, which suffering, or which event, which appears to us as accident, can best serve for the extension of his Kingdom on earth. We have to trust in our Father, in his divine providence that orders everything that happens in this world for our sanctification.

Later on during my studies of theology I read a lot of Teilhard de Chardin in order to complete my understanding of where the Spirit of Jesus is leading the evolution of the world by means of his actual grace in all human beings. Even during my philosophate, the base of my spiritual life was always to try to be a real Ignatian "contemplative in action," finding God in all things, in all events, and abandoning myself into our Father's hands in order to be guided by the Spirit of Jesus living and acting in me. I am telling the truth when I state that the greatest pleasure in my life in these last twenty-five years has been to contemplate the action of God's providence not only in me, but in all people. I can see his Holy Spirit directing the evolution of the whole universe, of all nations, and of each person toward himself, toward his Kingdom of love and brotherhood.

This is the same spirituality that I found and enjoyed in Charles de Foucauld. My favorite prayer, one that I have sent to many of my friends, was written by Foucauld when he lived alone among the pagan bedouin in the African desert about fifty years ago:

Father, I abandon myself into Your hands,
Do with me whatever You want.
For whatever You do, I thank You.
I am ready for, I accept, all.
Let only Your will be done in me and in all your creatures,
And I'll ask nothing else, my Lord.
Into Your hands I commend my soul;
I give it to You, Lord, with the love of my heart,
For I love You, my God,
And so need to give, to surrender myself into Your hands
With a trust beyond all measure,
Because You are my Father.

This prayer should be said slowly, with rhythm, pausing after each line to listen to the Spirit of Jesus in your soul. To abandon yourself to the providence of God is the secret of peace of soul. It is what helped me at last to control (at least in part) my nerves and headaches, leaving aside the worries about the thousands of things over which I have no control anyway, trusting that God knows best and that he will enlighten me in his due time about how to solve the problems that I face.

Another important basis of my spirituality is the idea of voluntarily identifying oneself with the poor, of incarnating oneself as much as possible in the poor, the working class. This idea is directly from the gospel, and it is also in the Spiritual Exercises of Saint Ignatius, but it was René Voullaime's book of the ideas and writings of Charles de Foucauld, *In the Heart of the Masses,* that brought it home to me. Foucauld, the French bourgeois soldier, sinner, penitent, Trappist, hermit, manual worker, priest, missionary, martyr, put it into practice, and inspired the founding of six religious institutions in different parts of the world based on his ideas.

Foucauld said that he did not understand how anyone could call him- or herself a Christian and have a comfortable living. How could anyone be a disciple of Christ and live with a comfortable, bourgeois house and food while the great masses of humanity, our brothers and sisters, do not have a decent house or sufficient food? He said, "I do not know about others, but I cannot imagine a love of Jesus that permits me to live in comfort while he lived in poverty and crowned with thorns." God freely chose to be born of a poor campesino woman in order to incarnate himself in the poor, workers' class that makes up most of humanity. Jesus identified himself with this poor class and shared their life with them from birth till death.

Neither Foucauld, nor I, while I was still in the philosophate, understood that poverty and the division of society into social classes is because of the capitalist system of exploitation of the workers. He and I only had the idea of incarnating ourselves into this poor, workers' class, like Jesus, in order to love them. We did not understand then that Christ came into this world in order to liberate the poor from their poverty and oppression—in this world, not after death—that he wants to take away the sin, the injustice, of this world; that he wants to change this world. I was enlightened by the Spirit of Jesus about what we have to do to really love the poor only when I was finally incarnated and identified with them in Honduras.

The other book that helped me very much during many years is the autobiography of Gandhi, *My Experiments with Truth,* in which three principal ideas of his spirituality stand out: First, practice self-control, mortification, asceticism; live as simply as possible, and do not possess anything that is not really necessary for your life or your work. Gandhi never ate meat. He went around on foot as much as possible instead of using buses and cars. When he was thirty-five years old, he and his wife took a vow of chastity, to abstain from sexual relations for the rest of their lives. Second, for Gandhi God is Truth. One who is seeking the Truth will not admit any kind of deception or lie in relations with others. Third, we will only change this world and eliminate injustice by using nonviolent methods.

Since my days in the army when I decided not to kill any German, because we are all brothers, I have been a pacifist. During the years that I was in the philosophate, there was a lot of organized passive resistance and civil disobedience by the blacks in the United States to gain their civil rights. The basis of this great Christian (principally Protestant) movement were the ideas and methods of Gandhi, which had achieved by nonviolent means the independence of India. The idea of Gandhi is not to conquer your enemies in order to force them to grant you your rights, but rather to make them conscious that their actions are unjust and inhuman Then they will be converted and voluntarily stop their injustice. "The truth has more power to conquer him than the gun."

So it was that the British government finally admitted that treating India with colonial imperialism, with unjust discrimination and exploitative laws was wrong. It was a long, hard struggle, with many years in jail and many weeks of hunger strikes by Gandhi and his followers, before the British admitted their injustices and granted India its independence. Gandhi, of course, wound up assassinated. This was the same course that Martin Luther King and his followers took to achieve better laws against racial discrimination in the United States.

Many of us philosophers liked this "Christian" method of nonviolence for overcoming injustices. We thought that you could not be a Christian and use violence, that all war is unjust and un-Christian. The crusades of the medieval popes were certainly un-Christian. We thought it was more Christian not to defend yourself or your family with violence. Later on I will explain how these ideas about violence evolved and changed during my metamorphosis.

Another thing that the study of Gandhi helped me to understand is that the Holy Spirit obviously works in non-Christians also. This is not only to save them, but to use them, like Gandhi, to spread the ideas or the Spirit of Jesus, of the gospel, in the world. Gandhi lived for many years in England studying to be a lawyer. He read the Bible a lot, and many friends tried to convert him to Christianity. "I have fallen in love with Jesus Christ," he said, "but I will never become a Christian, because I do not want to be like the Christians." He remained a devout Hindu all his life and tried to change the system of inequality and social castes that religion practices. Gandhi is as much a saint as Saint Ignatius Loyola, our wonderful founder of the Jesuits.

6. The Formation of a Jesuit - III

A new phase in my metamorphosis was started in June of 1955 when I got on the plane in New Orleans with Charlie Woods and Jack Ruoff to begin my life as a missionary in Belize, British Honduras. It was not entirely a new chapter. I more or less continued in the same rhythm of evolution in my thinking and my consciousness as in the previous years of study. It was not until after becoming a priest and returning to the Republic of Honduras after Third Probation in Colombia that a new chapter in my life started, that of being a revolutionary. In 1955 I was still a real "gringo," very middle-class, very selfish, very anticommunist, without any understanding of the structural causes of the poverty that certainly worried me. My three years in Belize helped me to deepen my love for the poor and my desire to incarnate myself with them.

In 1955 the name of the country was still British Honduras, one of the last of the English colonies, with a British prime minister and the army and police force under British officers. The name of the capital and largest city was Belize City. In recent years, England agreed to give them their independence, and they already have a native of Belize as prime minister and have changed the name of the country to Belize.

Guatemala claims this whole country as a historical and legal part of its territory and threatens to annex it to Guatemala by invading it as soon as the British pull out. They will not be able to do it, however, because almost all the people of Belize want an independent country within the British Commonwealth.

I really enjoyed my three years of regency in Belize. It is a very small country with a long coastline on the Caribbean Sea and about 150,000 inhabitants. The most interesting thing is that there are five "races," each with its own language. The greatest number are Creoles, a mixture of black, Indian, and English, who speak a Creole English that it took me a few months to understand. Then there are the Latins, or "Ladinos," who came from Mexico or Guatemala, speak Spanish, and live close to the borders of those two countries. There are Mayan Indians, who speak Spanish and Mayan, and Ketchi Indians, who speak their own language and know very little Spanish. And there are blacks, called Caribs, who speak English and their native African language. They are fishermen, live together in villages all along the coastline, and have a love of study (many of the grade school teachers in the country are Caribs).

The official language of the country is English, and all the children of all the races who go to school learn it; nevertheless, there are many older folks who only know Mayan, or Ketchi, or Spanish, or Carib. Another characteristic of Belize is that almost all the children of the whole country finish the eight years of grade school and more than half of them go on to at least part of high school (called college in Latin America). Illiterate persons are practically nonexistent.

In spite of all this emphasis on education, Belize is an extremely poor country. There are not enough paying jobs available for those who graduate from high school each year. The great desire of these young graduates is to go to the United States or to England, because there are very few natural resources or good farmlands and almost no industry in Belize. Up to now, stressing education for the populace has not helped much in the economic development of the country.

Nonetheless, it is admirable how the British government not only helps even the smallest villages have their complete grade schools (even if there is only one teacher for all the eight grades), but also how it promotes religious education. There are various big Protestant sects in Belize, the principal one being the Anglican Church, the official religion of England (under the queen as head of the Church). I think that practically all the primary and secondary schools of the country belong to one or another church. They all receive help from the government for the construction of buildings and the salaries of the teachers, secretaries, and even of the priest, nun, or Protestant pastor who directs the school.

About half the population of the country belongs to the Catholic church. Almost all the Mayan and Ketchi Indians and the black Caribs are Catholics. More than half the Spanish-speaking Ladinos, and the Creoles belong to the Protestant sects. There are good ecumenical relations among the different churches, and with the government.

The American Jesuit David Hickey was the Catholic bishop in my time, and almost all the priests in the country were Jesuits from the Missouri Province. The goal of the Jesuits was correctly set at forming a native church with native priests. In 1955 there were five native diocesan priests, and now, in 1981, under Bishop Hodapp, S.J., there are three times that number.

As for the number of priests to take care of the Catholics, Belize is almost as well off as the United States, with one priest for every thousand Catholics, whereas in Honduras, for example, there is only one priest for every twenty thousand Catholics. This was one of the reasons I and a couple of other fellow Jesuit scholastics teaching in Belize wanted to return as priests to work in our mission in Honduras instead of in Belize. We saw the great injustice, the unfair distribution of the spiritual riches (of the priests) in the Church.

To go back to the day that I arrived in Belize: as has been quite typical of me, I shot off my mouth as soon as I shook hands on meeting my new superior, Father Urban Kramer, S.J. Pointing my finger at the big building where the Jesuits of Saint John's College (SJC) in Belize City live, I asked him, "Do we Jesuits live in that palace?" He became very angry with me right away and told me that if I did not like the house, I could turn right around and go back to the States. So began three years of problems with this superior, also. I recognize that my capital sin of pride was at work again! As if I, who had just arrived, were a better missionary than the priests who had been working there for years!

This Father Kramer was really a great man, very self-sacrificing. I did not like him as a superior, but of much greater importance he was a very good missionary. He personally went to clear an area of the jungle in the Stann Creek district in order to start an agricultural school.

In my time, SJC was not only our Jesuit high school for the Belize boys, but also had boarding school facilities for boys from all the Central-American countries. It was the job of the five Jesuit scholastics who were making our three years of regency to take care of these fifty boarding students day and night, under the direction of Father Francis Cull.

In general, these were rich men's sons from Spanish-speaking Guatemala, Honduras, El Salvador, and Nicaragua, who wanted their boys to learn English. A good percentage of them were problem adolescents who had been expelled from other high schools in their own countries. The rule was that they always had to speak English, and we used to punish them if we caught them speaking Spanish. Father Cull was very hard on them, but they were very spoiled and disobedient and made our lives plenty hard. I was happy to hear that the boarding school was dropped a few years later.

I was the head coach for all sports at SJC during my three years there, and through this I not only won the friendship of the students but also of most of the people of Belize City, who were great sport fans, especially of basketball. Right from my first year as coach, our high school basketball team won the championship, not only of the country's high school league, but also of the men's national league.

I never liked teaching school, but since I had these fine diversions, sports and other activities outside of the school, I spent these three years very happily. My closest friend was Tom Quiery, who was a scholastic one year ahead of me. During free days we would go fishing and swimming off the cayos, which are beautiful little islands in the Caribbean Sea close to Belize. We used to go with Charlie Woods, a native of Belize City, who had been my classmate ever since the novitiate and was a great hunter of snakes, crocodiles, and many kinds of animals.

Charlie once took us in a jeep to hunt deer at night with shotguns and headlamps. We went slowly along the mountain road without using the headlights of the car, with Charlie and me seated on the two fenders with our headlamps lighting up the forest on both sides. The eyes of any animal shine out in the night when a light strikes them.

Suddenly Charlie jumped off the moving jeep and ran into the forest; I went after him without knowing why. He fired both barrels of his shotgun, and I arrived just in time to see a big wounded deer give Charlie a strong kick in the chest with his hind legs (just like mules do), which sent Charlie sprawling on the ground. The deer ran off, and Charlie got up without his shotgun and ran after him.

Without taking off his clothes, he dove into a deep river in which the deer was swimming toward the opposite bank. On reaching him, Charlie tried to strangle him, but the deer escaped and came swimming back to the bank where I was standing and watching all this with great wonder.

It was easy for me to kill the animal in the water with one shot, and Charlie dragged it out of the river to take it to the car. I thought this over later, and it made me sick to my stomach to think of killing such a beautiful, defenseless animal in that way. I swore I would never go hunting again. For Charlie it was great sport, and he could not understand it when I told him that I would not go hunting with him anymore.

During the long summer, school was out and Tom Quiery and I went with Dr. John Cull, the brother of Francis of SJC, on his yearly visits to the villages that belonged to the parish of Stann Creek. Most of them were villages of the black Caribs on the seashore to the north and south of Stann Creek. We reached them by using a small inboard motorboat that the parish had.

This boat and its motor were so old that it was now dangerous to go out to sea in it. Once, the motor died on us when we were out in a storm; by the time we finally managed to fix it, we could not see land—the wind had taken us out to sea. It took us several hours to find the coast again.

Another time, when we were on our way for a fifteen-day mission in a village on the Sittee River a little upstream from the sea, the motor failed again, and we could not get it started. Dr. Cull taught us a rule for missionaries that we never forgot: never turn back; always go on, even if it is on foot or swimming, leaving the car or the boat behind. That way you will get to your destination, even though you arrive a day late.

Well, in order to move our boat along the coast about fifteen miles to the south to the mouth of the Sittee River, we hoisted two hammocks as sails and started to row. We finally reached the river at nightfall and pulled onto the bank to cut some long poles in the forest. With these we poled the boat upstream against the current to finally reach the village.

The Caribs are an interesting people. Their religion is Catholic, but with a mixture of African spiritism and voodoo. Their language, which they have preserved from when they came from Africa as slaves more than a hundred years ago, has many words used only by the men, and other words that only the women use among themselves. All this makes apostolic work among them very difficult. A missionary priest would have to really incarnate himself with them if he wanted to evangelize them. He would have to learn their language and completely share their lives with them for a number of years, not just visit them a few times a year for a few days.

What continued to really strike me was the great contrast between how the priests and nuns lived, in their comfortable houses with good beds and good food, especially in the Catholic high schools in Belize City, and how the majority of the people, Indians, blacks, Ladinos, and Creoles lived so poorly, their families barely subsisting. The Caribs were the healthiest of all because they ate a lot of protein in their daily diet, fish. Their teeth are among the most healthy and perfect in the world. However, the great majority of the people in Belize, the same as in all Central America, hardly ever get meat, milk, fish, or vegetables, but only rice, red beans, corn tortillas, coffee, and fresh fruit.

This contrast would anger me, especially on returning to live in the big residence of the Jesuit high school after sharing a little bit of the poverty of the people in the villages. Compared with the building that is the philosophate of Fusz Memorial in Saint Louis, the residence of the Jesuits at SJC is poor; but compared with the houses and style of life of most of the people of Belize, it is very rich and bourgeois. The Jesuits in the parishes in the districts certainly lived more poorly, but after visiting the poor, they return to their more comfortable priests' houses.

The last summer vacation that I had in Belize I spent with Charlie Woods and Jack Ruoff in the parish of San Antonio among the Ketchi Indians of southern Belize. There was a rough dirt road from Punta Gorda on the coast to San Antonio in the interior, but there was none from Belize City to Punta Gorda. So we boarded the passenger ship *Heron H* with three bicycles, and in two days we reached Punta Gorda. The rocks on the twenty-five miles of road to San Antonio practically ruined our bikes. The three of us were very impressed with the good work that the

Jesuit pastor did with the Indians there. Jack Ruoff was so impressed that, when he returned to Belize as a priest four years later, he asked to work there.

To return to the States after our three years of teaching in Belize, Charlie, Jack, and I asked for permission to make the trip by land. We wanted to visit our other Missouri Province mission in Honduras, and also the other countries of Central America and Mexico. I had continued studying Spanish ever since the juniorate, and I wanted to try it out. (It was forbidden to speak Spanish with the boarding students at SJC.) Two of the Jesuit scholastics who had taught in Belize ahead of me, Tom Quiery and Paul Van Vleet, had been to visit our mission in Honduras and had asked to return there instead of to Belize to work when they were ordained. The Belize superior did not like that and forbade any other scholastics to visit Honduras.

We had a hard time convincing him that he should let us go. Ruoff and Woods assured him that they would return as priests to work in Belize. I told him that I was going to work as a priest in Honduras anyway, because that was my reason for joining the Jesuits, and he should let me take advantage of the opportunity to see it. Besides, we showed him that we would save money traveling by land and sleeping and eating free in the houses of the Jesuits along the way instead of going by plane.

So it was that I had my first visit to Honduras and was confirmed in my desire to return to work there. In 1958 when we passed through Honduras, it had only a few Jesuits, about ten. In 1947, at the request of Archbishop Humbach of Tegucigalpa, the pope asked the Jesuits to help out in Honduras by taking charge of the whole department of Yoro, with its five huge parishes and the parish of Minas de Oro in the department of Comayagua. Our Jesuit Father General in Rome assigned the mission to the Missouri Province under the Belize superior, at that time Father Knapp.

When the first two Jesuits arrived to start the mission of Yoro, there were only two priests in all these six parishes. They were both elderly Hondurans. One of them was in El Progreso, Yoro, the third largest city in the country. He was a bad priest who went around on a big horse with his woman riding behind him, a pistol in his belt and a bottle of whiskey in his hand. At least that is the way the people describe him, and for sure everybody in Progreso knows the few sons and daughters he left there. Father O'Neill, from Wisconsin, who was to replace him could not enter Progreso until the archbishop managed, at last, to move the other priest to Tegucigalpa.

The only other priest in all this huge territory during twenty years was Father Escoto, then an old man. He had visited by himself all the bigger towns of the parishes of Olanchito, of the town of Yoro (which is the capital of the Department of Yoro), of Sulaco, and of Minas de Oro, but only for their patron feasts once a year. (This explains why so few Catholics learned much about Christianity in this part of Honduras.) He lived in the town of Yoro, but he was happy to receive a pension from the archbishop and retire to live with relatives of his in Minas de Oro. One Jesuit started living in Yoro, but soon six more came from the United States in order to have two priests in Olanchito, two in Yoro, two in Minas de Oro, and two in Progreso. In 1958, when we passed through, they then had their own superior, Father Francis Xavier Hogan from Iowa, and it was a mission independent from Belize.

As soon as I saw the situation of the Church in the Yoro Mission, I knew that the need for priests was much greater there than in Belize. Just the two Jesuits in the parish of Progreso, including its eighty villages and twenty banana camps, had more Catholics under them than approximately forty priests had in the whole country of Belize (about seventy thousand Catholics). The challenge of evangelizing in Honduras was not merely beginning from zero, but rather with a lot of people being anticlerical. After ten years of honest, self-sacrificing labor by the first Jesuits, however, by 1958 the people had a different image of priests.

Father Al Smith, S.J., had given his life, drowned while trying to cross a swollen river on horseback. He is buried in the church in the town of Yoro. Father Ratterman was famous for starting in Yoro one of the first coffee-growers' cooperatives. Father John Newell, who in 1981 is still working on the mission at the age of 74, founded two famous cooperatives in Minas de Oro, one of shoemakers and the other for consumers. I really admired these great missionaries; they inspired me. With the ideal of following in their footsteps, maybe I could return to the States and endure the four years of theological studies to become a priest.

After spending about ten days visiting our Yoro Mission, we moved along. We got to know some of the works of the Jesuits in El Salvador, Guatemala, and Mexico, traveling always on public buses all the way up to Saint Louis, Missouri. The trip lasted more than a month and was worth more than two years of studying about Central America and Mexico from books. I was deeply impressed by the visit we made to the Basilica of the Virgin of Guadalupe in Mexico City, with its miraculous picture that Mary left on the *tilma* (rough cloak) of the Indian Juan Diego.

During my studies in theology, I read everything I could find about this legend. Scientifically it is inexplicable how there could be such a delicate, beautiful picture on such a coarse cloth (like a burlap sack), or how this fragile and crude material could have been preserved for more than four hundred years. But the irrefutable miracle is the historical fact that before the apparition of this image of the Virgin of Guadalupe, the millions of Indians of Mexico and Central and South America refused to accept this new religion that was brought by the Spaniards who had conquered them, killed thousands of them, and then made them work as slaves. In Mexico most of the Aztecs went right on adoring the sun and the stars as gods and offering hundreds of young virgins in human sacrifices to their snake god.

When the Indians saw in the picture that the mother of Jesus Christ, who the missionaries said was the God-Savior of the world, was an Indian like them, that she was crowned as the queen of the universe, that she was more important than the sun and the stars, which served as ornaments for her, and that she was squashing the snake god beneath her feet, they accepted that they ought to adore her son Jesus Christ as the only God. In the next twenty years after the enthroning of the picture of the Virgin of Guadalupe in a small new church in Mexico City, eight million Indians from all over Mexico, Central America, and South America asked for instruction in order to be baptized in the Catholic church.

This is one of the most important events shaping the history of Latin America. Because of this, one third of all the Catholics in the world live today in Latin America. I am all for trying to explain scientifically things that happen in this world without resorting to calling them miracles, including the events or marvelous "signs" that Jesus and his apostles produced in the New Testament. Little by little we are learning about the literary forms that the ancient authors used, who described almost all the pagan kings as also working "miracles." But of all the so-called miracles, the one I like the most is this one of the Virgin of Guadalupe.

7. The Formation of a Jesuit - IV

It was sad for me to have to separate myself again from the world for four years of theological studies at Saint Mary's College in Kansas. Formerly this had been a boarding high school for upper class Catholics, well out in the country near the little town of Saint Mary's. But many years ago the Jesuits had closed down the high school and converted it into a theologate where some two hundred Jesuits from various provinces studied.

I wonder if you can guess which of my former superiors was now the superior of the Saint Mary's theologate, waiting there to welcome me. None other than my friend from the philosophate. With him, with the isolation from the activities of city life, with the dry study of theology, with the textbooks and the classes all in Latin, and all this for four long years, you can imagine why I had another great trial in my vocation. I was already almost thirty-four when I started theology in September of 1958, and I felt that I was wasting the best years of my life on these long and purely theoretical studies.

I endured them because I had the great dream of being a missionary in Yoro, and, thank God, the provincial finally did formally assign me to Yoro Mission at the end of my first year of theology. I believe it was Father Linus Thro, who had been one of my philosophy teachers and who knew that this had been my desire ever since entering the Jesuits. At this same time Paul Van Vleet and Tom Quiery were also assigned to Yoro Mission. My brother, Pat, after we were ordained together as priests, was assigned there also. He had done his three years of teaching experience at Saint Louis University High.

Although I still had the problem of headaches when I studied too much, it was easier to control them in the theologate; we had more freedom to study when we wanted, as long as we did not miss classes and could pass the exams. As though we were adolescents, sports again were our big pastime. Saint Mary's College had a golf course, but in the philosophate I had sworn that golf was one sport I would never play again; I considered it a sport for the bourgeoisie. This was a continuous mortification for me during these four years, because Tom Quiery and the rest of my best friends played a lot of golf.

During this time I had already developed the beginning of a class consciousness. At least, I had firmly decided to identify myself with the working class, "with the poor," more than with the higher social classes. I still did not identify myself with the struggle of the working class for their liberation.

To be "like the poor," I wanted to smoke (and I did secretly, for it was still forbidden). I had also sworn never to use fancy clothes, never again to wear a necktie or shine my shoes. I had many conflicts with my classmates for calling them bourgeois for playing golf and wanting good whiskey and expensive food.

After seeing the poor in Belize, to me it seemed sinful the way Jesuits in the United States often ate as well as rich people, especially when they were celebrating feasts of the Church or of the Society. Of course, to openly criticize my classmates and our priest-teachers about this, as I did, was a sign of my great pride again, as though I were more saintly, more Christ-like than they. My classmates accepted it because they were my friends, but the priest-teachers and superiors became very angry with me for such talk.

How could we develop "class consciousness" or at least make the "option for the poor," when our studies and the way of life, the praxis, of Jesuits in the United States included absolutely nothing of liberation theology? Worse still, our studies and our apostolic work had nothing to do with the great social problems of the United States. We never analyzed the reality of the world that surrounded us. Our theological studies had no connection with the social injustices, the social sins, that abound in the United States in its national as well as its international policy.

I do not say that the Jesuits did not have any interest in social injustice or politics. Most Jesuits did study something about these problems, and some of them wanted to dedicate themselves to social studies. But the philosophy and theology that is still being taught in the United States to the seminarians and religious men and women is alienating, theoretical, apolitical. It is apolitical in the sense that it is not related to this real world and its great problems, but in truth, this very unrelatedness makes it political, because it implies an option for the status quo.

It is true that moral theology considers modern-day problems of nuclear war, abortion, terrorism, the manipulation of the masses by the communication media, and so on, with special emphasis on the sexual problems, but theology in general, the reflection on the gospel of Christ, does not. "Salvation" refers to the soul, after death, in the next world. This is what I call alienating. The gospel of Christ, instead of being a motive for getting involved in the political struggle to change this world, is interpreted in the "bourgeois theology" that we learned as dealing with the "supernatural." We were taught about the Holy Trinity, the Sacraments, grace, and the Church, as the road to heaven in the next world.

It would not be correct to say that Catholic theology in the United States is the same today as it was in 1960; some bit of political theology and liberation theology has penetrated. In general, though, it is still bourgeois theology: salvation in the next world, conformity with this world, eliminating personal sins. Even though the theological theory has been changing since Vatican II, with its constitution on "The Church in the Modern World," the praxis, the way of life of the priests and religious theologians, often is so apolitical and bourgeois that their theory at times turns out to be a justification of their lifestyle.

In the Central American Province, by contrast, Jesuit theologians, both professors and students, are being persecuted, imprisoned, and expelled from their countries for actively helping the poor in their struggles for liberation. It is precisely their *theology*, liberation theology, that impels them to get "involved in politics."

The basic tenet of liberation theology is that one can only reflect under the light of the gospel on the liberation, the salvation, that Christ brought (that is, do theology), when one is involved in the praxis, the practice of the political struggle for the liberation of the oppressed in this world. I will talk more about this when I come to that point of my life when I began to understand it. When I was in the theologate I did not understand anything about liberation theology. I could even say that there was very little that I understood or learned of the true gospel of Christ. The poor campesinos of Honduras were the ones who taught me the real gospel, the good news that Jesus brought. As Jesus said, it was "good news for the poor," the bourgeoisie cannot understand it.

There were some things in the gospels that I began to understand in the novitiate, especially that Jesus was one of the poor masses of the world. The meditations on the birth of Jesus in a stable were an enlightenment of the Holy Spirit for me. God freely chose his mother; he chose a poor campesino woman. He wanted to be one of the poor; that I clearly saw in the gospels. I also understood right from the novitiate that to be a disciple of Christ you have to sell all that you own, give it to the poor, and follow the poor Jesus, becoming one of the poor also, identifying yourself with the poor, incarnating yourself in the poor.

What I did not understand until I was living it in the praxis was how to truly love the poor as Jesus did. During all these first years of my Jesuit life I had the idea of Charles de Foucauld, that for loving the poor it was enough to just be one of them, share their life with them, be present among them as a witness of Christ, helping them in their sicknesses, and so on, without getting involved in politics, without criticizing or denouncing the injustices that they suffer. Later on I learned that a Jesuit has to love his neighbor more efficaciously by working to eliminate the causes of poverty.

If I love a poor person, I will help him or her get out of poverty. If I love a sick person, I will help find a cure, not just give that person a tranquilizer, but go to the cause of the sickness in order to completely get rid of it. In the Spiritual Exercises of Saint Ignatius, a Jesuit learns that he should use all means necessary to achieve a goal. And so, for a Jesuit to love the poor, he has to do all he can to help eliminate the poverty of the poor masses of the world. All Jesuits want this. Later on I will explain more clearly the two methods that are used for this purpose: one is reformist and the other is revolutionary.

The most interesting part of my four years in Kansas was my apostolate with the North American Indians of the Pottawatomie tribe, who lived principally on their "reservation" about forty miles from Saint Mary's. There was also a colony of them living in a poor section of the capital city of Kansas, Topeka, about seventy miles from Saint Mary's. A team of four of us Jesuit theologians, one from each year of studies, ministered to the Pottawatomies. The fourth-year man, who was already a priest, was the pastor of the mission, and the other three were his assistants. There was an old Ford pickup exclusively for this Pottawatomie mission work. My friend Tom Quiery was already part of this team when I arrived at Saint Mary's, and he arranged for me to be named to it also. What a joy it was for Tom and me to go every Sunday to the reservation, and sometimes to Topeka, to spend the day with these poor people, some of the poorest in the country!

Imagine it: the Pottawatomie Indians were the recognized owners of half the state of Kansas when the soldiers of the new republic finally conquered them after many battles in the early years of the nineteenth century. In the following decades the pioneers and soldiers went on killing these Indians in attempts to take away their best land. At last, in order to save the few thousand Pottawatomie survivors, the tribal chiefs signed a treaty with the U.S. government. It granted them forever the lands called the Reservation of the Pottawatomies, where the whole tribe was supposed to live and work. Naturally, it was just about the worst land in Kansas, not much good either for agriculture or for raising cattle.

Practically the same thing happened to all the Indian tribes who originally owned the whole continent. The Indians of the state of New York sold to the early Dutch pilgrims for twenty-four dollars the entire island of Manhattan, which today is part of New York City and must be worth thousands of dollars per square yard. The great tribe of famous warriors, the Sioux, who were the last to be subdued by the U.S. Army, were the proud owners of the two states of South Dakota and Iowa. Today they live miserably on two reservations in the Black Hills of South Dakota, and their lands produce hardly anything for them. The Jesuits of Wisconsin Province have the mission among them. The Missouri Province has another mission on the reservation of the Arapahoe Indians in Wyoming. I spent several weeks there getting to know it in the summer vacation of 1960.

Early in the nineteenth century, the famous Jesuit missionary, Pierre de Smet, who was one of the founders of our Missouri

Province, had converted the whole tribe of Pottawatomies to Catholicism. But in 1958 very few of them attended our Sunday masses in the old wooden church on the reservation. A few of them now belonged to one or another of the Protestant sects. Most of them were still Catholics, but very indifferent. We tried to organize catechism for the children and sports for the youth, but without much success.

We visited their poor wooden houses, which during the cold winters were like refrigerators, impossible to heat with small wood stoves. We used to get some help in money, food, and clothing to give to the poorest of them, and we tried to get jobs for some of them in Topeka. There were always some in jail in Topeka, and we would visit them and try to talk to the judge for them. This was all very frustrating, because the poor Indians had lost their self-respect. They were and still are discriminated against and looked down on as worthless by many whites. Worst of all is that some of them look upon themselves as worthless.

Because of this discrimination and contempt, most Indians cannot adapt themselves to modern "civilization," to the capitalist culture of the United States, and not being able to adapt themselves, they are more and more discriminated against by the whites. The same thing is happening with the Latin-American Indians. What injustice! What inhumanity! What a lack of Christianity in the white Christians!

In the United States the whites have done the same with the Native Americans with red skin as they have with the "freed" slaves with black skin. Today, following the example of the blacks, Indians are beginning to organize themselves to demand their human rights. May God help them!

On November 30, 1958, a Sunday, my father died in Saint Louis, on his sixty-fifth birthday. His last day at work for Burroughs Adding Machine Company was the Friday before. They were retiring him with a monthly pension and had a party in his honor at the office to bid him farewell. Shortly after the party, back at home, he suffered a ruptured artery, and two days later died in the hospital. For months before his retirement all he talked about was what he could do now that they said he was too old to work. He could not stand the thought of sitting around the house all day long. I believe it was the fear of retirement that killed him. Pat and I went from Kansas to Saint Louis for his funeral.

The saddest part of it was that my poor mother was suddenly all alone. All her seven children now had their own lives apart: the girls with families living in Michigan, Ohio, and Massachusetts; Pat and I with the Jesuits in Kansas; Eileen out west (later returning to Saint Louis to study psychology at the University); and Maureen teaching in Salt Lake City, Utah. But my mother was very holy and learned to carry this cross of widowhood for her greater sanctification. My father's pension and life insurance gave her enough to live on independently in Saint Louis. After a time, Eileen and Maureen returned to live in Saint Louis and were able to visit her frequently.

Since I was now officially assigned to Yoro Mission, I got permission to go to El Paso, Texas, with my brother, Pat, to practice Spanish and work during the three months of summer vacation in 1959 with Father Harold Rahm, S.J., in his Spanish-American Center. The big city of El Paso is on the very border of Mexico, and a big part of its population is of Mexican descent and speaks only Spanish. Father Rahm had a special talent for attracting the youth to his center in order to save them from the drug addiction and crime that dominated the streets of the Mexican slums in El Paso. Besides helping him with his program of sports and talks for the youth in his center, Pat and I visited the families of these adolescents and tried to help them with their problems.

Many of these young people were in trouble with the law: for stealing, drug addiction, prostitution, and so on, and we would try to help them get out of jail when they were taken in. This is another case of the great social injustice, or social sin, of the dominant whites in the United States. There are millions of Mexicans in the United States in all the towns near the border with Mexico. Just Los Angeles, California, has more than two million people of Mexican descent. In addition, there are more than a million Puerto Ricans in New York, and there are millions from all the other countries of Latin America scattered throughout the United States. Almost all these, just like the blacks and the Indians, suffer a lot of discrimination and contempt from many whites.

The Latinos suffer because it is hard for them to learn English, which makes it hard for them to get jobs. Besides, a large percentage of the Mexicans and Central Americans have entered the country illegally by sneaking across the Rio Grande at night. That is why Mexicans have the nickname "wetbacks." They can only get the hardest jobs, without any protection from the labor laws. Hundreds of these wetbacks are farm laborers working to harvest grapes, lettuce, sugar cane, and other crops for wages that are much below the minimum wage in the United States, and the living conditions for them and their families are miserable and inhuman.

One of the most wonderful and famous struggles for human rights in the United States in recent years is that of Cesar Chávez and the United Farm Workers Union (UFW), who are trying to organize these oppressed and exploited farm laborers. The local authorities, in general, have backed the exploiting owners who refuse to allow a labor union of the harvest workers, and Cesar Chávez and other promoters of the UFW have been thrown in jail a number of times. Chávez is a disciple of Gandhi and uses Gandhi's methods of nonviolent active resistance. When they throw him in jail, Chávez, like Gandhi, goes on a complete hunger strike. He is a tremendous Catholic, and one of the banners always used in UFW demonstrations is the standard of the Virgin of Guadalupe; when he goes on a hunger strike, the only food he takes is the daily Sacred Host of Holy Communion.

The tactic that has been most successful in winning the consent of the owners for unionization of farm workers in the UFW has been the boycott. By means of great propaganda across the whole United States, backed by all the progressive organizations and by the churches, the UFW convinced a large number of Americans not to buy grapes or lettuce from the farms in California whose owners fight unionization and collective bargaining with their workers. Today, in 1981, these efforts to organize the most exploited workers in the country, the migrant farm workers, still go on. Cesar Chávez, Martin Luther King, Jr., and Dorothy Day of *The Catholic Worker* are three modern saints that God has produced in the United States.

The fact that I had some apostolic experiences with the poor does not contradict what I said before about our not receiving much formation of our social conscience as part of our thirteen years of preparation to be Jesuit priests. I had these experiences because I insisted on it, but most of the philosophy and theology students had no apostolate; nor were they encouraged to have any. They spent the three months' summer vacations each year in one of the Jesuit villas or doing more studying.

In the summer vacation of 1960 I spent six weeks with the Mexican seminarians at Montezuma, New Mexico, in order to practice my Spanish. This seminary of the Mexican bishops, which was established in the United States during the persecutions in Mexico in the 1920s, is still functioning. These young Mexicans helped me try to perfect my Spanish, but after thirty years of studying and speaking it, I still have not perfected it. It is difficult for a grown person to learn another language and speak it without some accent.

During this same summer of 1960, I went directly from New Mexico to Saint Steven's Mission, which the Jesuits of our province have on the reservation of the Arapahoe Indians in Wyoming. I was only there a month getting to know the fine, self-sacrificing work of my fellow Jesuits among these Indians. The Arapahoes are not as poor or as lost as the Pottawatomies, but they suffer the same discrimination and contempt from some whites. The difference is that they discovered some petroleum on the reservation of the Arapahoes, and each family receives a check every three months with their part of the profits from the oil. This they obtain without working. This is the special problem that the Arapahoes have: receiving money without working, even though it is not enough to support their families. With this support now they do not work, and that can ruin a person more than being unemployed because of being unable to find a job.

At last the hour arrived for me to be ordained a priest for the rest of my life! Since I had already been assigned to the Yoro Mission, I had no doubts about making the written request for ordination that Canon Law requires. First we received the subdiaconate; the following day, the diaconate; and a few days later, the priesthood. It was June 15, 1961, in the big church of Saint Mary's College, when Bishop Hunkeler of Kansas City, Kansas, ordained about thirty of us Jesuits who had just finished the third year of theology. It was a very joyful day; all of our families had come to Saint Mary's to celebrate this great occasion with us. After the long ordination ceremony and mass, the families marched up to receive the first blessing of the new priests and to kiss the priestly hands just consecrated and anointed with the holy oils.

Our family was doubly joyful because Pat and I were ordained together and went with them to Saint Louis to celebrate our first masses there. It was only after our ordination that our mother told Pat and me that this is what she had asked for sixteen years ago. It was in 1945, while I was in the army in France and Pat in the navy in the Pacific. She sent, with a friend of hers who was going on pilgrimage to Mexico, a written note to be placed at the feet of the Virgin of Guadalupe in the basilica in Mexico City. She asked that the two of us return safe and sound from the war and that both of us become priests. She cried with joy when she told us about this. Our mother always had great devotion to the Virgin of Guadalupe, and after visiting Mexico and studying the history of the image, I did too. The holy card remembrance of my ordination that was given to all my friends had a photograph of it. I had selected this card a number of weeks before our mother told us about her petition.

This summer of 1961 was full of joy for me, because in July the provincial let me go to Progreso, Yoro, in Honduras to help in the parish for two months as my first priestly work. I had to be back at Saint Mary's again in September for our fourth year of theology, but I thought only about Honduras, so for me there was no better way to spend this vacation than helping out there. The theology students and many Jesuit priests spent two months of vacation each year in the Jesuit villa at Beulah, Wisconsin. I am glad that I have never even seen Beulah. There are very few rich people even who can spend two months of summer vacation at a villa beside a beautiful lake.

In the parish of Progreso, Father Murphy was the pastor and worked in the city; Father Fred Schuller visited all the villages and banana camps. I helped Murphy with masses and catechism classes for the kids, helped in the Jesuit high school, Instituto San José in Progreso, with religion classes, and went out with Schuller as much as possible to get to know the villages and banana camps. In 1961 there were hardly any roads into the villages; the paved highway from Progreso to Tela did not yet exist.

Schuller traveled free on the trains of the United Fruit Company, called the Tela Railroad Company in Honduras. This company owned about half the land in the big parish of Progreso; besides many big banana farms, they had huge ranches with thousands of head of cattle and other plantations of African palm trees and ornamental flowers for export. Besides their holdings in the municipalities (townships or counties) of Progreso and Negrito in the department of Yoro, they owned even more in parts of the departments of Cortés and Atlántida.

The priests in Progreso did not think it was so bad to be closely identified with the officials of this big Tela Railroad Company (called the Tela). Ever since their arrival in Progreso the Jesuits had been friends of the general manager and other American administrators who were sent to manage the enterprise in Honduras. The administrators had offices, big houses for their families, a golf course, swimming pool, and dance hall right in the center of Progreso, exclusively for them. Various Jesuits used to like to play golf and visit with these Americans and with the top officials who were Hondurans and who also lived in this "Company Zone" in Progreso. The Jesuits, visiting the different banana camps, used to eat and sleep in the big houses of the top administrators. We also received gifts of entire wooden buildings from the Tela to be taken apart and put up in the villages as churches. The parish received all its gasoline free from the company, and even a monthly donation check.

I myself traveled free on the company banana ships so I shouldn't just criticize others. I did not say anything, because I still did not understand much about the class struggle and the exploitation of the workers and of Honduras itself by the U.S. transnational companies.

These U.S. Jesuits were only following the line of their predecessors in the parish of Progreso. During the big strike of all of the twenty-five thousand workers of the Tela in 1954, priests went around with the soldiers and with the officials of the Tela looking for the "communist" leaders of the strike. Even though they paternalistically helped the workers with food during the sixty days that the strike lasted, some of the worker leaders accused the "gringo" priests of being identified with the company owners and with the army against the strike.

Before this famous strike by banana workers in 1954, in Honduras there was no work code, no labor laws, no minimum wage, no right of the workers to organize themselves in labor unions to make collective bargaining contracts with the owners. This strike, which finally spread to include the fifteen thousand banana workers of the Standard Fruit Company (subsidiary of Castle and Cooke) in the region of La Ceiba, Olanchito, and Isletas and the five thousand miners of the Rosario Mining and Resources Company (U.S.-owned as well) in the department of Santa Bárbara, achieved all these labor goals. Their labor unions were legally recognized, and the National Congress finally approved a work code.

What a mistake of the priests to identify themselves with the gringo owners instead of with the workers, for fear of "communism"! The parish of Progreso is partly made up of these banana workers, along with thousands of campesinos, and the Church has lost the workers. Most of them are completely indifferent to religion. If they continue to baptize their babies it is more as a custom than out of faith. After the strike many more of them became anticlerical. It is true that Marxist propaganda fostered this, but the priests lost their golden opportunity to win over the workers when they did not back them up in the strike, and did not openly denounce the transnational banana company for its exploitation of the workers and repression of the incipient labor union.

Instead of preaching against the injustices of the U.S. company, they preached against the dangers of communist infiltration in the unions. So once again religion served (unconsciously, perhaps) to justify the repression of the workers, to support the capitalist system of exploitation. With good reason some of the labor leaders said that the gringo priests were bought off by the company. It is very compromising for the clergy to receive gifts from the rich, especially from the bosses of their worker parishioners. Later on I will describe the labor unions, the transnational companies, and their relationships with the Church in more detail.

My first priestly experiences with the good people of Honduras, most of them illiterate and lacking knowledge of the basic tenets of Catholicism, really impressed me. I was impressed by how different is the culture and mentality of the Hondurans. It is a shame that foreigners, who do not understand them well, have to be their evangelizers. The U.S. Jesuits go to evangelize without any practical preparation for that work. I had spent thirteen years as a Jesuit; all those years of study were useless for teaching the gospel in a simple manner to the Hondurans. Rather, so much intellectualism, the habit of thinking in scholastic categories with words that are used only in universities, is a huge obstacle. This training only makes it very difficult to adapt oneself and to think as the masses of poor illiterates do and to teach them with the words and mental categories that they use and will understand.

Some American missionaries never learn Spanish well. Some of them have been many years in Honduras, but since they came as adults without having studied Spanish, speak it always like gringos. Also, in Honduras some of the Jesuits live apart in Jesuit houses separated from the people. They speak English there and follow the customs and even prepare the food as in the United States.

To me it was clear that to be a missionary one has to do what the documents of the Church and of the Society of Jesus say about this: one must inculturate, incarnate, oneself in the new culture in order to acquire the same way of thinking as the people. It is not Ignatian to be a missionary without theoretical and practical preparation as a missionary, and then on the mission to live apart from the people in a small American colony, as some Jesuits have done in Honduras, and as almost all foreign religious men and women missionaries have done. Whether they live in U.S. colonies, or German, or French, or Spanish, it is not Ignatian. This approach does not use the best means to achieve our goal, which is to better evangelize the people.

This criticism does not mean the U.S. missionaries, who live more comfortably than most of the Hondurans, do not love the poor. On the contrary, all the Jesuits in Yoro impressed me very much with their holiness, their love of the poor, their spirit of self-sacrifice. The missionaries are really giants, heroes. If they are not revolutionaries, it is not so much their fault but rather that of the whole capitalist formation that they received in the United States. It would be a miracle if they were not anticommunists, antisocialists, counterrevolutionaries. The first step for an American priest who wants to be a missionary in Latin America is to take all his studies for the priesthood in one of the more progressive seminaries in Latin America, not in the United States.

I had come to Honduras by airplane, but in September when I had to go back to Saint Mary's, Kansas, for my fourth and last year of theology, Father Murphy got free passage for me on a United Fruit Company ship that took bananas from Puerto Cortés, Honduras, to New Orleans. The banana ships had staterooms for about fifteen passengers, who ate during the voyage with the ship's officers. I have always loved the sea; its extent and profundity always make me think of God, the Infinite. This two-and-a-half-day voyage was lovely, and over the years I repeated it several times.

On returning to Saint Mary's, you can imagine how much desire I had to spend another year studying outdated theology. Nevertheless, I enjoyed very much this fourth year with the Pottawatomies, because I was now their priest, pastor of the mission, and had more freedom to be with them.

It was not part of our studies, but rather the fad at that time among the theologians, to read and discuss the theories of Teilhard de Chardin, also a Jesuit. The books of his that I read that year, especially *The Phenomenon of Man,* impressed me deeply. They helped me to clarify my vision of God's plan for this world. For me, the evolution of the world is evident, and Chardin shows so beautifully how this "Divine Milieu," the universe in which we live, is guided by the Holy Spirit in its evolution toward an "Omega Point," the perfection of the universe incorporated, at last, in Christ. We are now in the stage of the humanization of the universe under the progressive dominion of intelligent and free people, the universe tending always toward the greater unification of humanity. Some years later in Honduras, on reading the theology of Juan Luis Segundo, S.J., I completed my personal synthesis of God's plan for this world.

With great joy we finally graduated with the Licentiate in Theology in June of 1962. We had a big farewell party at Saint Mary's College before my classmates took off for their new apostolates in different parts of the country and of the world, wherever their provincials sent them. Most of these new priests were assigned to teach in one of our Jesuit high schools or universities. Several of them were going on to some other university to finish higher studies for a doctorate degree. Three of my classmates were from the Central American Province and returned there. My brother, Pat, had also asked to be a missionary in Yoro. So that he could practice his Spanish, he was sent directly to La Ceja, Colombia, to make his Third Probation, together with Tom Quiery, who had completed one year of work in Honduras. Charlie Woods and Jack Ruoff were sent to Belize. And I, thanks be to God, was sent to the mission of Yoro.

After a week's visit with my family, I took a train from Saint Louis to San Antonio, Texas. I remember sitting in the section for the blacks, explaining to the ticket taker on the train that I was a black man. "Can't you see?" I asked him. At last I felt like a missionary. I was thirty-eight years old. At last the Society of Jesus trusted me enough to send me forth into the apostolate. I still lacked one more year of formation, the Third Probation, but we usually made this after one or two years of apostolate.

Before going to Honduras I wanted to take a *"Cursillo de Cristiandad"* (a short course in basic Christianity), because I had read so much about its method and the spectacular results it was having in Spain and all over Latin America in converting nominal Catholics into active Christians. I got permission from the provincial to take one on the way to Honduras; that is why I went to San Antonio. I knew they were having a *cursillo* in Spanish for Mexican women, and the director had invited me to take part as his assistant. I became very enthusiastic about this method of evangelization when I saw the sincere conversions of these women. I resolved to introduce the *Cursillos de Cristiandad* in Honduras, where they did not exist as yet.

PART IV. A MISSIONARY IN HONDURAS

8. First Missionary Learnings

The superior of the mission of Yoro, Father Francis Hogan, met me at the airport in Tegucigalpa, capital of Honduras, and took me to Centro Loyola in Barrio Palmira, where he had bought a big building and converted it into a retreat house. He lived there giving spiritual retreats to men and women of the capital and had quite a bit of influence on some of them. From Tegucigalpa he would go every month to visit some of the other five Jesuit houses we had in our parishes of Progreso, Negrito, Yoro, and Olanchito in the department of Yoro, and Minas de Oro in the department of Comayagua. In my opinion he was the best superior we have ever had on the Yoro Mission.

Also living at Centro Loyola was a young Jesuit, John Fisher, who had permission from Archbishop Hector Santos to study and teach in the national university of Honduras without wearing the cassock or the clerical suit (which all the rest of us priests had to wear always, even in the mountains). This priest got involved in the life of the students as it should be done, by becoming one of them. The university was dominated by Marxists, and the environment was one of great anticlericalism. There was no priest or any Christian influence in this, the only university in the country. But he not only managed to enter and be accepted by the students and professors in general, but besides that soon had a group of young Christian students who met with him to study the Social Doctrine of the Church.

John went to Venezuela for a short course on the social doctrine of the church and brought back to Honduras Father Aguerre, S.J., and his team of Venezuelans, who gave the same course to this group of Christian university students. Then John and his group started giving this course to many other Hondurans. I took it with them in 1964, and I really liked it.

It was practically my first introduction to an economic-social analysis of the Honduran reality (although it was not a revolutionary, but a reformist, analysis). I doubt if John knew it when he brought them, but these Venezuelans were Christian Democrats and later on interested John's whole group in organizing a Christian Democratic Party in Honduras. Among the young university students who started this new party were Alfredo Landaverde, Fernando Montes, and Rodolfo Sorto.

The eternal gossipmongers of Tegucigalpa, "Catholics" of high society and of the leadership of the two traditional political parties, the Nationalists and the Liberals, always had the ear of the archbishop. They told him that this Jesuit priest in the university was teaching "communist" ideas and forming a new political party. The archbishop did not call John in to ask him about this, but rather called Father Schuller, who was then superior of the mission, to tell him that he no longer wanted John to work in Tegucigalpa. How sad and how typical of the bishops of Honduras! This happened in 1964; John had to return to the United States.

John was one of the two priests, both North Americans, whose work did most to cause the rejuvenation of the Catholic church in Honduras that was so notable in the decade 1965–1975. His influence, through his group of Social-Christian university students, had repercussions in the whole Church of Honduras and even in the movements to form popular organizations of the masses. The other priest of great influence was Vincent Prestera, a secular priest from a diocese of the United States, lent to the archdiocese of Tegucigalpa precisely for the purpose of starting the *Cursillos de Cristiandad* in Honduras. This was in 1964, and I will treat it later.

Our superior Father Hogan had the tactic of training new missionaries on the mission by sending them to visit the mountain villages to get to know once and for all the hardest job we have. He threw young priests into deep water, and they had to swim or drown. I agree with this system. For me, at least, it helped to learn how the majority of Hondurans live. So, after a few days in Tegucigalpa arranging for my residence papers, Hogan put me on a transport truck for Minas de Oro with a letter for the pastor, Father John Newell, naming me assistant priest in the parish.

This man had been pastor, and king, of Minas de Oro since 1948, shortly after the Jesuits started the Yoro Mission. In his fourteen years there he had founded a high school run by three Franciscan sisters, and two cooperatives, one of shoemakers and the other a co-op store. He also had a library for the people and a parish clinic with a Franciscan sister as nurse. Each week in the town plaza on the white wall of the church he showed a full-length movie sent to him from Tegucigalpa. For Christmas and on other occasions he would receive food, used clothing, and toys to give away.

He organized all those works not only as a service to the people, but also to win their allegiance. He was in competition with an American Protestant sect that had Minas de Oro as its major center, with a boarding high school, a medical clinic, and a lot of gifts of food and clothes for the people. They were like two capitalist businesses in competition. "But what could I do?" explained the pastor. "They (the Protestants) had won over many Catholics to their side with these methods."

If a census were made in Honduras, 4 percent of the people would say that they belong to one of the forty or fifty Protestant sects that exist in Honduras; 1 percent would say that they have no religion; and 95 percent would say that they are Catholics. I like what the Bishops' Conference said in a pastoral letter: "In Honduras 95 percent are baptized Catholics, and maybe 5 percent are Christians." I pray for the day when all Christian churches will no longer compete with one another for parishioners, but support and complement each other in their service to the poor.

In the beginning, John Newell and George Prendergast covered the whole territory of the two parishes of Minas de Oro (in Comayagua) and Sulaco (in Yoro), which also included the municipality of Marale (in the department of Francisco Morazán). When I arrived there, George had been transferred to Olanchito, and Joe Hebert and Mario Budzinski were helping Newell in this huge territory. Hebert practically lived in the parish of Sulaco, visiting the villages of the three municipalities of Sulaco, Marale, and Victoria, over sixty-five miles from one end to the other, all on muleback. There were no roads or cars there at that time. The only road in the whole parish of Minas de Oro was the dirt road that came from Tegucigalpa and ended in the town of Minas de Oro. It was impassable in the periods of heavy rain.

The parish had a huge mule, called Margarita, capable of carrying big, heavy Padre Mario to each of the fifty villages of the three municipalities of Minas de Oro, San José Portrero, and Esquias two or three times a year. Horses are no good in those mountains, with their steeply inclined, rocky trails that become very slippery with mud when it rains. Mario was about sixty years old and very witty. I recall a telegram he sent to the very elderly woman who cared for the church in Esquias: "I will arrive for mass on Tuesday. A thousand kisses, Padre Mario." It was a great pleasure and joy to go around with him getting to know the villages for the first time. After that I would go by myself. On one of the trips by mule, we were going down a very steep, rocky trail when poor Mario fell off Margarita and was seriously bruised on the rocks.

When I was in Progreso for the two months right after my ordination in 1961, I took the name of Mario in honor of Mary, the Virgin of Guadalupe, and I was called Padre Mario. My given name is James, which in Spanish is either Jaime or Diego or Santiago. I did not like Diego, and I did not want to be Padre Jaime, because in Progreso we had a Brother Jaime (O'Leary), or Santiago, because we had a Padre Santiago (McShane) in Progreso. But in Tegucigalpa when I learned that I would be working with Padre Mario Budzinski, I told our superior, Father Hogan, that I wanted to be called Padre Guadalupe, because I had a great devotion to the Virgin of Guadalupe, whom the pope has proclaimed Patronness of the Americas.

So I arrived in Minas de Oro as Padre Guadalupe. I told the people that they should not call me Padre, that I was no one's father, but rather their brother in Christ, and so they should call me Brother Lupe, or simply Lupe. In the parish of Minas de Oro and afterward in other parishes where I worked, many people called me Brother Lupe, but most of the people cannot change their customs that quickly, and they still call me Padre Guadalupe. When I was working later on in Yoro, I told the Laurita sisters to call me Brother Lupe, and the good Sister Amalia spontaneously answered, "Si, Padre."

Since I was the only young priest among the four in the parish, I became very popular with all the young people in the parish. There was a guitar in the parish, and in the evenings I often used to sit out in the park in Minas de Oro to play and sing with the young people. I started asking in each village that I visited if there was a guitar they could let me use during mass, and for the first time, at least in that part of Honduras, Catholics sang the hymns praising God and the Virgin Mary to the rhythm of the guitar. I would sit down to play for the songs at the beginning, the end, and at several points during the mass. The youth were attracted to the mass by the music, but the elderly ladies had their doubts about it, associating the guitar with the barroom.

In 1962 in Honduras, the people knew very little about the changes in the liturgy that were coming. All the masses were still completely in Latin, with the priest's back to the people, "looking at the saints," with the altar against the wall. I hated Latin. In the United States in our fourth year of theology, we were already saying private masses in English and facing the people, even before Vatican II in 1963 and its decree to celebrate mass in the language of the people.

In Minas de Oro I celebrated mass in Spanish several times in private with the Franciscan sisters in their convent. I wanted to try it in the church with the people, and the sisters encouraged me to do it. One Sunday the pastor (who would not have approved) was in Tegucigalpa for a few days, and another priest (who would have ordered me thrown in jail if he had known) was out in the Sulaco area, and Mario was left in charge of the parish. Mario didn't openly forbid me, but only advised me not to do it, so with the sisters, I arranged a table as the altar in the middle of the big church and moved all the benches into a semicircle around the table. We had the first mass in Spanish in Minas de Oro, facing the people and with guitar accompaniment.

Almost all the huge crowd who attended the mass liked it very much and wanted the mass always like that from then on. However, a group complained, not only to the pastor, who was not very upset about it because he knew that all over the world masses like that were being said, but also to Archbishop Santos in Tegucigalpa. He reacted, typically, by sending a letter to all the parishes in the country absolutely forbidding the celebration of mass in Spanish without his express permission each time. The other young priests in the country who had also been saying masses in Spanish in private were angry with me for provoking the archbishop.

Another stupid problem that almost all of us young priests in

Honduras had was with regard to the cassock, or clerical suit, that ecclesiastical law and Archbishop Santos demanded that we wear at all times in public. Many of us went around in ordinary shirt and pants, especially when we had to go by mule to the mountain villages. We simply wore a small crucifix on our shirt to identify us as religious. The people in all my villages already knew that this tall gringo was the priest Lupe. Nonetheless, the bishops continually sent pastoral letters throughout the whole decade of the sixties demanding the use of clerical garb. From 1965 on, however, none of us paid attention to these letters, and other than on trips to Tegucigalpa, hardly anyone wore the cassock or the clerical collar anymore. By 1970 only Archbishop Santos and a few other bishops and priests used clerical garb in Honduras.

When I was a young missionary, as I said, I was very popular with the kids and the teenagers, playing soccer and other sports with them. Some of them used to go along with me when I went by mule to visit some villages. I always carried my harmonica along in my saddlebags and used to play it as we rode along. On reaching a village, I would let the people know that the priest had arrived and that they should get ready for mass by riding around past the houses playing some of their popular hymns on my harmonica.

It was hard for me to leave the parish of Minas de Oro and my many friends there when, in October of 1962, Hogan sent me to the parish of Yoro, the capital city of the department of Yoro. The pastor there was quite sick and had to go to Progreso frequently for medical treatment. It seems that the cool and humid climate of Yoro, which is in the mountains at about 5000 feet above sea level, bothered the arthritis in his back; he could no longer go by horseback to visit the villages. This left Father Bill Brennan alone to visit on horseback the 150 villages of the municipalities of Yorito, Jocón, and Yoro, including the extensive districts of Subirana, Locomapa, Jimía, and Mejía. All of these belong to the Yoro parish, which totals nearly forty thousand Catholics.

The town of Yoro had (and still has today) about three thousand inhabitants, but it is the big commercial center for all the villages in the area. When the priest is in Yoro he celebrates two masses every day and three on Sunday. The pastor there put great pastoral emphasis on the Eucharist, on daily visits to the Blessed Sacrament, and on receiving Holy Communion. We even had to carry a hand counter with us as we gave out communion in order to mark down the number on a sheet after mass. This was to stimulate the priest to encourage the people to receive frequent communion. As if this were the sign of Christianity in a person! As if this should be the apostolic, pastoral priority in Honduras!

I now recognize that this was an alienating kind of religion: drawing the people to Jesus in the Blessed Sacrament, instead of teaching them to imitate Jesus of Nazareth, the Liberator of the oppressed. There was nothing like conscientization (developing a critical social conscience) of the oppressed to struggle for their liberation. The parish of Yoro was (and still is) one of the regions of Honduras where the campesinos and workers are the most exploited and least organized to defend themselves. A mafia of the National Party, all big landowners, live in Yoro and control everything that happens in the region. All the military and other local authorities obey them. They always watched over the religious activities, also. They used to receive Holy Communion every Sunday; they liked the religion of Jesus in the Blessed Sacrament, because it legitimized their lifestyle, soothed their consciences, and *made them feel Christian without having to act Christian.*

There was no denunciation of the great injustices against the ten Jicaque Indian tribes that were in the parish and whose lands were being fenced in by these big landowners. The parish helped these "poor little Indians" by handing out to them food and used clothing. I did not think much about this at the time; I still wasn't anything of a revolutionary; I was merely rebellious.

I did not like giving communion in Yoro to those rich landowners dressed in suit and tie in a church full of barefoot campesinos and Indians, but I still did not know how to analyze Honduran society to recognize the social sins. We only denounced the personal sins, which also were abundant, of drunkenness and of living in concubinage, or having a family without getting married. Our whole pastoral plan consisted in encouraging the people to receive the sacraments.

Helping in the pastoral work of the parish of Yoro were (and still are) four Laurita sisters of the Congregation of the Missionaries of the Immaculate Conception, which was founded by Mother Laura in Colombia in the 1920s to work in the most difficult missions among the Indians of Latin America. Of all the religious that I have seen, the Lauritas are the most self-sacrificing and the most willing to share the life of the poor in the mountain villages where the majority of Hondurans live. Almost all the Lauritas are young peasant women from Colombia, Ecuador, and other Latin-American countries.

Two of the Laurita sisters always used to go out either with Bill Brennan or with me to visit villages on trips of four or five days at a time. We would go by car as far as the roads went, and from there on horses or mules. I remember how I used to ask these sisters to get all the married men and women, all the single youth, and all the kids over ten to go to confession and receive Holy Communion in my masses in the villages. This was the main part of our pastoral plan for forming the Church of Christ and helping the people live "in God's grace." We helped them receive the sacraments three or four times a year when we came to their village for mass. I worked enthusiastically in this system without any preoccupation with solving social problems. We did help take sick people to the hospital, or visit them in their homes to give them medicine or used clothes, especially the Indians, who live so hidden away in the mountains of Yoro and who are the poorest of the poor in Honduras, but we did not work at changing the system that perpetrated these problems.

But Bill Brennan had more vision: he was a true pioneer missionary. We became close friends, and he, little by little, opened my eyes to the fact that we had to do more than just give out the sacraments if we wanted to form the Honduran church of Christ: we had to form Honduran laypeople to be the leaders of their own Church.

He tried to organize the Legion of Mary in all the towns and villages so that these lay men and women could be in charge of moving their community to receive the sacraments by visits to each home. To have monthly contact with at least the board of directors of the different *praesidia* (or groups) of the Legion of Mary, they had to come from their villages to a center one Saturday a month, returning to their homes on Sunday. The first Sunday of each month they met in Yorito, the second in Jocón, the third in Ocotal of Locomapa, and the fourth in the town of Yoro for all those of the Yoro Valley, and from Subirana, Jimía, and Mejía. The parish of Yoro still follows this same basic system today, except that now they have at the same time the monthly meetings of the Delegates of the Word of God and of the catechists.

Either Brennan or I would go with two of the sisters to one of these centers on Saturday to have rosary in the afternoon and confessions that night. Not only those of the Legion of Mary, but hundreds of others from the surrounding villages, would come to these centers to go to confession and to receive Holy Communion in the mass on Sunday at 9:00 A.M. After mass we would have baptisms, and then the meeting of the *curia* of the Legion of Mary with the leaders of all the praesidia of that area.

The best thing about the Legion of Mary is that, as long as there is one member who can read, the group in the village just follows the detailed instructions in the manual of the Legion in order to run their own meeting and write up their own minutes for each of the seventeen points on the agenda. They start with the rosary and end with special prayers of the Legion. An important part of the weekly meeting is when the president assigns the apostolic work to be done in couples, such as visiting the sick, teaching catechism to the children, encouraging a certain couple to get married by the Church, leading novenas or funeral services, and so on. Before getting the new assignments, each couple gives a report on the apostolic work done the previous week. The written minutes of the weekly meetings, with all these detailed reports, are turned in to the curia at the monthly meeting in their center.

You must realize that in 1962 there were no popular organizations in most of the towns and villages of Honduras. Only the two political parties, the Nationalists and the Liberals, had their leaders or political chieftains in each village, the army its official representative, and the municipal mayor his representative. Thus, the Legion of Mary, which started in the parish of Yoro, was the beginning in the north of Honduras, not only of the lay movement in the Catholic church, but also of the first popular campesino organization in many villages.

Only around Progreso and Tela did there already exist a campesino labor organization, the FENACH. The same thing was happening in southern Honduras, in Choluteca, where the French-speaking Canadian Xaverian priests formed the Apostleship of Prayer organization, which later was the basis for forming the Radio Schools in Honduras.

The negative aspect of the Legion of Mary was its traditionalist pastoral approach of trying to get people to receive the sacraments and, thus, "save their souls." But you cannot blame the Legion of Mary for this approach. In 1962 in Honduras no one had any idea of liberation theology, of basic Christian communities, or of Delegates of the Word of God. The Legion originated in Ireland in the 1930s and has spread all over the Catholic world. Each country and each parish should adapt it to its own particular reality, but the strict following of the manual in all its details did not permit much adaptation. Another negative aspect of the Legion was that it was often dominated by pious elderly ladies, which made it unattractive to younger people and to men. In Yoro we made great efforts to also get the youth and men into the Legion. Some of our praesidia were run by men who later became Delegates of the Word.

After the Sunday curia meeting in a center, I would take off with the sisters for a three- or four-day trip on horseback to visit some of the villages in that region. The horses were lent to us and were sent from the village to which we would be going. In our saddlebags we carried the mass and baptism equipment and a sleeping bag, because in the mountains of Yoro it got pretty cold at night.

The people in the village always gave us our meals and a bed to sleep on in one of their houses. Sometimes I slept alone in the schoolhouse or church, if there was one. I always preferred this latter arrangement because the houses in the villages were so small, so poor, so full of people, and so full also of chickens, dogs, rats, fleas, cockroaches, and mosquitos. The beds were full of bedbugs. You can see why it was preferable to sleep on the wooden benches in the school or church.

Some campesinos have beds with mattresses, but most of them have beds with light rope strung across the wooden frame, or a cow's skin, or wooden boards, or (worst of all) just sticks, on top of which they place a reed mat or some empty burlap sacks. We spent many a miserable night in these mountain villages of Yoro, not only because the people there are very poor, but also because their houses are very dirty, with dirt floors. That is how they grew up. They do not even feel the need for a better house. We gringos arrive and think: "Oh, they have to fix up their homes, put in cement floors, make latrines, boil the water, keep the animals out of the house, make separate rooms in the house for the parents and for the grown daughters." But no, these are our felt needs, not theirs, at least not until they have gone to live in a bigger town where most of the people do fix up their houses and have better hygiene.

I recall one night in one of these poor houses when I was sleeping on a cowskin bed full of biting bedbugs, surrounded by the whole family with two or three persons in each of the other three beds in the small room that was itself the house. So that the rats would not eat the corn, they had it tied in bundles hanging down from the beams of the roof, which was made of palm leaves. Well, early in the night a big rat fell down from a beam right on top of my chest and scurried off, waking me up. All the rest of the night I lay there waiting for another rat.

I have killed many a snake and many poisonous scorpions, not only in the houses of the villages, but even in churches and in the latrines in the towns. You have to look your bed over and even your chair before you sit on it. In the morning you have to shake out your shoes and your pants before putting them on. But, really, I have never been bitten by a snake or a scorpion (not yet, at least). God protects me. May God continue to protect me!

In Yoro was one of the first coffee cooperatives in Honduras, organized around 1956 by Father Ratterman, S.J., of the Yoro parish. When I arrived in 1962, all that was left of this cooperative that had been so famous six years earlier was its big cement-block building with offices, warehouse, ovens, and outside cement patios for drying coffee—and a debt at the bank of around a hundred thousand dollars. Ratterman had died, and Bill Brennan was trying to buy and sell coffee in order to pay off the debt.

The Agricultural Cooperative San Isidro Limited (CASIL) no longer existed. The hundred and some coffee growers from all over the region of Yoro who had been members still existed, and all of them owed money to CASIL, but they refused to come to a meeting or to pay their debts to the co-op. Many problems still had to be solved in starting effective co-ops.

The government's Department for Promoting Cooperatives always mentioned Father Ratterman as one of the founders of cooperativism in Honduras. What Ratterman did to start the cooperative was to get a big loan from the bank so that the co-op could lend thousands of lempiras (the Honduran currency) to each member to cultivate individual coffee plantations and to pay for the picking of the coffee. The members were supposed to pay their debt by turning in their coffee to CASIL to be dried and sold collectively. The idea was good: to avoid the middlemen (whom they call wolves), who bought the coffee at a very low price by paying the producers in advance, before the harvest. All the profit from the coffee went to these wolves. CASIL failed because of lack of understanding among the members as to what a cooperative is. So, when members had any economic problem, they did not pay their debt to CASIL. Some of them, after getting a loan from the co-op, went ahead and sold their coffee in advance to the wolves instead of turning it in to CASIL.

A part of the hundred-thousand-dollar debt that CASIL had in 1962 was fifteen thousand dollars that the Society of Jesus had lent them. Brennan worked very hard at buying and selling coffee for three or four years before he managed to pay off almost all the debt to the bank. The way I understand it, the Jesuits finally, around 1968, paid off to the bank what remained of the debt, about ten thousand dollars, and in return for this and for the other fifteen thousand dollars that CASIL owed them, took over complete possession of the big building of CASIL in Yoro to use it as a formation center for lay leaders of the Church. Watching and talking with Bill Brennan that year I was in Yoro I learned from him about the dangers of being a paternalistic priest-organizer of co-ops.

In Yoro I also learned a lot about the popular religion of the people: I learned to respect it. Often, as youthful enthusiasts, we only learn from our own mistakes, instead of listening to the veterans in order to avoid mistakes and avoid offending people. A gringo Jesuit with all his years of study naturally tends to automatically judge the popular religion of the simple Catholics of Latin America as just superstition, and to condemn it. I was not as naive and simple as some new missionaries who come up against this problem, because I had seen plenty of this in Belize, especially among the Caribs.

Popular religion includes all those beliefs and customs of the masses of Catholics who have not studied much of the Bible or of theology. The poor, uneducated Catholics of Latin America, who make up the vast majority of the population, like to go to a novena to one of the saints or to the Virgin Mary. These are generally held in a private house, especially if it is the novena for the dead in the house of the family of the deceased. Other popular religious customs include going to a procession of the patron saint of the town or a procession during Holy Week, to the burial service for a dead friend, preceded by an all-night vigil, or on a pilgrimage to carry out a promise, walking in groups to visit a sanctuary of some saint—the Virgin of Suyapa in Tegucigalpa or the Black Christ in Esquipulas, Guatemala, for example. The uneducated Catholics prefer these devotions to assisting at mass and communion or Bible study.

They are not to be blamed for preferring these devotions that do not require a priest for they had been without a priest for so long. As an example of the general situation in all of Latin America, recall what I said about the department of Yoro in 1947 when the first Jesuits arrived there. The two existing priests for almost a thousand communities only went once a year to the bigger towns or centers for the patron feast.

The Spanish missionaries in the seventeenth century started almost all the Catholic customs that the people of Latin America have. Afterward, in the nineteenth century, the "secular" governments, dominated by anticlerical Masons, expelled almost all the religious and foreign priests, especially the Jesuits, and confiscated the extensive properties of the Church. The Catholics were left practically without priests and had to carry on their religious practices as best they could. They baptized their children, buried their dead, carried out their processions and novenas to their patron saints, all without the help of a priest. It is admirable the way the Catholic faith was preserved almost without priests in Honduras from its "independence" in 1821 until

1950, when the pope requested that many foreign missionaries go to help the Church in Latin America.

The idea of naming a patron saint with the date of his or her annual feast day for each town or bigger center, where the people of the surrounding mountain villages could gather came from the first Spanish missionaries. This was so that everyone would know, without having to give them notice each time, which day the priest was going to be in their town, especially to baptize their babies, but also for mass, confessions, and marriages. On this day all the people were there for the procession of the patron saint, accompanied by big fireworks displays, a musical band, and a lot of merriment. And a lot of drunkenness!

I had a problem during my first participation in the exceptionally large patron feast that they celebrate for fifteen straight days in Yoro each year in July in honor of their patron, Saint James. Each day the people of a different region of the parish come into Yoro to celebrate their day with mass, baptisms, procession with the band, great noise of fireworks, and a big dance at night.

In 1963 I was named to give the sermon at the biggest and most solemn mass of the year, on the feast day of Saint James, July 26, when the thousands of pilgrims from all over the parish try to squeeze into the huge parish church of Yoro. I mentioned previously that young priests often make mistakes that offend people. Well, not only did I offend all the great crowd of people devoted to Saint James the Apostle, but they were very angry with me. I was told later that the people were murmuring among themselves in the back during my sermon, planning on throwing me out of the church.

I wanted to take advantage of this big concentration of parishioners to correct some of the superstitions they had. For example, many of them would enter the church without paying any attention to or genuflecting before the Blessed Sacrament, nor even the mass, if they happened to enter during mass. They would go directly up to the big statue of Saint James and kneel down before it to pray to him. Then they would touch it, kiss it, smell it, and finish by lighting and sticking on the bare floor in front of the statue a few, or even a few dozen, candles. They would then march out of church, or maybe sit down in a pew to rest if mass were going on.

I explained to them in my sermon who the saints are, and who Jesus Christ is, and that we should only adore God, not a saint. Besides, I told them, the statue is not the saint, but only a representation of him. Saint James is in heaven and not in this statue. Therefore, you should not pray to the statue. This statue of Saint James cannot hear you; it is merely a piece of wood that an artist has carved to represent the apostle.

I went up to the statue to knock on it with my knuckle like one does on a door. This is what the people did not like, and after mass and the procession many told me so. Because I was very popular with the people of the parish, especially the youth, they forgave me. However, I never again touched a statue disrespectfully, and I resolved to try to understand what the people meant to express with their popular religious customs before condemning them.

Each custom has its history and contains something good of faith and devotion, however much of superstition it might contain. For example, in Latin America being baptized a Catholic is so much a part of being a citizen of the country that many people, including the rich and some of those who openly claim to be atheists, baptize their children. To baptize their sons and daughters is more a custom than a personal conviction. The simple people say that a baby is not a human being until he or she is baptized. They also have the faith and the superstition that baptism can cure a sick baby, and that some babies get sick because they are not yet baptized. In each village there are some women, prayer leaders, whom you can get to "put the water on the baby" if it is sick; and most of the babies who are presented to the priest for baptism have already been baptized in this way.

The priests and nuns used to teach that a baby who dies without baptism could not enter heaven, but would go to a place called limbo (a state of happiness without the sight of God). The Bible teaches us that God wants to save all people, so nowadays we teach that a baby who dies goes to heaven whether baptized or not. The great majority of humanity up to now has died without baptism. God has ways of saving us besides the sacraments.

These popular village prayer leaders are usually older women who learned all the customs and prayers, like the rosary and the novenas, from their mothers. In a novena or an all-night vigil before burying a dead person, the men do not enter the house to take part. They remain outside "to accompany the family" and to see if they will be given whiskey or at least a cup of coffee and food during the night. They often become drunk while accompanying the all-night vigil. The men are outside playing cards and talking and drinking, while the women and children are inside the house praying and singing on and off.

Latin Americans have a real cult of the dead. It is an inheritance from the Indian religions and from the Africans who came as slaves. Almost everyone believes the "souls wander around," that a dead person's soul can return to its house to bother people, and that it cannot find rest because it had not carried out some promise made to a saint. Many will swear that this dead person spoke to them or that they clearly saw it.

During the all-night vigil for a dead person, they always light four candles, one at each corner of the coffin, and they put out a glass of water for the deceased. Many believe that the next morning there often is less water in the glass. They feel they have to pray the novena for the souls in purgatory for each dead person; this is more important to them than a mass. They spend a lot of money preparing food and drink (even whiskey) for everyone who accompanies them in the vigil for the corpse, and also on the last night of the novena.

They believe in fairies also, and in witches and spiritists who can do them harm through magic or charms. If they think that someone has paid a witch to do them harm or make them sick, only another witch can save them or cure them. For these cures the spiritists often use pieces of the blessed altar stone containing a relic of some saint (which used to be inserted in the altars of all the Catholic churches). They make a powder out of the stone and put it into healing drinks. A number of campesinos have come to me to ask for a piece of the altar stone, offering to pay me well for it. At times a church is broken into in order to steal the altar stone.

One must distinguish between spiritist witches and spiritist healers, who, besides their superstitions and secret prayers and even possible communication with Satan, know plenty (after so many years of experience) about healing sicknesses with medicinal herbs. They also know how to massage the limb or finger that is fractured and out of place in order to rectify it, and the stomach that has indigestion because one "is full of air." I have seen several cases in which the doctor in the government clinic could not cure a sick person and afterward the spiritist healer did. Holy water is always a part of these spiritist healings; that is why the people ask us to bless so many bottles of holy water for them.

Another superstitious practice of the masses of simple Catholics is to make promises in order to obtain favors, not so much from God, because they hardly ever pray directly to him, but from the Virgin Mary or some other saint. They promise to, for example, make a pilgrimage to the sanctuary, or to light so many candles, or to offer a mass, or not to cut their little boy's hair until he makes his first Holy Communion, or to dress him up as the patron saint for the procession if the saint grants the favor. If not, no deal. I tell the people that the saints are not wolves, not commercial middlemen who demand payment for giving us something. It is hard to make them understand that we can and should pray principally to our Father-God, as Jesus taught us to do.

The early Spanish missionaries—or someone—gave these people a false idea of God from a narrow, limited understanding of the Old Testament of the Bible. They see God as a judge who is watching us to see if we break some commandment, in order to become angry with us and punish us. The earthquakes, the floods, the diseases are all punishments from God, according to most of these Catholics.

As I mentioned early in this book, I really became angry when I read what Cardinal Casariego said. He was head of the Catholic church in Guatemala and famous for being with the oligarchy and against the struggle of the people of Guatemala for their liberation. After the great earthquake a few years back, he said that God had sent it to punish the people for their sins. How could he explain, then, that more innocent children were killed in this earthquake than adults?

Many mothers also teach this false idea of God from a literal, harsh understanding of the Old Testament when they tell their children, "Don't do that or God will punish you!" In the New

Testament we learn from Jesus what God is really like: the loving Father of the prodigal son, who never punishes his children but waits for us with open arms to forgive us.

On July 31, 1963, the feast of Saint Ignatius of Loyola, a new superior was named for the Yoro Mission. This superior was a magnificent missionary (of the pre–Vatican II style) and is a classic example, which I have seen repeated many times, of how to ruin a good missionary and a good companion by making him a superior.

This superior had many times heard me criticize the high schools the Jesuits ran in Progreso, Negrito, Yoro, and Olanchito. After being in Yoro about four months, in February of 1963 when classes were about to begin, he flatly ordered me to teach English and religion in the Instituto Santiago, our parish high school. I just as flatly told him that I did not want to teach in that high school, which was for the few sons and daughters of the wealthy in our parish. He insisted that he was the superior and that I had to obey him, and that only by teaching in Instituto Santiago would I learn to appreciate the value of the educational apostolate. I had to obey finally, and taught classes three days a week, but you can imagine how (just as with the extra year of juniorate forced on me) I learned to criticize more seriously our Jesuit high schools.

I still was not a revolutionary capable of criticizing the whole capitalist system of education, but I did criticize the injustice of having a high school for about three hundred teenagers of both sexes, when our parish had at least eight thousand teenagers who could never go to high school. I felt it was unjust that where there was a priest for every fifteen thousand Catholics, the priest should spend so much of his time on three hundred privileged young Catholics. Especially in our Instituto San José in Progreso and in the Catholic high schools of Tegucigalpa and San Pedro Sula, I was convinced that most of the students graduated with a repugnance toward religion and a marked anticlericalism. There are better ways of influencing the youth than being owners, administrators, and disciplinarians of a high school. I think it has been proven that forcing religion classes is not the best way to give a knowledge of Christ to an adolescent.

In Yoro, to tell the truth, the few rich coffee growers and businessmen were not so bourgeois and did not live so much more luxuriously than the masses of the poor, as those of Tegucigalpa and San Pedro Sula did. I do not deny that they have a right to have a high school for their children. My criticism was not aimed at doing away with the only high school in Yoro, but rather that it should be for everyone, not just for those who can pay the fees.

The Church should not perpetuate this injustice of helping just the rich have a Catholic education for their children, instead of helping in the education of the masses of the poor, who are also Catholics. I always suggested that we give away all our Catholic grade schools, high schools, and universities in Latin America to the governments. The religious who want this apostolate of education should work for the government with salaries as teachers, student counselors, or social workers. In Central America it would be better for these religious to dedicate themselves to popular education of the poor adult masses who have not been able to attend even primary school.

The Jesuits of the Yoro Mission in Honduras make more efforts for educating the poor than those of the province in the rest of Central America. For example, the Jesuits have the most luxurious high schools that exist for the sons of the richest families of El Salvador (Externado San José) and of Guatemala (Liceo Javier). The theory is the same that they use in the United States. They say they are forming the elite, the future leaders of these countries, and that if these are good Christians, the country will be more Christian. These schools have been working now for enough years to measure the truth of that theory.

To me, at least, it is clear (now that I am a revolutionary and can judge it in the light of the gospel which is the good news of the liberation of the oppressed) that these high schools and Jesuit universities in Central America have formed a good part of the oppressive oligarchy of all these countries. It is true that some of our alumni are revolutionaries in Central America, but they are exceptions; it is a miracle of the grace of the Spirit of Jesus that they became revolutionaries in spite of their formation (like myself).

I admire tremendously the contribution that many of the Jesuits of the Central American Province are making to the fight for justice in these countries, but I do not understand how the province can justify these schools. How can so many men and women religious continue to dedicate themselves to the education of the bourgeoisie, the rich, in Latin America, where the Church says it has made "the option for the poor"?

In Yoro, just as during my three years of teaching in Belize and in the parish of Minas de Oro, I became very popular with the youth. Outside of classes I played sports with them, sang with them in the park at night, and played the guitar I had bought.

Charlie Prendergast had been appointed the new pastor at Yoro. Since I can never go for long without some kind of conflict with my superiors, I had my first one with Charlie just a few days after he arrived in August. Always it was the same theme. He wanted to repaint the big priest's house, or parish rectory, where we lived. I told him that I was not in agreement. In fact, we should look for a poorer house in which to live instead of this big one, which was one of the five best dwellings in the town of Yoro. He became angry with me and said that, quite to the contrary, it was too poor and dirty and that we had to fix it up.

Little by little, I was learning that almost all Americans, including the Jesuits, measure things by comparing them with the United States. Surely, compared with the huge, comfortable buildings that the Jesuits have in the United States, our parish rectories and our high schools in Honduras are poor. Compared with what most Hondurans have, they are luxurious.

At any rate, our new superior was arranging for me to go to Colombia for my Third Probation, which started in November of that year, 1963. I was to go with Father Jim O'Brien who had just arrived on the mission after finishing theology in Kansas. Before we left there happened an event of historical transcendency in Honduras. You will understand it better if I explain a bit of the political situation in Honduras at that time.

After the sixteen years of continuous dictatorship under Gen. Tiburcio Carías and his National Party (controlled by big landowners and other conservatives) and after President Manuel Gálvez and the big strike of the banana workers in 1954, a junta of three military officers, with Col. Oswaldo López Arellano as head of the armed forces, took over the government of Honduras. They did this in a bloodless coup d'état in 1957, in order, they said, to assure free elections. This coup was planned by the armed forces, the U.S. embassy, various American interests, and the Liberal Party.

As was foreseen, Morales won the elections and started a liberalization of the country with some important reforms, such as the work code and the Agrarian Reform Law. On finishing their term of six years, the Liberal Party was almost sure to win again in 1963 with Modesto Rodas Alvarado as their candidate for president.

October third is Soldiers' Day, a feast day for the Honduran army. Early on this morning in 1963, Charlie Prendergast and I were asleep in the rectory in Yoro and heard the traditional early morning fireworks and rockets (as on all feast days) around 4:30 A.M. I was supposed to say the 6:00 A.M. mass in the church this day. When I did not hear the usual ringing of the church bells by our sacristan, Siverio, at 5:30, I went out to ring them myself. You could still hear a rocket explode now and then. On crossing through the town park from the rectory to the church, imagine my surprise to see behind each tree in the park a soldier with his rifle ready to shoot.

I asked them what they were doing, and they answered, "We are saving our country from communism." Then I realized that those had not been fireworks and rockets that I heard, but a lot of rifle shots. I asked them if there were any wounded, and one of them said that there might be some in the house of the Civil Guard a few blocks down the street.

I got the holy oils from the church and went there, only to find eight of the Civil Guard on the floor, all dead. About 4:30 A.M. the army had broken down the door of the house and shot them in their beds. A few had escaped, and the soldiers were going from house to house searching for them. They also had a list of the principal leaders of the Liberals of Yoro and were looking for them to kill also.

I returned to the rectory to let Charlie know and then went to the nun's house and the house of our sacristan, Siverio, to see if he was all right, because I knew he was a Liberal. They told me he had been taken prisoner, so I went to the prison—just in time to identify him as our sacristan. They might have killed him; I learned afterward that they had killed ten men in their houses just because they were Liberals with a reputation of being leftists.

There were soldiers in all the streets, and during all this time sporadic shots could be heard.

As I was returning to the church, Gazy Bendeck shouted to me from his house to please come in because his father was dying. What a horrible scene! The old man's face was all torn open and jets of blood were squirting out. You see, Gazy was a Liberal and, besides that, the richest man in town. His old father made the mistake of sticking his head out of a second-story window, and a .30-caliber bullet from a soldier's M–1 ripped right through his face. (All the Central-American armies bought weapons from the United States and used the uniforms and arms that were left after World War II.) I gave him absolution and put the holy oils on a piece of flesh of his forehead, and he died immediately. This is the only rich family in Yoro who always remained my friends.

What happened in Yoro was typical of what happened in all the towns of Honduras where there were Civil Guards. The army massacred them in their beds, and also massacred all the known "leftists" they could find. I do not recall how many hundreds were murdered in this cowardly fashion on that bloody morning and during the following days. Just in Progreso, its villages, and banana camps, more than a hundred were said to have been murdered and around three hundred taken prisoner.

There were many more than this in Tegucigalpa and in San Pedro Sula, the two principal cities. All the leftist workers, campesinos, students, professionals, and so on, and the principal leaders of the Liberals were on the list and were being persecuted by the army. Those who surrendered after the first massacre were prisoners. Those who hid out and escaped secretly left the country, because the search for them went on for months.

What happened was that the National Party agreed with the highest officers of the armed forces and with the U.S. embassy in Tegucigalpa to make a coup before the elections in November, otherwise the voters would surely give the victory to the Liberal Party again and allow "the advance of communism in Honduras."

It is true that under the government of Villeda Morales there was plenty of freedom of thought and of expression, and the

Marxists had acquired quite a bit of influence in the university and in a number of labor unions. The U.S. embassy was content with the Liberal government, which carried out all the ideas of President John F. Kennedy's Alliance for Progress, but the many agents of the CIA in Honduras insisted that they had to eliminate the "communists" who more and more were infiltrating everything.

The plan was for the armed forces to take over the government and, by decree, name Colonel López Arellano president of Honduras. Nationalists or trustworthy military officers were named to all the government posts in the whole country, as cabinet ministers, judges, departmental governors, mayors, managers of the state enterprises (like electric energy), and so on. Naturally, they in turn named trustworthy Nationalists to replace all the Liberals who were working in these organizations, even the janitors, watchmen, and chauffeurs.

The military promised to carry on with the social reforms that the United States wanted under the Alliance for Progress, for the purpose of avoiding the revolutionary explosion of the hungry masses. That is why they chose Colonel López Arellano for president; he was a military man favoring reforms and very popular. He knew how to win personal friends and also the masses. The Nationalist capitalists and landowners trusted the colonel because he also was already a big landowner and cattleman and had shares in a number of business enterprises.

The gringos insisted that they should not kill President Villeda Morales in the coup, because he was a friend of theirs and had been elected with their help. However, they would have to completely destroy the Civil Guard, which was the police force formed by Villeda with men who were loyal to him. It was like a private army of the Liberals (even as the Honduran army was like a private army of the Nationals), which several times during the previous six years had saved them from other attempts at coups d'état.

Everything went off as planned. Half the Hondurans were left crying for their dead, and half of them were rejoicing. My superior sent word about a week after the coup that I should help out in the parish of Progreso for a month before going to Colombia. I found that the whole of Progreso was under military vigilance and a state of seige, with a curfew from 6:00 P.M. to 6:00 A.M. There was none of this in Yoro, because the town was predominately Nationalist and without popular movements, but Progreso was the third largest city in the country, predominately Liberal, and a center of leftist labor union activity.

Just one block from the parish rectory the army had confiscated a big saloon and dance hall from a Liberal, and there they kept the three hundred political prisoners. We could see them from the second floor of the rectory. They did not give them any food; the families of the prisoners had to bring it to them twice a day. When I left for Colombia a month later, most of these political prisoners were still there.

I did not know it then, because the Jesuits in Progreso had no contact with the popular movements of the workers and campesinos, but one of the principal aims of the U.S. embassy was to destroy the FENACH, the National Federation of Honduran Campesinos, which had its main force in the Progreso area. There was a witch hunt in all the villages of our parish worse than in any other part of Honduras, and the army wiped out the FENACH once and for all. All the leaders had been killed or were being persecuted. Those that escaped left the country or hid out in other parts of the country. I will relate later the history of this campesino organization and of the new one, the ANACH, which the U.S. embassy with its American Institute for Free Labor Development (AIFLD) promoted to replace the FENACH.

The parish of Progreso got food from CARITAS (the national Catholic charity, usually supported by Catholic relief services) to give to the political prisoners, and the priests spoke up for some whom they knew to obtain their freedom. But I do not recall any of them (priests or bishops) daring to publicly denounce this horrible crime, the massacre and persecution of hundreds of Hondurans by the army. The labor unions were so beaten and threatened that they did not dare to make public protests either. The masses of the poor in Honduras, who were unorganized and accustomed to suffer injustice and oppression in silence, were still very much conformists. Neither did I myself do anything to denounce, or to encourage the masses to denounce, these great sins and injustices.

9. The Formation of a Jesuit - V

In November of 1963, Jim O'Brien and I took the plane from Tegucigalpa to the island of San Andrés, where we changed planes for Bogotá, Colombia. I remember spending one of the coldest nights of my life sleeping without blankets or any kind of heating in a school run by the Benedictines in this big city high in the mountains. The next day we flew to Medellín and traveled from there two hours in a bus to La Ceja in the department of Antióquia, where the Jesuits of the Northern Province of Colombia had their novitiate, juniorate, and Third Probation house on a big cattle farm close to the small town.

It was like going back to the novitiate at Florissant, Missouri, again, where I made my First Probation (the first week of novitiate) and my Second Probation (the two years of novitiate) before taking my first perpetual vows. After so many years of study and formation and a little bit of active apostolate, the Society of Jesus gives us a Third Probation before we take our final vows. We again make the full month of the Spiritual Exercises of Saint Ignatius, we study thoroughly the constitutions and the documents of the latest General Congregations of the Society, and in general we go deeper into the spiritual life before being completely thrown into the apostolic life.

Today Third Probation lasts only four or five months, but in 1963 in the conservative Province of Colombia it lasted a full year, and with rules almost as strict as we had in our novitiate. We had to always wear the cassock, and all the Colombian Jesuits had the tonsure, a small shaved-out circle on the very top of the head. This was to identify a clergyman easily, even if he took off his cassock.

The department of Antióquia in Colombia is the most religious region in all of Latin America, a lot like Spain, I believe. Everyone gets married in the Church; practically everyone goes to confession and communion every month for First Friday; each little town has its big church with one or more priests and nuns; there are numerous religious vocations; the campesinos give a part of all their harvests to the parish, and so on.

Colombia has a concordat with the Catholic church by which the government agrees to give a decent monthly salary to all the parish priests and to provide salaries for teachers of Catholic religion classes in all the grade schools, high schools, and universities in the country. One result of this is that the Church is submissive to the State. The bishops almost never criticize the government or denounce the flagrant injustices of the rich oligarchy who run the country and exploit the working class. There have been a few exceptions, like Bishop Valencia and the famous priest-guerrilla-martyr, Camilo Torres, but in general, the Colombian Church is one of the most conservative in the world.

Third Probation would have been very hard for me if we had not had as director one of the best Jesuits I have ever known, Father Jaime Martínez, who until that year had been the director of CIAS (Center for Investigation and Social Action) of the Jesuits in Colombia. It was a real pleasure to hear his talks and to discuss reflections on the gospel with him, because it was the first time for me that a spiritual director applied all the teachings of the Bible, the popes and bishops, and the Society of Jesus to the social problems of Latin America.

Since Jaime Martínez was an economist and his main interest had been the social apostolate, analyzing and seeking solutions to social injustice, he infected us with this same preoccupation, too. He was one superior with whom I never had a problem; we looked at things in the same way.

The worst problem in Colombia in 1963 was the tremendous violence, especially in the mountains, between the followers of the two big rival political parties, the Liberals and the Conservatives. Tens of thousands had died in recent years because of this great hatred among fellow Colombians, and worse, among poor fellow campesinos. If a member of one band was killed, they had to seek vengeance and kill two of the other band. The Church tried to convince the people that these were great mortal sins and that they were killing their brothers-in-Christ, but with little success.

The Jesuit Father Pacho Mejía, who had worked in the social

apostolate for many years with the labor leaders of the UTC (Union of Workers of Colombia), was carrying on a campaign to end the violence among the campesinos of the mountains around the Cauca Valley in southern Colombia. He asked Father Martínez, our director, to allow the thirty of us priests in Third Probation to help him by giving eight-day missions in the villages of the whole region around the city of Buga. He hoped to conscienticize the campesinos, so that they would put an end to the vengeance and the violence, by getting them all to go to confession.

We went two by two, staying eight days in a village and then giving another mission in another community before returning to La Ceja. I clearly remember the mission at which one of the principal leaders of the largest Colombian campesino organization, the FANAL, helped us. He and I slept on the cement floor of the school during the eight days and became great friends. This grand campesino, named Gastón Jiménez, gave me my first lessons about the importance of popular organizations, especially the labor unions of the workers and campesinos. We used to talk for hours each night about the popular organizations in Colombia, and after the mission he introduced me to many other leaders of the FANAL and of the UTC (Union of Workers of Colombia) who happened to be in Buga. I resolved to learn all I could about the labor movement and about cooperatives.

This campesino had graduated from "The Campesino University" in Buga, which, along with "The Worker University," had been founded by Father Pacho Mejía to give a basic cultural training to worker and campesino leaders, who often had not even finished the six years of grade school. The "university" consisted in giving them the equivalent of a primary education, but with more studies on leadership, cooperativism, unionism, and the social doctrine of the Church. They called it a university to give more prestige to its graduates.

What a tremendous work! The bad thing about it was that the gringos entered by means of a grant and loan from AID. Later on, the American Institute for Free Labor Development (AIFLD) had a lot of influence in these two universities and in the FANAL and the UTC, forming anticommunist and reformist, not revolutionary, labor leaders. I will explain all these terms more fully later.

Ever since my philosophate, meditating on the life and the ideas of Charles de Foucauld about incarnating oneself in the working class, and reading about the priest-workers in France and Spain, I had toyed with the idea of being a priest-worker in Honduras. After visiting the banana farms that made up about half of our parish of Progreso, I got the idea of possibly living on one of them after Third Probation as a priest-worker. With the stimulus that I received in Buga, getting to know the work of Pacho Mejía and of the FANAL and the UTC, I wanted to specialize in cooperativism and unionism in order to be able to help the working class by becoming one of them.

With all this the Holy Spirit was preparing me for my "election," or resolutions, in the month of Spiritual Exercises in La Ceja. I have already explained how these same month-long Exercises in the novitiate had changed my life, giving me the assurance of the existence of God that I have never doubted again. Each year we Jesuits repeat these Exercises during an eight-day retreat; therefore, in Third Probation these Exercises were not so sensational for me. They were more tranquil; I now always practiced the "prayer of simplicity." Ever since the novitiate, my problem with headaches had forced me to make my daily meditations more tranquilly, just resting in the presence of my Father and of my great companion and model, Jesus, abandoning myself to the Holy Spirit to use me as his instrument in the salvation of the world.

Saint Ignatius describes the Jesuit as a "contemplative while active." Some religious are just contemplatives, like the Trappists, the Carthusians, and the ancient hermits. Secular priests sanctify themselves in apostolic work, while active. The Jesuit is supposed to be a synthesis of the two.

I certainly find myself each year since the novitiate more and more a contemplative. I even consider myself a kind of hermit (something like Foucauld), but always involved in apostolic action. I find God in all things; I am with him all day long. More than anything, I contemplate God in daily happenings, reflecting on them, admiring how the Holy Spirit works in me, in those around me, and in the world's events. Nevertheless, more and more I have learned to like being alone, as though separated from the world, even if only for a few hours each day, in order to rest in God. But from this history of mine you are reading you can see that I am also a very active person, very involved in the things of this world. I want it to go on record here how much my love, my gratitude, and my admiration for the Society of Jesus grows in me more and more each year, because sometimes I am so critical that you might not believe that fact.

During the month of the Exercises in Third Probation I advanced more in the mystical life of abandoning myself into the hands of God with complete trust. I read a good deal of the works of Saint John of the Cross and of Saint Teresa of Avila. At the same time, with the new (for me) social viewpoint that Father Jaime Martínez gave to the Spiritual Exercises, and with my experience of having lived with the poor campesinos in their villages in Honduras, I received many new intuitions about Jesus and his gospel. As I said, I made my election in this retreat about the type of apostolate I should carry on in Honduras, and I decided to ask the superior of the mission two things: first, permission to become a naturalized Honduran citizen in order to be more incarnated with the Hondurans, and second, permission to be a priest-worker in the banana farms of the Tela Railroad Company in Progreso, at least for a year, and only then to start a plan of evangelization of these worker companions who have been so abandoned by the Church. I was deeply impressed by what Pope Pius XII wrote: that the working class of Europe has been lost to the Church.

Father Martínez encouraged me to follow this inspiration. That is why I dared to ask him that, instead of spending a month as a chaplain in one of the big hospitals in Bogotá, as all those of Third Probation do, he let me spend this month as a day laborer in the banana farms around Santa Marta on the north coast of Colombia in order to prepare myself for my work in Honduras. He agreed, but he had to get permission from the provincial superior and from the bishop of Santa Marta because in Colombia a priest is never allowed to take off his cassock and live away from ecclesiastical control, as I was asking to do. Because of his good reputation in all of Colombia, Father Martínez obtained the required permissions and personally took me to a town near the banana camps and left me with a priest of the local parish.

This priest took me to one of the farms and introduced me to the owner as a priest who wanted to work as a day laborer for a month "to study the religious life of the workers." Not only he, but also the owners of two other farms, said that they did not want any priests coming in to create more problems for them with the workers. The fourth owner, a Protestant, answered yes, but that I should not cause him any problems with the workers. I accepted, thanked the priest for helping me, and moved into one of the wooden barracks of that camp, where about forty workers and their families lived.

To understand why the owners were afraid of labor agitators coming into their farms, it is necessary to explain that the United Fruit Company in Colombia (precisely on account of labor problems) had divided up into smaller parts and sold all its banana farms to Colombians, with contracts to give them technical assistance in production and to buy all their exportable bananas. Thus the gringos of the transnational company get all the fruit for marketing without any more labor problems or production problems or accusations of being foreign landowners.

The idea of dividing up the big farms (even though the same person could be owner of several of these small farms) was to avoid unionization of the workers and the necessity of making a collective contract with them. The Work Code required twenty-five permanent workers at the same enterprise for organizing a labor union. Some of the bigger farms already had a union, like the farm where I worked, but on most of the farms they laid off the workers before finishing their sixty-day trial period so they would not have to give them severance pay, and so that they would never have twenty-five permanent workers on the farm. Since the owner of my farm had already signed a collective contract with the union, his fear of my presence on his farm was not so great.

I lived in a small room in one of the barracks with several other bachelors, and we bought our meals from a woman. Everyone knew I was a priest, even though I had no apostolate and did not wear a cassock. I mentioned that I was going to celebrate mass each day after work at 5:00 P.M. in the little schoolroom, if anyone wanted to attend. In Antióquia, everyone, without doubt, would have gone to daily mass and communion, but Father

Martínez had told me that the north coast region was religiously the coldest part of Colombia.

Almost everyone was Catholic, but they were like the people in Honduras on the north coast, very indifferent to and very ignorant about religion. Most of the couples lived together unmarried and had not made their first Holy Communion, for lack of priests in the region and also because many of them had come from other parts of the country and had no roots here. So I was not surprised that only a few of them ever showed up for my daily masses.

With Father Martínez, I had planned an experiment that I wanted to use as an apostolic tactic later on with the workers in Honduras. It was never to bring up the subject of religion in a conversation with them but just to live and work with them. I would preach the gospel by my manner of living, leaving them to take the initiative of speaking about religion if they wanted to.

I spent two weeks getting to know the work and getting to know by name all the people in the camp, as well as many people from other camps who visited ours. The soccer games on Sundays in other camps were good opportunities to get to know all the people in the region. I also attended all the union meetings in my camp and in others.

This last activity of mine soon reached the attention of the different farm owners, and I found out that if I had not left when my month was up, my boss would have fired me and no other owner would have given me work. I did practically nothing with the unions, but just the presence of a priest encouraged the workers to fight for their rights.

After I had gained the confidence of my fellow workers, they gave me a surprise! I would no sooner be alone with one of them, maybe digging a ditch, cutting off the flowering tail of the bunch of bananas, cutting and hauling on our shoulders to the wagons the ninety-pound bunches of ripening bananas (the hardest of all the work on the farms), or sitting in the barracks or wherever, than they would start asking me something about our religion. Many of them asked me if I could fix up their marriages. I spoke to the pastor of the nearby parish, and he agreed that I could marry them without charge. On hearing this, many workers from other nearby farms also sought me out to arrange for their marriages. Almost all of them had been living together unmarried for many years and had a number of children.

I met with these couples to prepare them with a little instruction about matrimony and about their first confession and Holy Communion, which most of them were going to make. Therefore, for my last day in the banana region, as my farewell, we had one of the nicest masses of my life under a huge tree alongside the soccer field. It was Sunday; all the people from the surrounding farms, around a thousand people, were there to accompany the thirty couples who were getting married at this mass. They stayed for the big dance afterward in order to say good-bye to me, because the next day I had to leave for La Ceja.

In this way my theory was proven that a priest does not have to tell the people that it is a sin to miss mass on Sunday, to fornicate, or to commit adultery, or to get drunk. Everyone knows this. What they do not know is Jesus Christ; nor do they know any real Christians. These workers had never talked with a priest as with a friend. They were afraid of the priest, the same as they are afraid of God (instead of loving and trusting him). Once again, my conviction was confirmed that the first step toward helping the people to save themselves is to incarnate yourself with them, live with them, win their confidence and friendship. Only then will they listen to you.

Another rare experience I had during Third Probation was of the fanaticism of the Antióquians about going to confession and communion on the First Friday of each month in honor of the Sacred Heart of Jesus. Each month that we were in La Ceja, we priests all went out to the different parishes of the department of Antióquia to help the pastors with the hundreds or thousands of confessions and communions they had. It started on Thursday afternoon with all the students of the grade and high schools (including the public schools) being marched over to the church by their teachers. On Thursday the campesino families from the surrounding villages also poured into town to go to confession and stay up waiting for the 6:00 A.M. First Friday mass, after which they returned to their villages. Do you know how long it takes two priests just to give communion to more than seven hundred persons? And to hear each one's confession each month?

My brother, Pat, had made his Third Probation in La Ceja the year before I did, and this superstitious practice was the straw that broke his back, that left him completely discouraged with being a priest only two years after ordination. Before finishing his year in La Ceja, Pat refused to hear more confessions. On returning to Honduras he took my place in the parish of Progreso when I left for La Ceja. He had already told me that he could not stand this giving out of sacraments, like pills, to people who did not understand their meaning. While I was in Colombia, Pat asked for a dispensation from Rome to leave the Society of Jesus and the priesthood, and he went back to the United States.

I could certainly understand why Pat became discouraged with hearing those hundreds of First Friday confessions in Colombia. Most of them were pure routine, habit, an automatic ritual like taking a bath, and generally lacked any real repentance. I endured it because I always remembered my goal of being a priest-worker in Honduras.

Many priests and religious of these years felt a crisis of identity. In ten years thousands of priests all over the world asked to leave. The number of Jesuits in the world went down from thirty-six thousand to thirty thousand during this vocational crisis. Vocations to the seminaries and novitiates went down to practically zero in many congregations.

It did not surprise me much when Pat wrote me that he was leaving the priesthood. He is so sincere and honest that I felt sure he was just carrying out the will of God, and that is what I wrote to our mother, to whom the news about Pat was a hard blow. A couple of years later she said she was content as long as she had one son who remained a religious. After she wrote that to me in one of her letters, I answered that she should not be surprised if she one day got a letter saying that I had been expelled from the Jesuits.

Thanks be to God that I have never doubted my vocation to be a priest. But what I wrote to my mother about being expelled from the Jesuits has been a real possibility ever since the novitiate and right up to the present day. Several times since Third Probation I have been tempted to request permission to leave the Society of Jesus to be a secular priest in one of the dioceses of Honduras if, with the Jesuits, I could not carry out my most basic calling, which is to live with and as the poor. But I have always loved and do love very much the Society of Jesus. I feel that the spirit of the Society is my spirit. I cannot imagine a group of men in this world more wonderful and saintly, in general, than the Jesuits!

When I finished Third Probation and returned to Honduras in October of 1964, I was in the throes of a complete metamorphosis of my whole mentality, becoming a revolutionary. I involved myself in the struggles of the campesinos, and there was a qualitative leap forward in this metamorphosis. It was now natural that I would have clashes with all the status quo societies, including the Society of Jesus. That is, a true revolutionary wants to change everything: envisions the utopia, the ideal of a society of perfect brotherhood, and criticizes everything that does not meet this ideal. The revolutionary is in continuous conflict with those who do not want change, and with those who do not want change in the same way as he or she does. So the next part of my life is the history of this qualitative leap in my metamorphosis, which caused so many conflicts, and, vice versa, of how the conflicts caused that leap forward in my metamorphosis. It is a dialectical process.

PART V. THE METAMORPHOSIS OF A NORTH AMERICAN THROUGH THE PEASANT STRUGGLES FOR JUSTICE

10. Parish Work in Progreso

On my return to Honduras, our superior, Fred Schuller, assigned Jim O'Brien to the parish of Negrito to help Father Bill Ulrich take care of the municipalities of Negrito, Morazán, and Santa Rita. I was assigned to the parish of Progreso to take the place of Father Jim McShane, who was sick and had to return to the States for an operation. Ramón Alberdi was the pastor and took care of the big city of about thirty thousand Catholics with the help of Miguel Renobales, who had just come to Honduras after many years of work in the Jesuit Landívar University in Guatemala.

Miguel wanted to work with the poor, and I admired how he, an aristocratic Spaniard, left the rectory every day on foot to visit and help the people in the poorest sector of Progreso, called Pénjamo. For one who had spent his whole life in the comfortable, rich universities of the Jesuits in Spain and Guatemala, this was a great sacrifice.

Ramón Alberdi was the best preacher I have ever heard. He had the gift of speaking in the language of the people with such vivid examples of the reality of injustice and exploitation that surrounded us and that he continually denounced, that he roused the consciences of a lot of people. At the same time some of the big landowners criticized him and denounced him to the military authorities who governed them. Nonetheless, Ramón was a great friend of most of the rich families of Progreso; he visited their homes, belonged to the Lion's Club, and went to the stadium every Sunday with them for the big professional soccer games.

More than for the rich, however, Ramón had great love and friendship for the poor, the labor leaders, the youth, indeed, every class of person, including the diocesan priests and the religious women of the whole country. All these groups invited him for talks and spiritual retreats, and the theme of his talks almost always was the Social Doctrine of the Church.

Ramón was a Basque, had left Spain after criticizing the dictator Franco and later Nicaragua after criticizing the dictator Somoza. After three years in Progreso, in 1964 he was the most famous priest in the country. The military authorities, the bishops, and our superior feared him, persecuted him, and warned him not to criticize the military government so much, not to be so "involved in politics." Besides his sermons at two of the Sunday masses, which attracted more and more people, especially the men and the youth, and his talks to different groups all over the country, he also spoke often over the radio and wrote articles for the newspapers. I learned a lot from Alberdi.

In those days in the parish rectory alongside the big church in Progreso lived Alberdi, Renobales, and myself; and in the Jesuit Instituto San José on the outskirts of Progreso lived other Jesuits, including Brother Jim O'Leary, Fred Schuller, Paul Van Fleet, who was the director of the high school, the teaching scholastics (Jesuit seminarians) Ray Pease, Steve Gross, Bill Barbieri, and my closest friend Tom Quiery, who was in charge of the Apostolic School. Father George Toruño had started this Apostolic School for boys who had finished grade school and aspired to be Jesuits. They boarded at the school for their high school studies and for some spiritual formation as future priests; it was like a minor seminary. But it never gave fruit. At one time they had up to twenty boarders, but they were mostly young fellows who were taking advantage of this opportunity for a free ride through high school. In the ten years it functioned, five boys went to the diocesan seminary and another five entered the Jesuit novitiate, but none of them persevered; not one reached the priesthood.

With Alberdi and Renobales taking care of the big city, I was left with the eighty villages and twenty banana camps that also belonged to the parish. Some of these communities were big, like Urraco Pueblo with its twenty-five hundred inhabitants, and Agua Blanca Sur, Quebrada Seca, Toyos, Finca Birichiche, and Finca Monterrey, each with more than a thousand; and some were small, like San Antonio, in the mountains, with some twenty houses, Arena Blanca with thirty houses, and others. The idea was to visit and form the Church in all of these hundred communities with approximately thirty-five thousand Catholics.

There were four Spanish sisters, Missionary Crusaders of the Church, who were still wearing their long habits and headgear. They had a sewing school in the big hall of the parish clinic that Father Murphy had started, and they helped us with the pastoral work in the city and at times in the villages, going out with me in our old International Scout jeep.

Progreso is in the Sula Valley on the banks of the Ulúa River; that is why it is called the Pearl of the Ulúa. This valley has probably the most fertile land in all of Central America. There used to be more swampland before the Yankee engineers of the United Fruit Company had them drained by a system of canals, which also serve for irrigating the banana farms with pumps. About half of this great valley was ceded to the Tela Railroad Company (subsidiary of the United Fruit Company) by the unpatriotic, bought-off presidents of Honduras at the beginning of this century. The rest of the best lands of the Sula Valley were in possession of the big cattlemen, principally of San Pedro Sula and Progreso.

The tens of thousands of campesinos in the valley, many of whom were former workers on the banana farms, had no land of their own. Year by year they rented small plots from the landowners or moved onto the marginal land that was not used for banana or cattle production. Just a very few campesinos had been able to buy small plots of their own for their corn and bean crops.

Practically all the villages of the parish in the valley could be reached by car, and there were only eight villages in the mountains that I had to visit on horseback. From Agua Blanca Sur to the south, near Santa Rita, out to Pavón at the northern extreme of the parish was about seventy miles. Every afternoon I used to leave Progreso for one of the communities for mass and baptisms and to notify other communities which day I would visit them. Just to go around like this to all of my communities to get to know them for the first time took me about four months. At the same time I was making a kind of written census of all of these communities so that I would be able to know them better and remember the facts about each one.

Even in this first visit I tried to promote the idea of forming the Legion of Mary in each community, as we had in Yoro. Up to then, the priests had visited the villages and camps only for the sacraments and to personally teach catechism to the children for their First Holy Communion. In many places, however, they had named "majordomos" to help them with the visits, and in some places they had organized the Apostleship of Prayer with its *Celadores* who distributed the monthly leaflet of the Apostleship. There was no other kind of church organization.

Jim O'Brien, who had the villages of the Negrito parish, Tom Quiery, who had the Apostolic School and helped O'Brien with his villages, and I used to meet frequently as good friends. We would reflect together about an apostolic plan for the evangelization of the villages, which were so many that we could visit them personally only a few times a year. We studied together an article in *Maryknoll* magazine that explained how the Maryknoll priests in the mountains of Perú formed men "catechists" for each village to get their community together on Sunday for a kind of a Catholic Bible service. They had songs, prayer, and readings from the Bible with a dialogue explanation. Once a month the priest would meet with these catechists to prepare with them the Sunday gatherings of their communities for the following month.

Near the end of 1964 we agreed to have as the main object of our visits for mass to try to pick out about three men from each village who could read and who had the good will to be "apostolic leaders," as we decided to call them. I was still making my first round of visits to get to know all the villages, but I started to explain at mass that Catholics should not come together only when the priest comes, that is, a few times a year. They could fulfill the third commandment, "Sanctify the Lord's Day and the Holy Days of Obligation," meeting together by themselves every Sunday and Holy Day to hear the Word of God; for that, however, we needed some men volunteers to form as apostolic leaders.

By the end of January 1965, I had a list of ten villages with their chosen apostolic leaders. Jim, Tom, and I prepared "Sunday celebrations" (as we called them) on mimeographed sheets for four Sundays, and in a three-day course in the hall of the parish clinic in Progreso, we showed these first fifty apostolic leaders of the two parishes how to lead the Sunday celebration by themselves, following the sheet for each Sunday. We also taught them about the Legion of Mary, so that they would interest the people in organizing it in their village.

Six months later some of our friends, Canadian priests in Choluteca, in the south of Honduras, bettered our system. They formed the leaders of the Apostleship of Prayer that they had in their villages as "Delegates of the Word of God" (as they called them). The Delegates would lead the "Celebration of the Word of God" every Sunday, following a handsome booklet that they had printed with the schemes for all the Sundays of the following six months.

After this, we too used the same names, "Delegates" and "Celebration of the Word," and the booklets from Choluteca. The bishops liked the idea; there were several pastoral meetings at the national level, and little by little all the rural parishes in Honduras started to organize Delegates of the Word. The idea spread from Honduras to Guatemala and El Salvador and, later on, around 1970, to Nicaragua, Panama, and Mexico. At least, that is how I understand the history of the "Celebration of the Word."

For the apostolate in the city of Progreso I tried to interest Alberdi and Renobales in the *Cursillo de Cristiandad* (little workshop in Christianity) movement. Ever since I took the Cursillo (workshop) in San Antonio, Texas, in 1962 on the way down to Honduras, I had wanted to promote them. But, as I mentioned before, it was the American secular priest, Vincent Prestera, who had started giving these Cursillos in Tegucigalpa in 1964 with great success. They really caused a rejuvenation in the Church there, in the bourgeois sector at least. Very many men and women in the capital "were converted to Christ," lived *"de colores"* (song of the Cursillo movement), received Holy Communion even daily, and started to help give these cursillos in other cities. Miguel Renobales, Paul Van Vleet (director of our Instituto San José), and I went with twenty men from Progreso to take one of these Cursillos in San Pedro Sula, and later Father Prestera came to give one in Progreso for fifty more men.

Since I had too much work with so many villages, Van Fleet became the spiritual director of these *cursillistas*. The movement in Progreso advanced and did a lot of good for many families. In general, though, it was a movement for the bourgeois class; a few poor workers entered but did not persevere.

Since I was not very revolutionary yet, I supported this movement in the Church and used to go to many of their *"Ultreya"* (followup) meetings. A few years later, when I understood more about the class struggle in the world and within the Church also, I realized that the Cursillo movement can be alienating if it is too individualistic. By putting the most emphasis on avoiding personal and matrimonial sins, one calms the conscience so there is no worry about the larger social or structural sins and injustices that are what most ruin this world. Not only does it often fail to instill a social, revolutionary conscience, but rather it is a substitute for this, and so it is counterrevolutionary.

The same thing happens with the charismatic or Pentecostal renewal movement within the Catholic church. It is often alienating by putting too much emphasis on personal conversion, on the personal relationship with Jesus and his Holy Spirit, thereby keeping the people from getting involved in politics, in the struggle to change the sinful structures of society.

This whole trend of false spirituality says that to change the unjust structures of society you have to first change people. If individuals are just and loving, society will be just. They do not realize the great fact of reality: that a selfish, unjust, society inevitably produces and forms selfish, exploiting, violent men and women. We must change at the same time the person and the society, with its structures for exploitation of the workers. We have to have a continual, double revolution: the economic-social-political revolution and the cultural-spiritual revolution. I have recently read several serious studies showing that a great deal of money comes from the United States, from the CIA and its front foundations and agencies, to foster the charismatic Protestant and Catholic religious movements in Latin America in order to challenge and counteract the movement of liberation theology. But in 1964 I did not understand all this.

I recall a funny incident during my first months as an innocent priest in Progreso. One day when I was alone in the rectory a man came in his car looking for a priest to bless his new hotel. I went with him down by the river where there were a lot of bars and whorehouses. He had a huge picture of the Sacred Heart hanging on the wall of the big room where we entered. I blessed the new building and threw holy water around in the big entrance room and in all the small, empty guest rooms. I still had some doubts and asked him again if he was sure that this was a decent hotel and not a brothel, because it was in the heart of a kind of red light district. He assured me that this was precisely why he had built it, to have a decent hotel for the decent people who came to Progreso and did not want to sleep in a brothel.

I passed by there a week later and there was now a huge neon sign over the door that said: "Bar 51." It was the biggest brothel in Progreso that I had blessed and that the Sacred Heart of Jesus watches over from the wall of the dance hall. I became angry when I realized that the "fine gentleman," who had his sons in our Instituto San José and his daughters in the sisters' Instituto Notre Dame, had fooled me. From then on, every time I passed by there on the way to the bridge to San Pedro Sula I would hurl maledictions and curses at the "Bar 51," asking God to burn it down. But my curses did not have much power as yet; rather, within six months this brothel had so much business that he built an annex to his big "hotel." Later on I will tell about other maledictions of mine that did take effect.

I had not forgotten my two resolutions of Third Probation, to be a priest-worker on a banana farm and to become a naturalized Honduran citizen, but on being assigned as the only priest for a hundred communities, I did not even mention to the superior the idea of dedicating myself to just one banana camp. I did ask him for permission to nationalize myself; he said that he was not in agreement, but that I could write to the provincial.

Our provincial superior, Linus Thro, answered me like a politician, neither yes or no, but suggested putting it off because I had only been in Honduras for a short period and I would perhaps regret it later. Besides, he wrote, he could not give me permission if the mission superior was not in agreement. I decided to wait until we changed superiors and then ask again.

I was not the only one to have conflicts with religious authorities and/or needed adaptations in our Jesuit apostolate in Honduras. In 1964 the great missionary of Yoro, Bill Brennan, left the mission to work back in the United States. Bill is working as a Jesuit today in a Peace and Justice center in Milwaukee. After him, the great missionary to the university students and politicians of Tegucigalpa was practically thrown out of Honduras at the request of Archbishop Santos of Tegucigalpa for being "involved in politics."

In March of 1965, Ramón Alberdi, because some rich people complained to the archbishop against him, was forced to leave Honduras. He went to Germany, where he works as a secular priest in Münster with the Spanish emigrant workers.

Once again, just as during the novitiate, the best elements, the most active, the most nonconformist, were rejected by conservative religious authorities. The Honduras Mission lost the three best apostles of Christ that it had.

When Ramón left the mission, Renobales wanted to return to Guatemala to work. The superior closed the Apostolic School and named Tom Quiery pastor of Progreso. Tom and I were close friends, and so we were delighted. To think about a pastoral plan for the parish, we asked for permission to go together to visit the famous model parish of San Miguelito in Panama to study their system for forming basic Christian communities (BCCs). We wanted to go for two weeks while Renobales was still in the parish. The superior was afraid of us because we were innovators. He said no, that we should follow the tried-and-true customary missionary methods instead of always looking for innovations.

We insisted time and again that we should learn from the experiences of others in order to better our parishes. At last he told us that for a good Jesuit the mere manifestation of the opinion of the religious superior should be enough evidence of the will of God. He added that in order not to fight with us anymore, he would no longer forbid us to go, for he had made it clear that he was not in agreement. The next day Tom and I left for Panama.

I am not exaggerating when I say that I learned more real theology in the eight days with the parish team of San Miguelito than in four years in the theologate in Kansas. It was April of 1965 when Tom and I had the providential good luck of learning how the new Latin-American church is formed, "the Church born from the people" in small basic Christian communities (BCCs) that later, in 1968, the bishops promoted in their documents of Medellín.

San Miguelito was a new suburb of poor workers that Panama City was developing on its outskirts. Bishop McGrath of Panama

asked the diocese of Chicago to send a team of priests to start a
new parish in this big new suburb. In 1963 Father Leo Mahon
arrived with two other American secular priests and four Maryknoll sisters. Leo was a true genius in modern theoretical and
pastoral theology. Every morning the parish team of priests and
nuns got together to reflect about the gospel and to make a synthesis of theology that they would then teach to the people. They
visited all the families in their homes and helped the people of
the new suburb make their own school, get water and light, and
so on.

Then each priest, with a sister, took a small zone in the parish
to start inviting the youth and the adults, especially couples
(whether they were married by the Church or not), to get together with them one night a week in one of their homes for a
Bible reflection. Each study group had about ten couples and a
few single persons. They had adapted for Panama the basic gospel initiation course they had used in Chicago with Spanish-
speaking people there, called the Family of God course. There
are fourteen themes for dialogue with people in small groups.
This course is the most simple and beautiful synthesis of the gospel of Christ and of the plan of God for this world that I have
ever seen.

The people discuss Bible texts to see how God wants this world
to be a paradise, a society of brothers and sisters all united as one
big family, the family of God, with everyone sharing their possessions with each other. Sin, or more clearly expressed, "injustice"
and "selfishness," is what goes against this plan of God; living in
the grace of God is living according to this plan. Christ came to
teach us to live like that, and left a model community of the New
Society that we want to form, the primitive Catholic church, the
first BCC, which indeed lived like the family of God. We are
supposed to imitate Christ's model community by forming a BCC
in every zone or neighborhood. This BCC will be "a light" for the
rest of the people, a "ferment" or "leaven" in the mass of people
to stimulate them to form the New Panama (and the New Honduras).

After fourteen weeks of meeting like this, the group has a
sense of unity and friendship among themselves. To solidify this
even more and for the personal conversion of each one of its

members, the whole group lives together, as in a retreat, during two and a half days on a weekend for an adapted *Cursillo de Cristiandad*. This retreat uses the techniques of the Cursillo that promote repentance and conversion and union and joy among themselves, but it changes completely the theological content and the passive method of the traditional Cursillos and uses instead the message and active methods of the Family of God course, repeated now at a more profound level.

After this Cursillo almost everyone goes to confession and starts receiving communion every Sunday, and those who lived together unmarried get married. The group continues to meet in one of their homes each week for a prepared Bible reflection and to plan actions for helping their neighborhood, but now they coordinate the dialogue themselves in rotation. On Sundays all the different groups in the parish, which are now basic Christian communities (BCCs) in formation, come together in the big parish church for mass. They sing the *"Misa Panamena,"* which one of the musicians of the parish in Panama wrote and which all Panama afterward was singing.

When they had a number of these BCCs functioning, the parish team started to give special courses for the formation of the coordinators named by each BCC. When we were there, they already had two hundred of these "brothers and sisters" (coordinators) meeting each week with a priest to plan the weekly dialogues and practical activities of their BCCs. A few years later the bishop ordained twenty of these "brothers" as married deacons. The "brothers and sisters" gave the Family of God course to start new BCCs.

Tom and I had the opportunity to participate in the daily reflections of the parish team, in several meetings of the Family of God course with new groups, in zonal meetings of the BCCs, in the "brothers and sisters" meetings, and even in one of their Cursillos de Cristiandad. We returned to Honduras with written material about all of this, convinced that San Miguelito had the correct theology and pastoral plan.

We decided to follow this same pastoral plan, adapting it to our parish. Since the Crusade sisters in Progreso were all occupied in their sewing school, on the way back from Panama we stopped in Tegucigalpa to talk to our friends the School Sisters of Saint Francis, Americans and Hondurans, who no longer used habits or veils, to see if we could get at least two of them to work as a team with us in the pastoral plan of forming BCCs. We approached them at an opportune moment, because several of them were dissatisfied with work in Catholic schools and were looking for something more pastoral. Within a few months four of them came to the parish.

Meanwhile, I took advantage of the time that Renobales was still in the parish to visit my family in the United States. We were supposed to make these visits every three years for six weeks of vacation. I got free passage going and coming on the banana ships of the "Great White Fleet" of the United Fruit Company. The two-and-a-half-day voyage from Puerto Cortés to New Orleans was again very restful and a great opportunity to feel the grandeur of God in contemplating the immensity of the sea and of the heavens.

I spent my time in the States visiting a few days with my mother and sisters, Eileen and Maureen, in Saint Louis, and then going to visit my other sisters in their homes in Michigan, Ohio, and Massachusetts. At that time my brother, Pat, was living in Massachusetts with my sister and her family while he studied at Boston University after leaving the Jesuits. I returned to Saint Louis to make my annual eight days of the Spiritual Exercises before going to New Orleans and returning to Honduras.

My sisters always insisted on paying my trips to their homes so I could spend a few days with their families every three years. I always finished my visits to the States by giving thanks to God that I did not have to live there in that "rat race," that life in the "consumer society." I always returned to Honduras with renewed enthusiasm for sharing the life of the poor campesinos.

When the four Franciscan sisters arrived, Renobales was already gone; Tom was left alone to care for the city, and I, the one hundred rural communities. We lived in the rectory, and the sisters lived in the house that belonged to the parish clinic, bought for a doctor who had been there at one time. Every morning our team met for prayer, reflection, and planning, and we all ate together at noon in the rectory. In the afternoon I always went out to the villages. The other Jesuits, the Crusade sisters, the Notre Dame sisters in their high school, and especially the superior, criticized us a great deal for working so closely with the Franciscans. But we formed a magnificent team together, the best I have seen anywhere.

Since we had so many villages, banana camps, and neighborhood zones of the city, we decided to start the BCCs first in just four villages and two neighborhood zones and continue promoting the Delegates of the Word, the catechists for the children, the Legion of Mary, and the Apostleship of Prayer in all the villages. In not even one of the banana camps could I get any of this organized; whereas by the end of 1965, we had Delegates, catechists, and Legionaries in thirty villages. Right from the start we had decided to accept only men as Delegates of the Word, and to incorporate the women in the apostolate as catechists for the children.

Tom and I always talked about having married priests and women priests in the Church some day, but because of the situation in our Honduran Church it would not be good to have women leading the Celebration of the Word. Our reason was that the Church in Honduras is a women's church. Very few men go to mass or even show up for the baptism of their children, and when they do go, they stay out by the door. Women lead the traditional popular religious ceremonies like the novenas, the burial services, and the processions, while the men (if they go at all) stay outside without participating.

This tactic of ours of insisting from the beginning on finding men to celebrate the Word of God has changed the Catholic church in Honduras. The other parishes, in general, have followed this same policy, and right now in Honduras there are around eight thousand men Delegates of the Word who feel responsible as leaders of the Church in their communities and who attract other men to participate in the Church. Other movements also tried to incorporate the men into the Church, like the Caballeros de Cristo Rey, the Celadores of the Apostleship of Prayer, and the Cursillos de Cristiandad. If we had allowed women to be Delegates of the Word, in many communities there would never have been any men participating in a Celebration of the Word.

Tom and I used the same tactic for the Legion of Mary. It, too, had always been a women's organization. Bill Brennan in Yoro encouraged the men to join, but the women always dominated it.

In my villages in Progreso I insisted that the president and at least two of the five-person board of directors of a praesidium and of the curia of the Legion had to be men. When I explained to the women the reason for these rules, they were very much in agreement; we had to get the men involved in the Church. In our Progreso villages we also changed the apostolic line of the Legion by giving them as their principal apostolic work a visit to all the homes to get the people to attend the Celebration of the Word. Wherever we had the Legion, it was much easier to organize the Celebration of the Word and maintain a good attendance, always putting the emphasis on getting the men and the youth to participate.

Let me go back and explain how God's providence gave me, as a gift from heaven, a campesino apostle of Christ who would help me in all of this. He was José Ayala. It was in December of 1964, when I was making my first visit to Toyos, one of the bigger villages of the parish. When I went to announce the coming mass, the old woman majordomo of the church there told me that there were hardly any Catholics left in Toyos. Everyone had gone over to the Protestant Pentecostal sect that rented a house near our church for their daily services.

We had the mass, and a small group of people assisted with great devotion. It was more than a year since a priest had visited Toyos. After mass a campesino, José Ayala, introduced himself to ask me if he could start teaching catechism to the children. He had been a catechist in Guatemala, although he had been born in El Salvador. He told me he had been living in Toyos now for six months and it was a shame to see the Catholics go to the Protestant services just because there were no Catholic services for them. He hoped I would return very soon and promised to go from house to house to invite the people for the next mass. I told him that I would not be back very soon for mass, but that if he could get ten more men, he should send me word and I would return to organize the Legion of Mary in Toyos.

In a few days I received a letter from José telling me that he already had a good group of men ready. When I went to Toyos, there were twenty men with José waiting for me at the church. We organized the Legion just with men, with José as president and with the task of getting more men.

When I returned the following month, they had forty men. They eventually had a praesidium of sixty men in Toyos, and José organized another one just for women with about sixty women. He went around to the other nearby villages organizing the Legion of Mary, and afterward, when we started the Sunday Celebrations, he helped me organize them in many villages.

Later on I organized my first agricultural cooperative with these sixty Legionaries from Toyos as its base. It was wonderful for me to have these campesinos as my personal friends. Quiery, O'Brien, and I gave them courses on the Bible, but they were the ones who actually taught us. These Christian campesinos opened the gospel for me. I did not really know the true Jesus Christ, the campesino of Nazareth, until these apostolic leaders commented on the verses of the gospel in our common meditations. I did not understand anything about the humble life of Mary, the campesino girl from Nazareth, until I contemplated the Honduran campesino women splitting wood and bringing it home on their heads to light the fire and cook. I fell in love with the Honduran campesino, and this love increases in me with each year of my life. I want to live and die with them and for them.

Toyos was the first place I started (in November of 1965) the Family of God course for forming the BCCs. Our parish team had rewritten and adapted it for the Honduran campesinos. (Later on, in 1968, we again rewrote the fourteen dialogue themes to include in them the ideas of liberation theology and of the Christology of Jon Sobrino, S.J.) There were so many who wanted to take the course that Mary Colgan, the Franciscan sister who worked with me, and I chose fifteen of the most faithful Legionary married couples to start with and formed other groups later.

With the help of the 120 Legionaries of Toyos, we organized the Apostleship of Prayer with all the people who were to receive Holy Communion at the mass I promised for the last Friday night of each month. The Legionaries got practically the whole village to attend this mass each month. The crowd did not fit in the old church (a big wooden barracks building up on cement pillars that Father Murphy had obtained from the Tela Railroad Company and had reconstructed in Toyos); therefore, we always had the mass under the building, allowing the crowd to spread all over the yard. I would play the guitar during the mass using a portable loudspeaker system. I taught the people to sing the *"Misa Popular,"* which Tom Quiery had written and which became popular in many parts of Honduras. Up to five hundred adults, youth, and older children belonged to the Apostleship of Prayer in Toyos and received communion each month at this mass.

The Family of God course was very successful, and when we ended it with a common meal under the church for the whole family of participants, everyone in Toyos wanted to take the course. Sister Mary Colgan formed a new group of married couples, and I did too. The first group continued to meet as a BCC once a week for the Bible reflections we gave them. José Ayala and Santos Alvarenga were coordinators who helped these incipient BCCs in Toyos and in four other villages where Mary and I had also given the Family of God course.

I have described more or less the kind of spiritual or ecclesial work that I did from 1964 to 1970 in the one hundred rural communities of the Progreso parish, but I did not limit myself to spiritual work. Sharing the campesino's life and struggle for material betterment is what caused the leap forward in my metamorphosis into a revolutionary during these years, as I will explain later. However, it seems best to relate my story year by year, so I will continue with my activities in the year 1965.

That was the year our superior was negotiating with the Tela Railroad Company. They had offered to sell us the main part of the Company Zone in Progreso, because they wanted to concentrate their offices in La Lima and in Tela. They would sell for only eleven thousand dollars (practically a gift) all the part where they had offices, big houses for their top officials, a club with dance hall, a swimming pool, and a part of the golf course—thirteen buildings in all. The other part of the golf course they sold to a rich former official of theirs who divided it into lots for homes to sell to the rich people of Progreso. The poor, the workers, could not even enter this Company Zone.

When I heard that the Jesuits were going to buy it to live there, I could hardly believe it. I went to ask the superior, and he said that everything was already arranged for the purchase. I told him that it would be better that he break the vow of chastity that we take and live with a woman—all the Hondurans would understand that and forgive him—rather than break the vow of poverty in such a way. If we made this purchase we Jesuits, who are the only ones in Progreso who proclaim we voluntarily want to be poor, would wind up being the owners of the best property in Progreso, and the "Zone of the Company United Fruit" would become the "Zone of the Company of Jesus." No Honduran will understand this and the masses of the poor will never forgive.

Well, the Jesuits bought the Company Zone, and we are still living there today. I privately swore that I would never live there. (I will come back to this later.)

Shortly after this incident, I had a similar clash with the School Sisters of Notre Dame (Americans and some Hondurans), who had the other high school in Progreso just for girls (the Jesuits' Instituto San José was just for boys). I heard that one of our Brothers was going to build them a private swimming pool, not for the students, but for the nuns, in the large yard behind their convent. The cost would be twenty-four thousand dollars (if I remember correctly).

Again, I was scandalized and unbelieving, and so I went to ask Sister Superior if it was true. She admitted it but added that I had no right to stick my nose in her affairs. I told her that, like Christ, I had to denounce sin and try to save people from their sins. I said that building a swimming pool for the sisters' recreation here in Honduras where most of the people did not even have enough to eat would be a mortal sin. I told her to look through the window at the poor shacks in which their neighbors lived (in 1965) and asked her if she was not ashamed to live here in this residence that was their convent and high school.

In response, she told me that houses of the Notre Dame sisters in hot climates in the United States had swimming pools for the sisters, and she already had permission to put one here. Besides, she said, many of the Jesuits were in agreement and could come here and use the pool. She was very angry with me, and I learned afterward that she informed our superior that I had told her that she was in mortal sin.

A few months later I received a letter from the provincial superior telling me they were holding off my final vows until I was more docile with my superiors and learned the spirit of the Society of Jesus with regard to the vow of poverty. I received the notice very tranquilly. It did not surprise me at all. It was the same as in the novitiate with my first vows and in the philosophate with my minor orders. Besides, I already had made perpetual vows, ever since the novitiate. These last vows were for binding us more closely to the Society of Jesus, but they did not bind me more closely to Jesus.

In addition, I have never agreed with the distinction of grades or classes of priests in the Society: the "professed fathers" of four vows (with an extra vow of special obedience to the pope), who can be superiors, and the "spiritual coadjutors" of three vows, who are like second-class Jesuits because they are not so intellectual. For me this was like the anti-Christian distinction that I experienced in the U.S. Army between the officers and the troops. I have always preferred to be of the troops; I also knew that most of the canonized Jesuit saints, the martyrs, were "spiritual coadjutors." I like to think that Christ, if he had been a Jesuit, would have been a simple "spiritual coadjutor" priest: one who serves, not one who commands.

These incidents had a comical epilogue. When the Brother was just finishing the Notre Dame swimming pool and before they filled it with water, I went up to the big cement block wall around the pool and cursed the pool, asking God to destroy it, not to let it ever be used. Well, you can ask Brother Jim whether it is true or not. When they filled the pool with water for the first time, the bottom of it split, the water ran out, and the black sewage waters of Progreso seeped up into the pool. How I rejoiced, and how I praised our God who can play such a joke! It makes no difference that afterward, with another sinful waste of a large sum of money, they fixed the pool, and the sisters and some of the Jesuits used it. Everyone knew that the pool was cursed and that God did not want it. Today this swimming pool is never used, and many of the sisters wish it had never been built.

When I saw the result of my curse on the sisters' pool, I did the same with the swimming pool of the Jesuits in the Company Zone, which was already being used by the Jesuits and the youth of Progreso. The big dance hall that the Jesuits bought was also used for dances every Saturday and Sunday night. This was not so bad; what was bad was that the Jesuits were (and still are) the owners. Today this pool is also in disuse, and at last some of the Jesuits even talk about selling all that we have in the Company Zone.

11. The Campesino Movement for Agrarian Reform

The other big event that the Holy Spirit provided for me in 1965, and the most important one for my metamorphosis as a revolutionary, was my meeting up with the ANACH, the National Association of Honduran Campesinos. Right from my first visits to the villages, when I returned from Third Probation at the end of 1964, I started to ask the campesinos where they worked, how they made their living, how much they earned, how many years of school they had, who the owners were of all this good farmland that surrounded their villages, where they were born, how long they had lived in the village, if they had land to farm, what they planted, why they were so poor, how much they had earned this year, and so on. I would visit their homes, at least some of them, to speak to them in this way before and after mass in each village I visited.

The Sula Valley, where the parish of Progreso extends all along the righthand bank of the biggest river in Honduras, the Ulúa, has the richest farmland in the country. Nevertheless, in its villages most of the people live in frightening, inhuman poverty. "Why?" I kept asking myself, and kept asking the people in each village. I was collecting a lot of facts, the answers to the questions I asked in each village—not to write them down, but for my own information, and as a way of making conversation with the campesinos. They were pleased to have someone show an interest in their way of living.

This is a summary of what I learned, written as approximations, not as scientific or exact data, about the inhabitants of the seventy villages of our parish in the valley in 1965. I am not including the twenty banana camps where the families of thousands of the permanent workers of the Tela Railroad Company lived or the eight villages in the mountains above Progreso where the people lived a little better because each family had a small plot of their own land. But this description is more or less valid for the rural population and the poor *barrios* (neighborhoods) of the cities throughout Honduras, which account for about 85 percent of the population of the country. The situation of most of these people has not bettered since 1965. In the opinion of many people, it has indeed worsened.

First of all, most of the houses were what are called *champas* (shacks) with dirt floor, roof of palm leaves, and walls either of sticks tied together by vines, or of mud plastered on a network of sticks tied together. These champas consist of only one room about six yards long and five yards wide. Generally there is a small kitchen shack apart, or if not, the mud stove for firewood has to go in one of the corners of the house. Fitted into the house might be two or three beds of heavy cord strung on a wooden frame and covered by a reed mat, or a canvas folding cot on which the whole family, maybe eight kids plus parents, have to sleep. An older boy might sleep in a hammock.

Their food consists of rice, red beans, corn tortillas, and coffee —three times a day. They eat a little meat, maybe in soup, about once a week, or a little bit of white cheese. The milk for the babies is from their mothers' breasts. Often this is the only food a baby gets until it is two years old. That is why so many of the children start out their lives physically debilitated, which scientists say even affects the development of their brains. I do not know what the infant mortality rate was, but many families told me that they had, for example, fourteen children and that only seven were still alive.

The health of the people in the Progreso villages is just about the worst I have seen in the whole country, with the exception of the Jicaque Indians in the mountains of Yoro, who are in even poorer health. The reason, besides the lack of good food from childhood, is the lack of hygiene in the house and kitchen and the contaminated water that everyone drinks from the rivers or creeks close to the villages. In these rivers, the people all take their baths, the clothes are washed, and all the cows, pigs, and dogs wander. A big village like Toyos, which has more than a thousand inhabitants, still, in 1981, does not have a piped-in water system; everyone hauls water from the river, and almost no mother boils it, in spite of all the campaigns to teach them to do this to kill the germs.

The small children go around naked because of the tremendous heat around Progreso, crawling around and playing on the dirt floor of the house, the kitchen, and the yard, and sticking into their mouths any object that interests them. Some small children eat dirt, which naturally makes them sick. The doctors say that they eat it, not only because they are hungry, but also because the dirt contains some iron, which is what is most lacking in their diets. They are all anemic. Almost all the campesinos lack iron in their blood.

It is remarkable how a man, undernourished, anemic, and maybe with tuberculosis (which is quite common) can work all day long under the tropic sun, swinging a big machete (knife), cutting the weeds in the pastures of the rich cattlemen. I, who am strong, have tried it, and I cannot take eight hours like that. The campesinos and Indians of Latin America are not lazy, but they are sickly. Father Murphy started a parish medical clinic in Progreso, which the Notre Dame nurse, Sister Charles, now runs. But it must be very frustrating to cure a child of worms in its stomach and to see it two months later in the clinic full of worms again; or to give a pile of vitamin and iron pills to a child for profound anemia, knowing that it is food, good nourishing milk, meat, and vegetables that this little brother or sister of ours needs.

The diet that I have described is that of a campesino family that has a father who has a job. Maybe 10 percent of the families are without a man; he may have abandoned his woman and children and joined up with another woman. These abandoned women, and also the widows, wash clothes or sell tortillas, or oranges, or the lottery—or who knows what—to halfway feed their children. Another 30 or 40 percent of the families cannot afford even the ordinary diet because the man does not have a steady job, can only find work a few days a month. These are the campesinos who could not rent a piece of land, even only an acre, to plant their *milpa* (cornfield) or their beans. Another 30 or 40 percent of the campesinos of the parish do not own land, either; however, they do manage to rent some, maybe three or four acres, for one crop of corn planted by the same system used by the Maya Indians, namely, first burning the brush and weeds, and then throwing four or five seeds in a little hole made with a pointed stick.

Only about 10 percent of our campesinos have their own piece of land and, thus, some security. They can at least plant, even though floods or insects or plant diseases leave them little certainty of having a good harvest. Another 10 percent or so have more or less steady jobs as cowboys, grass cutters (with a machete), and milkers for the rich cattlemen who have almost all the good valley land that does not belong to the Tela Railroad Company (and also much of the land of the Tela which they can permanently rent).

Why are the campesinos so poor who live in this rich valley? They are farmers who have neither land they can plant nor a steady job to earn a salary. If they do get a few days' work chopping the meadows or helping cultivate someone else's crops, they make very little. In 1965 they earned seventy-five cents for an eight-hour day's hard work. Since 1981 they earn the new minimum wage of two dollars (U.S.) a day, but because of inflation, with that two dollars they can buy just about what they bought with the seventy-five cents in 1965, that is, practically nothing.

The prices in Honduras (of food, clothing, medicine, etc.) are about the same as in the United States. Then how do those live who do not find a job, who earn nothing? The official statistics for 1980 put the average annual income of all the Hondurans (including the millionaires) at $450, but half the families (like our campesinos) earn only $90 a year. How do they subsist? Only God knows.

Those who have not lived with the campesinos in their villages, or with the campesinos who live in a poor, jobless barrio in the cities do not believe these figures that I am giving. Well, here is another unbelievable fact: 6 percent of the human race, those that live in the United States of America, consume half of all the world's riches. Many Americans cannot believe this statistic; it is against their interest to believe that 80 percent of humanity is undernourished. It also took me a long time to comprehend that the *rich, developed countries live well precisely because they exploit, or more correctly, rob the riches of the 80 percent of the world that remains poor and underdeveloped.*

Let us take Honduras as an example. (However the case is

more or less the same for all the countries of the third world.) Bananas are among the principal riches that Honduras produces. The owners of practically all the banana plantations and the owners and controllers of all marketing for bananas are the two U.S. transnational companies, the Tela (United Brands Company) and the Standard (Castle and Cooke). The University of Honduras published a study to show that of every dollar of Chiquita (of the Tela) or Cabana (of the Standard) bananas that are sold in the supermarkets of the United States, only seventeen cents was spent in Honduras for everything: for production (including irrigation), for labor, for transportation inside Honduras, for taxes to the government of Honduras, and so on. The other eighty-three cents goes to the United States for transportation and other marketing expenses there, and for profit to the shareholders.

The study also showed something of the shameless robbery of hundreds of millions of dollars that these two companies have been perpetrating over the years by evading a big part of the moderate taxes that Honduras has established. In a later section of the book I will talk of the political control that these two United States companies, backed up always by the U.S. State Department and embassy in Tegucigalpa, have over Honduras. They have installed and they have taken out most of the "democratic" governments of Honduras.

Coffee production in the decade of the seventies rose to equal the value of that of bananas in Honduras. Most of the coffee plantations do belong to Hondurans, but since almost all the coffee goes to the United States, the greatest part of the profits from Honduran coffee goes there, too. The profit is not so much in the production but in the marketing of the product. It would be interesting to know how much the U.S. importers of coffee pay the Honduran exporters, and then, how much the consumer pays for this coffee in U.S. supermarkets.

Cattle (beef) is the next important rich product of Honduras, but five of the seven butchering and packing houses for exportation of this meat belong to U.S. companies, and again, almost all export is to the United States. Until the late seventies the Tela was the owner of the biggest herds of cattle in Honduras on the best farmland of the Sula Valley.

Wood used to be the second largest business of the country

after bananas. Practically all the sawmills were U.S.- or European-owned. Since two thirds of the whole territory of Honduras is forest of good pine and hardwood, this is the country's greatest natural resource. The government finally nationalized the forests in 1973 under the state-owned COHDEFOR (Honduran Corporation for Forest Development), but the wood still goes principally to U.S. middlemen for marketing there.

Gold and silver were once the most valuable natural resources in Honduras, but the Spanish imperialists stole most of this, leaving only a few mines still functioning in El Mochito, Santa Bárbara. These mines belong entirely to the Rosario Mining and Resources Company of the United States, which, of course, sends all the gold and silver to the United States, and pays very little in taxes to Honduras.

Sugar cane and cotton are two other important Honduran products that wind up in the United States, even though rich Honduran landowners own these plantations. The main product of agrarian reform in Honduras is African palm, planted in tens of thousands of acres by new campesino cooperatives. The campesinos produce the nut whose oil is needed by the processing plants of the Tela ("Clover Brand") and of the Standard ("La Blanquita") to produce vegetable cooking oil and margarine.

I worked a lot with these cooperatives, and later I will explain how the United States banks and these two U.S. transnational companies are the principal beneficiaries of the Honduran "agrarian reform." It is worth adding here that these two U.S. banana companies are also the major shareholders in almost all the main industries that exist in Honduras, like breweries, cigarette factories, polymer plastics plants, the cardboard box factory, meat packing and exporting houses, and so on. Who are the real owners of Honduras?

Even of the products produced by Hondurans, like coffee, cattle, wood, sugar, cotton, and African palm oil, the final owners and the ones who set the prices, who control the international markets, are always North Americans. As I have repeatedly said, the big profits are not in the production but in the marketing of these products. A small decrease in the price of coffee in the States, for instance, can mean a 30 percent lowering of the dollar reserves of Honduras. We are a country completely dependent on the United States. We are a colony of the United States—economically and politically. I have pointed out here only a few aspects of this sad reality; the financial dependence of Honduras on U.S. banks is still more profound.

The biggest business in the world is international banking. Lending money for interest is easy profit. The Latin-American bishops have said that for each dollar that the United States gives or lends to Latin America, at least two dollars return to the United States in interest and in the purchase of U.S. goods. All international bank loans are conditional: you have to spend a big part of this money in the United States, for technicians, machinery, and so on.

The external debt of the Honduran government in 1980 (according to IDB) was $918 million, owed to U.S. private banks and to international banks like IDB (Inter-American Development Bank) that are made up fundamentally of U.S. capital. Supposing that the rate of interest was 12 percent annually, Honduras would have to pay to these banks 12 percent of $918 million, which is $110 million each year, just in interest. In 1982 foreign debt was $400 per capita. Where do the riches of Honduras go? Why is the United States rich, and why does Honduras remain poor? Is Honduras a free, independent, sovereign state? Honduras is a perfect example of what the bishops in Medellín called "neocolonialism," and condemned as "a situation of sin."

The bishops used another example of the terrible exploitation under this neocolonialism. They explained that the primary materials, like wood and minerals, and the agricultural products, like bananas, coffee, sugar, and meat, that the poor countries export are continually decreasing in value compared with manufactured items that they have to buy from the industrialized countries. In this way, conclude the bishops, the rich, industrialized countries are always becoming richer, and the poor countries are always becoming poorer. As an example, in Honduras in 1970 you could buy a Ford truck imported from the United States with so many sacks of Honduran coffee; now, in 1981, this same truck will cost you four times as many sacks of Honduran coffee.

When someone becomes a revolutionary, it is because he or she understands that the basis for getting a poor country out of its underdevelopment is for it to liberate itself from the exploitation of the rich countries. The necessary prerequisite for the development of Latin America is for it to free itself from foreign imperialism. These countries are rich. Honduras has great riches, but most of these riches leave Honduras to make the United States richer. It is easy to understand why we Honduran revolutionaries are very anti-imperialist. We are not against the people of the United States, but against the imperialism of the United States. The liberation of the oppressed Hondurans, which Christ came to announce and to put into practice, starts with liberation from the effects of this great sin of neocolonialism. *Christians of the United States have the serious obligation to help get rid of this greatest of all U.S. sins.*

Imperialism means to have an empire, to have other countries under your control, as colonies, for the benefit and enrichment of your own country. England was imperialistic in the last century, Spain, in the sixteenth century. The Roman imperialists ruled supreme in the time of Christ, with Palestine and practically all the countries of the civilized world under their yoke. The Jews of Palestine had to pay huge taxes to the emperor Augustus Caesar in Rome, and a big part of the riches of Christ's country of Palestine went to Rome. Rome had its soldiers and its governor, Pontius Pilate, ruling the nation of Palestine.

Many Jews wanted to liberate themselves from this imperialism that despoiled them of their riches. There was a guerrilla movement of liberation, called the Zealots or the Canaanites (one of Christ's twelve apostles was Simon the Zealot, a member of the guerrillas). One of the principal bases of the Zealot guerrillas was in the mountains of Galilee, only five miles from Nazareth; that is why Jesus knew many of these people.

As a trap, the Jewish Pharisees asked Jesus if they should pay taxes to Caesar or not. When Jesus was captured and finally brought before Pilate, the Roman ruler of all Palestine, the Jewish authorities accused him, saying that he was "stirring up the people, saying that we should not pay the taxes to the Roman emperor, and he also alleges that he is the Christ, that is, a king" (Luke 23:2). They involved Jesus in the anti-imperialist politics of his day in order to assure his death. Nowadays in Central America they would accuse Jesus of being a communist in order to assure his death at the hands of the government security forces (the secret police), the death squads, or counter insurgency military forces. But the financing, training, and "advisers" for the killing of Christ would, sad to say, most likely come from the United States for the sake of preserving its Central American colonies.

I have already explained that at the beginning of this century about half of the great Sula Valley, the best farmland in Honduras, was given away to the United Fruit Company by several unpatriotic, bought-off presidents of Honduras. One condition was that the banana company build a railroad line from the north coast of Honduras to the south coast, passing through the capital, Tegucigalpa. To the present day, the railroad line has been extended only from the banana farms to the ports on the north coast for exporting their fruit.

I have already spoken, also, about the big strike of the workers of the Tela Railroad Company (United Fruit Company) in 1954. After the strike the Tela reduced the number of workers from about twenty-five thousand to twenty thousand by mechanizing many of the jobs. Some years later the "Panama" disease attacked many of the banana farms of the Tela, and they were abandoned, leaving another ten thousand workers without jobs. A large number of these fifteen thousand former workers of the Tela lived in the villages I visited. Each year the Tela would rent them some of the land of the abandoned farms so that each one could plant a small milpa (cornfield). That is the way it was in all the sectors of our parish, from Toyos to Urraco Pueblo, the sector called Guaymas, and from Progreso south to Santa Rita, the sector called Guanchías. Besides these former workers, thousands of poor Honduran campesinos from all over the country had settled in these abandoned lands in the rich Sula Valley, looking for a place to work. Many of my villages had been founded only about thirty years ago.

The great strike of 1954 was promoted to a large extent by a small group of workers of the Tela who belonged to the forbidden and clandestine Communist Party of Honduras, founded or reorganized by Juan Pablo Wainwright and others in the 1920s. During the strike these Marxist leaders were persecuted by the army after being denounced by a group of "democratic" worker leaders, whom the U.S. embassy, with the AFL-CIO and the ORIT, (Inter-American Regional Organization of Workers) were preparing to be the leaders of the new labor union (the *Sindecato de Trabajadores de la Tela RR. Co.*—SITRATERCO), with whom this U.S. banana company finally signed the first collective contract.

Many of these Marxist workers were fired after the strike and lived as campesinos in the villages of Progreso. They started, in 1959, the first campesino organization, the Central Committee of Campesino Unity, which later became the National Federation of Campesinos of Honduras (FENACH). Its principal groups were in the villages of Progreso and Tela. The organization grew, managed to get some land for several villages by invading idle fields, and managed to defend some of their other groups, which the Tela and some cattlemen were trying to evict from the land with military force. The destruction of the FENACH was one of the objectives of the U.S. embassy and the Honduran military men who made the deal with the conservative National Party for the bloody coup of October 3, 1963. All the leaders of all the organized groups of the FENACH were hunted; many were captured and put in jail. Several were killed.

Some of these leaders of the FENACH and others from the industrial labor unions, who belonged to the secret Communist Party and who had escaped the massacre of 1963, hid out in the cities and in the mountains. Little by little they formed the first guerrilla organization of Honduras. In 1965 they were ready to start their first operations and had an armed band in the mountains of Jute in our parish, about twelve miles north of Progreso. A campesino traitor informed the army in Progreso, and Lt. Carlos Aguilar, with some thirty soldiers, surprised a group of them in the early morning while they were sitting around a table in a house on a coffee plantation near the village of Jute. The soldiers opened fire and killed all seven of them in cold blood, including the former president of the FENACH, Lorenzo Zelaya. These are the famous "martyrs of Jute," who are remembered in campesino meetings and in Honduran protest songs.

The U.S. embassy started destroying the FENACH in 1961.

Their American Institute for Free Labor Development (AIFLD), with the help of the presidents of SITRATERCO and of the FESITRANH (Federation of Labor Unions of Northern Honduras), Oscar Gale and Celeo Gonzales, organized courses in the towns of La Lima and Tela, with all expenses paid. Their purpose was to form a new "free and democratic" campesino organization, the ANACH (National Association of Honduran Campesinos), and they brought to these courses campesinos from the same villages where the FENACH existed. By 1963 the FENACH was completely destroyed.

The U.S. embassy, the transnational banana companies, and the big landowners preferred to have the campesinos organized, like the workers, in unions under AIFLD and the ORIT (Inter-American Regional Organization of Workers, dominated by the AFL–CIO of the U.S.) with capitalist, reformist labor union ideology, instead of the Marxist, revolutionary ideology of the FENACH. So the president, Ramón Villeda Morales, and his Liberal Party, which controlled the National Congress, greatly promoted the organization of the ANACH when in 1962 they issued the first Agrarian Reform Law.

With great demagoguery, they brought together (with the help of trucks and trains from the Tela) all the campesinos already organized in the ANACH for a big mass rally of Liberals in front of the SITRATERCO offices in La Lima. President Villeda Morales handed over the new Agrarian Reform Law to the executive committee of the ANACH, telling them that it was for them and that they should demand its fulfillment. He also presented them a month later with their legal recognition documents as an agrarian labor union.

In reality, the Liberal congressmen, who were practically all big landowners, agreed to the passing of this law (they never agreed to carry it out in practice) in order to be able to get the significant financial help of the Agency for International Development (AID) of the U.S. government. President John F. Kennedy, with his Alliance for Progress, demanded—in the agreements of Punta del Este, Uruguay, in 1961—that if they wanted help, all the countries of Latin America had to make social reforms, including agrarian reform, for the purpose of stopping the advance of the "communist" revolution in Latin America.

For this same reason, the new military government of Colonel López Arellano, in union with the National Party after the coup in 1963, tried to be populist and reformist. This was the agreement they had with the U.S. embassy. That is why they, too, permitted the development of the ANACH and of "free and democratic" labor unions under AIFLD and the ORIT and destroyed any revolutionary labor union.

There was a feeble effort at agrarian reform, but in the first place, this capitalist law of private property was no good for Honduras. It said that all national and *ejidal* (township) lands (without touching any belonging to big landowners or the U.S. banana companies) would be given out in 25-acre plots to native-born campesinos who had no land.

Former governments had given out some family plots also, but sooner or later these always wound up in the hands of the rich cattlemen. The campesinos would have no other recourse but to sell them to cover some family emergency. That is what happened a number of years ago in our parish near Toyos in the Guaymas sector, and also in the Monjaras sector of Choluteca in southern Honduras. This Law of 1962 was truly useless, however, because it was never carried out. With great demagoguery the National Agrarian Institute (INA) handed over just a few parcels of farmland to groups of the ANACH when the groups made too much trouble and invaded idle fields.

Honduras is the country in Central America that has most faithfully followed the U.S. policy of making small social reforms in order to calm the revolutionary fervor of the exploited masses. That is why up to now Honduras has had practically no guerrilla movement like the ones in Nicaragua, El Salvador, and Guatemala. The theory is that if a child is crying and bothering you a lot, you have to give it a piece of candy to quiet it down. López Arellano was an expert at this, giving something to the campesinos, to the workers, to the big cattlemen and rich industrialists, to the journalists, and to the gringos; he knew how to win everyone over to his side. Meanwhile, he became a millionaire.

It is interesting to analyze how the labor movement in Honduras, which has the reputation of being the strongest and best organized in Central America, was promoted by the very U.S. imperialism that exploits the workers. The principal Honduran labor leaders have been bought off by being taken to the United States or to Puerto Rico for courses, and in this way the "free and democratic" labor movement has been controlled. Thus, instead of changing the capitalist system, the labor movement serves to fortify the system, under the slogan of "peace between the owners and the workers" by means of contracts formed through collective bargaining. By increased production, they say, both owners and workers will profit.

The giant labor organization of the United States, the AFL–CIO, through its international institute AIFLD, is controlled by agents and funds from the CIA and by the labor attaché of the U.S. embassy in each country (usually a CIA agent). It has the role in U.S. State Department policy of promoting in all the countries of the "free world" (nonsocialist world) the formation of this kind of "free and democratic" labor movement among the workers and the campesinos. Honduras is one country where their plans have borne perfect fruit over many years. Only in recent years have the revolutionaries of Honduras (including me) been unmasking this deception of the working class by the so-called free labor movement, which pacifies the working class by giving them a bit of candy while they are being exploited.

So AIFLD and the U.S. labor attaché, with the approval and help of the U.S. transnational companies and the Honduran armed forces, had eliminated the revolutionary labor leaders and maintained control of the leaders of SITRATERCO and of the ANACH. In the same way, they managed to form and control the labor unions of the Standard Fruit Company and the Rosario Mining Company and the construction workers, the railroad workers, the bank employees, the cigarette, beer, margarine, clothing, and other factory workers, and the federations of these "free and democratic" unions, the FESITRANH in the north and the FECESITLIH (Federation of Free Labor Unions of Central Honduras) in Tegucigalpa.

These two federations, along with the ANACH, form the CTH (the Confederation of Workers of Honduras) under the perpetual presidency of the U.S.-controlled leader, Andrés Víctor Artiles. The CTH is affiliated with the ORIT and the CIOSL (International Confederaton of Free Labor Organizations), which are the biggest workers' organizations in the world and are completely dominated by the AFL–CIO. There are two other big international labor organizations, one of the Christian Democrats and the other of all the communist labor unions of the world.

The ANACH, of course, ever since its foundation had joined the FESITRANH, the CTH, the ORIT, and the CIOSL. The first National Convention of the ANACH was rapidly organized for September 29, 1962, by the AIFLD and the FESITRANH in order to have it legally constituted with bylaws before the big "show" of Villeda Morales giving them the Agrarian Reform Law in La Lima. The first president of the ANACH was a campesino from the department of Olancho, whose name I have forgotten.

You have to understand that I am writing these "memories" literally from memory in my shack in the village of Mozonte, near Ocotal in Nicaragua, forcibly expelled from Honduras by the military government and without notes, or books, or scientific data about Honduras and its history. The only thing I have from Honduras is a small file of newspaper clippings that treat of my problems from 1966 to 1980. So you will have to forgive me if I make a few errors in recalling the facts that I relate.

The second president of the ANACH, elected in their national convention of 1964, was Efraín Díaz Galeas. He had been the campesino mayor from the Liberal Party of the town of Santa Rita, Yoro, before the military coup of 1963, and I got to know him early in 1965 when I visited his own ANACH group. This group had invaded the abandoned Finca (Farm) 18 near Agua Blanca Sur in the region in our parish called Guanchías.

That was when I was asking the campesinos all those questions before and after mass in their villages, and they began to invite me to their weekly meetings of the ANACH. I started going every Saturday to these meetings of the "subsections" of the ANACH (which is what they call a village group of from 25 to 150 members) in the thirteen villages of the Guanchías region to the south of Progreso.

It was very inspirational to watch these unlettered campesinos in their meetings as they discussed their problems, collected the dues, wrote the minutes of the meeting, and planned their projects. Sometimes a member of the executive committee from the national office in San Pedro Sula would come to a meeting, and little by little I got to know the ANACH, its leaders and its activists or promoters.

Many of these poor campesinos of the villages of Guanchías had been workers on the banana farms of the Tela before they were abandoned (around 1945) because of the Panama disease. After that the campesinos planted their milpas each year in these abandoned lands.

In 1965 the Tela was selling to the Colombian, Arcesio Echeverry, the parts of these lands to which the Tela claimed legal title. At the same time, the Tela was returning most of the land to the Bográn family, with the explanation that this land had been rented to the Tela for the last fifty years by the Bográns. The Bográns claimed to have the legal title, given to them by their grandfather, Luis Bográn, when he was president of Honduras. They say that he flew over this region of the Sula Valley and chose all the lands from the mountains to the Ulúa River, and from Progreso to Santa Rita to leave as an inheritance with a legal title of complete dominion for his sons. Now, in 1965, the Bográns wanted to recover all these tens of thousands of acres of good flat farmland to extend their cattle ranches, and they tried to expel the thousands of campesinos who for many years had been living in villages and farming on these lands.

But this conflict was just beginning in 1965. The Bográns were important figures in the National Party and had the backing of the military government in power. The campesinos were already organized in the ANACH in all the thirteen villages of Guanchías. They had a copy of a decree of President Paz Barahona, issued before the remeasuring and legalizing of the Bográn title, granting all these same "national" lands for parceling into family farm plots for the campesinos of the region. In 1966 the class struggle broke out into open war between these two forces in Guanchías, and with me out on the battlefield, as I will explain later.

In 1965 I was just getting to know the movement, without as yet understanding it well. I was mostly interested in getting to know the leaders of the ANACH in each village in order to get them to be Delegates of the Word. I did achieve this in several villages. But little by little the Spirit of Jesus was showing me that these campesino brothers and sisters of mine needed more than the Word of God. I had to put into practice the Word of God, which clearly explains that love of neighbor means to give food to the hungry, clothes to the naked.

My investigations and questions clearly demonstrated that the reason 90 percent of my campesino brothers were hungry was that they did not have any place to work. "How can one be a farmer, a campesino, without land for planting?" the Spirit of Jesus asked me. He enlightened me to see that giving food to these hungry neighbors meant giving them land so that they could plant and harvest their own food. By the end of 1965, it had become my obsession to help these hungry brothers of mine to get good land. I became completely involved with the ANACH.

I used to visit the national headquarters of the ANACH in San Pedro Sula once in a while. It was in a room of the big FESI-TRANH headquarters' building. Céleo Gonzales, the president of the FESITRANH, and the American representative of AIFLD in Honduras were in the office of the ANACH practically every day. Frequently the American labor attaché of the U.S. embassy was there to "advise" the campesino leaders and to plan the projects that the ANACH was supposed to carry out with the money given to them by AIFLD.

The thousands of affiliated members of the ANACH were supposed to pay monthly dues in order to self-finance their organization, but the fact was (and still is) that very few paid their dues, and most of the money for salaries for the executive committee, for the activists, and for the secretary, as well as money for putting on courses, was (and still is) openly received from AIFLD. SITRATERCO and FESITRANH also gave something each month to the ANACH in those first years.

Efraín Díaz Galeas, the president of the ANACH, was not allowed to really run the campesino organization and did not really make the decisions. It was Céleo Gonzales who planned and decided for the ANACH, together with the two U.S. "advisers." Efraín was one of the geniuses that God has given to the Honduran campesino movement. Besides being very intelligent, he was very courageous. He was determined to get these Guanchías lands for the ANACH groups. He was willing to fight the Bográn family and, if necessary, the whole military government, in spite of advice to the contrary from an anticommunist (with reputed CIA connections) AIFLD representative. I knew this AIFLD representative well; we were friends. I, too, was still anticommunist.

Before finishing his two-year term as president, Efraín left the ANACH in an extraordinary convention because this AIFLD representative accused him of being a communist. Ramón Flores Molina, who was not even a campesino but a FESITRANH workers' activist, assumed the direction of the ANACH in the interim.

Efraín returned to Santa Rita and, with the help of Marco Virgilio Carías and others at the University of Honduras, organized the first collective cooperative of the ANACH (the "Guanchías," in Finca 18) to plant corn for the concentrated food plant of San Pedro Sula. Efraín was mysteriously shot in the face one day and disappeared. A year later, near the end of 1967, it was heard that the new director of INA (the National Agrarian Institute), Rigoberto Sandoval Corea, had sent him to Israel to study their system of cooperatives.

This new director of INA knew that the Agrarian Reform Law was no good for Honduras, that giving individual plots of land to the campesinos was not real agrarian reform. He wanted to form collective cooperatives of campesinos to be like large, modern agro-industries, and he wanted to form his own campesino organization to put into practice his ideas. Sandoval very wisely chose Efraín Díaz to be the promoter of his new organization of campesino cooperatives. When Efraín returned from Israel, Sandoval sent him to Guanchías to reorganize his old ANACH cooperative of Finca 18, converting it into the first co-op of INA. This was in 1968, and I will talk more about it later.

It is important to notice here how Efraín Díaz gradually came under the control of the INA and the military government of López Arellano and all the successive governments. He is not the only campesino leader who has allowed this to happen, as we will see. Power compromises almost everyone. Many of the higher military officers, worker and campesino leaders, politicians, and professional people, including some of the clergy and the bishops, sooner or later are tempted to compromise themselves.

The second campesino organization formed in Honduras was not that of the INA cooperatives, but rather the one formed by the Christian Democrats, the UNC (the National Campesino Union). The group of Christian university students that Father John Fisher had in Tegucigalpa gave several courses on the social doctrine of the Church in 1964 to campesinos from the departments of Choluteca and Valle who were *Monitores* (practical teachers) of the Radio Schools. The campesino Monitores who took these courses constituted the basis for organizing in 1964 the ACASCH (Social Christian Campesino Association), which in 1968 became the FENTCH (National Federation of Farm Workers), and in April of 1970 changed its name to the UNC (National Campesino Union). This same month the CGT (Centralized Worker Organization) was organized with the campesino UNC and two labor union federations organized by the Christian Democrats, the FASH (Authentic Federation of Labor Unions of Honduras) and the FESISUR (Federation of Labor Unions of the South).

The basis for organizing the Radio Schools, which started in these two southern departments, were the *Celadores* of the Apostleship of Prayer that the Canadian Xaverian missionaries had organized in almost all the villages of the south. Our Father Fred Schuller was one of the initiators of the Radio Schools in Honduras. In 1962 he went to Colombia with Father Pablo Guillet of the Xaverian missionaries of the south and with the Honduran director of Radio Católica (the Church's radio station) in Tegucigalpa, Father Molina. In Colombia they studied the system of the famous Radio Schools of Sutatenza.

The Radio Schools were promoted by the Catholic Church to teach illiterate campesinos who live out in the hills, where there are no schools or teachers, to read and write by means of a class by radio every afternoon after work. They meet around a radio in one of their homes and a campesino who already knows how to read, called the monitor, helps them put into practice what the teacher on the radio tells them to do. Each pupil has a simple reader, a notebook, and a pencil. Hundreds of thousands of

Colombian campesinos studied in these Radio Schools, which not only taught them reading and writing, but also ideas about agriculture, hygiene and health, the Bible, and the necessity of becoming organized together in the village for community development projects.

On their return Father Schuller and the others had to adapt all this material for Honduran campesinos. They organized ACPH (Honduran Popular Cultural Action) with the auxiliary bishop of Tegucigalpa, Evelio Domínguez, as president and enthusiastic promoter, and they were backed up by the whole Episcopal Conference. The Radio Schools started as a direct work of the Catholic church in the south and then spread all over the country through many of the parishes, which were their promotion centers.

As far as illiteracy goes, just as in every other field of development, Honduras has been the worst of all Latin-American countries except Haiti. Officially, 55 percent of Hondurans in 1965 were completely illiterate; now, in 1981, they say they have lowered this to 45 percent. However, in the villages, especially in the mountains, 90 percent of the adults still cannot read or write. Some of these campesinos went to school a year or two when they were small; but afterward they never practiced and are now illiterate again. The Radio Schools have helped tens of thousands of these campesinos to learn to read. Sad to say, however, they have not appreciably changed the overall picture of illiteracy in Honduras.

The literacy campaigns, the campaigns for vaccination of the children, for making agrarian reform by giving some national lands to the most violent campesino groups, for constructing roads, schools, or outhouses in "community development" projects, for forming savings and loan cooperatives, or coffee coops: all this is what we now call developmentalism. It is also called reformism, an effort at trying to give the poor masses some participation in the capitalist economy of the country. It is an attempt to better, to reform, the capitalist system instead of changing it.

The fact is that the masses are so poor, ignorant, sick, isolated, and backward that they are "marginated," on the sidelines, out of the game, excluded from the economic and social life of the country. They neither produce anything significant for the economy, nor significantly consume the products of "the consumer society."

That is why, besides calming the revolutionary spirit of the masses, the Alliance for Progress and all the big loans of AID and of the international development banks are set up to incorporate these poor masses, the "marginated," into the process of production and consumption of the capitalist international market. The great majority of Hondurans cannot buy cars, refrigerators, radios, watches, television sets, cosmetics, expensive clothes, whiskey, magazines, all of which come from the United States. They are "marginated," out of it; they have to be incorporated into the market. They have to be taught to read, to work better, to earn more money, so that they can buy these products of "civilized living" (and so that all this money can go to the United States).

In 1964 and 1965 when there was so much developmentalism in Latin America, I was enthusiastic about the ideas that I learned in the course on the social doctrine of the Church that I took in San Pedro Sula led by the Christian Democratic group. Fernando Montes, Orlando Iriarte, and Adan Palacios (the last two are still national leaders of the Christian Democratic Party of Honduras) sketched for us the facts of Honduran reality in the following manner: Only 3 percent of Honduran society live well, earning more than $500 (U.S.) a month, and some of them earn many thousands a month. This is the upper class, the bourgeoisie, the big landowners, doctors, engineers, lawyers, industrialists, big commercial dealers, top government workers, top politicians, and higher military officers. This is the oligarchy who control the economy, the armed forces, and all the power of decision in the country (dependent on the U.S. embassy, of course).

Another 12 percent of Hondurans form a poor middle class, who earn between $100 and $500 a month. These are the teachers, agronomists, small businessmen, medium-sized farmers and cattlemen, some of the skilled workers organized in unions like SITRATERCO, and so on. These people naturally work very hard to see if they can climb up a few rungs of the socioeconomic ladder to enter the upper class. That is the goal in life that the capitalist educational system has given them.

Statistics show that the remaining 85 percent of Honduran families do not earn even $100 a month, and, as I have mentioned, more than half these families do not earn even $100 *a year*. These are the bulk of the campesinos, the Indians, and those who live in poor barrios in the cities and towns, those oppressed and marginated by the present capitalist system in Honduras. This is the great injustice in Honduras, they told us in their social doctrine course, that instead of distributing them more equitably among the whole population, a handful of Hondurans grab up for themselves most of the riches that are left in the country (after the continual plundering by U.S. imperialism through its transnational enterprises).

They told us that to rectify this it was necessary to change the whole capitalist system. If we reject the capitalist system, we should analyze the only other economic system that exists, communism. After a whole day of looking at the lack of liberty under Stalin in Russia, we rejected this system too, as an even worse evil than what we have in Honduras. The conclusion was that we have to use "a third way," a new system, neither capitalist nor communist, that they called Christian socialism, or communitarianism. This new system would be a kind of cooperativism, in which the riches of the country would be distributed more equitably, in which the poor masses would have land, education, good food and housing, and so on. To achieve this the people have to be organized, and so we should help the campesinos to organize Radio Schools, co-ops, committees for community development.

They convinced me and many others, too. Tom Quiery and I and other priests and nuns who took these courses started to teach this same Social Doctrine of the Church to our Delegates of the Word. We were even more deeply converted by another course of five days in Tegucigalpa in 1965 given by the Belgian Jesuit, Roger Vekemans. The famous DESAL Institute of the Catholic University in Chile, which formed many of the principal Christian Democrat leaders of Latin America, was organized and directed by Vekemans. Vekemans explained to us his well-known book on "the marginated masses and development." It contains the whole theory that I have just set forth, about the unjust distribution of the riches under the capitalist system that leaves the masses of poor marginated, and the necessity for a third alternative, a Christian socialism in which the poor masses who are marginated will be incorporated, little by little, into participation in the economy and in the political decisions of the country. For this, the first step is to help the masses of campesinos, workers, slum-dwellers, women, and students get organized to demand their participation. The social doctrine of the Church, he said, demands the "natural right" of private property; all persons have this right to some of the private property. The campesinos must be given land, but that is better done "communitarily" in co-ops. The worker must be given participation in the profits and decision-making process of the companies through the system of co-management and self-management.

This is the peaceful revolution that the Church wants, Vekemans said. He demonstrated this by reading parts of the latest papal encyclicals. The changes will come when the masses are organized to make their voices heard in the government, in the elections. We do not want a violent revolution; this is forbidden by the Church. This is Marxist, not Christian. We have to start the radical changes that the Church looks for by organizing the campesinos in Radio Schools and cooperatives so that they can participate in society.

These were the ideas that I was preaching from then on. I became very anticapitalist: "We have to change the system." And also more anticommunist: "We want a peaceful, Christian revolution." "You have to be organized in order to be able to participate in the riches and decisions in the country," I was teaching the campesinos.

Only later on, about eight years later, did I begin to seriously re-think and challenge this so-called "third way," this "peaceful revolution," as a way to help the "marginated" masses to "participate" in society. I then began to realize that this is not a change of system; this is not any revolution; this is simply to help the masses "participate" in the first way, the capitalist and imperialist system. This is not a third way. In those days I was still far from being a real revolutionary, even though the big landowners of Progreso were then calling me a communist for preaching these reformist, Christian-socialist ideas.

In 1966 and 1967, some of the priests in the south and in Olancho with these same ideas were encouraging the campesinos to join the new UNC, the organization that followed the social doctrine of the Church, instead of the ANACH. These priests were helping to teach these ideas of "the third way" in the courses for leaders of the Radio Schools and for those of the UNC. In this way, the UNC grew rapidly. This was especially true where the Radio Schools and the Celebration of the Word were already organized in a village of the south, or in Olancho, where the campesinos had already been organized in the ANACH. Many of these groups decided to pass over and join the UNC instead, "because it was more Christian."

I had several arguments about the UNC with these priests. I continued with the ANACH, trying to convince the groups in the whole northern part of Honduras not to pass over to the UNC, but rather to work at bettering the ANACH, which was ten times the size of the UNC. It was obvious to me that the division of the campesinos into several organizations was very harmful. I tried to convince the priests and Delegates of the Word from other parts of the country to get involved with the ANACH in order to help it have more of a Christian spirit. The ANACH leaders noted that the priests and the Radio Schools were promoting the UNC, with the result that the UNC was stealing away many groups of the ANACH, and they resented it. If I, as a priest, had not been so involved with the ANACH and a friend of all its leaders and activists, the ANACH would have become much more anticlerical.

At that time Fernando Montes was the director of the Radio Schools. With his Christian Democratic companions he did a great job of raising the critical social consciousness, not only of thousands of campesinos, but also of the clergy and the hierarchy of the Catholic church. The Church actually began to be preoccupied, for the first time in the history of Honduras, with the lot of the masses of poor campesinos.

CARITAS was reorganized in all the parishes to promote community development projects. (The national and local offices of CARITAS were also mostly under the control of Christian Democrats.) Capacitation or training centers for campesinos were started by the Church in every part of the country: first in Choluteca with the Colmena (the "Beehive," directed by a Christian Democrat); then Santa Clara in Juticalpa, Olancho (directed

by Adán Palacios); Las Milpas in Pinalejo, Santa Bárbara; La Fragua in Progreso, and so on. Today practically all the rural parishes
in the country have their training centers (even though nowadays
they are no longer used as much for developing a critical social
conscience in the campesinos).

In February of 1966, Father Jarrell "Patricio" Wade, nephew
of the old missionary who founded our Institute San José, Joe
Wade, finished his theology in Mexico and his Third Probation
in Argentina and was assigned to the Yoro Mission and to our
parish team in Progreso with Tom and me. Here is another example of the lack of practical missionary formation in our Missouri Province Jesuits. Father Wade got his master's degree in
Latin! The superior's idea in assigning him to our parish was for
him to organize CARITAS and a campesino training center, using some of the big buildings we owned in the Company Zone in
Progreso. He and Brother Jim lived there, and rented eight of
the big houses to different families. A priest who taught at the
Instituto San José used the large hall in our Company Zone for
youth dances every weekend, and the swimming pool was open
every day for the youth who could pay the entrance charge.

Several of the houses were reserved for the parish CARITAS
offices and for the training center, and since neither Tom nor I
wanted the poor campesinos to go to the luxurious Company
Zone, Father Wade was told to start these works. Tom and I had
been giving many courses and spiritual retreats to the campesino
Delegates of the Word, catechists, and Legionaries, using the hall
of the parish clinic or the abandoned Apostolic School at Instituto San José, or one of the churches that we had in the villages like Toyos, Urraco Pueblo, and Agua Blanca Sur. We put on
these three-day courses in poverty, with the campesinos bringing
the food we ate together during the course and everyone sleeping
on the floor. This was more like the style of life of the campesinos.

The superior, on the other hand, decided to fix up three dormitories with about eighty beds, two classrooms, a kitchen, and a
dining hall in the biggest of all the houses in our Company Zone.
He named the Jesuit residence Casa San Ignacio (Saint Ignatius
House), but the people continue to call it the Company Zone, just
as when it belonged to the Tela Railroad Company.

Jarrell had an interesting contest. He asked all the parishioners to suggest names for the new campesino training center. The winning name was La Fragua (The Forge). "To forge the New Man," said Jarrell.

Before starting short courses for the campesinos in the Fragua, Jerry prepared himself well. For several months he studied and visited the Colmena in Choluteca and other training centers of the Church that were already functioning. He became a real technician in the new method of popular pedagogy, the active method of Paulo Freire, which the Christian Democrats in the south and in Olancho were using with great success in conscientizing the campesinos. Instead of the old capitalist "banking" method of "depositing" ideas of the "teacher" in the heads of the passive students, Freire says that "liberating education" should simply encourage the oppressed to have a dialogue together about the reality around them and always ask themselves why it is like that.

They divide into small groups and sit in a circle (instead of in rows like in a classroom), and the "animator" merely, for example, shows his or her group a photograph of a campesino family, or proposes to them a word like *poverty,* so that each in the small group will say whatever comes to mind with regard to that. In this way it is surprising the conclusions that uneducated campesinos come to about the oppression and exploitation that they personally suffer. In this way they are as though awakened, they begin to realize that they are unjustly exploited by others and by the capitalist system. They conclude that their poverty and lack of land and of work is unjust, is a sin—that God does not want the world like this, some of his children eating well while their brothers and sisters are dying of hunger. They decide among themselves that they should unite and organize themselves in order to demand their human rights, get land, fix up the school, dig wells for drinkable water, and so on.

Many of us priests and nuns in Honduras learned to give this kind of course for the campesinos. We used the Bible to illustrate that God wants the liberation of the oppressed. This liberation theology really only penetrated with force into the Honduran Church after the Latin-American Bishops' Conference in Medellín, Colombia, in 1968. Nonetheless, many of us were already interpreting and teaching the gospel of Christ in this liberating sense long before that time.

From the beginning, Jarrell fit in well with our team in the parish rectory. He started working very well in several of the poor barrios of Progreso with Bible reflection groups for forming the BCCs. I was still alone for all the villages and camps.

The Franciscans helped in everything. They were also in charge of forming the women catechists to teach the children in the whole parish. As soon as we took over the parish, Tom and I had given over the parish grade school, San Jose, to the sisters of Instituto Notre Dame. For us it was unjust to be teaching only a few children in Catholic grade schools and high schools (and these were principally the children of the richer families of Progreso), leaving thousands of children and youth who also were Catholics in the public grade schools and high schools without any Christian instruction. The Franciscans tried to get catechists at least for the children of all the grade schools in the city, villages, and camps.

You can imagine the continuous clashes I had with the superior and with Jarrell about constructing the campesino training center, La Fragua, in the Company Zone. I was all for having a center for the formation of the campesinos, but I wanted it out in some village, or in the abandoned Apostolic School of our Instituto San José. I told them right from the beginning that I was not going to invite campesinos to the luxurious Company Zone, especially now that the Center La Fragua was right next to the big swimming pool where young women in their bikinis sunbathed each day for everyone to watch. How could the Delegates of the Word concentrate on studying the Bible with such distractions? The Jesuits there were Americans and were accustomed to these styles of life, but the Honduran campesinos were not.

When Jarrell started giving courses in La Fragua, few campesinos came. I never told anyone not to go, but neither did I collaborate by inviting them to go. Jarrell has always been very angry with me for this, and rightly so, I now recognize. After more than a year of boycotting La Fragua like that, holding my monthly meetings of Delegates and giving some courses myself in other places in the parish, I finally realized that I could not change the decision of the Jesuits nor the fact of having La Fragua in the Company Zone. It was probably good for me that I did not get my own way in some of these conflicts. Therefore, I resolved to stop my opposition to Jarrell's work in La Fragua, and I began rather to help him with his courses there, which was a more brotherly and effective way to act.

12. The Land Struggles

In May of 1966, the crisis of the campesinos in the sector of Guanchías was greatly intensified; this was when the contract of the Tela Railroad Company for renting these lands from the Bográns ran out. As mentioned earlier, these lands had been abandoned by the Tela years ago and now were occupied by about twelve thousand persons, campesino families who lived and planted their milpas on these lands. Without even taking into consideration these poor families, the Bográns sold about half to the rich Colombian, Arcesio Echeverry, who had a deal with the Standard Fruit Company to plant bananas there. He immediately tried to throw the campesino families off the land. The Bográn Fortín brothers, Luis and Fausto, and the Bográn Paredes family wanted to extend their existing cattle ranches over all the rest of this land.

I have in my file a letter that I wrote June 25, 1966, to the director of INA, Angel Araujo. I sent a copy to the American ambassador in Honduras, Joseph John Jova, who had come to Progreso to the parish rectory to see me after this whole affair came out in the national and international newspapers. This is the letter:

Dear Sir:

I am writing you as Director of the National Agrarian Institute so you can confront the serious problems blocking agrarian reform.

In the municipality of Progreso there are four big land problems. In the last months thousands of poor campesinos have been evicted from these lands and do not have any place to plant their crops. For them this means a future of hunger and misery. In each of these four problems it is INA that must find the solution according to the Agrarian Reform Law, which exists, it says, to distribute more justly the lands of Honduras so that the poor campesinos become owners of a family plot. Up to now INA has not found a solution to the four problems that follow:

1. The biggest problem is between the Bográn Fortín family and the campesinos of the thirteen villages between Progreso and Santa Rita: Pajuiles, Arena Blanca, La Mina, Guacamaya, La Sarrosa, Urraco Sur, Balsamo, Agua Blanca Sur, La 14, La 6, El Socorro, El 4 de Marzo, and Virtiente de Progreso. The president of Honduras and INA promised to put the exact boundaries and measure the land, which the 1927 decree of President Paz Barahona gave for family plots for these villages. They promised to do this right away. After months of conflicts and injuries to the campesinos of this sector of Guanchías, the boundaries still are not determined. An engineer is now measuring the eastern boundary back in the mountains instead of measuring and deciding the disputed western boundary in the valley with the Bográns and Echeverry. Meanwhile, with soldiers from El Rancho, Bográn Fortín evicted many campesinos from the cornfields they have been cultivating for many years, and with tractors he has planted corn there. After many complaints from the ANACH and from us priests of the parish, Bográn signed an agreement that gives the use of nine fields to the three villages of La Sarrosa, La Mina, and Guacamaya. This calmed down the ANACH but left the campesinos in their misery, because practically all the land of these nine fields was already being used by campesinos, and what was not being used was swampland. Thus, one half of the campesinos of La Mina and Guacamaya are still without a place to plant their milpas this spring. And the part of the fields destined for Guacamaya has just been flooded with the rains. If a campesino cannot plant his milpa, or he loses the crop, he faces stark hunger. Therefore INA should measure and distribute these valley lands immediately. To do so, INA will also have to reject the illegal titles of other big cattlemen there and evict them. Just in La Sarrosa, La Mina, and Guacamaya there are more than three hundred families. About two hundred of these have not been able to plant their crops this spring and are suffering real hunger.

2. This same decree of Paz Barahona affects the lands that Arcesio Echeverry bought from Bográn Fortin last year in this same sector of Guanchías. Echeverry is planting bananas to sell to the Standard Fruit Company. It seems illegal to have a sale of lands that INA is measuring or studying under this decree for family plots. But Echeverry is planting his banana farms now very rapidly, while INA is back in the hills delaying the measuring of the western boundary. As always, it is the poor who suffer. On May 13, Echeverry burnt the ripe milpas with corn still on the stalks and also some piles of picked corn on the ground. The municipal police of Progreso have a list of thirteen campesinos of the villages of La 6 and La 14 who lost a total of about 700 quintles (35 tons) of corn worth about L. 3500 ($1,750). For them, this represents their whole income of the last six months. When they denounced Echeverry to the police in Progreso, Echeverry denied he had burned anything, and it was then too late to prove it. This millionaire refuses to pay a cent to these poor men. Also a few weeks ago Echeverry sent his tractors to plow under the new cornfields that many campesinos from the village of La 14 had just planted. Again he denied that there was corn planted there, and it is now too late to prove it because he has banana trees already planted there. Just to lose the corn seed is a tragedy for a poor campesino. INA should make Echeverry respect the Agrarian Reform Law and stop the forceful eviction of campesinos.

3. At this moment the most explosive problem of all is that of the family of Antonio Bográn Paredes with the villages of El 4 de Marzo and El Socorro. These villagers published two complaints in *La Prensa* on June 24 that give a good résumé of the ugly events there. The first complaint is against the two military representatives and the representative of the mayor of Progreso in the village of El 4 de Marzo, whom all the villagers consider their enemies. For more than a year they were against the people of the two villages, having beaten up several, and having threatened to kill others. A number of times the villagers have asked for a change of these authorities, but they continue on. These same three men, plus two more, were the ones who signed a contract

with Bográn saying that the people of the two villages together would buy 300 manzanas (about 500 acres) for L. 150
a manzana. And thus the two villages would be reduced to
live and work within these 300 manzanas. All the villagers
rejected this contract and have signed a document for INA
stating that only the ANACH is their representative, and
that these men who signed the contract were not their representatives, but their enemies. The second complaint was
about what INA did last Sunday in a mass meeting with the
two villages. Three officials of INA, their lawyers, and an
engineer, arrived with Luis Bográn Paredes and with six
uniformed soldiers armed with rifles to tell the people
that INA had the final solution to this conflict on orders
direct from the presidential palace. The engineer would
immediately start measuring 400 manzanas in which all
the people of the two villages would have to live and work.
The villagers and the parish priest from Progreso
(me), whom they had invited to this meeting, spoke up
against this solution. Luis Bográn Paredes called the priest
(me) a communist and afterward published in *La Prensa* a
very offensive and disrespectful article against this priest.
According to the villagers there are around four hundred
poor campesino families in the two villages. They have been
working in about 1000 manzanas. All this land is either cul-
tivated by them or is useless swampland. It is true that a few
of them are Salvadorans and that some of those who farm
there live in Progreso. But an attempt to force all these
families within 400 manzanas (taking away from them 600
manzanas), without having made any study of how many
people really work there and how much land they have in
crops, seems irrational and will hurt many campesino families. Well, at last, after so many insults and clashes and complaints, maybe INA will make the study of the land and the
people. The villagers fear that the study can even be used
against them, if it is not objectively done and interpreted.
The people there live in a state of great fear, and it could be
said that there is great unrest among most of the campesinos
of the whole northern part of Honduras.

4. In the sector of Guaymas there are hundreds of cam-

pesinos from the sixteen villages around the Batan Farm of the Tela Railroad Company who are without land this spring because they were evicted from the Batan lands. The Tela Railroad Company has decided to increase its cattle herds there, taking back the land that these campesinos had always rented each year from the Tela for their milpas. The general manager of the Tela told me that the company had given to INA thousands of manzanas of land in other places to distribute to the campesinos, and INA has not done it. He said that the immediate solution would be for INA to investigate the illegal titles of the other big landowners in the Guaymas region. The priests of the parish in Progreso have a list of a hundred campesinos of Toyos who couldn't get land for their spring planting, of fifty from Naranjo, of about two hundred from Mezapa, fifty from Zamar, seventy from Río Abajo, etc., etc.

It seems as though no one wants to help the poor campesinos, but rather many are hurting them—and the campesinos make up 60 percent of the Honduran population. INA was created to carry out the Agrarian Reform Law and redistribute more justly the land of Honduras so that these campesinos could better their lives.

> Sincerely yours,
> (signed) Padre Guadalupe

This Luis Bográn Paredes (nicknamed "Toto") who called me a communist in an interview in the newspapers was like the black sheep of the aristocratic Bográn family, the heirs of the former president of Honduras, Gen. Luis Bográn. In this famous meeting of Luis and INA and the soldiers with all the people of the village of El 4 de Marzo and El Socorro, my intervention caused such a controversy afterward in the newspapers that it stopped the eviction of these campesinos. The only thing I had said was that it was not just to take away 1000 manzanas (1700 acres) that four hundred campesinos had in crops and force them all into only 400 manzanas (510 acres); that they ought to first make a good study of the situation before evicting them; that this was not agrarian reform to take the land away from the campesinos.

"Toto" Bográn, in another letter published in the right-wing newspaper *La Prensa,* said that "the curita Guadalupe is a subversive foreigner who stirs up the campesinos to rebel against the armed forces' government." The executive committee of the ANACH came out with a pronouncement in the newspapers defending me. What follows is one part of their statement:

To clear up the charges made by Mr. Bográn Paredes accusing Reverend Guadalupe ("Curita" Guadalupe, he disrespectfully called him) of inviting the campesinos in the above mentioned villages to start a revolution, and saying that this is subversive action against our constitutional government, we think it good to state that the only thing Mr. Bográn Paredes is doing is using the dirty tactics that the capitalists and big landowners always use to confuse the public and governmental opinion with regard to the reality of problems we are trying to solve.

We believe that Mr. Bográn, who claims to be a good Catholic and who is so worried about Padre Guadalupe's activities, has forgotten or is ignorant of some of the biblical precepts, and so we want to remind him that when the capitalists and big landowners told Christ that they wanted to follow him he told them: "Distribute your riches among the poor and come follow me." We also want to remind him that Pope Leo XIII said in his encyclical *"Rerum Novarum"* that the worker and campesino should receive better salaries, better working conditions, and a better standard of living, which has moved the clergy to participate in these activities to help solve the problems of the poor.

With this, we want Mr. Bográn to understand that Padre Guadalupe is not inciting the campesinos to start a revolution or engage in any subversive activity, but only trying to put into practice the principles of Christianity that Christ left us and to change the mediocre and backward mentality that up to the present day the capitalists and big landowners have."

I wonder who wrote this pronouncement that the whole executive committee of the ANACH signed on July 1, 1966? I did not have anything to do with it, but I really appreciated the support.

Other articles and editorials came out in the newspapers, especially in the extreme right-wing *Correo del Norte,* about the priest who is a "duped tool of the Communists" and who "is involved in subversive politics." My superior Fred Schuller and Tom Quiery also made the following pronouncement, which came out in the national and international press.

CHURCH AUTHORITIES DEFEND PRIEST

Seeing that a Catholic priest of the parish of Progreso, Padre Guadalupe, has been unjustly attacked in the newspapers by some members of the Bográn Paredes family, we feel obliged to defend the good name of Padre Guadalupe who always has been and is a good priest, and to condemn the disrespectful manner in which they referred to him.

This is not the first time that someone who defends the poor has been subject to calumnies. But the Church cannot be silent when she sees that her sons need help and defense. As the Holy Father Paul VI said in Rome a few days ago: "The Church recognizes her obligation to be involved in the world of the workers, to be on the side of the defenseless, and to seek with them and for them better living conditions."

The Church has always defended the rights of the poor. To do this is not being an agitator or being involved in politics. There is an urgent need for agrarian reform in our country and of a better distribution of the riches of Honduras among all the citizens; and, besides that, the Church teaches that the campesinos should be helped to organize themselves to get their rights.

With God's help and the cooperation of all men of good will, let us dedicate ourselves to find a just solution to the serious problems of the campesinos of our country.

(signed) Padre Federico, Superior of the Jesuits
Padre Tomás, Pastor

I went to visit the Bográn family a number of times to see if the problems could be settled by dialogue. Luis Bográn Fortín, who later on in 1969 was one of the precandidates for the presidency of Honduras for the National Party, spoke with me several times at his big cattle ranch Hacienda el Rancho in Guanchías. He did not like it when I told him that he had more love for his cows than for our brothers and sisters, the campesinos, because he was giving food to the cows by taking it away from the campesinos. I mentioned that the good economists all say that the cattle should be on the hillsides while the good, flat valley lands should be for agriculture. Later on he did not even visit Guanchías; he stayed in Tegucigalpa and left his brother Fausto, who was a hard man and always went around armed with a pistol, to arrange for the eviction of the hundreds of campesinos from "his" land.

During this same period we were trying to find a solution to the big problem of the campesinos in the sector of Guaymas. The Tela Railroad Company was evicting campesinos to put cattle on "their" land (the way the Bográns were in Guanchías). I especially wanted to help my poor Legionaries of Toyos, who this year (1966) had no place to plant their milpas. I went to La Lima to speak to the American general manager of the Tela, but he explained to me that the Tela had just given back to INA a lot of land in other places where all these people of Guaymas could be sent. If he could not continue renting these lands to the campesinos, I asked, would he sell their cooperative about 500 manzanas (850 acres), as the Tela had done in Santa Rita, Yoro, with the Subirana Cooperative, and in San Manuel, Cortés with the cooperative there? He told me that he had orders from the central office in Boston not to sell any more land.

In a big meeting under the church at Toyos with all the men Legionaries of the four nearby villages, Naranjo, Las Delicias, La Colorada, and Toyos, I explained how the general manager had answered me. These men had told me before that they would be delighted to form a co-op to buy 500 manzanas of land from the Tela. When they heard what the general manager told me, they all agreed to form the co-op anyway. They would buy any land they could around there, because they no longer could find land to rent. I promised to write to the very heads of the Tela Railroad Company and of the United Fruit Company in the United States to ask them to sell us some land in Guaymas. To form the co-op, I told them, they would have to meet every Saturday to study about cooperativism, and at the same time, each week they should put something in savings, even if it was only twenty centavos L. 0.20 (ten cents U.S.) in order little by little to save enough money to buy the land.

That is how our first co-op started. The members, all Legionaries, chose the name of the parish, Las Mercedes (from Mother of Mercy), for their co-op. After a few weeks of study sessions, the 120 members from the four villages elected a provisional administrative council, or board of directors, with José Ayala as president. From then on, he directed the study of cooperativism, following a Radio School pamphlet I lent him.

Meanwhile, I wrote to the general manager of the whole United Fruit Company (of which the Tela is a subsidiary) in Boston, explaining to him the sad situation in which his company had left the campesinos by refusing to continue to rent the land to them for their cornfields, which were their only income. I told him that the general manager in Honduras had said that he could not authorize the sale of more land. I explained about the formation of the Las Mercedes Agricultural Co-op and how the members were saving up in hopes of buying 850 acres from the Tela Railroad Company.

He also answered no, that they did not want to sell any more land, because they needed it for their cattle herds. But, surprisingly, a few months later I received another letter from Boston. It said that, after investigating the great need of the campesinos, the company had approved the sale to the Las Mercedes Co-op of 800 acres of land close to Toyos for only six lempiras ($3) an acre, the same symbolic price they had charged the San Manuel Co-op.

The union leaders of SITRATERCO told me later that with all the noise in the newspapers about me and about the ANACH in Guanchías, the general manager of the Tela was afraid that, if they refused to sell us some land, not only the Las Mercedes Co-op, but all the sixteen villages of Guaymas would organize themselves in the ANACH and invade these lands where they used to plant corn and that were now cattle pastures. (That is exactly what did happen, but in 1970.)

We received this letter from Boston about a year after starting the co-op and the weekly savings. To become a legal entity so that the co-op could buy the land, I asked for the immediate help of FECOAGROH (Federation of Agricultural Cooperatives of Honduras). This was a new movement promoted and financed by AID (the U.S. Agency for International Development) for forming cooperatives of small and medium-sized farmers and cattlemen who owned their own land. Elías Villegas and Gustavo Chávez, promoters of FECOAGROH, came to give us a course for legally constituting the co-op, and in August of 1967, after a huge outdoor mass with practically all the people of the four villages present, the representative of the government's Cooperative Development Office handed over the legal documents to the first president of the co-op, Marcos Del Cid. José Ayala was the vice-president, Santos Alvarenga the treasurer, and I, as a member of the co-op, was elected president of the Vigilance Committee.

With this we could now legally buy the land. Each of the 120 members had to have forty lempiras ($20) in savings as his part of the 4800 lempiras ($2400) that the 800 acres cost. Those who still had not saved that much after a year had to sell their pigs or chickens to get it. We no sooner bought the land and got the title of full dominion when we had a big fight within the co-op.

I insisted that not only had we bought the land collectively, but that we should work it collectively as we had agreed on doing right from the start. But the FECOAGROH promoters convinced the majority of the members that it was better to work individually in plots of five acres of good land for each member, distributed each year by drawing lots. AID would give the co-op a loan for each member to plow his plot, to buy selected corn and bean seed and fertilizer. Each member would pay back his part of the loan with the harvest, which the co-op would then sell collectively.

Sounds like a good plan, doesn't it? This is the system of the farm co-ops in the United States, I told them, which is fine if each one of the members is at least a medium-sized modern farmer, as they are in the United States. But if some of you lose your crop, as happens here in Toyos every year, how will you pay back your loan? By dividing up the land and working individually, this co-op becomes like a savings and loan co-op. I told them in the assembly of the co-op, with Villegas and Chávez there, that the savings and loans cooperatives for campesinos started by the Radio School in southern Honduras had failed. If money is lent to a poor campesino and he does not have a good harvest, he remains in debt for the rest of his life. Many campesinos wind up selling their little plots of land, or all of their animals, or their small coffee plantation, or even their house, to pay off the debt. "You people know that this region of Guaymas every year suffers from floods, or insect plagues, or something that ruins the harvest. Of the last three corn harvests in this region, how many were good harvests?" I asked them. "None," said one member. "One good harvest and two bad ones," said another.

Since farmers in all parts of the world are traditionally the most individualistic of humanity, the majority of our members voted to follow the FECOAGROH system of working individual plots. I really was sorry for having invited FECOAGROH to help us.

Before returning to describe other events of 1966 and 1967, I will finish the history of this first of the farm co-ops I was involved in. Just as I feared, many of the members had bad harvests and could not pay back all of their loan. By refinancing with another loan for the next harvest, some of them went deeper into debt, either because they had another bad crop, or because they had a serious illness in the family and a big medical expense. Some of these left the co-op, and their savings did not even cover their debt. Each year I tried to convince them in the co-op assemblies not to take out more individual loans, to work collectively, to plant plantain together or pasture cattle instead of just growing corn and beans. Many agreed with me, but FECOAGROH, AID, and the majority of the co-op members still wanted individualism.

I, too, used to make a small milpa twice a year, in the spring and in the fall. I love to work in the fields with the campesinos. When I was too busy to cultivate my milpa personally, my co-op companions helped me. My crops were always given away to poor families of the area.

In 1969 there occurred one of the worst tragedies in the history of Honduras: the war with El Salvador. José Ayala and practically one half of the Las Mercedes Co-op members were Salvadorans and had to flee for their lives, as I will explain later, leaving the co-op with their debt. The war had only one good result: FECOAGROH never returned to Toyos.

To pay the big debt that the co-op had to AID, we decided, at last, to work together and plant seventy acres of plantain collectively just for paying off the debt; each would plant his own milpa, but without any more loans. We did it, and then in 1971 they took out a bank loan to buy two hundred head of cattle. I was then no longer in the parish or in the co-op, but I visited them from time to time, especially for the mass on the anniversary of the co-op's foundation in August each year. After the departure of the Salvadorans, many of the members from Las Delicias, La Colorada, and Naranjo also left the co-op, and from then on it never had more than fifty members.

Later, in 1974, Hurricane Fifi completely destroyed the plantain trees, and the Guaymon River flooded and left a thick coat of sand on a large section of the co-op's land, rendering it useless even for pasture. To pay off the debt that they still had with the bank, the co-op sold part of the land and some of the cattle. The co-op at present continues with forty members, again working individually on their corn and bean plots on the part of the land that is good. Their plan is to collectively plant all their land with African palm as part of the INA Guaymas Project, which I will talk about later.

Back in 1966, after helping the campesinos of Toyos and the other three villages to organize Las Mercedes Co-op, I tried to do the same in thirteen other villages, all of which were already organized as subsections of the ANACH and trying to get land. Almost all the subsections of the ANACH in the region of Guanchías started using my system for forming a poor campesinos' co-op. They met each week to study the lessons about cooperativism in the Radio School pamphlet, to put into savings ten cents a week each, and to plan their ANACH activities for getting land.

The Agrarian Reform Law promised to give plots of 14 manzanas (24 acres) with full-dominion titles to each campesino (which is what the U.S. advisers of the Honduran government wanted). I convinced some of the leaders of the ANACH in the executive committee to insist on acquiring the land under one single title for the subsection as a cooperative, with projects for cultivating it collectively. If they receive individual family plots, I said, they will stop paying dues to the ANACH once they get their land title. They will wind up being small private property capitalists, getting loans to hire other campesinos as their workers in order to be able to cultivate, at most, ten acres. The rest of their plot will remain unused. They will probably have to sell their land to a rich cattleman someday (even though the law forbids it) in order to pay off their debts, as practically all those who received family plots in Guaymas and in Choluteca have done.

The executive committee of the ANACH in 1967 started discussions in their office in San Pedro Sula with Céleo Gonzales of the FESITRANH, with people from AIFLD, and with me to organize a National Cooperative Plan for the ANACH. We had a five-day workshop with the National Directive Council of the ANACH, all the activists, and the leaders of the ANACH co-ops already existing in the country to decide the structure of this plan. I again presented to them the arguments for changing the Agrarian Reform Law so that land would be given to the campesinos, not as individual family plots but only as land to be farmed collectively in cooperatives.

First of all, I told them, collectivization is necessary in order to form modern agro-industries belonging to the campesinos, instead of uneconomic minifarms. Second, it will promote the unity and equality of the campesinos working collectively and then distributing the harvests according to the amount of work each one did, instead of promoting individualism and the use of hired workers, which is always an exploitation of one by another. Third, besides these economic and social reasons, for political reasons the ANACH should be strengthened with a National Co-op Plan that would continually provide services to the subsections as collective cooperatives. Then the campesinos will not get their own family plot and leave the ANACH. I explained the failure of cooperatives that give loans to campesinos working individually, like Las Mercedes Co-op.

Everyone wanted a co-op plan, but not all agreed with me that all the subsections should receive their land collectively under a single title, instead of being divided up into family plots. The majority voted for a co-op plan for the subsections that wanted to receive their land collectively under a single title. The rest of the subsections could get individual family plots for their members, as the law stipulates.

The experience of the ANACH has proven that I was right about the campesinos leaving the ANACH once they had their title to a family plot of land. Some of those with individual plots still paid dues in the ANACH, however, for protection against the cattlemen or military men who wanted to grab their land. It is interesting to note that right from the start, of the future presidents of the ANACH, Antonio Julín Mendez agreed with me about the collectivization, but Reyes Rodríguez Arévalo, who became more and more compromised by the government's power, wanted the individual family plots for the campesinos.

By 1967, I think that most of the campesino leaders agreed when Rigoberto Sandoval came in as director of INA and started the policy, in spite of the law, of not giving out any land individually, but only collectively, to organized campesino groups. The evil of individualism, nevertheless, continued in many groups who received land collectively, because they then divided it up to cultivate it in individual plots (as the Las Mercedes Co-op did in Toyos). But at least if a campesino left the organized group, he lost his right to work on this land, and another campesino could join the group to take his place.

There was another point of debate that I had with the leaders of the ANACH and with Céleo Gonzales of the FESITRANH that lasted from 1967 to 1978, when my point of view finally prevailed. I maintained that each subsection co-op in the National Co-op Plan of the ANACH should be its own legal entity, an autonomous agricultural co-op, in order to legally receive its own land title and that the Co-op Plan of the ANACH should be a federation of co-ops. But no, up until three years ago Céleo Gonzales insisted with the leaders of the ANACH that the Co-op Plan must be one big national cooperative. It should use the same legal entity that the agrarian labor union, the ANACH, received from the Ministry of Labor, just as the Co-op Plan of SITRATERCO did. This idea, he claimed, had the advantage that the local groups of the Co-op Plan would stay affiliated with the ANACH in order to receive the loans and other services of the National Co-op Plan.

Since 1972, however, when INA started to give out provisional land titles and the banks gave loans only to the co-ops that were organized as separate legal entities, it became obvious that the ANACH, a national union, could not be the legal owner of all the lands of the hundreds of subsections and of all their tractors and so on. Many local subsections of the Co-op Plan were leaving the ANACH to join FECORAH (the Federation of Agrarian Reform Cooperatives, which INA had founded) to become their own legal entities and get land title. Later I will explain how the ANACH, in 1978, finally changed its National Co-op Plan.

In 1966 we were just starting some of the first ANACH co-op groups. The thirteen that I was organizing were five subsections in Guanchías: Arena Blanca, La Mina, Guacamana, La Sarrosa, and Agua Blanca Sur. Two were in the municipality of Santa Rita, Casiano and Plan Grande; and six were around Morazán in Yoro, La Esperanza, Mojiman, Portillo Gonzales, La Estancia, La Cruz, and the town of Morazán. I was extending myself beyond our Progreso parish because the ANACH activists asked me for help with these subsections that were being organized to demand land from INA.

The veteran co-op organizer, Father John Newell, was the pastor in Morazán. He kindly lent us the big parish hall for the monthly assemblies of the six subsections around Morazán that agreed to form one big regional co-op, as we had in Toyos. The difference was that here each subsection would try to get collectively from INA some land close to their village, which they would cultivate collectively. The big co-op would get loans, seed, fertilizers, and a good market for their corn and bean crops.

There were 160 members in all in this regional co-op, which they named Suyapa (the Virgin of Suyapa is the patroness of Honduras). After a year of studying cooperativism and saving their weekly minimum of ten cents in each subsection without getting any land from INA, we tried to get a loan from the bank to buy about 350 acres of land that was for sale near Morazán by the Oloman River.

Thanks be to God that we never got the loan, first of all, because that land was too dry to give good crops without irrigation and the co-op would have been a failure, and second, because with the war against El Salvador in July of 1969 this co-op fell apart completely, when more than half its members had to flee back to their homeland, El Salvador. What remained were the six subsections of the ANACH as cooperatives apart. All of them, with time and after great struggle and repression by the military authorities, who always favor the big cattlemen, got some land near their villages.

As for the two subsection co-ops that we organized in the municipality of Santa Rita, Plan Grande began to struggle for land but the members became discouraged after a frustrating year and a half without getting any land, and the co-op folded. In one town we had one of the best fights. Practically the whole village joined the co-op of the ANACH to try to get back some of the traditional village lands along the bank of the Cuyamapa River, lands that had been fenced in by the big landowner.

From the beginning he and his hired gunmen threatened to kill me and the leaders of the subsection co-op. He told the military authorities in Progreso that I was a communist stirring up the campesinos. Soldiers came to the village late one night with a list of all the leaders to take away as prisoners. They captured seven in their homes; another three fled the village and never returned. The ANACH got the lawyer, Rodolfo Jiménez, to defend the prisoners, who were accused of having killed one of the landowner's cows. After three weeks they were freed and returned to their village and to the fight. Now, however, the villagers were afraid, and many of them left the ANACH.

The thirty who continued the fight reached an agreement with INA. The landowner would have to give them 35 acres to plant some corn in the spring of 1967, while INA measured the lands of his title to see if he had fenced in an excess of several hundred acres as the ANACH claimed. The campesinos of the co-op sent word for me not to visit them anymore until they told me to, because he had a gunman hired to kill me if I entered the village.

After a few weeks I continued visiting this fine group of fighters, who at last saw something of a victory. INA got the landowner to grant them 120 acres, but without having measured his title to prove that his excess was more like *600 acres*. Before the coming of Sandoval as director, INA always made secret deals with the big landowners instead of carrying out the Agrarian Reform Law.

This co-op has always worked collectively. After a few years this co-op left the Co-op Plan of the ANACH and joined INA's FECORAH in order to become a legal entity and obtain a loan. In 1974 INA gave them more land for new members as a branch of their co-op, but in the Lower Aguán Valley Project in the Department of Colón. There they had crop failures every year because of floods, and in 1977 all of them returned to where they still have their 120 acres producing plantain.

The sad history of the five co-ops I helped organize during that period in Guanchías is more complicated, and I will tell that story later. I mention now only that all during their long and even bloody struggle to get some of the land that the Bográn family had acquired, they went right on studying cooperativism and saving their ten cents each week. The only one of the five co-ops, however, that was successful and still exists today is the Lourdes Co-op of Agua Blanca Sur. Their struggle was different from the war with the Bográns. The ANACH finally got them agrarian reform land close to their village, but with the INA pressure on all the co-ops to join its FECORAH if they wanted help, the Lourdes co-op also left the Cooperative Plan of the ANACH in 1968 and joined FECORAH. They wanted to become a legal entity and obtain a loan to plant 350 acres of plantain. A few years later, everyone in this region was planting sugar cane, and since their plantian gave them little profit, they, too, changed to sugar cane, which is what they still produce.

Besides Lourdes, Auxiliadora in Casiano, Suyapa in Morazán, and Las Mercedes in Toyos, another co-op that took the name of the Virgin Mary was the Agricultural Cooperative Fátima Limited, in Guacamaya (which no longer exists). The governmental promoters of the Office of Co-op Development and of INA started calling the co-ops that I organized the Guadalupanas. In the following years, from 1966 until I was finally deported from Honduras in 1979, I helped organize at least a hundred agricultural co-ops of the ANACH in the departments of Yoro and Colón, and about sixty consumer sections of co-op stores belonging to these co-ops.

To start these co-op stores and for collective agricultural projects of new co-op groups, I got permission from our mission superior to ask my family and friends in the United States for money to start a rotating fund for loans without interest. For example, in 1967 I lent $300 to the Las Mercedes Co-op of Toyos to start its consumer section, and ten years later this store was worth more than $8000. I taught them a simple bookkeeping system for control of the money, the goods bought, the sales to each member of the co-op, the distribution of the profits to them each year according to what each one had spent, and a monthly inventory. I learned all these things about cooperatives, book-keeping, and modern agricultural methods by doing them, but also I read a lot and visited practically all the other cooperative projects in the country.

In 1967, I could no longer personally visit the many cooperative groups as often as they needed (and still do all my parish apostolic work). I sought the help of my Christian Democratic friends in Tegucigalpa, who had founded an agency called the Association for Human Promotion. It was directed by Fernando Montes, and it organized all kinds of co-ops and gave loans and technical help, especially to the UNC, the National Campesino Union (which they helped organize and which has always followed the Christian Democratic ideology).

They were overjoyed to have an opening into Progreso in the north and sent Alfredo Landaverde to open, as co-director with me, a Center of Agricultural Services (CESA). From Father Joe Fisher, our new mission superior, we obtained the use of one of the big buildings of the Company Zone that was outside the zone along the railroad line and had a big storeroom. Landaverde may be a good politician of the Christian Democratic Party, but he is not so good as an administrator of a farming operation like CESA. However, besides Landaverde, the Association for Human Promotion sent us the American Peace Corps agronomist Vince Morabito and his wife, Jan, to work for two years in CESA. They turned out to be the best possible helpers for these new co-ops.

José Ayala of Toyos also worked with us in CESA (until the war in 1969) driving one of the two tractors that CESA had for plowing the land for the different cooperatives. CESA also helped the co-ops with modern farming education, bookkeeping, loans from the Association for Human Promotion, and marketing of their products. I went on organizing new co-op groups. The Morabitos ended their two years in 1969 and left us, and with the war and everything, CESA little by little disappeared. But it had been a great help during the critical years when we were organizing so many ANACH co-ops around Progreso and Morazán.

Now I will pick up again the thread of the history of the whole agrarian reform and of the campesino movement in Honduras. I

go back to the key problem in this history and in the metamorphosis of this revolutionary, which was the struggle of the
ANACH in the region of Guanchías in our parish of Progreso.

At the insistence of the ANACH, President López Arellano
ordered INA to mark the boundary between the Bográn lands and
the lands that Paz Barahona had decreed for family plots. The
Bográns appealed to the Supreme Court of Justice and, naturally,
the judges, all Nationalists and all big landowners, stopped
the measuring of these lands. Without doubt, they were under
pressure from the Standard Fruit Company, which wanted
Echeverry's bananas.

Meanwhile, to avoid bloodshed, INA and the ANACH made a
deal with the Bográns to let the three hundred campesinos of La
Mina, Guacamaya, and La Sarrosa use nine pasture fields for their
milpas. Since these fields were already full of campesinos (or else
were swamplands), about two hundred of these families could not
plant their milpas in 1966 and suffered famine. AID's solution was
to give them food through the ANACH.

For International Workers' Day, May 1, 1967, there was a big
rally of the FESITRANH labor unions, along with thousands of
campesinos of the ANACH, in San Pedro Sula. The ANACH
invited me to speak at this rally, and I denounced the great injustice of the rich landgrabbers in Guanchías and all over Honduras
who left thousands of campesinos without land to produce the
only food that their families could get. The next day in the rich
landowners' newspapers I was again accused of being an "agitator," and again the executive committee of the ANACH had to
publish a public pronouncement defending me.

For months now the hired gunmen of the rich landowners and
of the military security forces had been threatening the leaders
of all of the subsections of the ANACH in Guanchías, and they
always included me in their threats. Nevertheless, these leaders
continued their clamoring for the measurement of the lands decreed for family plots.

Meanwhile, Echeverry was not only hastily planting part of
these disputed lands with banana trees (protected by a squad of
armed soldiers under his orders), but he was even secretly buying more of the disputed land from the Bográns. The govern-

ment knew he was buying the land full of the corn and plantain crops of the campesinos of four villages (La 14, La 6, El 4 de Marzo, and El Socorro), but the ANACH did not know this.

On May 12, 1967, hired gunmen with the two military representatives in the village El 4 de Marzo, came to the house of Arcadia Luna, one of the leaders of the subsection of the ANACH in this village. While her whole family were sitting there eating supper, without warning, the gunmen suddenly opened fire on them, killing two of her grown sons and wounding her, her husband, and another son.

The next day we had the funeral mass for them in the church in Progreso with thousands of campesinos of the ANACH, and afterward a huge procession to the cemetery. Instead of frightening them, this brutal incident helped to strengthen the determination of these campesinos of Guanchías in their struggle, or rather in their war, to get a piece of land. We priests of Progreso never go to the cemetery for a burial (because we might have up to five funerals a day in our church), but for the first and last time in Honduras, I went to the cemetery with these companions killed in this war.

These same gunmen had threatened to kill me several times, and so the burial of these two young campesinos instead of me made an especially deep impression on me. I believe that this was one of the important moments in my metamorphosis as a revolutionary. Ever since the novitiate I have asked Christ for the grace to imitate him, even to martyrdom, to be killed for his cause. Now, with this funeral, I was completely sure that I wanted to give my life for the poor campesinos, so that no more of them would be killed in the class struggle. I strongly felt that Christ would grant me this great grace of being a martyr for the sake of justice. I felt completely committed to identifying myself with the campesinos in their fight for land.

In spite of the fact that many Jesuits criticized me, advised me, and even warned me that I had to stop taking part in these land problems, I was sure that Jesus wanted me to get even more involved, even unto death. I remember that I felt a real joy when the campesinos of the village of La Mina sent me word not to visit them because the Nationalist politician, a Mancha Brava gunman, was telling everyone that he was going to kill me. For answer, I went to La Mina, passing by his place just about every day to let him know that his threats would not deter me.

In June of 1967 the biggest battle of the war of the Guanchías between the rich and the poor broke out. The poor (and not only the men) were disposed to fight until death. I was astonished to see that it was the women who urged their husbands not to be afraid. These women, like lionesses defending their cubs, marched out ahead of the men with the flags of the republic and of the ANACH in all the operations that followed, against the rifles and bayonets of the soldiers of the rich.

I have a small file of documents and newspaper clippings about these events. A letter that I wrote on July 15, 1967, to the then military commander of the north coast, Colonel Melgar Castro, to the new director of INA, Rigoberto Sandoval, and to the president of the ANACH, Rolando Núñez, is a good summary of these events:

Dear Colonel Melgar, Licenciado R. Sandoval, and Rolando Núñez:

The peace of Christ be with you! Because Padre Tomás, the pastor of Progreso, and I are accused of having instigated the campesinos to invade properties, it seems necessary to write to you everything I know about the recent case of the Guanchías campesinos versus Arcesio Echeverry. According to what I have personally seen and what other witnesses have told me, this is the history.

Last month Echeverry sent machinery to level and plow up dozens of acres of land in front of the village La 14 that the villagers for many years have been using for their milpas. Echeverry also permitted Engineer Lúque to take down the fences and plow up more than 85 acres of small pasture fields, not belonging to rich cattlemen, but to poor campesinos of the village La 6. And finally, Echeverry also sent his tractors to plow up many acres that the villagers of El 4 de Marzo and El Socorro for many years have been using, and that were either already in crops or were ready for planting. I personally saw, along with other witnesses, that many crops had really been destroyed.

Céleo Gonzales of FESITRANH and Oscar Gale of SITRATERCO invited Padre Tomás and me to go with them and others in a commission to witness on June 26 the operation that about five hundred campesinos, from seven villages organized in the ANACH in Guanchías, were going to carry out: replanting the land belonging to the village of El Socorro that Echeverry had plowed up. During this planting a government commission finally arrived, which included Colonel Melgar. They held conversations with Echeverry's and Bográn's lawyers and with the executive committee of the ANACH and arrived at a provisional agreement that for now no one should continue plowing, or leveling, or planting in the land of El Socorro, La 14, and La 6.

I was told two days later, Thursday, that Echeverry had sent in his machinery again and was destroying more crops of the villagers of La 14. The campesinos told me they had decided to all go there to replant the corn in La 14 as they had done in El Socorro, because Echeverry had not kept his word to wait until the government commission arranged a definite solution to the problem. Once again they invited Padre Tomás and me to go simply as witnesses of what went on. I deny that I in any way instigated the campesinos or their leaders to any of these actions they have taken. On the contrary, Padre Tomás and I decided between ourselves not to even talk or pray with the campesinos gathered together for these actions. We did accompany them as witnesses, because it seems that very few public leaders around here want to help the campesinos when they are in danger. Well, Monday, July 10, we went to La 14 and saw that armed soldiers there kept their distance and didn't intervene while the two hundred campesinos replanted the land. But I personally saw this same day that simultaneously two big bulldozers and a tractor with plow continued their work of destroying the crops of the poor campesinos. I was convinced that Echeverry had broken the agreement.

I gave neither advice nor speeches to the campesinos about what actions they should take. I was simply there as a witness, the same as I was on Wednesday, July 12, along with Juventino Sandoval, who edits *El Sindicalista,* and with

Rolando Núñez, the president of the ANACH. And we were not the only witnesses; Rigoberto Sandoval, the director of INA, and Oscar Gale, the president of SITRATERCO, saw and took photos of the crops of La 14 that the campesinos had replanted on Monday and that were again being destroyed by plows on Wednesday.

I don't have any hatred toward the rich landowners, but I do have great love for the poor campesinos.

> Sincerely yours,
> (signed) Padre Guadalupe Carney, S.J.

Tom Quiery signed this note that was added on: "According to my knowledge the above letter truly describes the events."

The reason for writing this letter was that our superior received the following telegram, dated July 12 from the subdirector of INA in Tegucigalpa, Alejandro López Cantarero:

> The central office of this Agrarian Institute has reliable reports that, instigated by a priest of the parish of Progreso, the campesinos invaded the Farm La 14, property of Arcesio Echeverry, and planted corn in fields prepared for agriculture by his company. This violates the agreement made with the commission that recently visited that zone and seriously obstructs the negotiations that we are carrying on with the owners of these lands. To reach a satisfactory solution to this problem, we ask you to influence the campesinos to desist in their attitude and avoid any actions that could lead to situations that we would all lament.

Father Hogan, who was acting superior, called to caution me to lay off, but Quiery, the pastor, spelt out the facts as explained above. This same day I received a telegram calling me to the offices of INA in San Pedro Sula the next day. When I arrived, Randolfo Discua, the regional director of INA, took me to the Military Zone of San Pedro Sula to talk with Col. Juan Alberto Melgar Castro, the military commander of the north (and future president of the republic). He warned me not to continue involving myself in agrarian affairs, because I was a foreigner and a priest and the constitutions of the republic forbade these two classes of persons to take part in politics.

Well, thanks to the opportune intervention of the new director of INA, Rigoberto Sandoval, there were no further killings of campesinos for a while, and the rich capitalists entered into dialogue with INA to solve the problem. Everyone, rich and poor alike, looked at this newcomer as having dropped from heaven, and hoped that he would be the savior of Honduras, at least in the rural area.

This Honduran genius returned to his country in June of 1967 when the war of Guanchías between the rich and the poor was at its hottest. He was called by President López Arellano to be the cabinet minister for economic planning and, at the same time, director of INA. Sandoval had worked for seventeen years in different parts of the world with the FAO, the United Nations Organization for Agricultural Development, in his specialty, agrarian reform, but the previous year he had worked in Washington as an executive of IDB (Inter-American Development Bank).

What changed the picture of this war was, in the first place, the complete backing that Sandoval had from President López Arellano; second, that Sandoval personally went to the battlefields of Guanchías a number of times and, right there, talked to the campesinos, listened to them, and promised to solve their land problem for them; and third, his way of inspiring confidence in both the rich and the poor that he would solve the problems for the benefit of all.

However, he did not do it. After a month the campesinos saw that Echeverry continued to take away their lands and was again destroying their milpas in La 14. So on September 5, for the third time, the union of all the subsections of the ANACH in Guanchías, went out with the women in front with the flags. This time, with a platoon of soldiers with fixed bayonets threatening them, they pulled up the little banana trees that Echeverry had planted in the fields where he had destroyed their corn. They say that the soldiers, on receiving the order to fire in the air over the heads of the campesinos, refused to do so.

Almost all the Honduran soldiers are poor campesinos recruited by force for two years of military service. Would that all soldiers had enough class consciousness not to kill their brother and sister campesinos! But no, most soldiers are afraid to disobey the orders of an officer, even though it be to kill in cold blood.

Once again, Sandoval arrived on the scene of conflict and talked and listened with the campesinos out there in the fields of La 14. Once again, he managed to calm them down with promises.

In October of 1967, a poor cattleman, Alfredo Ramírez, was ambushed ("deer-hunted," as they say in Honduras) and shot to death as he was entering his pastures in La 6. Alfredo was a friend of mine who lived in Progreso, had a few cows, and belonged to the ANACH. A well-known gunman was captured and publicly confessed that the son of Arcesio Echeverry, Jaime, had paid him to kill Alfredo. Jaime was arrested, but within two days he was free again. Thanks to the influence of the rich landowning judges of the Supreme Court (of Injustice), he has never been punished. The campesinos of La 6 warned me that this Jaime Echeverry had hired gunmen to kill me, too.

Before all these massive actions of the ANACH, I had twice gone to the home of Arcesio Echeverry, who was an old man of eighty years and lived on one of his big banana farms near La Lima called Colombia. I asked him why he had destroyed the milpas of the poor campesinos. "You are already a millionaire," I told him. "Why do you want more, when these campesinos don't even have enough food for their families?" We talked a long while, but finally he told me flatly, "Guadalupe, for me the only god there is, is money. This is the all-powerful." What sadness I felt; how I prayed for this old fool who died a few years later (as I had told him he would) without being able to take his money with him!

During these months, Sandoval was having discussions with the Bográns and Echeverry to arrange for the government to buy some of the disputed land from them to give to the campesinos. Although he spoke to the ANACH leaders about giving out family plots in Guanchías, Sandoval knew this was not real agrarian reform and was secretly making plans to form his own organization of campesino cooperatives with collective production. He was even talking to the Standard Fruit Company about having these future campesino co-ops plant banana farms with the technical help and marketing of the Standard. He had already secretly sent the former president of the ANACH, Efrain Díaz Galeas, to Israel to study cooperativism for six months and then return to direct his new campesino organization.

Sandoval organized several high-level workshops on agrarian reform for the big landowners, labor union and campesino leaders, politicians, military officers, and religious. I attended two of these workshops and became quite friendly with Sandoval, whom I had met on the Guanchías battlegrounds. In a very wise campaign he was conscienticizing all these different classes of leaders so that they would all accept his plan for agrarian reform.

He finally revealed this plan as a system of big agro-industrial projects in Guanchías, in the Lower Aguan Valley, in the Lean Valley, in Baracoa, and so on, with campesino cooperatives on the idle lands that INA would buy from the big landowners with government bonds. These bonds could be redeemed after twenty years–or immediately, if the money was invested in industrial enterprises.

In January of 1968 Sandoval announced the final solution of the Guanchías problem with the purchase from Echeverry and the Bográns of a total of 8000 manzanas of land (about 14,000 acres: 800 manzanas, or 1400 acres, for El Socorro and El 4 de Marzo, and the rest close to Agua Blanca Sur). The newspapers acclaimed this a wonderful solution. Echeverry and the Bográns were happy because they kept all the lands they had grabbed, from Progreso to La Sarrosa and from the Santa Rita highway to the Ulúa River. But the poor campesinos of Arena Blanca, La Mina, Guacamaya, La Sarrosa, Urraco Sur, Balsamo, La 6, and La 14 had been deceived and were still without land.

The Paz Barahona decree for family plots was never carried out. These subsections of the ANACH, after many further struggles and other mass invasions of the Bográn lands and those of other big cattlemen of the region, have obtained small portions of bad land. It is all they have up to the present day. A big part of the Guanchías lands are now planted in ten banana farms belonging to Echeverry and his company and five banana farms belonging to agrarian reform campesino cooperatives. Since all this production goes to the Standard Fruit Company of San Francisco, California, the U.S. embassy and IDB, which lent the money for the project, are quite pleased with the "agrarian reform" in Guanchías. The Bográns continue to have thousands of acres in Guanchías for their cattle and, recently, for sugar cane.

The agrarian reform cooperatives of INA began when Efraín Díaz Galeas returned from Israel. Sandoval sent him to reorganize his old subsection cooperative Las Guanchías of the ANACH, which was planting corn in the abandoned Farm La 18 near Agua Blanca Sur. Efraín easily convinced his old companions to leave the ANACH and form the first co-op under INA, since INA promised them all these lands of La 18 to plant in bananas and a contract for marketing them with the Standard.

Efraín was elected president of the Agricultural Cooperative Las Guanchías Limited, and INA invested one million dollars in the rehabilitation of the three abandoned banana farms La 17, La 18, and La 19, including the system of irrigation. The Standard gave technical assistance, constructed two packing plants to box the bananas for export, and guaranteed a fixed price for each box of bananas.

Efraín Díaz did not limit himself to directing his own co-op but went around to different parts of the country, especially to other subsections of the ANACH, promising that INA would give them land and other help if they organized themselves as cooperatives under INA, as the cooperative Guanchías had done.

Sandoval also initiated PROCCARA (a Capacitation training program for campesinos), under the direction of a Brazilian agrarian reform expert, Clodimiro DeMorais, whom he had invited to Honduras. First, they formed a team of good "promoters" of cooperatives, who then went around giving intensive courses to the organized groups of campesinos about the advantages of collective cooperatives formed as big agro-industries. The thesis of DeMorais (another real genius like Sandoval) was that to form these big campesino agro-industrial co-ops that will transform the socio-economic structures of the country, the campesinos have to change their mentality.

In general, the campesinos have the individualistic mentality of artisans who perform by themselves all the operations of production: they prepare the ground, plant, cultivate, harvest, and sell the crop, all by themselves. To have a modern, efficient industry requires a division of labor: some workers drive the tractors, others plant, others irrigate, others are bookkeepers, others market the products, which requires a cooperative worker approach, not an artisan mentality. That is why DeMorais and Sandoval wisely chose the region of Guanchías to start these new agro-industrial co-ops, with the campesinos who were almost all former workers on the Tela Railroad Company banana farms and already had this proletarian, industrial mentality.

With just a little technical help from agronomists and engineers of the Standard, the Las Guanchías Co-op was soon producing bananas equal in quantity and quality to those of the Standard Fruit Company's own farms. The former banana workers knew perfectly well how to produce good bananas. On the lands INA bought from Bográn in Guanchías the Buenos Amigos Co-op was organized to plant bananas on the Farm La 15 (to do so, INA evicted a subsection of the ANACH from these lands). To plant bananas on the abandoned Farm La 16, the Agua Blanca Sur Co-op was organized. The Lourdes Co-op, which the ANACH and I organized, also received about 375 acres of this agrarian reform land for the production of bananas from their three farms. With a loan from INA, the Las Guanchías Co-op constructed their colony of one hundred modern, cement-block painted houses, all equally furnished with furniture, running water, inside bathroom, and television. This colony was to serve as a model for the other cooperatives.

With these first INA co-ops in Guanchías and some others that INA formed in Choluteca in 1969, FECORAH (the Federation of Agrarian Reform Cooperatives of Honduras) was organized, with, of course, Efraín Díaz as president, and with Benjamín Garméndia, a former member of the executive committee of the ANACH, as vice-president. They remained in these positions until 1980, when, at last, Efraín turned over the presidency to Garméndia, while he remained as "adviser" of FECORAH with a nice salary.

FECORAH has been the favorite offspring of Rigoberto Sandoval and INA, and also of all the military governments up to the present. Almost by force, the groups organized by the ANACH and the UNC had to pass over to FECORAH if they wanted to get land and help from INA for loans. The Nationalists and the military officers were afraid of the potential political power of the ANACH, and later of the Christian Democrats and the UNC, and wanted to weaken them. This fear was well founded, because in spite of losing many groups to FECORAH, the two organizations kept growing. Today the ANACH still claims around 80,000 members, the UNC, 35,000, and FECORAH, about 15,000.

DeMorais and many other "leftist" technical advisers brought in by Sandoval had to leave Honduras when he resigned as director of INA and left the country, disillusioned by the 1970 elections. However, PROCCARA continued giving courses for the formation of cooperative leaders and administrators. After the new coup in 1972, again by López Arellano, as I will explain later, DeMorais returned to Honduras with a new system of Associative Industries of Campesinos (EACs) instead of cooperatives, and a new kind of training course for changing the "artisanal mentality" of the campesinos, called experiential laboratories.

In these training courses, a whole group of campesinos is brought to one of the training centers of INA and left alone, so that they have to get themselves organized to obtain food, arrange for the cooking, cleaning, sleeping, instruction, and so on, for two weeks. This experience of working together collectively in an organized way turns out to be wonderful for the campesinos and helps change their individualistic mentality.

DeMorais and Sandoval were good friends of mine, and I went to see them in Tegucigalpa a number of times, especially with my complaints. I really liked their system of collective cooperatives and their training courses (in which I was often asked to give talks), but I did not agree with their work to weaken the ANACH and the UNC (which they always denied doing). Sandoval was the person who, at first, many of the rich and the poor wanted for president of the country. After three years of his "dictatorial" ways, the rich no longer cared for him, because he confiscated lands, and neither did the campesinos of the ANACH and the UNC, because they finally realized that he promised a lot, but everything went toward promoting FECORAH.

Only Reyes Rodríguez Arévalo, the continuous president of the ANACH, and some leadership of the ANACH, backed up

Sandoval. Arévalo wound up seeking the favor of the military authorities and of all the successive governments.

It is a shame that Reyes was co-opted by the military and the government. He was a great campesino leader when he started, with extraordinary courage for standing up against the rich land-owners and their gunmen. He never went to school even one day of his life, but he learned to read and write during six months that he spent in jail for his part in the agrarian conflicts of the ANACH in the Department of Santa Bárbara. A communist fellow prisoner taught him, he once told me.

I knew him from his very first days as the new president of the ANACH in 1968, when he could scarcely express himself during an interview with reporters and could hardly sign his name to documents. Within a couple of years, however, he could give a speech to stimulate the campesinos in a mass rally better than most university graduates. He had the gift of explaining things in the language of Honduran campesinos, and with examples directly from their lives.

I admired Reyes a lot, especially his courage; he was not afraid. What a shame that he so wanted to maintain himself in power! But I come back to this later.

13. Church and State Struggles

During all these years of the campesino struggles in Guanchías, I continued visiting the one hundred villages and camps I had, trying to form basic Christian communities in some of them. I have already explained that in 1965 our provincial held off my last vows in the Society of Jesus. Well, the following year he came to Honduras for his visitation and to talk to each Jesuit for what is called the manifestation of conscience.

When I spoke to him about my conflicts with some Jesuits on account of my antagonism toward the Jesuits as owners of the "luxurious" Company Zone, the provincial told me that he understood that my complaints were out of love for the Society and for the vow of poverty, and that I could take my final vows. Thus, on August 15, 1966, in the crowded Las Mercedes Church in Progreso, and with many Jesuits present, I promised, as a spiritual coadjutor in the Society of Jesus, to be poor, chaste, and obedient, like Jesus.

In those years there was much division and many disputes among us Jesuits of the Yoro Mission. Basically it was between us younger ones who wanted to put into practice the changes and modern teachings of the recently finished Vatican Council II and the old-timers, who either did not do much reading and were not familiar with the Vatican II documents or just plain wanted to continue in the old style of missionary apostolate that had worked for them.

This division was so acute that the provincial decided to send us a new superior who was not from the mission and who could reconcile and harmonize the two bands. He asked for everyone's opinion, and the majority chose Father Joseph Fisher, the former novice master, former rector of the theologate, and former provincial who, besides having a reputation as a conciliator, had always manifested his desire to be a missionary.

So, once again I had Joe Fisher as my superior. In 1968, I asked him for permission to become a Honduran citizen. He refused permission, saying that ever since I had been a novice I had always wanted to be different, that I thought I was better than the rest and was always criticizing the other Jesuits. As I reflected on this afterward, the Holy Spirit helped me recognize that Fisher was right!

My basic capital sin is pride. I ought to humble myself and be silent instead of criticizing the Jesuits and the bishops. The Spirit enlightened me to realize that I should not spend any more of my energy on these internal conflicts among Jesuits and within the Church. The tremendous problems of the world would never be solved primarily by the Church anyway, but by revolutionary political parties and the labor movement. I was brought to see that the role of the Church was to be present within these institutions as a Christ-like "leaven in the dough." This was the important thing for a Catholic to do, not waste time on internal disputes.

I was not the only rebellious one who had these conflicts with superiors and bishops, who generally have the mission of conserving the faith and the healthy customs and are chosen precisely because they are conservatives. In the whole world after Vatican II the Church was divided and in crisis—the progressives against the conservatives. Thousands of progressive priests and nuns abandoned the fight to change the Church and left their ministries. But you cannot do much to change an institution from without. I clearly understood the importance of the Catholic church in Latin America. There cannot be a new society here without a new Church, because most Latin Americans are Catholics. There has to be a revolution in society as a whole, and also a revolution in the Catholic church.

Therefore, in spite of what I said about not wasting energy on fighting with superiors and bishops, I do have to help make the revolution within the Church, to make the Church once again like that of the first Christians. However, this will not be accomplished by the conversion of the bishops but at the base of the Church. As a matter of fact, the Holy Spirit is already forming the new Church in Honduras, the Church of the poor, the basic Christian communities (BCCs) in the villages. This new Church is involved in the popular organizations for the political fight for liberation, with the Delegates of the Word as its vanguard.

This is not taking place only in Honduras; in all Latin America the new "Church that is born of the people" is in gestation. In 1968 delegations of all the bishops of Latin America met in Medellín, Colombia, and their "Conclusions," which were approved by Pope Paul VI, are impregnated with the theology of liberation. The bishops, moved (at last) by the Holy Spirit, expressed in great measure what the Church of the poor, the basic Christian communities, are thinking and doing for their liberation. These documents repeatedly state that Christ came into this world "for the liberation of the oppressed" (as Jesus himself declared in Luke 4:18). He came to transform this world into the Kingdom of God, to take away the sin of the world, which is the injustice, the poverty, the ignorance, the "institutionalized violence," and the "economic neocolonialism."

The ideological line of Medellín was that of the Christian Democrats, of "a third way," neither capitalism nor communism. "The liberal capitalist system and the temptation of the Marxist system seem to be the only alternatives in our continent for transforming the economic structures. Both systems are against the dignity of the human person," wrote the bishops in paragraph 10 of their document "Justice."

The bishops clearly stated that the evangelizing role of the Church in Latin America includes the conscientization and the promotion of popular organizations of the marginated and exploited masses. They spoke of the necessity of a complete reformation of the educational system, so that it will provide a liberating education that helps youth, and also adults, to develop a critical consciousness of the unjust economic-social-political reality in which they live. They also opted for a new way of organizing the parish similar to the basic Christian community, with new ministries for laypersons like Delegates of the Word (which by then were being formed all over Latin America).

This blessing by the bishops in Medellín of liberation theology opened the doors for the Christian revolutionary movement. It also was a big stimulus for the Christian Democratic political movement in all of Latin America. Several different teams of priests under CELAM (the Latin American Episcopal Conference) came to Honduras to give courses on liberation theology. I attended one of these directed by two Colombian Jesuits that, together with my personal study of Gustavo Gutierrez's book, *A Theology of Liberation*, deepened in me the conviction that this is the theological line of Christ's gospel, the "good news for the poor."

It confirmed in me what I had already experienced: that theology is not studied, as we did at Saint Mary's, Kansas, but is rather "done," as we were doing it with the campesinos, especially with the Delegates of the Word in the villages that were fighting for land. First comes the "praxis," the practice, the living of the Christian life by working for the liberation of the oppressed. This is the only efficacious way of loving the poor. Only then can one "do" theology, reflecting on this praxis under the light of the gospel, the Word of God.

Those who are not committed to this dangerous work for the liberation of the oppressed cannot even understand liberation theology, as is the case with most bishops, priests, nuns, and lay-people in the United States and Europe. The bishops and priests of Latin America, Africa, and Asia who are committed to the governments and to the capitalist exploiters, not only cannot understand it, but use every means in their power to suppress it. CELAM today is controlled by conservative bishops who actually persecute the best theologians of Latin America and direct a strong campaign to exclude the teaching of the "Conclusions of Medellín" in our countries. Many bishops repent of having signed these documents, which have inspired to a great extent the Christian revolutionary movement that exists in all the countries, not only of Latin America, but of the whole third world.

In Honduras the bishops returned from Medellín with great enthusiasm, permitted those courses on liberation theology, and even brought Father Beltrán to help organize a national pastoral plan for conscienticizing the campesinos and promoting their integral development through the Church's training centers and the Radio Schools. A few years later, however, all the bishops of Honduras were filled with a great fear of violent revolution and communism, and they started marching backward to such an extent that last year (1980) they even forbade the "preaching" in Honduras of Dr. Enrique Dussel. He is the most famous historian of the Latin-American Church (a great Catholic layman), who was invited by the Conference of Religious to give them a talk at their annual assembly.

Right after Medellín most of the Church's campesino training centers, which existed in practically every department of the country, did a fine job of conscienticizing the campesinos by means of short, three- to five-day courses for the Delegates, catechists, and other campesinos. Also, the centers were lent to the Radio Schools for the formation of their Monitors, or to the UNC for the formation of its leaders, usually with the help of a priest. The executive committee of the ANACH was afraid of these training centers of the Church because they knew they were all controlled, including La Fragua in Progreso, by teachers who belonged to the Christian Democratic Party and wanted to promote the UNC instead of the ANACH. Because I helped to organize just about all the villages of Progreso in the ANACH, the UNC had no entrance there until later on when I moved out of the parish. This was true even though the Christian Democratic professor Roberto Vallejo was the subdirector of our Center La Fragua under Father Wade.

In this year of 1968, our superior, Joe Fisher, with the help of Father Phil Pick, who had been superior of the Jesuits in Belize and was an expert radio technician, arranged for the buying of Radio Progreso, with its frequency, from a local family. Thousands of dollars were then spent to install a strong transmitter for shortwave and medium wave broadcasts, which Phil brought from the United States and personally put together, piece by piece, in our Instituto San José. Father Jerry Tolle was named director of the station, and Phil Pick, technician, and Radio Progreso, "The Voice of a Marching People," began to broadcast with great success. Jarrell Wade had a good program of La Fragua ("The Forge") each night for the campesinos called "Molding a People."

I did not agree that the Jesuits should be the owners of one of the most powerful radio stations in Honduras. I suggested that we get the radio but give it away to the ANACH, with an arrangement to have some programs from the parish each day. Naturally, no Jesuit agreed with me. Some Jesuits already had me catalogued as half-crazy, and others believed the rich landowners who called me a communist. Thanks to the good team we had in the parish, with Tom Quiery and the Franciscan sisters always defending me, I was able to stay at Progreso.

The last day of March in 1968 was the first attempt at elections in the country since the military takeover of the government in 1963. The election was for mayors and other municipal authorities. Since the Nationalists along with the military officers, controlled all the positions of authority in the country, they thought they could easily control the "show" of democratic elections for the sake of international public opinion.

During the days immediately preceding the elections, I was a witness to the reign of terror unleashed in all the villages and banana camps of Progreso (and other priests told me it was the same all over the country). Bands of twenty or thirty armed men, some civilians and some uniformed soldiers, most of them drunk, went around at midnight from house to house of the Liberals, waking them up with shots in the air and demanding that they hand over their voting credentials. Many persons were beaten, some received machete (knife) wounds, and in Urraco Pueblo and in Toyos two poor campesinos of the Liberal Party who refused to hand over the credentials that gave them the right to vote were killed in cold blood.

I went to Toyos early in the morning just after they killed Fermín Alvarenga, a Legionary and member of our Las Mercedes Co-op. This poor campesino had tried to run away when they broke down the door of his house. I saw the body of my friend Fermín still lying in a pool of blood alongside the creek where he was murdered by a shot in the back. The women told me that they saw the gang of drunken armed men arrive at Toyos in the car of the Nationalist candidate for mayor of Progreso. They heard the shots and shouts of, "Hand over your voting card or your life."

In the village of Guaymitas, a bureaucrat went around, armed with a small machine gun and a gang, and took away the voting credentials from the Liberals. We Jesuits of Progreso made an investigation of all these outrageous happenings, which we sent to the American ambassador in Tegucigalpa. In my file I have a copy of this report that Wade wrote up for us. All the Jesuits, without exception, acted in complete union and agreement with Wade's report.

The day before the elections, several different commissions of the Liberal Party in Progreso, which had always held the majority in this municipality and would easily win in any free elections, visited our superior to ask for our help in avoiding a possible massacre. They said that the Nationalists with the army had hundreds of men and women armed in their paramilitary force, called the Mancha Brava ("the Angry Mob"), to impede the Liberals from voting. They planned to steal the voting boxes before the final counting and fill them with false votes. The Liberal Party asked that the priests and nuns be present at the polling places just to be witnesses of the events—and maybe stop a massacre by our presence.

Early on election day, all the Jesuits and all the Franciscan, Crusader, and Notre Dame sisters met and agreed to divide up and be present at all the voting stations. We priests decided to wear our long white cassocks for the first time in several years. In spite of the bands of soldiers and Nationalist gunmen in the streets, on the highways, and at all the entrances to Progreso trying to intimidate the Liberals into handing over their voting credentials and returning home without voting, by late afternoon it was clear that a large number of Liberals did vote and would probably win the election.

Some of the Nationalists actually told us afterward that our presence spoiled their plan to steal the voting boxes and fill them with false votes. The Nationalist congressman from Progreso, was obviously the one who was directing the soldiers and Mancha Brava in their fruitless efforts to scare us so that we would go home. They even hit one of the priests. At one point, a big group of Liberal campesinos surrounded me to protect me. They said that gunmen were looking for an opportunity to shoot me during the confusion. I really enjoyed hearing Jarrell Wade shout at the Congressman, "If you don't get these soldiers and the Mancha Brava out of here, we're going to scratch you off the list of the baptized Catholics."

The Liberals won in Progreso and in San Pedro Sula, but in very few other municipalities, and the armed forces and the Nationalists still really ran the whole country. This was so true that, after a few months, the Nationalist candidate was even "named" mayor of Progreso. The American embassy was officially invited to watch over the honesty of the election, but they never said a word about this, nor did they acknowledge our report from Progreso. "This," the campesinos told me, "was a typical Honduran-style election."

In the parish of Progreso I never had a dull or boring moment; something interesting was always going on. In this same year, 1968, it was my turn to go to the States again to visit my family. I went free on a United Fruit Company banana ship from Puerto Cortés to New York this time. So I first visited my sister and her family in Massachusetts and then each of the rest of the family, ending up in Saint Louis with my mother. I returned to Honduras by airplane on September 14. I have this date exactly, because in my file I kept a copy of a declaration I made for the U.S. ambassador, Joseph Jova, about all the events of the following days.

On September 19, 1968, a nationwide general strike took place in Honduras, called by the CTH (Confederation of Honduran Workers) in agreement with many big industrialists of the progressive wing of the Liberal Party. It was called in protest against a new law imposing more taxes on all items of popular consumption. The military-Nationalist government put out this decree in spite of the general discontent of the people and the threats of such a strike. All the unions in the country, including the ANACH, all the other popular organizations—of women, of students, and so on—the university, and many progressive professional and business people agreed on the general strike, and September 19 dawned with industry, business, and transportation closed down in the whole country.

With astonishment I analyzed afterward how the Honduran military apparatus and the police force could, in just one day, decapitate all the organizations that backed up the strike by calling a state of siege. They captured about five hundred worker, campesino, and student leaders, and also industrialist political opponents–practically all the leaders of the movement. A few of the rich political opponents, like Edmond Bográn, fled the country the day before, without doubt having been warned by a military friend what would happen. Céleo Gonzales of FESITRANH, a great friend of the president, General López Arellano, was arrested along with all the top leaders of SITRATERCO and of the ANACH. The strike ended the following day, and four days later all these leaders were freed, except those whom DIN (Department of National Investigation, the secret police) had in their files as "communists" and for a long time had been looking for a pretext to throw in jail.

Since I had been out of the country, I only heard about the threats of a general strike from the newspapers. In the five days after my return to the parish I was not at any meetings about the strike. On the nineteenth, after the 6:00 A.M. mass, three civilian gunmen of DIN in Progreso saw me out in front of the church and handed me a letter from the civil judge of Progreso. The letter informed me of the state of siege and ordered me to report to the judge's office at 9:00 A.M. Wade went with me for this date with the judge, who told me that they had proof that I had participated in the planning of the strike and had encouraged the workers of Progreso to back up this strike, which the government had declared illegal. He told me that I was forbidden to leave the city or have any kind of meetings during the thirty-day state of siege.

I immediately informed our superior, Joe Fisher, and the pastor, Tom Quiery, who decided that if we could not have any meetings or masses, they would close the church of Progreso in protest.

Father Ramón Alberdi happened to be visiting us in the parish rectory for a few days, having brought money and a new little Volkswagon car for the Crusader sisters and their new Women's Training School in Progreso. You will recall that Alberdi had been pastor with me before Quiery and had had to leave Honduras and the Jesuits because of conflicts with conservative religious superiors. It was only a coincidence—or such is the providence of God—that he and I, the only two priests on the list of "communists" in the files of the DIN (the secret police), had returned to Progreso almost simultaneously a few days before the big general strike.

At 10:00 P.M. that same nineteenth of September, a dozen armed agents of the DIN, dressed in civilian clothes, demanded that we open the door of the rectory. They told Alberdi and me that we were to go with them immediately to talk to the head of the DIN in San Pedro Sula, Lt. Hubert Bodden. They promised to bring us back to sleep in the rectory that very same night. We did not want to go, because they brought no orders in writing, but they insisted that such was the law under the state of siege. They told us not to take clothes or anything with us, because we would soon be back.

They put us into a car with four of them, and we took off for San Pedro Sula. Quiery and Wade tried to follow us in the parish jeep to see where we were being taken, but some soldiers at the bridge across the Ulúa River would not let them pass. Alberdi whispered in my ear that they were going to kill us. This idea filled me with great joy; I was invaded by such a profound spiritual consolation that I paid practically no attention to anything else that happened that night.

Alberdi was trying to convince the agents of the DIN in the car that it was a mistake. Didn't they know who he was? He feared that they were going to kill us. The thought of being a prisoner for Christ and maybe a martyr for the sake of justice gave me great interior peace. I looked on these agents as benefactors who were going to give us the greatest prize of all: martyrdom. I felt affection for these instruments of God.

We were taken to the big penitentiary of San Pedro Sula and put into a cell full of men. They told us that they would soon take us to talk to Lieutenant Bodden. Alberdi recognized a rich businessman from San Pedro Sula, a local dentist, and other Liberal political leaders. I lay down on the filthy cement floor but could not get to sleep because of the joy I felt at being a prisoner. I was very united with Christ that whole night, feeling his presence.

About 2:00 A.M. the same DIN agents took Alberdi and me to the office building of the DIN in the center of San Pedro Sula and locked us in a room with some prostitutes and drunks, telling us that we would soon talk with Lieutenant Bodden. Well, we never talked to him.

I had just fallen asleep on the dirty floor when four soldiers came at 5:00 A.M. to take us out. They put us in the back of an open truck with them guarding us, and we took off for Santa Rosa de Copán. We really felt the cold in those mountains, because we had left warm Progreso with just short-sleeved shirts.

In the army headquarters of Colonel Alvarado in Santa Rosa

de Copán we asked to be allowed to talk with the bishop of Santa Rosa, José Carranza. They called him by telephone, and he brought us some lunch. He said that the colonel had informed him that we were being expelled from the country as "subversive agitators" who had helped instigate the general strike. This was the first accusation we had heard. Bishop Carranza promised to inform the Jesuits and Archbishop Santos of Tegucigalpa.

Again, we were put on the truck, to go to Ocotopeque close to the two borders of El Salvador and Guatemala. Alberdi told the military commander that if we were going to be deported they should send him immediately to San Salvador because he had his Spanish passport with him. I had no document of identification with me whatsoever, having left our priests' rectory with just the clothes on my back and six lempiras ($3) in my pocket. They agreed to get rid of Alberdi, and an officer took him to the border of El Salvador.

The plan for me, they said, was to send me to Guatemala, but not until my passport arrived, which they were asking for by radio. The soldiers in the military camp of Ocotopeque, where I was held prisoner, treated me very well and let me sleep in the bed of a sergeant who was on leave. The next day, however, September 21, an officer told me he had orders to deport me immediately without my documents, leaving me on the border in Guatemala.

On the way to the border, he confided to me that he was a good Catholic and was going to take me to the town of Esquipulas in Guatemala. He would leave me with the American Benedictine priests there, because the Honduran army had informed the Mano Blanca, an anticommunist paramilitary group in Guatemala, that they were sending them a "communist" priest. I thanked him, and many times since then I have prayed to God for this honest soldier.

The Benedictines in Esquipulas received me with great hospitality, and that night I slept very well. I had the idea of waiting for my documents and clothes from Progreso, which the lieutenant promised to send me, and then going to Belize, where I had many Jesuit friends from the Missouri Province. However, the next day at 6:00 A.M. two soldiers from the Honduran Immigration Office came looking for me with the news that I could return to Honduras with them, if I so wanted. With tears in my eyes I told them, "With great pleasure, for I want to live and die in Honduras."

The army commander of Ocotopeque told me that the American ambassador had arranged with President López Arellano for me to return by plane to Tegucigalpa under his responsibility. I remained again a prisoner in the quarters of the soldiers, who treated me very well, sharing their food with me and giving me a bed in their dormitory. The whole day, the twenty-second, we waited for the airplane, which never came; the twenty-third was the same. The American Capuchins from the parish of Ocotopeque came to the soldiers' quarters to visit me, and the pastor, Father Rod Brennan, who was a friend of mine, asked the commander to let me sleep with them that night in the parish. This request was granted. The next day, the twenty-fourth, the small plane of the American embassy arrived, at last, and took me to Tegucigalpa.

I was taken to the luxurious residence of Ambassador Jova, where I ate lunch with him and his wife and related to them my experiences. He told me that as soon as he learned of my capture, through a telephone call from Father Fisher, he immediately called Archbishop Santos and President López Arellano to find out why and to demand my return. They cannot expel an American citizen from a country without a public trial giving the person the opportunity to defend himself against the accusations.

The ambassador gave me a photocopy of the declarations of two false witnesses before the civil judge of Progreso. They said that they were workers of the Tela Railroad Company and that I had talked to them early on September 19 in Progreso, as they were going to their customary jobs, and encouraged them to join the strike and not work. This was the only "proof" they had that I had "instigated the strike," and it was false.

With a secretary of the embassy I made a long public declaration of my activities, not only for the days since my return from vacation in the States, but also of my activities with the ANACH and with the farm co-ops. I included an explanation of the necessity for accelerating the agrarian reform to give land to the campesinos. I pointed out that the lack of a place to work was the cause of the misery in which the mass of campesino families live, and also the cause of the social uprisings in the countryside. Copies of this were sent to the president of the republic, to the archbishop, to my superior, Joe Fisher, and to the head of the DIN, who later in the day informed me that I was still under arrest while my case was under investigation.

I was to remain in the custody of Archbishop Santos, with the city of Tegucigalpa as my jail. The archbishop did not even let me have an interview with him. By telephone he told me that I was to remain at Centro Loyola, our Jesuit house in Tegucigalpa, until he told me I could leave, and that I definitely would not be able to return to work in Progreso. Certainly that is just what his rich landowner and military friends were asking of him. What a shame he does not listen to the poor!

In Progreso ever since the day of our capture, the Las Mercedes parish church had been closed, with a big sign on the main door that read,

> THE CHURCH IS CLOSED IN PROTEST.
> THERE ARE NO RELIGIOUS FUNCTIONS.
>
> We protest the kidnapping of two Catholic priests by the authorities late at night on September 19.
> It was signed, "The Parish Team" and, "The Jesuit Fathers."

There was an awful lot of publicity in the newspapers about this, not only in Honduras, but internationally. Alberdi, as soon as he reached San Salvador, gave an interview to *La Prensa Gráfica;* Tom Quiery sent articles to a number of newspapers in the United States defending me.

In my file I have a letter from the campesinos of Morazán, Yoro, to the newspapers (which was never published). I would like to have shown it to Archbishop Santos in those days so that he could hear the voice of the people, not just that of the rich. In part, it said the following:

A sad and painful day was September 19 when we heard the news of the capture and expulsion from Honduras of our Padre Guadalupe. We are 40 Monitors of the Radio Schools, 150 members of the Suyapa Agricultural Cooperative, 93 members of the Legion of Mary, 45 Delegates of the Word of God, and hundreds of other Christians of Morazán, Yoro, who sign this protest. His politics is that the campesino who is supposed to be a leader, like a Monitor, Delegate of the Word, Legionary, or member of a co-op must be a good, honest, responsible man, a real Christian son of God. . . .

We are thousands of Christians who back up Padre Guadalupe in his tireless work as an apostle of Christ. We ask ourselves: Where are we going? Isn't this a Christian, democratic country? Why do they treat a minister of God with such barbarity, as if this were a communist country where they despise those who preach the doctrine of Christ?

The co-ops around Progreso and the executive committees of the ANACH and SITRATERCO all sent protests against my expulsion to General López Arellano and to the press, demanding my immediate reassignment to my cooperative work in Progreso. The day after my capture the Jesuits called Ambassador Jova and Archbishop Santos, asking them to speak to the president of the republic to rectify this injustice. Jova did do so, but I do not know if the archbishop spoke to the president or not. Father George Prendergast of Centro Loyola sent the following communication to Archbishop Santos on September 21:

DECLARATION OF THE JESUITS OF THE MISSION OF YORO asking for the intervention and support of the very Reverend Archbishop of Tegucigalpa, your Excellency Hector Enrique Santos, in the case of Padre Guadalupe Carney, S.J., assistant pastor of the parish of Las Mercedes in Progreso.

On Thursday, September 19, 1968, at 10:30 P.M., Padre Guadalupe was taken from the parish rectory by agents of the DIN without any explanation. Since that time we have had no communication with him.

Therefore, the Jesuits of the Yoro Mission beg of your Excellency, for the sake of the country, of the people, of the Church, and of Padre Guadalupe and all those others who are so treated, that a strong protest be made to the government of Honduras, and at the same time a demand for an explanation from the government for the strange treatment given to our fellow priest, and finally for his prompt return to the parish rectory of Progreso. Meanwhile, we have closed the church in Progreso and suspended all public parochial functions.

With a sincere expression of our deep respect for you, and our hope for a rapid and satisfactory solution, we remain as always, The Jesuits of the Yoro Mission of the Archdiocese of Tegucigalpa.
(signed) George Prendergast, S.J., Secretary.

Two weeks later, while I was still a prisoner in Centro Loyola, Fathers Prestera and Amador handed over the following declaration to Archbishop Santos and to the newspapers. It was signed by twenty-six priests.

We priests of the Archdiocese of Tegucigalpa make this declaration of solidarity in conformity with the resolution made in our monthly meeting in the Major Seminary on October 8, 1968:
We want to give testimony of our solidarity with our brother-priests, Guadalupe Carney and Ramón Alberdi, who unjustly suffered in their own person and in their priestly dignity. We priests have felt this injustice as done to all of us, because we share the conviction that an attack against any priest automatically wounds the whole priestly community. We want our Christian people to know that the clergy is solidly united.

During the whole month that the state of siege lasted and that I was confined to Centro Loyola, the archbishop insisted to the Jesuits that I could not return to Progreso, that our superior should send me to some other parish. At last, Joe Fisher convinced the archbishop to let me return to Progreso when the state of siege was over, and there the Jesuits, in consultation, would decide where I should work.

It so happened that the Association for Human Promotion, under its director Fernando Montes, was also putting a lot of pressure on Archbishop Santos and on the Jesuits to let me return to Progreso. If I did not, then not only CESA (the Center for Agricultural Services for the co-ops around Progreso) would fall through, but also the big project with Misereor (of the German bishops), half a million lempiras ($350,000) for an agricultural school near Progreso to train the campesinos of the

ANACH co-ops. Representatives of Misereor had come to Honduras several times to talk to me, to the Association for Human Promotion, to Father Fisher, and to the ANACH about this project. The school would not belong to the Jesuits; we asked for it for the ANACH, under the direction of CESA. If I did not return to help the co-ops and CESA, this agricultural school would most certainly not be approved by Misereor.

Meanwhile, right from the beginning, I was very uncomfortable enclosed in Centro Loyola without knowing anything about the campesino leaders of the co-ops or the leaders of the ANACH and SITRATERCO who had also been arrested that same night. After a week of uncertainty, I decided to go secretly to La Lima to look for Oscar Gale (the president of SITRATERCO) in his home, since the newspapers said that he had been freed. I knew that there was always a DIN agent watching Centro Loyola from the gas station across the street, but it was easy for me to slip out the back door at 4:00 A.M. one day and, without passing by the gas station, walk down to the center of Tegucigalpa, catch a bus to Toncontin Airport, buy a ticket, and get on the 6:30 A.M. plane for San Pedro Sula, close to La Lima.

From the airport I walked to Oscar's home in the SITRATERCO colony just in time to eat breakfast with him and his family. I called Tom Quiery in Progreso, and he and Wade came to La Lima to see me and tell me how things were in Progreso and with its aldeas and co-ops. I stayed in Oscar's house for two days, coming to know him and his family very well. On the third day I returned to Centro Loyola in Tegucigalpa in exactly the same way I had left.

After the month of state of siege was up and I could return openly to Progreso, I had the happiness of reunions with the Jesuits, the campesinos, and the rest of the people of our parish. Joe Fisher informed me that they had decided to let me continue my work in Progreso so that they would not lose the projects already started for the campesinos, and to get the grant of money from Misereor for the agricultural school. There was no lack of advice, however, from him and other Jesuits that I should not get involved anymore in these conflicts, which caused a lot of problems for all of them. They told me that I liked to criticize them, but then afterward expected their solidarity and support. I admitted that they were right, and thanked them for their solidarity.

After having undergone imprisonment and deportation for my connection with the ANACH and SITRATERCO, I was now treated with more confidence by all the worker and campesino leaders. Before, many of them had had their doubts about me because I was a gringo, especially the leftist leaders, who were antiimperialist, antigringo, and anticlerical (I have already told of the experience of the labor leaders with the gringo priests at the time of the big strike of the banana workers in 1954). Now they accepted me as one of them, in spite of my being a priest and a gringo.

The labor unions, the co-ops, and in general all the organizations now invited me more often to give talks in their training courses and in their assemblies. Even the UNC, FECORAH, and INA invited me, though I was always identified with the ANACH. Each September 29 the ANACH held its convention, with representatives from all the subsections in the country. The inauguration of the convention was very solemn, with speeches transmitted over the radio by top government and labor personalities. I was always invited to start it off with an invocation to God.

More and more the executive committee of the ANACH, with Reyes Rodríguez Arévalo as perennial president, invited me to its meetings and study workshops. In those years I was studying the ideology of the Christian Democrats in the books of Lebret and Mounier. I read about the ideology and the strategy of the UNC, its vision of changing the capitalist system of exploitation for a New Society, and compared it with that of the ANACH, which was simply to fight for the immediate needs of the campesinos for land, loans, schools, roads.

In practically all the meetings of the leaders of the ANACH I would repeat that the ANACH had no ideology, that it was like the *babosa*, the worm that damages their bean crop each year. The babosa is fat, I told them, and appears to be very strong, but just smash it under your shoe and you see that it is practically all water, no bones, no skeleton. That is just like the ANACH, I said, which appears to be big and strong, but is really just water, without a backbone, without a clear ideology, easy to destroy.

14. A Tragic War

In July of 1969 occurred the saddest chapter in the modern history of Honduras: the war with El Salvador. I was visiting all my villages and camps again, and with CESA was organizing and bettering the collective farm co-ops and their consumer stores. The agricultural school project had been delayed but was practically ready, when the war broke out. Because of the war, CESA slowly disappeared. Thank God we had not started the agricultural school, because it was CESA that was supposed to direct and administer it.

In my file I have some notes and letters that can help me relate the history of this stupid war between the two most brother-like countries in the world, which the international press called "the football war." Honduras is an underpopulated country of 112,088 square kilometers and, in 1969, with 2.5 million inhabitants; El Salvador, on the southwestern border of Honduras, had only 20,935 square kilometers and more than 4 million inhabitants, the majority of which are poor campesinos without land.

The infamous fourteen rich families of El Salvador own most of the industry and good land in El Salvador and always control the government and the armed forces. Instead of promoting land reform or more industry to give work to the masses and to develop the country, *they prefer to leave the campesinos unemployed in order to have them available as cheap laborers for their coffee and sugar cane harvests. They say the campesinos should go to Honduras if they want land.*

Thousands upon thousands of Salvadoran campesinos, the poorest, crossed over the border in the years after World War II to look for a living in Honduras. Many of them married Hondurans. Most of the immigrants had no documents or legal residence papers, but had sneaked across the border through the mountains, and spread out into the villages and mountains of Honduras, especially along the north coast.

I have already mentioned that many of our best Legionaries and Delegates of the Word in our parish were Salvadorans. Half of the 120 members of the Las Mercedes Co-op of Toyos and of the 150 members of the Suyapa Co-op of Morazán were Salvadorans. When I was hearing confessions of the campesinos, I could immediately tell which ones were Salvadorans, because they knew how to pray and how to go to confession. Few Hondurans in our parish did. In El Salvador there are more priests and nuns than in Honduras, and the majority of them are natives of the country.

In 1969 it is calculated that there were at least two-hundred thousand Salvadorans living illegally in Honduras. In our parish about 25 percent of the people were Salvadorans. This, of course, increased the pressure for land. For many years the big landowners had been demanding that the government expel all these undocumented Salvadorans. The Agrarian Reform Law of 1962, in Article 68, stipulates that only native-born Hondurans can use national land or be subjects of the agrarian reform.

In order to explain some events that few historians know about, and that pertain to the immediate causes, or rather, *excuses* for the war, I am copying here a letter that I wrote to the director of INA on June 10, 1969, one month before the start of the war:

Dear Licenciado Rigoberto Sandoval,

Because of our friendship and mutual confidence, I want to describe for you a little more of the sad situation in Guanchías. All the people in the villages there, Hondurans as well as Salvadorans, feel threatened and afraid because of what INA did in Guacamaya. It was very ugly to throw human beings, our brothers and sisters, out onto the street, taking away their houses after only four days' notice. After talking to you last Friday, I thought you were going to pull the soldiers out. But I have been told that Saturday and Sunday they went around threatening to burn down the homes of those who had not left yet. They even told a poor, sick woman, who just a few days before had given birth to her baby, that they would throw her out if she did not leave immediately. A number of families could not sell their

houses and had to leave for El Salvador without a cent in
their pockets. Others sold their homes and their coffee or
plantain plantations for ridiculously low prices. There are
new people now living in these houses in Guacamaya, who
bought them to see if they too could get some agrarian reform land. A manager of INA, accompanied by five armed
soldiers, talked to the poor Salvadorans as though he was
one of the soldiers (who have become like brutes that have
no respect for other human persons). No Christian would
treat other persons as if they were cattle to be moved.

I have read articles in the Honduran newspapers, and
even some by INA, fomenting hatred against the Salvadorans who are in Honduras. A Christian must love his neighbor as a brother. Only racists, Nazis, or the Ku Klux Klan
foment hatred against those who are not of their same race
or nation. I know that you do not have this hatred, but
haven't you noticed how this hatred against Salvadorans is
being fomented now in Honduras? Please help Christ to get
rid of all hatred and put love into the hearts of the Hondurans.

I was told about another thing that is doing a lot of harm
in Guacamaya. The soldiers told the Salvadorans that they
had to leave their lands because these were to be given to
the cooperative. So many people are now saying that it is the
Fátima Cooperative, which I helped to found, that is to
blame for their losing their homes and lands. Thus hatred
and animosity are being fomented against cooperativism.

After these preliminary comments, which I hope you
won't interpret wrongly, I want to ask you to consider, if the
Salvadorans have to be evicted from the other villages, how
it can be done with more respect for their human rights.
You could give them notice in a personal letter that, after
they harvest their spring crop, in October they will have to
abandon the region of Guanchías, and therefore that they
should sell their home and the lot it is on. The letter to
those of Guacamaya only told them they had to turn over
their farmlands, without saying anything about leaving the
village. Most of the Salvadorans of the other villages have
not received any notice to move out, and so have already

planted their milpas. I beg you to let them reap their harvest.

I have the firm conviction that a more just social-economic order won't be accomplished by force and injustice, but by solving the problems with the Spirit of Christ. And I trust that this is your conviction also; that is why I have dared to write you so frankly and sincerely. I want to be your friend and help you make an agrarian reform really integral and Christian.

Your friend in Christ,
(signed) Padre Guadalupe

Most of the seventy Salvadoran families from Guacamaya fled back to their homeland and told what had happened to them. The newspapers and radios of El Salvador exaggerated these injustices, saying that the Honduran soldiers were going to burn down the homes of all the Salvadorans in Honduras and, in this way, incited hatred in the Salvadorans. When the thousands of Honduran fans reached the stadium in San Salvador for the famous soccer/football game between the select teams of Honduras and El Salvador on June 15, the aroused Salvadorans insulted and even beat up some of the Hondurans, going way beyond the punishment inflicted on the seventy families of Guacamaya.

The Honduran newspapers and radios, in turn, exaggerated these offenses and created more hatred in the Hondurans. On the night of June 15, gangs in almost all the bigger Honduran towns went around beating up Salvadorans, robbing them, and even burning down some of their homes and businesses, and threatening the lives of all the Salvadorans in Honduras. I was a witness to the mob of about a thousand men and women, led by some well-known gunmen, petty thieves, and barroom elements of Progreso, that was formed when some of the Mancha Brava of San Pedro Sula arrived to encourage them to destroy and steal.

The injustices that night and during the next days against the life and property of the Salvadorans in Honduras was again way out of proportion to what the Salvadorans had done against the Hondurans at the football game. The police and other authorities saw the mobs, but did not even try to control them, at least in

Progreso, where practically all the businesses and some of the homes of Salvadorans were ransacked and burned down.

The next day the reign of terror started in all the villages against the thousands of Salvadoran campesinos. The Mancha Brava, with the local authorities in almost all the villages, stole from, beat up, and threatened the lives of all the Salvadorans. We collected facts about many of the barbarous offenses perpetrated by soldiers and civilians of the Mancha Brava in our villages of Progreso. They showed special hatred against the Salvadorans who were Legionaries or cooperative members. The following are only a few examples:

In Nueva Florida an armed band, led by a soldier in uniform, drove from their homes forty complete families without giving them the opportunity to sell or take along any of their possessions. They came walking eighteen miles down the mountain, carrying their little children, to Las Delicias, where the president of the Legion of Mary, Agustín Cortés, gave them shelter for the night in his storehouse. The nicknamed "exterminator of campesinos," Sergeant López, who was in charge of the soldiers stationed in Batán (the Tela Railroad Company's cattle ranch), punched Agustín, who is a Honduran, for helping the Salvadorans. The families went to Progreso and stayed in our church until June 20, when they got together $125 to hire a bus to take them to the border.

In the village La 36 the soldiers from Batán went from house to house giving all the Salvadorans twenty-four hours to leave the country. They beat up several men and raped a young girl. They even forced the president of the Legion of Mary, the Honduran Evangelista López, to send his Salvadoran wife to El Salvador.

In Toyos the military representative, along with the worst of the Mancha Brava, and a uniformed soldier went around each night breaking down the doors of the Salvadorans' homes, hitting them, and giving them twenty-four hours to leave the country or die. They threatened to kill Elio Preso, the general manager of our Las Mercedes Co-op—several daughters of co-op members were raped during these attacks. They threatened to kill José Ayala, who worked with me in the apostolate and with the co-ops, on sight; so I sent him to Tegucigalpa to Fernando

Móntes, who gave him money to escape to El Salvador. *They even tried to destroy the personal documents of many Honduran leaders of the Church and of the co-ops in order to call them Salvadorans and force them to leave the country.* Against such an attempt, Fausto Orellana Luna, who also worked with me in Church and co-op affairs (and who is now the leader of the Associative Industries of Campesinos of Guaymas), had to defend himself with a machete. The military and the Mancha Brava of the National Party wanted to take advantage of this opportunity to destroy our work with the campesinos.

Between June 17 and July 14, before the war broke out, they say that more than twenty-five thousand Salvadorans fled to El Salvador and there recounted the abuses they suffered from the Hondurans. During these weeks the radios and the newspapers of both countries did a really diabolical job of fomenting hatred and exaggerating the outrages. The hundreds of thousands of Salvadorans, who remained as hidden away as possible in Honduras, feared for their lives.

Again acting in reprisal all out of proportion to the offenses, on July 14 at 6:00 P.M., El Salvador, in a surprise attack without declaring war, bombed eight cities and towns in Honduras and sent their troops across the border at Ocotopeque and other points. The war lasted six days, until both sides had used up most of their ammunition. The Salvadoran army penetrated up to thirty-five miles into Honduras, having planned to take Comayagua, Santa Rosa de Copán, and San Pedro Sula in two days as a result of the surprise air and land attacks. But the Honduran army stopped them on land, and in six days pushed them back across the border without crossing into El Salvador themselves. The Honduran air force shot down or bombed on the ground practically the entire Salvadoran air force.

Both sides followed the line of hatred and vengeance that the press and radio of both countries had traced out, killing with great brutality almost all the soldiers they captured, whether healthy or wounded. All over Honduras the Salvadoran men who had remained in Honduras were rounded up and kept guarded in the schools or football stadiums (as in Progreso) for a month, bringing great suffering to their abandoned families. CARITAS of the parishes tried to help them, but they were criticized, as were all of us who helped the Salvadorans in Honduras before, during, and after the war.

The military authorities and the rich landowners were always looking for an excuse to expel me from the country again. Here is a copy of a letter I wrote one month after the war, August 14, 1969, to the Progreso Committee for National Defense. The military authorities formed these groups in each municipality to organize the cooperation of all Hondurans in the war effort. My letter will give you an idea of the atmosphere in those days.

To the Committee for National Defense:

Friends have informed me that there are many rumors going around about the sermon I preached last Sunday at the 6:00 A.M. mass, in which I supposedly spoke against the Hondurans, calling them savages. This is false; and there were many witnesses at this mass, including the Crusader sisters and Dr. Kuhlman from Germany, who state that I said nothing more than the truth without exaggerating. Without doubt there are others who could interpret badly my words. That is why I decided to write you a summary of what I said in the sermon.

I started by reading the Bible from 1 John 3:13–19, which says: "My brothers, don't be surprised that those of the world criticize you. We have passed from death to life, and the sign of this is that we love our neighbor. He who does not love his neighbor is dead. Everyone who hates his neighbor is a murderer, and you know that a murderer doesn't have this eternal life in his heart. We know what love is, in that Jesus gave his life for us; and so we too should give our life for our neighbors. Thus, if anyone has the necessities of life and sees a person in need and doesn't have pity on him, how could he possibly have any love of God in his heart? My sons, our love should not consist in what we say, but rather in true love seen by what we do for others."

Commenting on this text, I said that we Christians have a great responsibility to help solve this great tragedy of the war. The Word of God should help clear up the great disorientation and confusion caused by all the hate propaganda. The Catholic bishops of Honduras in their meeting just before the outbreak of the war said that the press, radio, and television of the two countries have a big part of the blame for inciting hatred between the two peoples. Who should orient Catholics, the doctrine of Christ or some newsmen who probably don't even know Christ? Christ says to love, that hatred is a sin. He who hates his neighbor, the Salvadorans, is not a good son of God.

Here in Progreso they are passing around sheets that say that "if you are a good Honduran, make life difficult for the Salvadorans so that they will leave" and "you can't be friends with a Salvadoran; where a 'Guanaco' [Salvadoran] lives, lives an enemy; Guanacos, get out!" But you know that Christ says not to harm anyone, not even to wish to harm anyone; love even your enemy; forgive; to seek vengeance or reprisals is a sin. You also know that a good Honduran is a good Christian, and a good Christian is a good Honduran. Then don't be fooled into thinking that you have to hate Salvadorans in order to be patriotic. If we have to fight a war to defend our country and kill some neighbors, we should do this with sorrow, not with hatred. Some newsmen say that the Honduran "people" are demanding reprisals and don't want to see any Salvadorans here in Honduras. Well, I said in the sermon, don't forget that 80 percent of the Hondurans, the "people," live in great poverty, and most of them cannot read or write. This hate propaganda doesn't come from them, but from those who do know how to read and write. The "people" do not want war; they want peace; they want food for their children, decent homes, a plot of ground to cultivate. In the villages, in general, the Salvadoran campesinos got along fine with the Hondurans. Only now with this hate propaganda they are given the idea that they cannot be friends. "Love your neighbor as yourself," says Christ, "not only with words but with deeds." There are a thousand men, fellow human beings, held prisoners in the Progreso stadium simply for having been born in El Salvador, and have been suffering there for a month now. This also means that there are about a thousand women and several thousand children of these men who are suffering from hunger. Many of these women and most of these children were born in Honduras and are Hondurans. Many good persons in Progreso have helped them with food, but there are others, confused by the hate propaganda, who criticize and say they are traitors for helping the Salvadorans. "Let the Guanacos die of hunger," some have said.

I finished the sermon by saying, like Saint John, that it is no surprise that I am criticized for preaching love. They will say that Padre Guadalupe only loves the Salvadorans. Well, indeed I do love the Salvadorans, but I also love the Hondurans. I try to love everyone, even my enemies. And I forgive them the calumnies they spread about me. I have proven with deeds, not only with words, that I love Honduras, especially her poor campesinos. With great pleasure I would shed my blood for Honduras, to help Christ save her. That is my only reason for being here in Honduras. I am not a communist, as some say, but a Christian. And as a priest of Christ it is my duty to preach the gospel of Christ. Let us offer this mass for peace between these two neighboring peoples, and for those who have died in this war.

That is more or less a summary of my sermon. I also want to explain to you that I didn't touch any poster against the Salvadorans in Toyos. It was another Jesuit priest who did it, outraged at seeing the hate propaganda. He and I admit it was imprudent to tear it down. Along with this letter is the signed confession of the crime. With all due respect, and with love for Honduras, I remain your servant in Christ,
(signed) Padre Guadalupe

This hatred fomented by the mass media was what allowed the Salvadoran army to invade Honduras, but it was not the cause. The real causes of the war were, first of all, that both the Honduran and the Salvadoran governments were corrupt military dictatorships that repressed the people and illicitly enriched themselves, and second, both peoples were rebelling against their governments with strikes and public demonstrations. The war solved this problem for both governments, because both peoples now had to back up their armed forces.

Another cause of the war was that the border between the two countries had been in dispute for more than a hundred years, and this gave another pretext to the Salvadorans to invade and permanently occupy the Honduran territory that El Salvador had always claimed. With these lands the pressure of the landless campesinos in El Salvador would be alleviated without touching any of their big landowners.

Even though the war ended, Honduras and El Salvador did not sign a peace treaty until October of 1980 (and this was finally done only because the military leaders needed it, as I will explain later). During these eleven and a half years there were no diplomatic or commercial relations between them. The Pan-American highway was closed at the border. The Hondurans and Salvadorans in Honduras could not visit their relatives in El Salvador, and vice versa. As soon as the war was over, almost all the Salvadorans who were not married to Hondurans rushed back to El Salvador with great fear for their lives. The big landowners bought up their lands for ridiculous prices. All our co-ops suffered with the fleeing of their Salvadoran members, and the Suyapa Co-op of Morazán broke up.

CESA also broke up little by little, not so much because of the war, as of bad administration in general. It had served well for the early years of many co-ops, but I was not sad to see it disappear, for I began to realize that it is the government that should give the services of agrarian reform to the campesinos, not private agencies like CESA.

Also, I was glad we never started the ANACH agricultural school. I am examining more and more critically the place of private or church-owned schools, universities, clinics, hospitals, and so on. Sometimes these great and wonderful services for the people prevent us from focusing our efforts on helping organize the marginated masses so that they can demand these services from the government. I am also examining the function of church-owned radio stations that say they are "the voice of those without voice." Well, we must, rather, help the masses get organized so that their voices will be heard, instead of speaking for them. Good Christian apostles, including priests and nuns, should work in all these governmental service institutions to give them a Christian spirit.

It seems that 1969 was the year for the breaking up of many things. Another union that broke up was our fine parish team. As soon as the war was over, Tom Quiery went to the States for a vacation. It could already be noticed that he was having a vocation crisis, as though he were just burned out and weary from his continual service to the poor and their struggle for human dignity. I hoped he would return from his vacation with a renewed spirit. Tom was one of my best friends, and I suffered seeing him in crisis.

When Tom returned to Honduras, he tried to carry on as pastor for another month, but he finally told me that he was thinking of leaving the priesthood, that he wanted to form his own family. He returned to the States and asked Rome for a dispensation from his vows as a Jesuit and as a priest. When Tom got his dispensation, he married and went to work with another former Jesuit from Honduras who was helping alcoholics to recover. I don't judge it as either good or bad that these fellows left the priesthood. What would be a shame would be to leave the service of others as a priest and then not work anymore for your neighbor, but just for your own family. But both men are helping other needy persons, maybe more than some priests are.

When Tom left, John Waters, who was teaching at the Instituto San José, was named pastor of Progreso parish. The Franciscan sisters in our team were having their problems, too. Only two of them remained, the other two had left their religious order some time before. After Tom left, these two went back to Tegucigalpa to work. One of them was Mary Colgan, who was a close friend of mine, after having worked with me in the villages for so long. She later returned to the States to study more philosophy (she was very intellectual) and to give retreats. I saw her again on several different visits to the States, but I do not know where she is now.

With Waters, Wade, and I in the parish rectory, and without the Franciscan sisters, we no longer had much teamwork. Waters is a wonderful person, and so is Wade, but we didn't make the best team. I still had all the villages and camps to care for, so I decided to live out in Toyos and, from there, visit the other communities in our Nissan jeep. I wanted to incarnate myself more into the life of the campesinos. I lived in a small room behind the altar of the wooden barracks church in Toyos. (By 1975, the wood had become so rotten that it was torn down, and a new cement-block church now stands in Toyos.)

I went to live in Toyos in October of 1969, and spent ten very happy months there. Every day at 4:30 A.M. I would ring the bell of the church, and about thirty men of the Las Mercedes Co-op, all Legionaries, would meet with me in the church for a gospel meditation before going to work. I frequently went to work with them too; but not every day, because I had a hundred communities to visit, besides the courses and meetings of the other cooperatives, or of the ANACH, or of the Jesuits, and so on.

It was in this same month of October that the violent war for the land of Guanchías broke out again in two different places. In Agua Blanca Sur, INA, with soldiers, was evicting all the campesinos and cattlemen of the village from the lands that INA had finally bought from the Bográns and Echeverry. INA (and FECORAH) wanted to give this land to their five new co-ops to plant bananas to sell to the Standard Fruit Company. The ANACH organized these small farmers and cattlemen to defend their rights, for they had occupied these lands for more than ten years. This started the conflicts between the different campesino organizations, the ANACH and FECORAH, that is so tragic.

Sandoval of INA was right to want agro-industrial cooperatives for agrarian reform, but all the campesinos have a right to some land. He finally listened to the ANACH and gave this subsection of individual farmers and cattlemen of Agua Blanca Sur some land on the mountainside, but only after one of them killed an army sergeant, a promoter of INA named David Fúnes Villatoro, who was trying to evict them from their land. The campesino training center of INA in Agua Blanca Sur is now called Center David Fúnes Villatoro.

The other zone of conflict at this same time in Guanchías (which also ended with a person being shot to death with a pistol, and in which I was indirectly implicated) was that of the four ANACH villages of Arena Blanca, Guacamaya, La Mina, and La Sarrosa. These villages still had not obtained any of the good land that Sandoval had bought from the Bográns and Echeverry, in spite of the many invasions they had made, which I have already described.

To reduce the pressure from these ANACH groups, INA was trying to relocate on the mountainsides all the medium-sized cattlemen of Progreso who long before had bought up the land around these four villages. These mountainsides were now unoc-cupied, since the Salvadorans who had previously planted their milpas there had fled the country.

After continuous strife, and invasions that again mobilized up to four hundred campesinos of the ANACH in Guanchías, each of these four subsections finally got some part of the rocky land of these cattlemen of Progreso (without touching, of course, the land of the Bográns or Echeverry), which amounted to only about two acres for each campesino. Then, for a whole year, I tried to get them to work collectively in co-ops, but after two successive crop failures collectively, they divided up the land into two acres for each one. To the present day these campesinos who struggled so hard are still without agrarian reform in that part of Guanchías.

The most tragic event occurred when the campesinos were in-vading the lands of one landowner from Progreso. He told Sister Josefa (of the Crusaders) that Padre Guadalupe was to blame, and that he always kept a bullet in the chamber of his pistol ready to put into the mouth of this communist priest. Sister Josefa told me this to warn me to keep away from this man. He had always been a good friend of these sisters and helped them a lot with their training school. Actually, I was not involved at all in these latest land invasions in Guanchías. This time I did not go with the campesinos; nor did I even know that they would invade the gentleman's land.

Well, one afternoon it just happened that I was visiting Pro-greso and was alone in the parish rectory when a woman arrived urgently looking for a priest; the son of this landowner had just shot his own brother. The father had gone to San Pedro Sula and left his pistol in the drawer of a table. His two sons, who were students of our Instituto San José, were with some other young companions in the house. They took out the pistol, a re-volver, to play Russian roulette, leaving only one bullet to spin around in the cylinder. The younger, sixteen-year old son pointed the gun at the face of his brother, slowly pulled the trigger, and the bullet entered his mouth and came out the back of his head, killing him instantly. This was such a shock for the boy with the pistol that he also fell over as though dead with a heart attack.

Since I was the only priest around at that moment, I had to go with the woman to the home. There I found the father doubled over in a chair, crying, next to the body of his eldest son. The younger son was recuperating in a hospital. The only thing I could do was to put my arm around him and tell him how sorry I was and that I would offer mass for his sons and for him. I walked away thinking how that bullet that was planned for my mouth wound up in the mouth of the son. I prayed a lot for this father during those days, and Sister Josefa told me a few months later that he had changed completely. He became converted to Christ and, though still a large landowner and commercial "coyote" ("wolf"), became a friend of the poor campesinos and my friend also. How strange and wonderful are the ways of the Lord!

It was really a great thing for me to live all alone in Toyos, especially for my spiritual life. I became more of a contemplative. I have always had trouble sleeping, but in Toyos I learned to take better advantage of the nights when I would wake up at maybe one or two in the morning and not be able to get back to sleep. I would get up for one, two, or three hours of reading, prayer, meditation, just being with God—my Father and I, my Leader and Model and I, the Spirit of Jesus and I. My prayer always concluded with my abandoning myself into the hands of my Father, as his instrument to help him form his Kingdom in this world. On the days that I was not going to work with the co-op, I would read tranquilly in the church all morning and then after lunch take off for some other community.

For my meals in Toyos I went to a different home to eat each meal with a different family. I followed a list made up by Santos Alvarenga, the new president of the Legion of Mary since the departure of the Salvadoran José Ayala. In this way I made friends with all the people. I still use this same system of eating with each family of the town here in Nicaragua, where I am writing this.

In this period of my life I started to read, by preference, all the books I could find about Marxism. Friends of mine at the University of Honduras used to lend them to me. The libraries of the Jesuits in Honduras did not contain Marxist books; American Jesuits had little interest in this. They were very anticommunist, whereas, by contrast, my contacts with Marxist worker and campesino leaders were slowly stripping me of my prejudices and leaving me, rather, with an admiration for the Marxists who struggled for justice. They had more courage and, it seemed to me, more love for the poor than most Christians. This made me very curious to learn more of their doctrine. My metamorphosis was advancing by means of my struggles for the poor.

I remember that it was during this year that I lived in Toyos that I planted two acres of cucumbers in my parcel of the co-op land. I was trying to get the campesinos to diversify their crops and plant other things besides corn, beans, and rice. I was also part of a project with Sister Leocadia (of the Notre Dames in Progreso) to form a co-op of women in Toyos to make and bottle bread-and-butter pickles, using the sister's secret recipe. I got the idea one evening when I was eating supper with the sisters in their convent, after having mass with them, and they served me some of Sister Leocadia's delicious bread and butter pickles. She and Sister Leticia promised to teach some women in Toyos how to make and bottle them for sale.

I knew the co-op land in Toyos was good for cucumbers for the pickles, because I was still trying to sell my tremendous crop of thousands of them. I wound up giving hundreds of them away in the villages close to Toyos and planting some more for pickles. Of the fifty women in Toyos who wanted to join the pickle co-op, I chose eight widows who had small children to start with as an experiment. The Radio Schools and Association for Human Promotion assured me of a market, not only in Honduras, but in all Central America.

After a lot of difficulties in finding all the condiments called for in the recipe and in getting bottles from the factory in Guatemala, we finally made our first batch of pickles and bottled them. They tasted superb, and we gave away these first bottles as samples to our friends in Progreso, San Pedro Sula, and Tegucigalpa, so that they would then promote their sale.

We placed them for sale only in the supermarkets of those three cities, because only foreigners or the Honduran bourgeoisie would buy pickles. We went on making and bottling them because some were beginning to be sold. The failure came after a few months. We were noticing that something was wrong with our crude bottling process in a rustic campesino kitchen in

Toyos; after a few months on the shelves, the bottled pickles were changing color, becoming white, and the supermarkets had to remove them. Several bottling experts went to Toyos to help, but without success. That is the way it was when I had to leave Toyos to go to the parish of Sulaco in August of 1970; and so the project was abandoned.

Another great project of mine also flopped when I left the Progreso parish. For several years I had been talking with some construction workers, carpenters, and bricklayers in Progreso about being united in a labor union or a co-op instead of being in competition among themselves for the jobs. All the bigger construction works in Progreso were always given to workers from San Pedro Sula. At last, in January of 1970, after I had explained the idea to each one personally, we had a big meeting of almost all the construction workers, carpenters, bricklayers, electricians, plumbers, and painters in the whole city of Progreso, about sixty men. All of them did rustic work with few tools, with difficulty getting construction materials, always having to rent trucks for transportation, and being many days of the year without work. No one in the whole city, for example, had a machine to plane the wood. United, they could get loans to buy a truck, start a cement block factory, and get an electric wood planer, electric saws, and so on.

So they decided to form the Construction Cooperative of Progreso Limited. Each week I met with them in a big open shed, which the mayor of Progreso, Juan Manuel García, lent to the co-op, to study cooperativism and to save at least a dollar a week. We planned to have a system for training older boys in the different branches of construction work. They started making cement blocks in the yard by the shed with two hand machines lent to us by Brother Jim, and they used their savings to buy the cement. We started proceedings to obtain the legal status for the co-op and to get a loan from the bank to buy a truck and a wood planer. Some of the carpenters brought their small home workshops together in the shed and started making furniture.

Within a few months, the co-op controlled practically all the construction work in the city, and the mayor agreed to give all the municipal work to our co-op. The idea was that the co-op would make all the contracts for construction or restoration of houses, schools, streets, bridges, furniture, and so on, and then give work contracts to some of its members to do the jobs. They always left a good part of the profit for the co-op to better itself, or to be distributed at the end of the year to the members according to the work of each one.

Artisan workers like these members of the co-op are even more individualistic and distrustful of their companions than campesinos, and right from the beginning there was some jealousy and strife among the members. These workers of the city are more materialistic, more selfish, and more full of vices, like drinking and gambling, than the campesinos; thus, their unification was that much more difficult. But little by little the members were doing their work within the co-op, and all the other construction workers of Progreso were joining the co-op.

I served the co-op as adviser and helped the vigilance committee check the treasury books and funds each week. The co-op was going along more or less well when I was transferred to the parish of Sulaco in August of 1970.

In May of 1970, Father Steve Gross returned to the Yoro Mission after finishing theology and was assigned to our parish team of Progreso with Waters, Wade, and me. Steve helped me with the villages and banana camps. He had taught at Instituto San José for three years as a scholastic and knew a lot of people in the parish. Since I was living in Toyos, Steve had all the communities to the south of Progreso, and I kept all those to the north, where Toyos was. He was very active and very capable, and I knew that he could very well take my place in everything. They did not need me so much in the Progreso parish now, and I could go to the frontiers of civilization where as yet there was nothing organized in the villages, neither Delegates of the Word for the Church, nor popular organizations, like the ANACH, to help solve their material problems.

For a long time, the activists of the ANACH and I had been talking about organizing the poorest and most exploited campesinos of northern Honduras, those around Yoro and Sulaco where the Indian tribes were. I knew that the parish of Sulaco was very isolated. The pastor had been there for fifteen years and had not adapted to the teachings of the Second Vatican

Council. He celebrated mass and all the sacraments in Latin. For him, all these new changes were a result of communist infiltration in the Church, and he did not accept them. I knew that our superior wanted to send him back to the States for a course in theological renewal; but the pastor did not want to go, and the superior had no one else who wanted to work in that difficult, isolated parish.

One night in Toyos the Holy Spirit asked me, "Why don't you go to Sulaco, to the hardest part of the mission? They no longer need you so much in Progreso. For the parish work, Steve will do very well. And for the struggles of the campesinos, all the campesino organizations and government agencies are already helping in this whole region; meanwhile, in Sulaco the campesinos are completely abandoned. As for the Church, it is hurting and as for the campesino organizations and government agencies, like INA, there is absolutely nothing there. Why don't you go there as a pioneer to extend the frontier of the new liberating Church, and of the ANACH for agrarian reform?"

At the beginning of July, I talked to our superior and he was delighted with my offer to go to Sulaco. He and other Jesuits preferred to have me far from Progreso so as not to cause them more problems, and for several years he had wanted to transfer me. He told me he would name me pastor of Sulaco starting August 1 and would call the other man to Progreso. I used the last weeks in the Progreso parish to show Steve everything about the Delegates of the Word, the basic Christian communities, the catechists, the Legion of Mary, the co-ops, and I even took him to the headquarters of the ANACH in San Pedro Sula to have him commit himself to help them.

Steve went to three meetings of the Progreso Construction Co-op with me, and hoped to continue checking the treasurer's books and funds each week with the vigilance committee. But after I left, little by little the vigilance committee stopped doing the weekly checkup. Two months later, when I returned to visit Progreso and the Construction Co-op, they told me that some members had left because the treasurer did whatever he wanted with the money. In a general assembly of the co-op, I tried to rectify this failure of the vigilance committee and of the administrative board, but when I returned a month later the situation was worse; more members had pulled out.

A group of workers continued in the co-op for another year, but it was probably best that they never obtained legal status as a co-op or the loan from the bank, for the co-op finally folded and the treasurer was left owing many of the members the amount of their savings, which he had taken. What a shame! This construction co-op would have been a great benefit for the city of Progreso and its workers.

My last participation in the big mobilization of the ANACH in the Progreso area occurred during the last weeks that I lived in Toyos before going to Sulaco. This time the battle was right in my area near Toyos, called Guaymas. I have already mentioned a couple of times the problem that approximately fifteen hundred campesinos and their families in sixteen villages of Guaymas had. They had always rented small parcels of land from the Tela Railroad Company for their milpas. In these last years the company had evicted them and was little by little filling these thousands of acres of good farmland around Batán in Guaymas with cattle.

Some of the campesinos still planted milpas along the borders of the canals or the roads or in the swampy, abandoned lands that were flooded each year. All of these sixteen villages were organized in the ANACH and for three years had been demanding that INA give them, under the Agrarian Reform Law, one thousand manzanas (1700 acres) of idle farmland that the Tela had in Guaymas. After many promises and lies by INA, some of the subsections had several times invaded the lands around Luzón, but they were always forcefully evicted and the milpas and huts they had made were destroyed by the soldiers that the Tela had in Batán.

This year they united the sixteen subsections under a single, regional leadership of the ANACH in Guaymas for a big operation. They prepared everything well, renting three tractors with plows and asking around for money for gasoline. (I lent them $750 from my rotating fund.) The rising sun of July 10, 1970, discovered about six hundred campesinos and their families building their champas (huts), plowing, and planting corn in eight different parts of Guaymas. There was a great movement of soldiers surrounding them and threatening to throw them out; the director of INA promised them land, but in an orderly fashion. They would have to leave these lands they had invaded (the campesinos say "recuperated," i.e. recovered), and INA would measure lands for them close to Batán (in the swampy part that was useless even for cattle).

The negotiations of the ANACH with INA and with the Tela dragged on for eight days. The soldiers started to capture the leaders of the subsections of the ANACH, but nonetheless, the campesinos were firm in their decision to never leave these lands. The truth is that the campesinos of Guaymas, in general, are the most conscienticized and politicized campesinos in all of Honduras. Most of them are former banana workers, and ever since the great strike of 1954, some of them have been Marxist revolutionaries.

Finally the military government ordered the eviction of all these families, and hundreds of soldiers arrived to capture all the leaders and throw down and burn the newly built champas. Many resisted and were cruelly beaten and arrested, including some women. Many of the newly planted cornfields were plowed under by tractors of the Tela. Nevertheless, the executive committee of the ANACH managed to get the Tela's agreement to leave many of the collectively planted milpas alone for the harvest and the military's agreement to free all the prisoners from Guaymas.

The people returned to their villages and started planning a better operation for the following year in case INA did not give them good lands. The ANACH did not accept the swampy lands on the other side of the highway from Batán.

That is the way things were when I left Toyos. I did not directly accompany the campesinos in their "recovery of land"; they themselves told me not to do so. Only afterward did I visit these poor, heroic families in their new champas in the eight different recovered areas, bringing them some food from CARITAS to help sustain them. All in all, the Tela Railroad Company, the military and civil authorities, the big landowners of Progreso, San Pedro Sula, and the whole north coast, all the bishops, and many of the Jesuits seemed very happy to hear that I was being transferred to Sulaco.

15. Pastor of Sulaco

On August 1 I was supposed to receive the parish of Sulaco. I already had my written appointment signed by our superior and by Archbishop Santos of Tegucigalpa, but the pastor refused to leave; he wrote to our superior that he would not leave the Sulaco parish until our Father General of the Jesuits in Rome answered his letter of protest at being replaced by a Jesuit "communist." In Yorito, on the way to Sulaco, I received a telegram from our superior telling me not to take possession of the parish until the other man had left, so I decided to stay in Yorito, a municipality of the parish of Yoro, for a few weeks until he left for Progreso. Well, the weeks turned into months; for five months I lived in the sacristy of the old church in Yorito, helping there.

Since I had worked in the parish of Yoro in 1963, I knew the villages and a lot of the people of Yorito. I ate with the family of Doña Chana when I was there in town, but I spent most of my days walking through the mountains visiting the villages of Yorito. After mass in each village, I would call a meeting of the men to encourage them to get organized in the ANACH in order to get land (which practically no one had) and in a cooperative to start a store (there were no stores in these villages and the people had to walk to Yorito to buy salt, soap, coffee, and other necessities), and to start some small collective agricultural project.

After a few weeks of walking through these mountains, which are covered with beautiful pine forests, a campesino of Pueblo Viejo, who was walking with me one day, gave me an inspiration. I asked him who the owner was of all these fine trees that surrounded his village and whether the villagers got some benefit from them. He told me that they belonged to the municipality of Yorito, and that only the rich owner of the sawmill, who was cutting the wood from this sector, mainly benefited from them. He told me that it was a shame that the campesinos could not get more benefit from these lands close to their villages. To plant their corn and beans they had to go way up to the top of the mountain where there are no pine forests, or else go down to the valley of Yorito to try to rent a couple of acres from the big landowners of Yoro.

The inspiration I had was that the kind of co-op that these campesinos of the mountains of Yorito needed was not for agriculture, but for timber cutting. With a small loan they could buy those long, two-man saws and even a portable chain saw. I started to talk to them about this, and the campesinos became enthusiastic. The pine trees were the great riches of their area; they wanted to get permission from the government to cut and sell them themselves instead of the rich lumbermen doing it; they would rent trucks to take the logs to the sawmills in Progreso. I promised to investigate all this for them with the government, but they would have to start meeting each week to study cooperativism and save at least ten cents a week in order to form their co-op.

In this way I started six pre-co-ops and tried to be at their weekly meetings: the villages of Pacayal, Vallecillo, Pueblo Viejo, and Portillo, the Santa Marta Indian Tribe, and the town of Yorito. The Delegates of the Word and the Legionaries of these communities were the basis and almost always the elected leaders of these pre-co-ops.

The group that most attracted my attention was the Santa Marta Indian Tribe. It was the farthest away from Yorito, way up in the mountains. Every Saturday afternoon I would meet with the Pueblo Viejo Co-op after a two-hour climb from Yorito, and on finishing there, I would walk another two hours farther up the mountain to Santa Marta to sleep in the nice church they had there. The people of this municipality were so poor that I did not even ask them to lend me a horse or mule. They all traveled on foot, so I did too. After mass on Sunday morning, I would meet with the tribe's pre-co-op, and after lunch, on the way down to Yorito, I would pass through Portillo for the meeting there. On Fridays I would visit Pacayal and Vallecillo, another round-trip of four hours on foot from Yorito. In this way I got plenty of physical exercise and felt good.

I spoke to the representatives of the Ministry of Natural Resources (in charge of the forests) in Yoro, but they did not have enough authority. I had to go to the central offices of the ministry in Tegucigalpa to talk to the head of the Forestry Department about the possibility of forming forestry cooperatives of campesinos to cut lumber. I was told to talk to Francisco (Chico) Borjas. He had just graduated in Mexico as a forester and had returned to Honduras with the idea of controlling the pine resin industry, which was destroying many good forests. He liked the idea of forming campesino forestry co-ops, but to extract resin from pine trees using the modern technique that does not damage the tree.

To profit most from a pine tree, you should extract the valuable resin with this modern technique for five years before cutting down the tree for lumber. There were two ancient plants in Honduras, near Tegucigalpa, for processing the crude resin into two products that are in great demand on the international market: turpentine and colophonia. (Colophonia is used for making plastics, paints, and medicines.) The owners of these two plants hired a number of campesinos to chop big, cavelike holes with axes into the heart of the wood of the pine trees. The holes served as receptacles that filled up with the bleeding resin. After six months of collecting resin like that, the trees were only good for cutting up for firewood. This work was what most of the campesinos did in Ojojona in the department of Francisco Morazán and in the whole region around Guinope in the department of El Paraíso.

I went with Chico Borjas to Ojojona to see how the resin workers destroyed the forests and to talk to the campesinos who had been working like this for years. They were being horribly exploited by the truck-owning middlemen who bought the resin and firewood from them very cheaply and thus got the biggest part of the profits. Chico had been thinking of organizing these campesinos into the first forestry coop of Honduras and teaching them to extract resin with the modern method. However, he did not believe they would change their system with the axe, which got all the resin out of a pine tree in six months, for the new system, which was slower. Therefore, he decided to go to Yorito with me to see if the forests there were good for a resinating project.

Chico visited all the six pre-co-ops of Yorito with me, explaining to them the system of extracting resin. Each co-op would have a sector of the forest, not only for resinating, but also to protect against forest fires. Fires have always caused great destruction of this, the most valuable natural resource in Honduras. Approximately half of the territory of Honduras is covered with good forests. There used to be even more, but they have been destroyed, either by fire, or by being exploited without control by foreign lumber companies, who left the mountainsides barren (like the ones around Tegucigalpa and Choluteca).

Chico stayed on in Yorito and taught the six pre-co-ops the modern technique of extracting resin without touching the wood of the tree. They cut off a strip of the bark, one inch high by eight inches long, close to the ground on the side of the tree most exposed to the sun. The heat helps draw out the resin. In this strip, which goes right up to the wood without cutting it, sulphuric acid is squirted on the wood from a plastic bottle. The acid stimulates the pores of the wood and attracts the resin. Below the cut-off strip is nailed a small zinc canal to catch the resin, which runs out of the strip onto the canal and into a plastic cup stuck onto the tree below the canal.

About once a week the campesinos come with a container to collect the resin in the cup, cut open another one-inch strip right above the first one, and squirt on the acid. In this way, each member of the co-op can take care of five hundred trees, which should yield about five big (54-gallon) drums of resin a month. Each barrel is sold for about forty dollars to the processing plant. Not all of this is profit, because the co-op has to pay for transportation, materials, and taxes to the government for using the forests. Each member left an additional 10 percent in the co-op treasury.

I believe that these six small co-ops of the municipality of Yorito were the first agro-forestry co-ops in Honduras; at least, they were the first to resinate with the modern method. Now, in 1981, there are more than a hundred of these campesino agro-forestry co-ops all over the country. They not only extract resin with this method, but they also extract liquidambar, cut hardwood lumber, and collect the seeds from the pine cones. (This is also done by six agro-forestry co-ops of the ANACH that I helped organize in the municipality of Jocón, Yoro, in 1973). They also have their collective agricultural projects.

One of the first reforms of the populist General López Arellano, after his second coup in 1972, was to decree the nationalization of the forests under the control of the new COHDEFOR (Honduran Corporation for Forest Development). This decree-law included the social use of the forest by forestry cooperatives of campesinos in the zone. This was exactly what we started with Chico Borjas of the Ministry of Natural Resources in Yorito and then in several of the other Indian tribes of the department of Yoro in 1970 and 1971.

To bring up to date the political situation in Honduras in 1970, when I was in Yorito, you will recall that Colonel López Arellano, with the army, in a secret agreement with the National Party and the U.S. embassy, made the bloody coup d'état against the Liberals on October 3, 1963. They massacred the Civil Guard and persecuted all the "leftists." They always promised free and democratic elections, and I have already told about the "free" election of municipal authorities in 1968.

The election for the presidency was programed for the end of 1970. López Arellano had the good idea of changing the custom whereby the party that wins the presidency fills all the public posts on the national, departmental, and municipal levels with members of its party and eliminates all government employees of the losing party. He called together the leaders of the two parties, the Nationalists and the Liberals, of the industrialists organized in COHEP (the Private Enterprise Council of Honduras), of the big landowners organized in FENAGH (National Federation of Cattlemen), of the workers in the CTH (Andrés Víctor Artíles, Céleo Gonzales, and Oscar Gale), and of the campesinos (Efraín Díaz of FECORAH and Reyes Rodríguez of the ANACH) to agree on the famous "National Unity Pact." By this agreement the people would vote only for the president of the republic, Liberal or Nationalist. All the other government posts, like cabinet ministers, congressmen, departmental governors, judges, and so on, would be distributed according to the percentage of votes that each party got in each department and municipality.

The candidates were Jorge Bueso Arias (rich landowner and banker from Santa Rosa de Copán) for the Liberals, and Ramón

Ernesto Cruz (distinguished judge) for the Nationalists. The Nationalists won easily, first of all, because the Liberals were very divided (Modesto Rodas Alvarado didn't really give his support to Bueso), and second, because there was plenty of fraud in the election since the Nationalists had held all the positions of authority since 1963.

López Arellano (now a brigadier general) turned over the presidential palace to "Monchito" Cruz, and remained as head of all the armed forces and administrator of the millions of dollars he had acquired during recent years. He was associated (for example) with his friend Somoza (dictator of Nicaragua) in some big business enterprises. Today, he is one of the richest businessmen and cattlemen in Honduras. A military career in Honduras and in many countries has been the easiest and quickest road to wealth.

Right from the beginning the "National Unity Pact" did not function. The Liberals who won government posts did not collaborate with the Nationalists, and vice versa. Worst of all for the campesinos was the appointment of Horacio Moya Posas as the new director of INA. He was an ultraconservative Nationalist from Olanchito who completely bogged down the agrarian reform and was one of the principal pretexts López Arellano (and the U.S. embassy) used for the military coup of 1972 (as I will explain later on).

When the election of 1970 was announced, with its "pact," Rigoberto Sandoval, disillusioned, immediately resigned as director of INA and left for Rome to work with the FAO of the United Nations in his specialty, agrarian reform in Latin America. With his departure, most of the foreign "leftist" advisers of INA, of the Ministry of Economic Planning, and of the university also had to leave the country.

The only good thing that the new director of INA did was to take a little interest in the Indian tribes of Yoro at my instigation and that of the ANACH. My five months of living in Yorito in the providence of God were principally so that I would get to know well and become profoundly interested in the problems of the Yoro Indian tribes. There were orginally twenty-one of them, but two have disappeared without any known descendents, and now only nineteen remained. Their communal land titles of

full dominion were all in the department of Yoro; the great missionary, Manuel de Jesús Subirana, got the titles for them in
1864.

In the municipality of Yoro were the tribes of Subirana,
Tablón, Mataderos, San Francisco, San Esteban, La Reinada, Ani-
sillo, Lagunitas, Siriano, and Jimía; in the municipality of Yorito
was Santa Marta; in the municipality of Negrito were Guajiniquil
and Pate; and in the municipality of Olanchito were Agua Caliente
de Guardarrama and Zapotal. Each tribe is now composed of from
seventy families, the smallest, to about three hundred families, the
largest, with a total of about ten thousand Indians on the lists of
these nineteen Yoro Indian tribes.

These are Jicaque or Xicaque Indians (another Indian name
for them is Torrupanes), descendents of the famous Mayas of
Central America. The ruins of their marvelous holy cities of the
twelfth century are now tourist centers in Mexico, Guatemala,
and Honduras.

After the apparition of the Indian-faced Virgin of Guadalupe
in the seventeenth century, all the Indians of Central America
accepted the new religion of their Spanish conquerors and, after
a little instruction, were baptized Catholics. I have explained how
the Spanish missionaries organized "patron feasts" to visit the
bigger towns of Honduras once a year.

With the French Revolution and the wars of independence in
Central America at the beginning of the nineteenth century,
however, all the religious and all the foreign priests were expelled from Honduras, leaving the country practically without
priests. At the same time, the new rich Creoles (native-born with
Spanish blood) were despoiling the Indians of all their lands in
the valleys of Honduras, even murdering them to do so, and the
Indians fled and dispersed into the mountains.

Thus, they lost their contact with the few priests left in Honduras, and by 1850 it could be said that the Indians of the departments of Olancho, the Mosquitia, Santa Bárbara, Copán, and
Yoro had practically lost their faith. The last generations had not
even been baptized. They lived dispersed in the mountains in
extreme poverty.

Then God sent the great Spanish missionary, Padre Manuel de
Jesús Subirana, from Cuba to Honduras, and the archbishop of

Comayagua (then the capital of the new republic) commissioned him as missionary to all the Indians of Honduras. It is unbelievable how this man of God, in about fifteen years of going around through the mountains of these five departments, where tens of thousands of Indians were hidden away, managed not only to convert them to Christ and baptize all of them, but to organize them again into tribes whose authorities and chiefs were then recognized by the governments of Honduras. He also left men "catechists" in each tribe to continue instructing new Christians and to bring them together for common prayer.

It was in the department of Yoro that the great missionary Subirana worked most and where he "got involved in politics"— in order to get land from the government (in 1864) with full dominion title in the mountains for the twenty-one tribes of the municipalities I have named. The plan of Subirana was what it says in each title: "that these lands with these boundary marks will be handed over when all the families of the tribe live together around a school and a church, which they must build." In this way he managed to bring together the thousands of Indians of the one Jicaque tribe dispersed in the mountains of Yoro into twenty-one towns, calling them tribes. This was the first effective agrarian reform in Honduras.

Padre Subirana lived only two more years and could not consolidate this work with the tribes. He died in 1866 and is buried in the big church in the town of Yoro. He is venerated, not only by all the Indians, but by all the people of the department of Yoro and, indeed, of all Honduras.

Nevertheless, his work did not last. When I was visiting, little by little, all the nineteen tribes left in Yoro in the years 1970, 1971 and 1972, I found them in almost the same situation as before Padre Subirana's agrarian reform. The big landowners were again taking their best land away from them, fencing it in for cattle or coffee plantations. Once again, most of the families no longer lived together in their own towns, no longer had schools, churches, or land for their milpas. They had spread out higher up in the mountains, outside their tribal lands, each one looking for a place to build a poor hut and plant some corn.

These are the poorest people in Honduras, in every sense—in food (all of them are undernourished), in health (most of them have tuberculosis and profound anemia, and most die as children or as teenagers), in education (98 percent of the adults and most of the children have never attended school), in religion (in general, they look for a priest only to baptize their children; practically none of them make their First Holy Communion or are married by the Church), and in culture (they have lost their native Jicaque language, except for a few old-timers, who remember some of it; and they have lost their Indian customs). Most of them are now mixed by blood with the Ladinos or Honduran Creoles, speak only Spanish, and look much like the rest of the Honduran campesinos, except that they are the very poorest and most looked down on of all.

When I visited a tribe and got a good number of them together for mass and baptisms, I would tell them that I was a missionary like Padre Subirana, with the same ideas he had for helping the tribes get their own land and live better together. To recover their lands with the legal title that Padre Subirana left them, they would have to organize the whole tribe in the ANACH, in order to have the support of all the organized campesinos in the country. We would talk about bringing together all the families of the tribe dispersed through the mountains, once they recovered their tribal lands, to live in two or three villages with their school, church, and health clinic, as Padre Subirana wanted. Only in this way could the tribe recover its pride and develop.

I explained to them that "tribe" means "a family," and that is how they should live, united as one big family, helping one another, instead of each one out on his own. I explained to them that "Indian" means "indigenous," that is, "native." They were descendents of the pure native Hondurans who had always lived in Honduras and were owners of all the lands of Honduras before the Spaniards came to conquer them, enslave them, and take their lands and other riches away from them.

"You should be proud to be Indians, native Hondurans," I told them. "Those who call you 'Indians' in a disparaging way are ignorant. You should not feel any shame for being an Indian, and so you should never hide the fact from anyone that you are an Indian, a descendent of the pure Hondurans."

But to recover the lands that Padre Subirana got for the tribes is very difficult, if not impossible, without changing the whole capitalist system in Honduras. Only a revolutionary government is going to worry about the Indians. I will relate some of the great, practically useless, struggles we went through to try to get INA to remeasure and return the lands to each tribe according to their legal titles.

One of the first problems was that many of the tribes had lost their copy of the title that Padre Subirana left them a hundred years ago. But we finally helped all the nineteen tribes to get authentic copies of their titles from the National Archives in Tegucigalpa.

Another big obstacle in organizing the tribes in the ANACH so they could fight for their land were many of the tribal chiefs, who had always been named as the supreme authority in the tribe by the governor of the department of Yoro. The town of Yoro, the capital, has always been completely dominated by big landowners and Nationalist politicians (even during the time of the Liberals). The governors have always been big land-owning Nationalists and have always named as chiefs of the tribes Indians who were sold out to them, who would help them get the votes of the Indians for the National party, and who would keep quiet when the big landowners fenced in more and more of the tribal lands.

Most of the Indians were in agreement with me and wanted to try to recover their lands. Many of them were enthusiastic about the idea of benefiting more from the good pine forest, which almost all the tribes had, by extracting resin in their own agro-forestry co-ops. Besides stealing their best lands, some of the big landowners, politicians, military authorities, and government agency men had stolen most of the money that was given to a tribe for the sale of their timber to foreign or domestic owners of sawmills.

For example, one big Ladino cattleman in the municipality of Olanchito fenced in almost all the valley land of the Agua Caliente de Guardarrama tribe as pasture for his cattle. A number of years ago he sold all the best pine timber that the tribe had, merely giving a few lempiras to the chief. The lumbermen have made contracts with other tribes to cut so many cubic meters of wood for so much money. They wind up cutting maybe four times that much for that money, and the authorities get a good tip for keeping it quiet.

Therefore, the Indians rejoiced when I arrived with promoters of the ANACH and of the new government forest agency, COHDEFOR, who promised to control these thefts. We planned to use the money from the timber sales for building schools and roads for the tribes, and to promote their own collective coffee-growing and cattle co-ops.

The first tribes that became organized in the ANACH and in agro-forestry co-ops, using the same system of meeting each week to study cooperativism and to save at least ten cents a week, were Santa Marta (of Yorita), Subirana, Tablón, San Francisco, and Lagunitas (of municipality of Yoro), Las Vegas de Tepemechín (of Victoria), and in 1972, when I started visiting the village of Olanchito each month, the tribes of Agua Caliente de Guardarrama and Zapotal. The first projects of all these tribal co-ops were resination, with the help of COHDEFOR, and small collective stores, with small interest-free loans from my revolving fund.

In 1971 I managed to take out to Yorito an old jeep (made in 1955) that had been brought into Sulaca when there was an attempt to open a nonexistant road. After fixing it up a bit, I used it to visit all these tribal co-ops every month.

As for the corrupt chiefs, by means of the assemblies of the tribal co-ops we managed to throw out some of the worst ones and to convince others that it is better to work for the tribe than for the exploiting politicians. You can imagine how much opposition, criticism, and threats I received from the big landowners and the military and civil authorities of the municipalities who had been used to doing what they wanted with the tribes of "poor, ignorant Indians." The Indians, especially the chiefs who joined the ANACH and the co-ops, were, naturally, often threatened too. Several were thrown into jail and even shot at by the big landowners, with the military authorities at their service. I will tell more about that later.

Now, at the end of 1970, I was living in the sacristy of the church in Yorito after being named pastor of Sulaco. As I said, the pastor was reluctant to hand over the parish, telling our superior that he had appealed to our Father General in Rome. I waited three months before starting to visit some of the communities of the parish of Sulaco.

I did not want to act insensitively by moving into the parish rectory (priests' house), so in November, when I knew the pastor was in another community, I made the four-hour trip by mule from Yorito to Sulaco for a mass in the church there, during which I read the letter of the archbishop naming me pastor. I did the same thing in Victoria, Las Vegas, and San Antonio, the other big towns of the parish (each had about a thousand inhabitants). I promised mass on a fixed day each month in each of these four towns and started to visit other villages, always using Yorito as my home base.

In January 1971 our superior requested the pastor to turn over the keys of the parish rectory to me, and I finally moved in. Father General Arrupe had written to the pastor telling him to obey his superior, but the pastor immediately wrote another letter to the General in Rome telling him about the Marxist infiltration in the Jesuits and that it would not be wise to turn the parish over to one of these Jesuit communists. Even though our superior requested him to go to the United States to talk to the provincial, he said that he had to stay in the parish of Sulaco until Father General answered his second letter. You can see how dedicated this man was.

Before all this, the pastor and I had been good friends; I greatly admired his austerity and life of poverty. Both of us were convinced that this was one of the bases of the Christian life, which consists in the imitation of Christ. We just disagreed on the future of the church. He had been living fifteen years in the villages of the Sulaco parish, going tirelessly from one to another in three-month-long trips before leaving the parish to see other Jesuits. It is understandable that he would have a hard time with the Second Vatican Council, with its changes in the ritual of the mass and the sacraments. In 1970 he continued doing everything in Latin and suspected that the changes were because of Marxist infiltration in the Church. The new movement of Delegates of the Word, he used to tell the people, was to form married priests and destroy the true priesthood, and all this about ANACH, campesino cooperatives, and agrarian reform was just plain communism.

So he went around until June of 1971 visiting the towns and villages of the parish with his masses in Latin, his sermons about fear of sin and of hell, and telling the people that the Catholic church in Honduras was infiltrated by Marxist priests who wanted to change the customs, the morality, and the true religion of the Hondurans. He carefully avoided me and I would arrive at a village after his visit. You can imagine how hard it was to encourage the people to accept the changes in the Church and organize, for example, the Celebration of the Word of God. But little by little the people, especially the youth and those who had been to masses in other parishes, came to prefer the mass in Spanish, the priest facing the people, with joyful music accompanied by guitar, and dialogued sermons about their everyday problems.

After about six months I had picked out and become friends with some of the best men in many of the communities, and I gave them an introductory three-day Bible course in Victoria to form them as Delegates of the Word. The people of the town of Victoria were more open-minded and had never listened much to their previous priest. I visited all the homes in Victoria and won over a lot of people. I spent more time there each month than in Sulaco and started the Family of God course for couples to form the first basic Christian community (BCC) in the parish. The other community that responded very well to me and formed a strong BCC, with six Delegates of the Word, was Las Flores. It was way back in the mountains, where it was easiest to enter through the town of Subirana, which belonged to the parish of Yoro and which had more influence on the people of Las Flores than the former pastor had.

During my first year in the parish of Sulaco, I did not even mention the ANACH or cooperatives or agrarian reform in the towns and villages. As a basis for change in the parish, I invited many good Christian men and women to be Delegates of the Word, who would study the bishops' documents of Medellín with me in order to learn something of the theology of liberation. Only afterward was I going to talk to them about how to solve the greatest problem they all had: the lack of land for their corn and bean plots because of the best lands in the parish having been fenced in by a few rich cattlemen.

This parish of Sulaco was one of the most difficult in all of

Honduras, partly because of its geography. The parish was made up of two municipalities: Sulaco, with about ten thousand inhabitants in fifteen different communities, and Victoria, with about twenty-five thousand inhabitants in some thirty-five scattered communities. From the town of Sulaco at the extreme eastern end of the parish to Bajo Grande close to Santa Rita at the extreme western end of the parish were more than sixty-five miles of high mountains and barren hills with small valleys between them.

When I arrived in 1970, there was not a single road of any kind, nor a car, in the whole parish. All trips were made on foot or on mule back. Horses were no good in those rocky mountains, and it was not just any ordinary mule that could get through the mud on the mountain trail to Las Flores during the rainy season.

With good reason the former pastor made trips of three months, going from one village to the next without returning to Sulaco. He finally left for the United States in June of 1971. Again I do not want to take away from the dedicated service of this man. We were both hard headed and just saw things differently. I got a mechanic to help me get the former pastor's old jeep out of Sulaco, and from then on I always left it in Yorito.

My system was to use Victoria as my home base for visiting the bigger towns of Sulaco, San Antonio, and Las Vegas, plus all the villages of the eastern half of the parish. Each month I would go by mule to Yorito, where there was a road, to leave by jeep to visit the Indian tribes and the other ANACH groups that I was helping in practically the whole department of Yoro. To visit the whole western half of my parish of Sulaco, one month I would leave my jeep in the town of Subirana (where my favorite Indian tribe of Subirana was) to take the hour-long mule trip to Las Flores and spend a week in this part of the municipality of Victoria, visiting some of the other villages around there. The following month I would leave the jeep in Terrero Negro (in the municipality of Santa Rita) and cross the Cuyamapa River on mule to visit for a week another good BCC in San Isidro and some of the other villages at this extreme western end of Victoria.

To come to our monthly study and planning meetings of the Delegates of the Word in the town of Victoria, those from Las

Flores, for example, had to travel thirty miles each way by mule; those from San Isidro took a two-day trip of fifty-five miles just to get there, and then, of course, had to make the same trip back.

In my last years in the parish, after 1973, I began having the monthly meeting of Delegates and catechists in three centers where I would go each month: Victoria, Las Flores, and San Isidro. In 1975, when I left the Sulaco parish, the whole west-central part of the parish, entering through Subirana, was given over to the Yoro parish, and the whole far western part around San Isidro was given to the parish of Morazán.

With all those long hikes up and down the mountains during the five years I was in the Sulaco parish, I was in good physical condition. Even though the people of a village would send me a mule to go to visit them, I always walked at least halfway. I really enjoyed those trips through the mountains, feeling myself very close to God in this beautiful, wild country. Now I do not like life in a big city at all.

To change the alienating religious customs and mentality of the people, and to plant the new, liberating Church in the Sulaco parish really cost me a lot of anguish and suffering. The strongest propaganda against me, against the Celebration of the Word of God, and against the campesino organizations was from the big landowners of all the towns of my two municipalities and of those of Yoro, Yorito, and Morazán where our people would go to shop and to sell their corn, beans, and coffee. Also, over the radio stations (controlled by the rich bourgeoisie of Tegucigalpa and San Pedro Sula) the campesinos in the most remote mountain villages heard about my problems with the landowners and the military authorities first in Progreso, and now in Negrito, Morazán, Yoro, Yorito, Jocón, and Olanchito. This was because of my work with the Indian tribes and other campesinos we were organizing in the ANACH and in co-ops in all these municipalities.

It was hard to convince the campesinos in my isolated parish that I was not a communist. To do so, I had to visit each champa (hut) in all the villages and towns to try to make personal friendships with all those thousands of brothers and sisters of mine, so full of prejudices. After two years of these visits to all the families, most of the campesinos of the parish were in agreement with me and with the idea of getting organized.

In those first years in the Sulaco parish, I was so alone, and faced so much opposition, trying to open this frontier for the Kingdom of Christ! But I had so much work and activity that I did not have time to worry about the difficulties.

Ever since I had been named pastor in August of 1970, I tried to get some religious sisters to work as a team with me. The Spanish Sister Africa of the Missionary Crusaders of the Church, who had worked a lot with me during my last year in Progreso and Toyos, wanted to go to Sulaco, but it was a year and a half before she had all the permissions and found a Crusader sister to be her companion. In 1972, at last, Africa and Sister Enriqueta. another Spaniard, came to Victoria and rented a small house on the main street. It was in true evangelical fashion that they shared in the daily life of this town and little by little went out to visit the other towns and villages of the parish.

From the beginning we three worked very well as a team. Their only gripe was that I spent very little time with them in Victoria, only a few days of the month. But each month we planned the work together and studied together the five volumes of the Uruguayan Jesuit, Juan Luís Segundo, *Open-ended Theology for Adults*. We wanted to be in agreement on how we would explain the doctrine of Christ to the adults and to the children. The sisters took charge of organizing the catechetical instruction of all the children of the parish and of the formation of the women catechists. Those books of Juan Luís Segundo were and still are my favorite manuals of modern liberation theology. I have read them several times and made summaries of each chapter for use in my courses.

The first volume about the Church presents the basic pastoral option: Are we trying to form the "Church of the masses" (trying to get everyone to be a Catholic with a very minimum of demands, like the actual Church in Latin America), or the "Church of the small communities" as ferment or leaven of liberation within the masses? The fact is that one does not have to be a Catholic, or even baptized, to be saved; one only has to love one's neighbor as oneself, as Jesus explained in Matthew 25:31–46 about the last judgment day.

Actually, most of humanity never knew, neither in the past nor in the present, about Jesus Christ; but as long as they helped their fellow human beings, they did it to Jesus and will be "blessed of my Father." Well then, if one does not have to be a Christian to be saved, why be a Christian? We Christians should be the "light" of the world; we should be the ones who understand, through the revelation of Christ, the plan of God for this world, where the evolution of this world is going. We should be a "ferment (or leaven) in the masses," a vanguard, an elite group that promotes the evolution of the world and of humanity according to this plan of God. We should form model communities of the New Society of brothers and sisters (without social classes) that will be the Kingdom of God. We are not Christians, then, in order to be saved, but in order to be saviors, like Christ.

Theoretically, today, at last, many bishops and priests (not all) admit these ideas, but in practice, only a few adopt the pastoral option of dedicating themselves principally to the formation of these liberating basic Christian communities—maybe with only a few committed families. Many still dedicate most of their time, energy, and money to campaigns to convince the masses to receive the sacraments, in popular missions, in preparing all the little Catholic children of a town for First Holy Communion (even though their parents never receive it), in radio and television programs, and so on. We cannot abandon the masses of Latin-American Catholics, but we have to put the emphasis on forming the "Church as sign, as ferment in the masses," and not the "Church of the masses."

This option is really a political option in Latin America. Most of the bishops want the "Church of the masses," in order to have "the new Christendom," with the Church as a political force in the country. That is why they adapt themselves and stay friendly to any kind of a regime, even though it be fascist and repressive, in order to have "liberty" to give popular missions, to have Catholic schools, and so on. On the other hand, the pastoral options that give priority to the formation of revolutionary, liberating BCCs among the poor and oppressed, that get involved in the revolutionary struggles for the liberation of the oppressed, end up as a new "classist" Church of the poor. This Church is identified with the oppressed class, the exploited, and of course, is persecuted by the dominating, exploiting, elitist class.

The great majority of the bishops and priests still want to be on good terms with everyone, with the rich and with the poor, with the oppressed and with the oppressors. They want to avoid this conflict, or class struggle; they do not want to choose one class against the other. That means that their option is for the status quo. This is the same as choosing the social class that is in power, the bourgeoisie, the exploiters, against the exploited class. Christ did not try to be on good terms with everyone. He plainly made his choice for the oppressed class and was killed by the oppressors.

In the Sulaco parish, our team also chose to form the Church identified with the oppressed class in its struggle against the oppressors. We put our priority in the formation of the BCCs and Delegates of the Word, which would be involved in the revolutionary struggle to change the capitalist system for a new socialist society. We saw this as an important step in the formation of the Kingdom of God in our part of the world.

We also studied the other volumes of Juan Luís Segundo, *Grace and the Human Condition* (everything is supernatural in this world), *Our Idea of God* (humanity is evolving a more correct idea of God), *The Sacraments Today* (they are not for saving us, but to celebrate our community life), and *Evolution of Culpability* (the revolutionary dialectic has to overcome "the sin" of the conservativism of the Church). We incorporated many of these ideas into the Family of God course that we used to start the BCCs.

We started at least something of a BCC in Las Vegas, San Antonio, Las Flores, San Isidro and Las Canas, and two of them in Victoria. The town of Sulaco was the only place where I could not even finish the Family of God course: first of all, because of the opposition and calumnies against me from the big landowners and Nationalist politicians of Yoro, who had some of their cattle ranches near Sulaco, and second, because there were some heavy drinking problems throughout the area. It was really for these reasons that I changed the headquarters of the Sulaco parish to Victoria and only visited Sulaco for two days each month. Also the town of Victoria was closer to the center of the parish.

Once the former pastor was gone, it was easier for me to become friends with most of the campesinos of the parish and to pick out Delegates of the Word in about thirty of the fifty communities of the parish. By the end of 1971 all the Delegates had taken at least one of my introductory Bible courses. In 1972 I insisted that all the Delegates take four days of the Spiritual Exercises of Saint Ignatius with me, enclosed and in complete silence. It was like a short Jesuit novitiate, where they learned to meditate and to listen to the Holy Spirit in their soul in order to know God's will.

I adapted the Exercises to these simple, honest campesinos who were already committed to Christ. We prayed that they would come out of the retreat also committed to help organize the campesinos of their village for the revolutionary struggle for a new society of brotherhood and equality. We prayed for a world without social classes, which will be more like the Kingdom of God toward which the Holy Spirit is directing the evolution of this world. I reinterpreted all the principal Exercises of Saint Ignatius to relate them to the reality of Honduras, using the theology of liberation and the documents of Medellín.

We meditated on, first, the existence of God, which we adults should accept for intellectual reasons and not because our parents told it to us; second, the end of humanity and of the universe, that is, the plan of God, which is that men and women should live happily in a paradise, in the Kingdom of God in this world, in a society of perfect brotherhood and equality where everything is shared with one another (the Holy Trinity is the model); third, what ruined and continues to ruin this plan of God, are not only the personal sins, the selfishness of each person, but unjust economic-social-political systems. Here in Honduras these unjust systems are capitalism and imperialism, with private ownership of the means of production, which promotes selfishness. This is a form of structural sin, social sin, the "sin of the world" that Christ also came to take away.

There are other economic-social-political systems in the world that have become unjust besides capitalism. Socialist and communist systems have "institutionalized sin" at times, as when the party or state takes too much power from the workers, when human rights are not respected, when religious freedom is denied. People need to work, fight, and die for liberation from the injustices of these systems even as they do against raw capitalism. The concentration of power in the state in socialism or communism has in itself a danger that people begin to exist for the party and state rather than the party and state existing for the people. Such corrupted socialist and communist states also become imperialistic. A good example is Stalin's Russia. However, such corrupt socialism is not our problem in Honduras. (Here we made a short Marxist analysis of the actual capitalist Honduran society, with the rich exploiting the poor and U.S. imperialism exploiting Honduras.)

We meditated on, fourth, "The Call of Christ the King" to help him transform this unjust capitalist society into his Kingdom by means of a truly liberating revolution; fifth, Luke 4:14–21, in which we heard Jesus explain his mission in this world, "the liberation of the oppressed"; sixth, the famous meditation of "The Two Standards," in which we saw the mentality of Satan as the selfish spirit of seeking riches, private property, and honors in order to dominate others; and we saw the mentality of Chirst as the spirit of a revolutionary who loves his neighbor, the poor, so much that he identifies himself with the poor class, disposed to suffer every kind of persecution in the struggle for the liberation of the oppressed. Christ humbly prefers others to himself and conquers selfishness. We saw the necessity of a double, continuous revolution: the economic-social-political revolution to change society, and the cultural revolution to change the person from the bourgeois, selfish mentality to the socialist, unselfish mentality.

Seventh, we reflected on and discussed why they killed Jesus; and eighth, we finished by reviewing the strategy of Jesus for transforming this world into his Kingdom. He organized a vanguard for the evolution of the world, a small model-community of the new classless society of brotherhood, a BCC, the true Catholic church. This is what we should do also in each town and village.

On this last point, we reflected a lot about the BCC of the first Christians described in the Acts of the Apostles 2:42–47. It explains that they shared their possessions with each other, handing over their money to be distributed according to the needs of each one. In Acts 4:32–34 it says, "No one said that his things were only his, but that all things belonged to all of them. There was no one among them who was needy." This was the liberation of the oppressed, the "good news for the poor," who gladly joined to form the primitive Catholic church, which thus spread rapidly. But this was bad news and "subversive" for the bourgeoisie and the authorities who persecuted and killed the early Christians.

With these reflections it became clear to our campesinos that the capitalist system of private ownership of basic tools of production, of individualism and competition to acquire personal gain, promotes selfishness. It is exactly the opposite of "loving your neighbor as yourself" and of the example of the first disciples of Christ. From that, they understood that it is Christian to work collectively in cooperatives and share the harvest, like brothers and sisters. We would finish the retreat thinking about how the New Society, the New Honduras that Christ wants, would be without social classes, without rich and poor, all persons being equal and deciding that it is necessary to have a revolution to make this change from a capitalist to a Christian socialist society.

The campesinos and I spent many hours discussing the type of society we wanted to build. We Christian revolutionaries dream of a socialist society in Honduras unlike any society presently existing in the world, "a quantitively distinct society." We do not want to copy the model of the Soviet Union, China, Cuba, or any other country. We want to create a socialism, fully true to Christ's teachings, born in and of Central America for Central Americans. We also understand it will take great heroism from generations of Central Americans to bring this new society to perfection.

In October of 1972 I gave the first of these retreats to my friends, the leaders of the Christian Democratic Party. The participants came from Tegucigalpa to be in the environment of the poor campesinos for five days of retreat in the church at Toyos. I kept the list of Christian Democrats who participated with me in six more of the same five-day enclosed retreats during 1973 and 1974, four for men and two for women in different places in the country.

In those years I was going to Tegucigalpa at least every other month for the problems of the Indian tribes. At the same time, I met with all these Christian Democrats who had made retreats with me, and with other friends of theirs, for private masses and discussions in some of their homes. In 1974 I went to Olancho to give two more retreats of these Spiritual Exercises to practically all the intermediate leaders, like the teachers, that the Christian Democrats had in the Radio Schools, the campesino training centers, and so on. On looking over the list of the participants in all these retreats, I am glad to see that most of them have left the Christian Democratic Party and are now in other parties that are more revolutionary. Many of them are in PASO (the Socialist Party of Honduras).

In November of 1973 I gave the first of these same spiritual retreats to labor leaders in the vacation colony of the SITRATERCO in Puerto Cortés. Those who took it were the president of the CTH, the president of the FESITRANH, the president of the SITRATERCO, with almost all the rest of the executive committee, plus other leaders of the SITRATERCO. In January of 1974, I had one with ten leaders of the principal labor unions of the FECESITLIH in Tegucigalpa in the Minor Seminary. In March of 1974, in the training center of the FESITRANH, close to San Pedro Sula, I had another one with the top leaders of five of the sections of the SITRATERCO, and in September of the same year in Tegucigalpa another one, with ten more leaders of labor unions of the FECESITLIH.

For all these labor leaders I focused the Spiritual Exercises around the theme of the social doctrine of the Church and held them only for three days on a weekend. I tried to organize some kind of follow-up by means of monthly study meetings with these labor leaders, but after many attempts I realized it was impossible. I will explain later how I started these same retreats for leaders of the campesino organizations; with them, the follow-up study circles were quite successful.

With all of this, and with my continual visits to the ANACH groups in almost the whole department of Yoro to help them get organized in the National Co-op Plan of the ANACH, it is understandable why I only spent about half of my time in the Sulaco parish. There, also, once I had won the friendship and confidence of most of the campesinos, I decided to openly encourage them to get organized in the ANACH in order to demand some agrarian reform in this part of the country. No campesino movement existed here as yet. This was in 1972, after the new military coup of Colonel López Arellano, when the

ANACH had some good revolutionary elements in its executive committee that were promoted by activists of the Communist Party in the San Pedro Sula and Progreso areas.

The ANACH played an important role in the new military coup to completely change the nonfunctioning government of Ramón Cruz and the "National Unity Pact." Especially brought to a standstill were agrarian reform and the INA under Horacio Moya Posas of the National Party, who helped the big landowners evade the application of the Agrarian Reform Law.

On February 18, 1972, there was a cold-blooded massacre of six campesinos of the UNC in La Talanquera, Olancho, by a platoon of soldiers who arrived to evict them from the land they had "recovered." Just a few days later all the sixteen villages of Guaymas (in Progreso), organized in the ANACH under a single regional leadership, again "recovered" about 1700 acres of idle land of the Tela Railroad Company near Batán (in Guaymas). About eight hundred compesino men and women entered these lands with tractors and started plowing, planting corn, and building their champas. A whole company of soldiers arrived to forcibly evict them again from these lands, as they had a year and a half previously, and threw about 50 of the main leaders of the ANACH of Guaymas in jail.

Rather than transfer these idle lands of the American transnational company, INA offered land to all these sixteen subsections of the ANACH, but in the lower Aguan River Valley in the department of Colón. This is where Rigoberto Sandoval had initiated the big agrarian reform project of the lower Aguan. Some of the subsections accepted, like Luzón, La Nueva Jerusalem, and San Francisco, which became cooperatives, and each received 1200 acres near Sava, Colón. I will talk more about this later, because I too was later transferred to the lower Aguan Valley.

In March of 1972 there was a nationwide wave of land "invasions" (as the landowners call them), or "recoveries" (as the campesinos call them). The campesinos explained that as the Bible says, God made the earth and gave it to mankind, to all men and women, not to just a few, so they are just recovering a little of their share of the land that the rich have unjustly grabbed for themselves. The Jesuits had to defend me with a pronoucement that was reported in the newspapers that I reproduce in part:

The Accusation Against Padre Guadalupe Is False

The Vicar General of the department of Yoro and superior of all the Jesuits in Honduras flatly denies the accusation of agitator that has been made against Padre Guadalupe. Father Joseph Fisher denies the news report in *La Prensa* (Tuesday, 14 March) that states that "Padre Guadalupe is one of the agitators" in the invasion of the ranch "Ganadera del Norte" in Negrito, Yoro. "Padre Guadalupe has not even been in the area of the invasion since the month of January," says Father Fisher, "and has not encouraged nor given orders to any of the campesinos in this invasion. . . ."

Not only the campesinos, but also the labor unions and even the progressive industrialists wanted a change of government. They made a new "Little Pact" with the head of the armed forces, Colonel López Arellano, with, of course, the approval of the U.S. embassy. The ANACH for months had been threatening a gigantic hunger march to Tegucigalpa of all its members, if the government did not change the director of INA, Moya Posas, and give land to the hundreds of campesino groups that had been making formal requests to INA. They would stay in Central Park in Tegucigalpa with their women and children to die of hunger there, where the government would have to see them, instead of hidden away in their villages. Since I came out of Sulaco each month to see the ANACH leaders, when I knew the date of the hunger march I wanted to go with them, but the executive committee advised me not to get involved in this; so I was back in Sulaco when it happened.

On the arranged date, from every point of the compass, twenty thousand campesinos started the march toward Tegucigalpa, without any opposition from the military forces until the biggest group of them, who came in trucks from the north and from the west, reached Comayagua. There they were stopped by the soldiers and told to return to their homes because the armed forces had taken over the government and put Colonel López Arellano in again as president of the republic. He promised to reorganize INA and give land immediately to the campesinos. Since the executive committee of the ANACH had been in on the new "Little Pact" with López Arellano and knew what was going to happen, they convinced the twenty thousand campesinos to go back home.

As a matter of fact, one of the first acts of the new military government was to name the progressive lawyer, Mario Ponce Cambar, as director of INA and to promulgate Decree Number 8 of the new government. This decree declared that organized groups of campesinos could request from INA any lands, whether held by the state or private property, that were idle. After it was proven by a commission of INA with a representative of the ANACH, the UNC, and the FECORAH that they were really unproductive, INA immediately had to give these lands to the groups to use for at least two years. With the new director of INA, Ponce Cambar, backed up by the government and armed forces, who were really serious about carrying out Decree Number 8, almost all the organized campesino groups, hundreds of groups of the three organizations, received some land within a few months.

This made the atmosphere at that moment in Honduras so favorable toward agrarian reform that near the end of 1972 I got a great friend of mine to make a ten-day trip with me around my parish to organize many of our landless campesinos. He was a former Delegate of the Word from the Guaymas region of Progreso, Fausto Orellana Luna, who was then one of the seven members of the national executive committee of the ANACH. In these ten days subsections of the ANACH were organized in nine communities, including the towns of San Antonio, Victoria, and Sulaco.

A subsection of the ANACH had formerly existed in Sulaco, but it was dissolved when their campesino president, my friend Santiago Reafios, was murdered. We reorganized this subsection and formed another new one in Sulaco.

After some of the hardest struggles of the ANACH, in 1973 these two subsections of Sulaco and that of San Antonio finally got some of the land fenced in by a big landowner and his wife (a big Legionary and daily communicant). I helped them get organized as cooperatives for collective work, and each one of the three co-ops bought their own tractor and plow with loans from the bank.

The landowner's family and that of his wife had illegally fenced in almost all the fine, flat farmland of the Sulaco Valley, which were really ejidal lands (lands belonging to the municipality). They have even more land in the Yoro Valley. Their son was very mean and threatened to kill me and the leaders of the sub-sections of the ANACH. (The gunmen of the Mancha Brava in Yoro were famous.) You should have seen how these and other big landowners who lived in the town of Yoro spread propaganda and calumnies against me.

The campaign against me in Yoro, for organizing the Indian tribes in the ANACH and the campesinos of Sulaco, Yorito, and of some of the villages of the Yoro Valley, reached a high level. One priest, with whom I had worked in 1963 and who was still pastor of Yoro, told me that I could not eat or sleep in the parish rectory or celebrate mass in Yoro, and that he did not want to even see me around there. I told him that I would not do any pastoral work in his parish, but that I had permission from our superior, Joe Fisher, to help form co-ops among the Indians and campesinos of the whole department of Yoro.

I had to be in Yoro a few days each month to visit the Indian tribes and other campesino groups we were organizing with an activist of the ANACH in the municipalities of Yoro and Jocón. Therefore, I rented a champa with a dirt floor in El Pantano on the outskirts of Yoro for five dollars a month and ate with a poor, friendly family in the town.

Something similar was also taking place with the pastor in Olanchito, who received many complaints against me from the big landowners around there. But since it was Father Valentín Menéndez, his assistant, who had precisely invited me to organize in cooperatives the Indians and campesinos of his villages of the parish of Olanchito, and since Valentín was highly respected by the archbishop and by all the Jesuits in Honduras, the pastor had to tolerate me.

There had been a number of subsections of the ANACH organized in the municipality of Olanchito ever since 1968. About five of these had obtained some land, and two of them, Méndez and Potrerillos, were working collectively in the Co-op Plan of the ANACH, and had obtained tractors and even irrigation equipment. During five years I helped different activists of the ANACH reorganize a number of the defunct groups and start new subsections and cooperatives, including the agro-forestry co-ops of the two tribes of Agua Caliente and Zapotal.

A "section" of the ANACH was organized with the twenty sub-sections of the area, and had its own rented office in Olanchito. Nevertheless, right up to today many of these groups still have not received land, though they have invaded the idle lands and their leaders have been thrown in jail several times.

PART VI. THE BIRTH OF A CHRISTIAN REVOLUTIONARY

16. How Can a People Be Liberated?

When I came out of Sulaco and Yorito each month, if I did not go to Jocón and Olanchito, I would go to Morazán, Negrito, Progreso, San Pedro Sula, and even to Tegucigalpa. Since I spent a few days in Progreso almost every month on ANACH affairs or for the retreat, and since I had sworn never to live in the Company Zone in Progreso, (where the rest of the Jesuits passing through always stayed), I had the problem of where to sleep each time. I sometimes slept in the parish rectory and, at other times, in our Instituto San José.

After two years of that, in 1972 I looked for a poor champa to rent in one of the slum neighborhoods of Progreso, but there were no empty houses. Looking in the villages closest to Progreso, I found in Camalote, (about three miles north of Progreso) a poor, dirt-floored house of wood that was rotting through. It was unoccupied or, more accurately, abandoned. It was without lighting or running water, but was alongside a lovely creek and exactly what I wanted for living with and as the poor campesinos. It belonged to the big landowner Julio Píres, of Progreso, who, for rent, asked me only to keep the grass cut in the big lot around the house. I used this house for seven years.

I was delighted to be there by the creek at the foot of the mountains, a little bit separated from most of the houses of the village. I called it my house of prayer, and indeed, I spent many solitary hours, especially when I got up in the middle of the night, in close union with the Spirit of Jesus living in me. I read a great deal at night by the light of a candle, preferably now books about Christianity and Marxism: books by Julio Girardi, the Italian Marxist priest, and Roger Garaudy, the former head of the French Communist Party. I have a type of insomnia and still get up almost every night for an hour or two of meditation and reading, or else I get up at 4:00 A.M. to do it. In this way I get in a lot of reading.

It was in this period that I wrote a ten-page document for the thousands of campesinos of the ANACH to study called "The Ideology of the ANACH." I distributed about a thousand mimeographed copies of it at the national convention of the ANACH in September of 1973, where, as always, I opened the convention with an invocation to God. The representatives there unanimously approved my document for study by all the subsections in the country, and each one took along a copy. Afterward, the military authorities learned about the document; they, the American embassy, the American Institute for Free Labor Development (AIFLD), and the controlled leaders of the CTH and the FESITRANH, Victor Artiles and Céleo Gonzales, were very angry with me.

In the document I explained how the ANACH had been born and nurtured as a child by the FESITRANH and AIFLD, but now, after ten years and a tremendous growth—to more than fifty thousand members—the ANACH should begin to think for itself as an adult. It should decide why it exists. What do the campesinos want for Honduras? I told them that their objective could not just be economic gains for themselves, like land and help for their farming and for their villages, leaving the campesino and worker class always exploited and dominated by the capitalist class and by Yankee imperialism. They are the big majority, 85 percent of Hondurans, who should unite themselves to take over the power in Honduras, which up to now had been controlled by a capitalist-military oligarchy for their own benefit and for that of the foreign companies. But take over the power and the government for what purpose? What is the ideology of the ANACH? It is now time to decide about it, so that the ANACH would not be an instrument of domination of the campesinos and of their conformity with capitalism, but rather of their integral liberation.

The document stated that we have to change the whole capitalist system that the Catholic church has condemned as a system of selfishness and of exploitation of one by another. The ANACH should define their long-range goal, the kind of new society we want. *The new Honduran society*, I said, *should be neither capitalist nor communist* (which the Church has also condemned for being atheistic). It should be, first, *egalitarian*, with laws fixing not only the minimum wage, but also the maximum wage. For the poverty-striken Honduras of 1973 I suggested that the minimum that a day laborer or a salesclerk or a hired housekeeper or any salaried person ought to earn should be $100 a month, and the maximum that a doctor, a military general, or the president of the republic could get should be $200 a month, in order to distribute more equally the small amount of riches available in Honduras. It should be, second, *communitarian*, a mixed economy of small private property and also of state property, with nationalization of the most essential services of the country, like the banks, energy, transportation, and so on. Most of the means of production should be social property in the form of cooperatives. It should be, third, *participative*, with autogestion, or self-government by the workers in the cooperatives and state enterprises, and with co-gestion, or shared direction and profits in the private enterprises. The whole population should belong to basic popular organizations, through which everyone will participate in the local and national government. It included goals of agrarian reform, urban reform, and free, obligatory education during one's whole life in order to form the *New Person in the New Society*.

Following the advice of my brother Jesuits who read it before it was distributed, the document did not mention the word *socialism*, so that it would not be automatically rejected by those who have prejudices. As can be seen, the ideology that I proposed for the ANACH in 1973 was the same as that of the Christian Democrats, of the social doctrine of the Church, and of the Medellín documents: "a third way," neither capitalist nor communist. The worker-campesino class would take over the power and radically change the capitalist system by using nonviolent methods, like those of Gandhi. That is as far as I had advanced in my metamorphosis as a revolutionary when I wrote this document in early 1973.

What principally inspired me at that time were the *nonviolent revolutions* of Salvador Allende in Chile and of the progressive military rulers in Peru, especially the documents of these latter revolutionaries (or reformists?). The Socialist Party of Allende, together with all the other revolutionary groups including the

"Christians for Socialism" and a big part of the Christian Democrats in the "Popular Union," took over power in Chile by winning free elections, and they started making socialist reforms little by little. All of us anticapitalists and antiimperialists in the whole world were looking at Chile with great hope as a model of how to make the revolution peaceful, without violence.

I studied and liked very much the document of the First International Meeting of Christians for Socialism of 1972 in Chile, and also the very advanced document of the Peruvian Bishops' Conference for the Bishops' Synod in Rome in 1971. The Rome document states on page 9:

There can be no political participation without economic participation. Also, we must affirm that work is what gives the legitimate and primary title of possession of goods. This implies a new, humanistic conception of the economic process, which surpasses the capitalist model, where capital was privileged, and work was considered just another merchandise. As a consequence of this conception of work, there follows the need to go beyond the exclusively private appropriation of the means of production and to promote social property, which is a more efficacious response to the meaning of human labor and to the universal destiny of the goods of this world. God, the Creator, put these goods in the world for all men. . . .

What we have said and also the experience of our people lead us to reject capitalism, as well in its economic form as in its ideological base, which favors individualism, personal gain, and the exploitation of man by man. We therefore have to create a qualitatively distinct society. . . . With the appearance of governments that seek to implant more just and human societies in their countries, WE PROPOSE: that the Church commit herself to help them by breaking down prejudices, by recognizing their good aspirations, and by encouraging them in the search for their own proper road toward a socialist society with human and Christian content.

In the retreats we studied this document and that of the Christians for Socialism. I also liked very much the book of Ernesto Cardenal, which he wrote about Cuba after he visited there to learn about their revolution. For a number of years I have been listening to Radio Havana as much as possible, especially the speeches of Fidel Castro. I have great admiration for this outstanding revolutionary. Since 1972, I have been listening almost

every day to the program "Voices of the Revolution" at 7:00 A.M.
over Radio Havana with parts of his speeches. He is a real
teacher, not only of all the Cubans, but also of millions of others
who listen to Radio Havana all over the world. In practically all
his speeches he is teaching, for example, the campesinos, the
small private landowners, with tremendous patience and with no
kind of threats, the advantages of working together in cooperatives, or he is teaching the doctors and professors that they
should not consider the privilege they had to study as a right to
live better than the campesinos, but rather as an obligation to go
out to the rural and mountain villages to share their learning
with the poor of other countries, like missionaries. I consider
Fidel Castro to be a person inspired and led by the Holy Spirit.

I liked it when Fidel went to Chile and told the priests that in
Latin America the alliance between Marxists and Christian revolutionaries is not a tactical but a strategic alliance, that is, not
temporary, but permanent and necessary. Also I liked the saying
of Che Guevara (another Marxist saint, who gave his life for the
poor guided by the Spirit of Jesus without knowing him) that
"when the Christians in Latin America take seriously the revolutionary teachings of the gospel, the revolution will be invincible."

In January of 1973, I wrote and distributed to my friends the
following document:

DOES THERE HAVE TO BE RICH AND POOR, THE CLASS STRUGGLE?

Do you think that there is no class struggle in Honduras? Do you
think all Hondurans are treated alike? that government money is helping everyone? that all eat the same? Why are there land invasions by the
campesinos and strikes by the workers in Honduras? Isn't that the class
struggle? We all know that there are a few rich and many, many poor in
Honduras. Indeed, all capitalist countries have this division into social
classes. The industrialized countries have a smaller percentage of poor
than Honduras, but they still have the class struggle. Do you think we
could better the capitalist system in Honduras, little by little industrializ-
ing the country, and then there will be no class struggle of the workers
against the owners? The fact is that at the rate Honduras is presently
trying to better the capitalist economy, the percentage of Honduran
families that have an annual income of less than $500 grows every year.
But even if we could lower that percentage from the present 85 percent

of the population down to 50 percent, do you think that would be a good situation?

What does God think of the class struggle, of having rich and poor classes, of some families eating better than others? Do you think God wants his children to live like that? Is that the way God made the world to be? Because some persons are more capable of earning money than others, does God therefore want them to have more than others? Well, I know that God doesn't want that, because that is unjust, is sinful. The system of life in Honduras is very unjust, is very much contrary to the will of God. After thirty years of daily meditations on the gospel of Christ, I am convinced that God wants everyone in the world to live as brothers and sisters. God doesn't want some of his sons and daughters to have more privileges than others. If we are brothers and sisters, how can I be content eating better than my brothers and sisters? It makes no difference whether God made me more intelligent, or with a more pleasing personality; if we are brothers and sisters we should share everything we have. We shouldn't call ourselves Christian until we are disposed to share everything we have with our brothers and sisters, our neighbors. It seems to me that the saying of Marx that "each one should give according to his capacity, and each one should receive according to his need" (which was the same as the system of the first Christians described in Acts 2:42–47) is another way of saying with Jesus, "Love your neighbor as yourself."

Why is this considered bad? What does it mean to "love your neighbor as yourself"? Doesn't it mean that I am not going to eat better than my neighbor? That I do not want privileges that my neighbor does not have? If I can prepare myself better by professional studies, it cannot be to earn more money than my neighbor, the illiterate, but in order to be better able to love and help my brothers, my country.

I am convinced that these are ideas of the Spirit of Jesus. After the first Christian communities, Christ has not been able to penetrate much into the mentality of most Christians (only of a minority in each generation), but the Spirit of Jesus is certainly penetrating lately into the mentality of millions of Marxists. Or do you think that the Spirit of Jesus only works in Catholics? The Church has always taught that God gives his grace to all persons to save them. I am also convinced that one does not have to be an atheist to have these ideas. These are Christ's ideas.

Eighty-five percent of Hondurans are poor, do not eat well, and would gladly accept the idea of everyone receiving according to his or her need and giving according to his or her capacity. But 15 percent of the Hondurans live a little better and have struggled hard in their lives to be able to earn more money than the poor campesinos. They definitely are opposed to these "communist" ideas (of Christ). And they are the ones who have all the power in their hands. The Church has always told them that they should share with the rest, and so once in a while they permit a law that helps distribute a little bit more of the riches to the poor workers. But who can imagine that this 15 percent will completely change their mentality and permit laws that would distribute equally the total income in the country from production among all the Hondurans? The saddest part of it all for me is that not even those who consider themselves the best Christians want this. Not even most bishops and priests would agree to such laws, so that all citizens would live alike, as brothers and sisters. Well then, how can we get a socialist, egalitarian society like that? How can those who think like Christ about this (even though they are not Christians) get the power of the government and of the army into their hands to force the 15 percent of the privileged class to accept a just society?

My document ended leaving this question hanging in the air because I myself did not know the answer in January of 1973.

Afterward, when Padre Ernesto Cardenal of Nicaragua and Bishop Sergio Méndez Arceo of Cuernavaca, Mexico, openly called themselves Christian-Marxists, I also started to consider myself a Christian-Marxist, but just a beginner. I decided that I had to study Marxism-Leninism more seriously, and, thanks to my many progressive professor and labor leader friends, I was able to borrow many books about this. Of course I had to obtain and read these books secretly. In Honduras there has never been freedom of thought and expression, which are fundamental rights of all people. You cannot openly teach or write Marxist ideas in Honduras, especially nowadays. Just for being a "communist" the police will throw you into jail and torture you, or throw you out of the country.

But what caused the biggest leap forward in my metamorphosis, a qualitative change, was the military coup d'état in Chile, with the murder of Allende and tens of thousands of "leftists" by the army, and the later revelations of the dominant role that the U.S. embassy in Chile, the CIA, and the transnational U.S. companies, like ITT, played in all this before and during the coup. The U.S. economic blockade, the CIA's fomenting of the counterrevolution inside of Chile, spending hundreds of millions of dollars for this, and the fact that Allende did not control the whole army made it impossible to carry out the Chilean revolution peacefully, following the rules of bourgeois democracy.

At last I and many thousands of other revolutionaries-in-formation in the world realized that Marx and Lenin were right when they taught that the anticapitalist, antiimperialist revolution is possible only by taking over power militarily and taking away the guns from the army of the bourgeois class by means of an army of the working class. The only way to eliminate the government of the minority, of the bourgeoisie (which is disguised as a "democracy"), is with the government of the majority, with the power in the hands of the people, "popular power."

I now seriously doubted that the nonviolent methods of Gandhi, of pacifism, of active resistance, of civil disobedience, of peaceful mass demonstrations, could change the capitalist system and liberate a country from imperialism. After the bloody military coup of 1973 in Chile, *it was obvious that the United States would never allow a country that is economically dependent on it to make a revolution by means of elections*—through the democratic process directed by the majority—at least as long as the country has an army that obeys the capitalist bourgeoisie of the country.

At last I was convinced that there was only one way for a dependent country to make a real revolution to liberate the people from capitalism and imperialism: by an armed revolution, by a popular war. "People's power" in a country will only be achieved by an armed struggle, a war of the masses of working people organized under a vanguard and fighting to defeat the army of the oligarchy that is helped economically and militarily by the United States. The intervention of the CIA to overthrow the revolutionary military officers in Peru, and the invasion by the U.S. marines together with other armed forces sent by the Organization of American States (including Honduran troops) to brutally smash the popular revolutionary insurrection in the Dominican Republic in 1965 were other obvious proofs confirming the Marxist-Leninist thesis.

I still had some doubts about how to reconcile this fact with Christianity. For one thing, Christ, in order to form the Kingdom of God in this world, a brotherhood and sisterhood of all humanity, wants the liberation of the oppressed. This was and still is one major purpose of his mission in this world. For this, he wants to keep away the great sin of the world, which is any exploitation of one person by another. This is the task of true love for the poor.

On the other hand, it is now more and more clear that this liberation is possible only by means of an armed struggle of the poor masses organized against their oppressors and their armed forces in order to take over the power in the country. But from still another point of view, we were always taught that Christ forbade violence, at least preferred nonviolence, to win the enemy over by love, to "present the other cheek"—"he who lives by the sword will die by the sword"; "Thou shalt not kill". Well, what does that mean, then? Can a Christian not actively participate in the liberation of his or her people? Or can he or she do so only as a medical doctor would, without a gun?

The Church has always taught that one can use violence and can even kill in self-defense, if it is necessary. It has even taught that there are just wars for the defense of the homeland in which a Christian certainly can fight (as they did in the war between Honduras and El Salvador in 1969). But most of the latest documents of the popes and bishops about modern problems condemn the use of violence as un-Christian. There is a passage, however, in "*Populorum Progressio*" of Pope Paul VI, repeated by the bishops in Medellín, that says that popular armed insurrection would be justified in the case of prolonged tyranny that has no other solution, and he adds, but violence always engenders more violence. So, after having sworn during World War II that I would never kill a person, and after being a disciple of Gandhi and his nonviolent methods of combating injustices, it still took me a couple more years to clarify my ideas about a Christian and his or her place in an armed revolution.

While I am on this theme, I might as well develop it further. Later, during 1975 with its violent repression, my ideas on the Christian use of arms became clearer. I was gradually and finally acknowledging to myself the truth that *love sometimes demands fighting back*. The book that most helped me to reflect on this and come to an understanding was Julio Girardi's *Christian Love and the Class Struggle*. It explained to me that the only true Christian love for the poor is an efficacious love, a love that helps them get out of their poverty once and for all, that liberates them. For this, one has to enter on the side of the poor in the struggle against the capitalist and imperialist exploiters, because the liberation of the poor will only come by way of the struggle to form a new socialist society without social or economic classes. Efficacious love for the oppressors also demands this armed struggle to take the guns away from them by which they are sinning, repressing the poor, and, thus, to liberate the oppressors also.

My studies of Chardin and Juan Luís Segundo made it clear that God's plan for the evolution of this world and of human society is obviously dialectical, involving conflict and at times even armed revolution.

Marx perceived part of God's plan (without recognizing God) for the evolution of human society. Human selfishness ruined a structural aspect of God's original plan for the "earthly paradise" and led us to fence in lands as private property and to use other people as slaves, or as day laborers, exploiting them for our own profit. We thus formed antagonistic classes, an exploiting minority and an exploited majority, and the resulting class struggle became a primary motor of evolution and of history.

The class struggle in a capitalist society will finally result in a recovery of power by the exploited majority in each country and in the entire world. Instead of the dictatorship of the bourgeois minority, in the socialist society there will be a government by the working class majority as a necessary step for forming the classless society. Then everyone will be a worker, and each will give according to his or her capacity and each will receive according to his or her need. This society of brotherhood and sisterhood will provide a structure upon which to build the Kingdom of God, a paradise, the "new heaven and the new earth" of the Parousia at Christ's second and final coming (described in the Apocalypse 21:1–8).

From this perspective I no longer found a contradiction between Marxism and Christianity, but rather a great convergence and complementarity. The writings of certain liberation theologians helped me to understand how the gospel needs the mediation of the social sciences in order to be able to apply it to our lives, that is, to learn how to put the gospel, the "good news for the poor," into practice in Honduras and the third world.

It is helpful to use the Marxist scientific method for making a structural and a conjunctural analysis of the society in which we live (whether this society be capitalist, socialist, or communist) in order to understand the reality and the sin from which Christ wants us to be liberated. Without understanding scientifically the reality of unjust societies that we have to transform, and also the technique for transforming them, we will not know how to form societies in which God's kingdom can flourish most fully.

The other part of Marxism, the global, philosophical vision of the universe that rejects the transcendental, that rejects everything that the natural sciences cannot study, that rejects the existence of God, the immortal soul, and the resurrection of the body, is clearly in contradiction with Christianity. *I fully reject this part of Marxism as every Christian must reject this part of Marxism.* Pope Paul VI, in his *"Octagesimo Adveniens,"* recognizes this distinction between Marxism as a social science and Marxism as a vision and philosophical explanation of the universe.

For me, Marxism explains a lot, but needs the Christian vision to complete it. It explains the world already made, but it does not explain where it came from, why it exists and evolves as it does, where the laws of dialectical evolution came from; it needs metaphysics.

Marx rejected religion and God because he correctly concluded that religion has historically at times been used as an "opium of the people," an ideological instrument of the exploiting minority to help dominate and control the exploited masses. The Christian religion has often been an ideological superstructure constructed and manipulated to justify the base or infrastructure of society. The base is the economic system, whether it be the ancient system of slavery, or the feudal system, or the modern capitalist system which justifies as "natural law" the right to private ownership of the means of production.

Thanks partially to the Marxist criticism of religion, the Holy Spirit has finally been able to lead many present-day Christians to an understanding of the gospel of Christ as the "good news for the poor" about their liberation from the yoke of exploitation. Only in recent years has the understanding of the teachings of Christ, and of the economic-political situation in which he and his disciples lived, evolved sufficiently to enable us to arrive at a renewed understanding of the gospel (with help from modern science) regarding the salvation and the transformation of this world into the Kingdom of God.

By the end of 1975, my metamorphosis was being completed; I was quite revolutionary. No longer was I anticommunist, no longer did I fear fighting back; rather, as a Christian revolutionary, I wanted to help the guerrilla war for the liberation of Honduras. This does not mean that I was a perfect Christian revolutionary, the new man, without any selfishness. Oh no, this would mean being a saint, and I still have a long way to go. But I continued growing in the Christian revolutionary spirit. I continued my formation as a good Marxist and as a good Christian, more and more like Christ, the Liberator of the oppressed. Later on I advanced through other important stages in my development as a Christian revolutionary; but my metamorphosis ended in the sense that I had my birth as a Christian revolutionary.

17. A Honduran Citizen at Last

Let us go back to my history in 1973. In this year Jarrell Wade was named superior of our mission and Valentín Menéndez was named by the Honduran Bishops' Conference as director of a national pastoral team in Tegucigalpa. For two years Valentín did a tremendous job of raising the consciousness of the bishops, priests, and religious and of unifying the pastoral plans of all the dioceses of Honduras. I participated in many of the national assemblies for studying and planning the apostolate. After one of these assemblies in Tegucigalpa with priests from all over the country, five of us from different regions decided to meet every two months to deepen and to unify on a national level our committment to the liberation of Honduras. These were wonderful meetings of progressive priests. The group grew and afterward included many nuns also.

We called ourselves a group of prayer and pastoral reflection, or "charismatic group." In almost all the countries of Latin America have sprung up organized groups of progressive priests, like SAL in Colombia and ONIS in Peru. The goals of the groups are, first, to conscienticize and unify progressive priests so that they will be more efficacious in their work for the poor, and second, to promote and coordinate the new "Church born of the people," the liberating BCCs.

Around this same time in my parish of Sulaco we started another Church organization that had great potential for helping the revolution within the Catholic church. In a three-day course in Victoria with all the Delegates of the Word of the parish, we discussed the need to have an organization of Delegates of the Word with some control and regulation of people who could be Delegates and receive official cards from the bishop identifying them as such. My idea was to form a kind of national labor union, or professional organization, with the more than six thousand Delegates of the Word in Honduras that would be able to pressure the bishops and priests to listen to them and to the poor people about what kind of a new Church they wanted. It could be an instrument of the hundreds of BCCs in the country for participating in the government of the Church in Honduras.

During this same course the Delegates formed the founding parish section of ANDEP (National Association of Delegates of the Word) and named commissions to write different parts of the bylaws of ANDEP. For several months these bylaws were discussed in the monthly meetings of the Delegates and finally approved. I do not have a copy on hand, but I remember that they established three phases: aspirants, candidates, and finally, Delegates.

An aspirant had to be a man at least eighteen years old, and able to read. If he faithfully fulfilled the rules for a year—receiving a short training course, helping every Sunday in the Celebration of the Word (after having prepared it well together with the other Delegates in his community), bettering his reading skill, overcoming his vices and fixing up his marriage if he lived in concubinage, and so on—then the assembly of Delegates could pass him on to the second phase, candidate.

For two years as a candidate he would have more serious obligations, like giving prebaptismal instructions to parents and godparents, receiving other training courses, being faithful in attending the monthly meeting of Delegates, and so on. If he fulfilled all of this well and had the approval of the assembly of Delegates, the pastor would finally name him Delegate of the Word and give him his identification card signed by the bishop.

In 1974, one of my best friends among the Jesuits, the American Bob Voss of Denver, Colorado (who had gone around to the villages of my parish with me for a number of weeks) was named pastor of Yoro. He organized the second parish section of ANDEP using the same bylaws. Later on, the parishes of Progreso and Olanchito also organized their sections of ANDEP. My companion priests in our "charismatic group" took the bylaws of ANDEP back to their parishes in different parts of the country to discuss with their Delegates, but I never got them to seriously help organize ANDEP on a national level, as I had hoped.

As soon as Wade was named new superior of our mission, I wrote to him and to our new provincial superior in Saint Louis, Missouri, Father Leo Weber (who had worked many years as a missionary in Belize) asking for permission to naturalize myself as a Honduran citizen. After ten years of asking for this permission from my former superiors, at last I got it. Leo Weber wrote me that he too had the idea of returning to Belize after finishing his term as provincial and naturalizing himself as a Belize citizen. So I immediately started the naturalization (or nationalization) process through the lawyer of the Christian Democratic Party of Honduras (PDCH), José Cisne Reyes.

The leaders of the PDCH who had made retreats with me got me this lawyer gratis and also the help of some of the employees of the Ministry of the Interior (of Gobernación y Justicia, they call it in Honduras). Without this help I never would have obtained the signatures of Colonel Melgar Castro, the minister of the interior, and of Col. Oswaldo López Arellano, the president of the republic, which were required for the decree granting me Honduran nationality. These two army officers knew me and personally had tried to expel Padre Guadalupe from the country in 1968. Maybe because the application forms were all with my original, true name, James Hanley Carney, they did not notice who the applicant was. I believe that not only my friends of the PDCH, but also God himself intervened to work this small miracle of getting the signatures of these two military enemies.

As a prerequisite for naturalizing myself as a Honduran, I had to get a document signed by the American ambassador in Honduras and by me, in which I would give up my American nationality and lose the rights and privileges of having been born in the United States. Several officials of the embassy talked with me in private in their offices, trying to dissuade me; they had never known an American who willingly gave up his citizenship. But at last they had to look for a Bible so I could put my hand on it and solemnly swear that I knew perfectly well all the consequences and that I freely relinquished my American citizenship in order to become more fully identified with the Hondurans with whom I intended to spend my life.

I got the document from the ambassador, and within two months I received my copy of Decree Number 2142 of the government granting me Honduran nationality. In the mayor's offices in Progreso in December of 1973, I received my Identity Card Number 18, Page 12, Volume 18, as a Honduran.

The funny part of it was that after a month of having all this, I received telegrams in Sulaco and Victoria, and even calls over Radio America, that they needed me urgently in the U.S. embassy in Tegucigalpa. I was making a trip to several mountain villages at the time and was not able to respond. The next time I went to Progreso, however, my superior suggested I go to the embassy because they continued to call me. When I finally went to Tegucigalpa, the embassy informed me that Washington was demanding that I sign with the ambassador a different official form, because the standard form that we had signed had been changed. After again unsuccessfully trying to dissuade me, they got out the Bible and again I relinquished my American nationality, and again we signed the document, the new form this time.

So I was no longer a gringo, but a Honduran. For my visits to my family in 1974 and in 1977, I went to the United States with a Honduran passport and a tourist's visa. For my family and friends I mimeographed the following letter, which was published in our Jesuit Missouri Province Newsletter:

MY REASONS FOR BECOMING A HONDURAN

1. Out of love of Christ and of the Honduran poor. Just as Jesus declassed himself and freely chose to become a man, to incarnate himself as one of the class of poor and humble men, I also want to imitate Jesus as much as possible and no longer be of the bourgeois middle class or of the religious Pharisees. Also, if I really love the Honduran peasants, I have to share their life with them as much as possible: I do not want to eat better than they do. For me, to follow Christ in poverty means to be completely dependent on God's providence, to trust him completely to take care of me. Therefore, I freely renounce all the security and privileges that come from being a U.S. citizen. I do not want social security, or life insurance, or savings in the bank, or medical attention in the United States, and so on.

2. I have freely chosen to belong to the oppressed class in order to be side by side with the peasants in their fight for liberation, and with Honduras in its efforts to liberate itself from the external dependence that oppresses it. Christ is working in the revolution for the liberation of the oppressed; I want to help him and not be with the bourgeois middle class or with the selfish capitalists who are in favor of the unjust status quo.

3. I want to identify myself with the third world and no longer be identified with U.S. imperialism. That is why I renounced my American citizenship. I do not want to be part of the unjust capitalist system of

competition, of exploitation of one person by another and of seeking personal profit, or of the materialistic consumer culture of seeking personal comfort. I want to help the third world form more human, more free, more fraternal societies, which will be a model for the United States, and in this way I will make my contribution to the salvation of the United States too.

4. I took out legal Honduran nationalization papers as a symbol of all this, the same as we religious publicly take a vow of chastity instead of simply living a celibate life. Also, with legal nationalization it will be a little harder to expel me again from Honduras.

I signed it with the date of December 1973.

To be able to legally call myself a Honduran not only gave me a lot of satisfaction, it also removed many of the barriers and doubts of the Marxists and other Honduran revolutionaries to accept me as one of them. With good reason they automatically distrust all gringos and all priests. But now they called me "companion" and "fellow countryman." The campesinos and Indians, especially, were very glad that I had become a Honduran. I always began my talks to the co-ops, or in courses and retreats, explaining that, even though I still had the face and the accent of a gringo, I was now a naturalized Honduran.

Another thing that pleased the campesinos was the fact that I lived in a poor champa in the village of Camalote whenever I was around Progreso.

In 1974 I just happened to be in Progreso when without warning the most horrible natural catastrophe of the century struck Honduras: Hurricane Fifi. It came out of the Atlantic Ocean and directly smacked the whole north coast of Honduras with a force of wind that tumbled a large percentage of the trees (including the rich plantations of banana and plantain) and houses, not only close to the seacoast, but up to fifty miles inland.

Fifi came with torrential rains that did not let up during five days and five nights, and that caused the greatest harm of all: great landslides on most of the mountainsides in the departments of Cortés, Santa Bárbara, Atlántida, Yoro, Colón, Gracias a Dios, and the Bahía Islands. These landslides of dirt, sand, rocks, and trees came down the mountainsides in flooded creeks, which emptied into the rivers, filling the riverbeds with all of this. This not only caused the biggest floods of the century, but even today these rivers and creeks flood very easily, because they are still full of the sand and rock from these landslides.

More than ten thousand people died, killed by this hurricane; most of them drowned in the sudden floods. How many thousands more were wounded or became sick! How many hundreds of thousands were left without a home, without their personal belongings, without their animals and their crops! The destruction of the agriculture and cattle along the whole northern coast of Honduras was tremendous. The losses were so great that seven years later the agricultural and cattle production still have not reached their pre-Fifi level. The Las Mercedes Co-op of Toyos, for example, not only lost all of its 70 acres of plantain to the wind and the floods, but the Guaymon River left more than 160 acres covered with about four inches of sand, land that now cannot be used for anything.

It so happened that both Wade and Steve Gross, who took my place in the villages and camps of Progreso, were in the States, so Brother Jim Cleary and I had to locate thousands of refugees in the Training Center La Fragua and in the dance hall of the Company Zone. All the schools of Progreso were also turned into refugee centers. For weeks, thousands of families from the villages and from the flooded parts of the city lived in these centers, and we had to organize emergency committees to help them with food, clothing, medicine, and so on. I stayed to help in Progreso for six weeks.

As soon as the first torrential rains slowed down, the United States sent six helicopters from Panama to rescue the victims of the floods throughout the whole north coast who were still in danger and to leave food for the tens of thousands of families trapped in the high spots near their villages surrounded by water. Two of these helicopters worked out of Progreso taking food, clothes, and medicine to the thousands of isolated families of the Progreso villages and banana camps, who were on the canal borders and even on the roofs of their houses. Since the pilots were from the U.S. Air Force, they needed guides who knew well all the villages and camps of the municipalities of Progreso, Negrito, Morazán, and Santa Rita, and who spoke English, to direct them.

I started going as one of the guides right from the first flights. After a few days, Steve Gross returned to Progreso and took over the whole tremendous operation of sending out in the helicopters tons of food, clothing, and medical brigades to about a hundred different isolated places. From the air the whole municipality of Progreso looked like a huge lake on both sides of the Ulúa River, with some islands here and there surrounded by water. On all of these "islands" there were people who were hungry, cold, and sick. For many of them it was two full weeks before the waters went down enough for them to leave these islands and walk into Progreso to get food. Only then did the helicopters return to Panama.

CARITAS was in charge of most of this huge operation of assisting about a half-million refugees in the whole north coast. In Progreso many of these poor families, who had lost their homes and everything, stayed in the refugee centers for more than two months. During another six months CARITAS had programs of food-for-work to rebuild the houses and roads, and to replant the crops in the villages. For six weeks I helped Steve and the CARITAS promoters organize community development committees in all the villages and camps of Progreso, so that the people could work collectively and get food from CARITAS for each day's work.

As a result of this, Steve started his big program of cheap houses for the poor villages of Progreso with a grant from AID (the U.S. Agency for International Development). The CARITAS community development committees constructed their own colonies of hundreds of cheap wooden houses with tin roofs and cement floors, for which each family had to pay five dollars a month. Brother Jim Cleary had previously started similar housing programs in several poor neighborhoods of Progreso. I admired these U.S. Jesuits for being such fine business organizers. Steve Gross later started a project of planting chilies in almost all the villages of Progreso to sell to an American, McIneny, who made "salsa del Diablo" ("The Devil's Chili Sauce").

You can see that all of the Jesuits (including myself) were deeply involved with efforts to help the victims of Fifi. How can you not help? The problem still remains for me and others, however. How can we best help the poor to help themselves? All of us missionaries in Honduras love the poor, have made "the option for the poor," in this sense of helping them with their material problems. But a few of us were beginning to understand that these problems of poverty will only be definitely solved when the cause of the poverty is eliminated, which in Honduras is the economic-social-political system of capitalism and imperialism. While more of the riches of the country go to a native oligarchy and to foreign companies, all this help for the poor to make their homes, to find work, to learn a trade, or to find a market for their products, while being necessary, Christlike and humane, is still putting a patch over a basic evil (which is the tragic exploitation of the workers and campesinos in Honduras).

These are developmental, reformist projects; they are not revolutionary, liberating projects that help to eliminate the cause of the unemployment and poverty. The same is often true of the labor unions, the agrarian reform, and the cooperatives in Honduras; they do not automatically change the unjust capitalist system, but often help incorporate the poor into the capitalist system. On the other hand, any kind of a collective fight for their rights, like the struggle to get land, or loans, or a plot of ground on which to build their homes, or better salaries, if it unifies the poor, is potentially revolutionary. It can serve as a magnificent opportunity to raise the moral, social, and political consciousness of the poor, and can be revolutionary in character.

After the new military coup of López Arellano in 1972, I was glad to see that INA, under the new progressive directors, first Ponce Cambar, and then the young army colonel, Mario Maldonado, had many promoters who were exceptions to the general rule I just mentioned about reformists. Many of the young officers of the armed forces of Honduras admired the revolution that the military leaders of Peru were carrying out after their takeover of the government; they were pacifically but energetically making good agrarian reform and nationalizing the natural resources. Ponce Cambar brought back to Honduras the great agrarian reform educator, who had been Rigoberto Sandoval's advisor in INA until 1970, Clodomir Santos DeMorais, to be the supervisor of PROCCARA (Program for Campesino Formation in Agrarian Reform). He also invited other advisers on agrarian reform from

Chile and Peru to profit from their revolutionary experiences in the collective organization of the campesinos for agrarian reform.

PROCCARA started to train as new promoters of agrarian reform hundreds of teachers and agronomists, many of whom were Marxists or at least progressive-minded. They were taught that cooperatives were like capitalist enterprises with a managerial group, the five-person administrative council, controlling the decisions; this often resulted in the president of the co-op making all the decisions alone, instead of all the members of the co-op participating in decision making. They were taught the system that was giving good results in Peru, *Empresas Asociativas de Campesinos* (EAC), where there is true autogestion, or self-government, with the responsibilities shared by all the members through many different work committees.

DeMorais and his team taught them to give the experiential laboratories to the organized groups of campesinos that were receiving land under Decree Number 8, in order to form them into EACs. Thus, by means of these experiential laboratories the promoters of INA in the whole north coast, and a little bit in Choluteca, stole many groups of the ANACH, which could have been co-ops in the Co-op Plan of the ANACH, and many collective campesino leagues of the UNC, to form them into EAC.

Since the ANACH and the UNC rejected the EACs, precisely because they were an instrument of the government for stealing their already organized groups to form with them a new, governmental campesino organization, these groups automatically left the ANACH and the UNC. Just as INA under Rigoberto Sandoval had given special preference in their help to the groups of FECORAH, now INA shared this preferential help between FECORAH and the EACs, openly trying to weaken the ANACH (because it was influenced by AIFLD), and the UNC (because it was influenced by the Christian Democrats).

After studying the new system of the EAC, and seeing that it was very good, I adapted it to the one hundred and some co-ops of the ANACH that I was visiting and helping, introducing in the co-ops the same division of working committees that the EAC had, so that all the members shared in the responsibilities. For this same reason, I had always insisted that the ANACH collective co-ops should have an assembly of all the members every week or every two weeks to decide their new work plans together, leaving for the administrative council the managing of routine operations. But now we formed in each co-op the different work committees, for example, of education, of corn (the production and the marketing), of beans, of cattle, of machinery, of the warehouse, of resination, of the consumer store, of housing, of formation of the women, of health, and so on, according to the projects of each co-op. The coordinators of each committee met once a week to coordinate the work together with the administrative council.

After a few months, when it was clear that the co-ops functioned better like this, in the 1973 national assembly of the Cooperative Plan of the ANACH I explained this system to the representatives of all the ANACH co-ops; many of them later introduced it into their own co-ops. Three years later, when I was working in Colón, not only all the coops of the ANACH in the Lower Aguan Valley Project, but also all those of FECORAH, were using this system of work committees.

From 1973 to 1976 (when the revolutionary foreign advisors of INA again had to leave the country), I used to frequently visit my friend DeMorais and also the directors of INA, to try to convince them that they did not have to destroy the ANACH. I explained to them the new system in the co-ops that had all the advantages of the EACs. They, of course, denied that they were trying to destroy the ANACH. I also taught this new system to help promoters of the production co-ops of the Direction of Co-op Development (of the government) and to those of COHDE-FOR (with the forestry co-ops).

In 1974 Bishop Jaime Brufau of San Pedro Sula asked the Jesuits to take over little by little all the four parishes of the Department of Colón. Tom Halloran, S.J., was the newly named pastor of Sonaguera when, near the end of 1974 shortly after Hurricane Fifi, I made my first visit to the ANACH co-ops in the Lower Aguan Project. I went especially to see my good friend, Ruben Erazo, who was president of the Luzon Palmera Co-op of the ANACH. This co-op had gone to Colón along with other subsections of the ANACH after being evicted for the second time by the army from the lands of the Tela Railroad Company in Guaymas of Progreso. The ANACH had no activist in Colón, and the few ANACH co-ops there were under continual pressure from the activists of FECORAH and the promoters of INA to leave the ANACH and join the majority of the co-ops of the Lower Aguan Project in FECORAH (as I explained before, FECORAH was organized and has always been completely controlled by INA).

Since I then had a Toyota jeep that could enter into Sulaco in dry weather by the new road opened in 1974, (it was practically the only type of car that could get through the roads of the department of Colón after the hurricane), Ruben Erazo and I started visiting all the co-ops in Colón that had once belonged to the ANACH. I used to go from Sulaco to Colón for a week just about every month, where I would stay either with Tom Halloran in Sonaguera or with Padre Jaime Pratisabal, a Spanish Vincentian missionary who was in charge of the Tocoa area under the parish of Trujillo. Little by little Ruben and I were encouraging about ten co-ops of the INA project to continue in the ANACH and to join the National Co-op Plan of the ANACH.

Two of these co-ops of the ANACH were made up of poor campesinos from villages close to Sonaguera and had received land from INA close to their villages, but the big cattlemen would not let them work in peace. When we visited for the first time the Quebrada de Arena Co-op of the ANACH near Sonaguera in 1974, they had only ten members left. All the leaders of the co-op had fled, because the cattlemen, with hired gunmen, had set fire to several of their champas in the village and had threatened to kill them.

The other one, close to Sonaguera, was the Tosca Co-op, which, when we visited, was still in the process of measuring with INA the 1200 acres of land they were receiving. In one of our visits to encourage this valiant group of thirty-five poor campesinos of the village of Tosca to continue the fight in spite of the daily threats they received from the big cattlemen of Sonaguera, the president of the co-op, Juan Ramón Triminio, a *sarco* (dark-skinned Honduran Creole with blue eyes), told me that they were going to kill him, that there was a gunman paid to do it, but that he could not run away and leave his buddies. He had a beautiful black-eyed wife and two little beautiful sarco children.

A week later the gunman "deer-hunted" him (as they say in Honduras) that is, ambushed him in the fields and killed him with a shot in the back. That same night about fifty armed cattlemen and hired gunmen from Sonaguera rode their horses into the village of Tosca shooting in every direction. All the families of the village immediately fled for their lives, leaving their homes, personal belongings, and animals behind.

Some of these big cattlemen and their gunmen put their cattle on the co-op land and used the abandoned houses of Tosca. At this time, as I said, INA had many revolutionary promoters, especially in Colón. They organized five hundred campesinos from the other co-ops of the Lower Aguan Project to invade Tosca with their tractors, to plow and plant with corn the co-op lands, and to chase out the cattlemen. In the confusion when they all entered the village, one of the INA promoters with a pistol killed a rich cattleman from Sonaguera. He was later captured and, I think, is still in the prison of Trujillo, while the cattleman who paid the killer of Triminio goes around free.

INA tried to persuade the people of Tosca who could be found, to return to their homes and to the co-op lands, but they refused. When I went back to Tosca two months later, INA had brought in a mixed group of campesinos of the ANACH and of the UNC from the Department of Choluteca to take over the lands and the houses of Tosca. Ruben and I convinced them that they should all belong to the ANACH and call their co-op Juan Ramon Triminio, in honor of the first ANACH martyr in Colón.

The national lands in the municipality of Sonaguera were the only ones left in the lower Aguan Valley that INA had not recovered for their project. The cattlemen refused to leave them because they knew that INA in 1975 (after the coup of General Melgar Castro, which I will talk about later on) could no longer get the backing of the army to evict them from the valley and move them onto the mountainsides with their cattle. That is why the big landowners could fight against the campesino co-ops in that area.

Another similar case was that of the Occidental Co-op of the ANACH, which INA had brought from the mountains of the department of Copán to occupy the national lands of the village of Juan Lazaro, very close to Sonaguera. I was visiting them every month also, but after the flight of the campesinos from the Quebrada de Arena Co-op and from the Tosca Co-op, after the murder of Triminio, and after many threats against them from the cattlemen of Sonaguera, these Indians from Copán also wanted to flee. INA had to move the whole cooperative to other lands close to Tocoa. The national lands that this co-op had received in Juan Lazaro are still occupied to this day by the big cattlemen of Sonaguera. You can again imagine the hatred and threats I received from the big landowners of Sonaguera for helping these three ANACH co-ops.

The other lands of the Lower Aguan Project in the municipalities of Tocoa and of Sava had earlier been recovered by INA more easily. Cattlemen many years before had illegally taken over and fenced in much of the 150,000 acres of abandoned lands that the Trujillo Railroad Company (an earlier subsidiary of the United Fruit Company, like the Tela Railroad Company) had turned back to the government of Honduras when their banana farms were destroyed by the Panama disease.

Starting in 1969, when Rigoberto Sandoval started the Lower Aguan Project, and then under Ponce Cambar and Mario Maldonado of INA from 1972 to 1975, the army helped evict these cattlemen. They were paid indemnity and offered national land to buy for their cattle on the mountainsides nearby or in the extensive, unoccupied flatlands out beyond Bonito Oriental, in the "Mosquitia."

In the municipality of Sonaguera are also the nine big banana farms with their central offices in Isletas that belonged to the Standard Fruit Company. Hurricane Fifi almost completely destroyed these nine farms, which left about fifteen hundred workers unemployed, because the Standard decided that it would cost too much to put these farms back into production. They also said that they might as well abandon them now because within a few years their concession of these twenty-five thousand acres in Colón (which unpatriotic governments had given them) would terminate. Another reason that moved the Standard to abandon these farms, but that they did not publish, was that their labor union, SUTRASFCO, was controlled by leftist leaders, especially in the Isletas area, who were giving this U.S. transnational company more and more problems.

Since Tosca is right next to these Isletas banana farms, each month Ruben and I passed through these farms and talked to the former SUTRASFCO labor leaders, like Porfirio Hernández and Efraín Pavon. At the beginning of 1975 these two were leaders of a large group of former workers on these farms who had not left the area. Though half of the former workers had gone to other parts of Honduras to look for work after they received their severance pay from the Standard, the other half stayed on, living with their families in the barracks of the nine abandoned camps, and planted milpas in the abandoned lands. They were waiting to see if the committee they had organized of their former labor leaders could get the support of INA for them to replant these nine banana farms as an agrarian reform project.

In Tegucigalpa and in the central offices of the Standard Fruit Company in La Ceiba, administrators, agronomists, and engineers told these workers that only with the "know-how" of the transnational companies could those nine farms be rehabilitated. They did not think that Honduras could do it without American technicians (like those who helped rehabilitate the banana farms of FECORAH in Guanchías near Progreso). Nevertheless, the progressive director of INA, Col. Mario Maldonado, and his foreign advisers decided to form a big EAC (Associative Agro-industry of Campesinos) of Isletas with the former banana workers and, with a loan from IDB, to start one of the most outstanding agrarian reform projects in Honduras. These men did trust in the capability of those leaders of the banana workers of Isletas who were requesting the project.

Ruben and I, like all the leaders of the ANACH and of the UNC, were afraid of the EAC, because they were directly under INA, and because they were dividing the campesino movement by forming a new, governmental campesino organization. We tried to explain this to Efraín Pavon and the other Isletas leaders and to convince them to join the Co-op Plan of the ANACH, with a co-op for each farm, united in a regional federation of the nine co-ops for buying and selling together. In the ANACH they would have the backing of most of the labor union movement in the struggle to get these farms and the financing they needed.

Efraín Pavon wound up convincing me that, besides being more efficient, it was more just and egalitarian to have just one big organization of the workers on all the farms rather than nine co-ops united as a federated agro-industry, because one of the co-ops would undoubtedly have more production and more profits than others, and thus some workers would earn more than others for a day's work. I therefore suggested that he form just one big co-op, then, with the nine farms in order to help us make the ANACH more revolutionary. But the promoters of INA were by then already giving the experiential laboratories to the workers who lived in each camp for the purpose of forming the big EAC of Isletas.

In the following months I observed with great admiration how these six hundred former workers of the Standard, founders of the EAC of Isletas, had the true revolutionary spirit of striving for equality among all the members. This EAC in the beginning was really a model of the new type of socialist enterprises that we want in Honduras. I was overjoyed to hear of their voluntary work, their daily study circles, and their mutual helping with the problems of the families, not only of their members, but also of the poor campesinos who lived in the villages close to the farms. They got this spirit from the teachers, promoters, agronomists, and even accountants of INA and of PROCCARA who were helping them rehabilitate the first five farms and who were all of revolutionary mentality (at least the ones that I know).

For the specialized technical help and for the commercialization (marketing) of the bananas, not only of Isletas, but also of the Garcia Birichiche Farm of Guaymas, the Farm La 3 of Guanchías near Progreso, and of other banana farms that INA bought after the hurricane, the government formed COHBANA (the Honduran Banana Corporation). COHBANA made contracts with the EAC of Isletas (to buy all their exportable bananas) and with the Standard (to sell them all these bananas and to use their railroad facilities).

Under the second populist government of López Arellano from 1972 to 1975, not only the forests were nationalized under COHDEFOR, but also all the wharves and the railroads of the country, which until then had all been constructed and owned by the Tela and the Standard. After paying indemnity to these transnational companies, the government turned right around and rented the wharves and railroads back to them for their use.

The two companies were happy with these arrangements, as were the U.S. embassy and the Honduran oligarchy, who always have as a top priority making sure that these two U.S. enterprises gain plenty of profits for their shareholders. Now, without being odious foreign owners of the wharves and railroads of Honduras, they could go right on using them for their own profit. After receiving from the Honduran government payment for all the roads, buildings, machinery, irrigation equipment, and so on of the Isletas farms, the Standard still gets all the select bananas from these farms to market across the world.

Since the biggest profit (not only from bananas, but from almost all primary products, like coffee, meat, wood, African palm oil, sugar, cotton, etc.) is in marketing, rather than production, the Standard always gains the bigger part of the profits from the Isletas bananas, and now without any problems from a labor union, without any risks from floods, hurricanes, or diseases, and without being hated as foreign owners of Honduran lands. All the transnational companies—bananas, cattle raising, mining, oil refining—would gladly sell all their lands and their installations to the government or to private businessmen of Honduras, as long as they could continue to market these products.

The last months of 1974 and the first months of 1975 was a time of rude blows for Honduras—not only Hurricane Fifi, from which it would take about seven years for the economy to recuperate, but also what happened in the political sphere. At the beginning of 1975 was the great scandal, the Honduran "bananagate," which was the occasion, not the cause, of the unbloody, military coup d'état of the then General Juan Alberto Melgar Castró against the populist government of newly-made General López Arellano.

Roughly, what happened was that the Latin-American banana exporting countries decided to imitate OPEC, the Organization of Petroleum Exporting Countries. Guatemala, Honduras, Nicaragua, Costa Rica, Panama, Colombia, and I do not know who else, formed OBEC, the Organization of Banana Exporting Countries. To get a little more of the profits for their countries, they decided to all put the same tax ($1 a box) on bananas exported by United Brands (Tela Railroad Company in Honduras) and Castle and Cooke (Standard Fruit Company in Honduras).

Ecuador, the world's largest banana exporter, under pressure from the transnational companies, never entered OBEC, and so receives preference from these companies. The pressure of the U.S. fruit companies was so great against OBEC that, if I am not mistaken, only Panama, under the progressive Gen. Omar Torrijos, did not weaken. Panama put in the whole one dollar tax; the other countries imposed only a part of this.

In Honduras the popular organizations and all progressive, patriotic Hondurans were happy about the organization of OBEC and with the idea of a dollar for each box instead of the measly five cents that the Tela and the Standard had been leaving in Honduras for taxes. The University of Honduras at that time published a study telling how many hundreds of millions of dollars these two U.S. companies had defrauded the state of Honduras of by evading the payment of these low taxes during the last forty years. Nevertheless, after great public debates and great pressure, the general consensus was pretty much that Honduras should start off raising the tax to just fifty cents a box. But the decree of López Arellano's government came out imposing only twenty-five cents, which would be augmented by five cents each three years until it reached fifty cents a box.

At the same time an article appeared in the Honduran newspapers from *The Wall Street Journal,* one of the most prestigious newspapers in the United States, with details of a bribe of $2.5 million given to the government of López Arellano by the United Brands Company to put less tax on the bananas. A few days later came the news that the president of United Brands, Eli Black, had committed suicide by jumping from the window of his office on the fifteenth floor of their building in Boston. The newspapers said it was because a U.S. Senate committee investigating monopolies had proven his guilt in the bribing of the Honduran government. All in all, the dirty profits of the bribe were still won by the United Brands. It is clear that, if with the bribe of $2.5 million the Tela Railroad Company saved twenty-five cents in taxes on each of the eight million boxes of bananas it exported each year, in a little more than a year it would cover the cost of the bribe, and from then on it would save about $2 million each year.

When all this became public, not only the people of Honduras but also those of the rest of the world criticized both United

Brands and the Honduran government. The Supreme Council of the Armed Forces of Honduras, shortly afterward, made a quiet and unbloody coup d'etat, changing all the cabinet ministers along with the president, López Arellano. The newspapers of the world called it "banana-gate," after the famous "Watergate" scandal in the United States the year before, which caused the resignation of President Richard Nixon. The new government of General Melgar Castró ordered a complete investigation of the scandal. In the United States they obtained some evidence that the minister of economy under López Arellano, had received and deposited in a Swiss bank one-half of the bribe, $1.25 million, as payment in advance.

The minister went to jail for a few months while the investigating committee tried to determine whether the money was in the Swiss bank in his name, or of López Arellano, or of somebody else. Since the Swiss banks, protected by the laws of their country, never divulge anything about their clients, the minister was released from jail with the prohibition not to leave Honduras while the investigations continued. The general prosecutor of the republic (as part of the military government) never could prove anything (naturally), and in 1980 in the general pardon of prisoners and criminal cases, the case of the "banana-gate" scandal was closed forever. General López Arellano quietly went on managing his multimillion-dollar business and cattle enterprises, without any need to involve himself more in politics. It was now General Melgar's turn to become rich, to become a big landowner and cattleman.

As I said, "banana-gate" was only the occasion, not the real cause, of the military coup against the populist government of López Arellano. The bourgeois Honduran oligarchy, with the American embassy, had been looking for months for a pretext to change the government, but the popularity of López Arellano and of Col. Mario Maldonado of INA did not permit a coup d'état before. It was, they said among themselves, urgently necessary, because the popular organizations of the workers, campesinos, women, slum-dwellers, teachers, and students were becoming too powerful, and worst of all, they were to a great extent dominated by leftist leaders. Even the government was infiltrated in almost all its departments by capable leftists.

With the help of its foreign advisers, the government had made a progressive Five-Year Development Plan, and was seriously trying to carry it out by, for example, nationalizing the forests, the wharves, and the railroads. The foreign advisers of INA also helped to make a new Agrarian Reform Law, which went into effect on January 1, 1975, and put a limit on the amount of land a landowner could have. For the land-owning oligarchy, "international communism" was clearly dominating the government of López Arellano, which would have to be completely changed. The older officers in the armed forces also wanted a coup, because they now feared the power and popularity that, under López Arellano, the progressive young officers who wanted a revolution along the lines of Peru and Panama had acquired.

The U.S. policy for avoiding the Marxist revolution in Latin America, ever since the Alliance for Progress agreements in 1961, has always been to promote economic and social reforms for the poor masses, while at the same time implacably repressing anything or anyone that smells of Marxism. Their embassy in Tegucigalpa was in favor of cleaning out all the leftist elements in the populist government, but insisted with Melgar Castro that his new government should continue following the reformist Five-Year National Development Plan already under way. They called the change of government the "second phase of the armed forces' government for the development of Honduras" and promised to carry out the Five-Year Development Plan, whose "principal task was agrarian reform."

Therefore, only after about ten months, when its power had been consolidated, did the new military government get rid of the progressive colonels. Col. Mario Maldonado of INA was sent as military attaché to the Honduran embassy in Washington with a very good salary and expense account. He was the most dangerous, because a large part of the popular forces in Honduras wanted him to be president of the republic. Leonel Fonseca and other progressive colonels were sent to other embassies in other countries.

To continue with "the principal task" of the government, Rigoberto Sandoval was brought back into the country in 1976 to be director of the INA again, but he became so frustrated at the government and the army no longer backing him (as they had under López Arellano) that he did not last even a year this time. For the new military hierarchy, Sandoval was too progressive and too slow in getting rid of the leftists in INA and PROCCARA. When the engineer Fabio Salgado took over as director of INA, the government immediately fired all the foreign leftists from INA, PROCCARA, the Economic Planning Office, and even from the "autonomous" University of Honduras. This, of course, included my friend DeMorais.

Fortunately, there remained in INA and PROCCARA a good many of the Honduran leftist promoters who were organizing the EAC. As I mentioned, the new Agrarian Reform Law went into effect January 1, 1975. Besides putting the maximum amount of land that one owner could possess at 350 hectares (about 830 acres), this law also legalized the EACs (the associative agro-industries of campesinos), but too much under the control of INA.

According to the law, INA can call assemblies of all the members and intervene in the assemblies and in the management of an EAC. That is why the ANACH and the UNC never accepted EACs in their organizations. The EACs, as I have explained, were really a new fractioning of the campesino movement and a planned tactic for weakening the ANACH and the UNC by stealing their already organized groups to change them into EACs.

The other factor that ruined the new Agrarian Reform Law was that, as usual, it was not put into practice. To avoid the expropriation of their land that exceeded the limit, almost all the big landowners, before the date that the law took effect, simply legally divided up their big properties among all the members of their family. They got INA to give each one full dominion title for the smaller property. For example, the Bográn Fortin family, which had tens of thousands of hectares of land (in Guanchías close to Progreso and in several other parts of Honduras) got titles for 350 hectares from INA for their wives, sons, grandchildren, nephews, and so on, including a couple of newborn babies. Thus, they did not lose any part of their huge properties.

In spite of these disadvantages, I liked the new law, and I wrote a study sheet about it that I distributed for use in many groups of the ANACH, and also of the UNC. (I then had a lot of opportunities to enter the UNC because of the retreats I led for many of its leaders.) The study sheet outlined four revolutionary ideas of this new law, which is still in effect today:

1. It puts a ceiling or limit on big properties (Article 25).
2. It requires the direct and efficient exploitation, the social function, of the land (Articles 23 and 24).
3. It gives out land only collectively, either to cooperatives (Article 104) or to EACs (Article 111).
4. The campesino beneficiaries have to personally work the land, without hired help (Article 82.a).

It is the third idea, of groups of campesinos collectively working their collectively owned land, that opens the door for a truly structural change in the system of private ownership of the most important means of production in Honduras, the land. Up to now practically all the best farmlands were in the hands of rich Honduran landowners or of the two U.S. banana companies, without any limit to the amount of land they could have and with no requirement to put it to good use. They could leave it idle or rent it to the campesinos, or do whatever they wanted with it. Now, the first idea of a ceiling or limit to how much land one person can own leaves a lot of leftover land to distribute to campesino groups in agrarian reform. The second idea is that if an owner does not cultivate land well, it can be expropriated. Thus, every kind of renting or leasing of land is now forbidden.

The fourth idea obliges the campesinos who receive land in cooperatives or EACs to work it personally without hired help. This prevents these new agro-industries from becoming like the previous landowners, exploiting other campesinos as their workers. The third revolutionary idea, of not allowing individual plots but promoting collective work, avoids the minifarms and forms modern agro-industries in which it will be easier to help the campesinos receive credit, technical assistance, machinery, education, and so on.

This is a new socialist kind of property, communitarian property. In Peru they call it "social property." The worker (not the state, as in communism) is owner of the means of production, not individually, but collectively, forming, with a minimum of twelve campesinos, a production co-op or, with a minimum of five campesinos, an EAC. The members do all the work, make all the decisions, and distribute all the profits among themselves according to the amount of work of each.

My study sheet included the following questions for discussion:

1. Why do many Catholic and Protestant thinkers say that communitarian property (socialism) is more human and more Christian than individual work?
2. Why do many say that collective work is more Christian than individual work?
3. Why do we say that with collective work it is easier to help the campesinos with credit, technical assistance, machinery, education, etc.?
4. If the new Agrarian Reform Law tends toward a New Socialist Society, what will the Christians say? Is that good or bad? Why?

I still had some of the Christian Democratic ideas about communitarian property instead of state property. Now, in 1981, when I am living the experience of the wonderful revolutionary process in Nicaragua, I understand very clearly that private ownership of the means of production, especially land, even though it be communitarian, as in the self-governing co-op enterprises we were forming in the ANACH, always leads to inequality.

The experience of Honduras in agrarian reform is proof of this. Some of the co-ops and EACs advance prosperously and become like capitalist corporations that have big profits to divide among their shareholding members, "the owners"; meanwhile, other co-ops and EACs fail, and the members continue in hunger and misery. With the means of production in the hands of the state, with "property of the people," as they call it in Nicaragua, you can distribute equitably for social works the profits of all the enterprises. All the workers of the country, including the top professionals, receive more or less the same annual salary.

With a capitalist government, like the one now in Honduras, which is the dictatorship of the bourgeois class with the armed forces at its service to control the exploited working class, it is better that the workers and campesinos be communitarily "the owners" of the property and of the production instead of the state controlled by their enemies, the bourgeoisie. But in a true socialist country where the state and the armed forces are in the hands of the working class, under the government of the workers, the property and the production are for the benefit of all the people and not just some individuals or groups of "owners."

Even in a system of socialism called "self-governing" (or autogestion) as they have in Yugoslavia and some other socialist countries, the state is always "the owner" of the industrial and agricultural enterprises that are self-governed by the workers. In this way the state can (and must in a true socialist country) allocate of the leftover profit of all the enterprises for public works that serve the people, like schools, hospitals, roads, new industries, and so on, without having to resort to so many loans from the transnational banks that make a country more dependent on the imperialists. Besides being the biggest and most lucrative business in the world because of the high interest rates, these loans always come tied to some economic and political conditions.

18. Apostolic Teams at Yoro and Tocoa

At the beginning of 1975, our superior transferred the pastor of Yoro, Charlie Prendergast. Charlie went for a year of Renewal in modern theological studies with the Jesuits at Berkeley, California. His assistant, Bob Voss, who was one of my best friends among the Jesuits, was left alone in this most extensive parish of our mission. José María (Chema) Tojeira, (who had taught during his regency period at our Instituto San José in Progreso) had just returned as an ordained priest to Honduras from studying theology in Spain, along with the newly arrived Spanish Jesuit scholastic, Juan Fidalgo Rodriguez. Both of them were fine, very progressive intellectuals. Bob, Chema, Juan, and I decided among ourselves to form an apostolic team, with no one as pastor but all as equal brothers, and ask our superior to give us the two parishes of Yoro and Sulaco to work as one single apostolic zone.

Since we Jesuits are encouraged to live in a Jesuit community as much as possible, and since I was alone in Sulaco, Voss alone in Yoro, and since Tojeira and Fidalgo insisted on working as a team, our superior agreed to the experiment and made the arrangements with Archbishop Santos of Tegucigalpa, to whose diocese the department of Yoro belongs. So I left the Sulaco parish at the beginning of 1975 and went to live with our new team in the priests' rectory in Yoro, leaving the Crusader sisters Africa and Enriqueta living in Victoria to work with Chema Tojeira, who would be visiting there.

In Yoro there were five Laurita sisters, four from Colombia and one from Ecuador, all from campesino families. These are religious with the old-time habits and veils and very strict rules, but, nonetheless, they go out in the mountains and live with the poorest of the poor, with the Indians. I have not run across any better missionaries than the Lauritas.

We made a wonderful team. We divided our apostolic zone of the two huge parishes into three sectors, with a priest and two nuns for each sector. Chema with the two Crusader sisters took the municipalities of Yorito, Sulaco, and the part of Victoria out to Las Vegas where cars could now enter. Bob Voss took the town of Yoro with Juan Fidalgo, the villages nearby in the Yoro Valley, and the areas of Jocón, Jimía, and Mejía. One sister directed a sewing school that the Lauritas had in their convent in Yoro for poor girls, and two worked with Bob. The other two Lauritas, my good friends Nohelia and Amalia, worked in the areas of Locomapa, Subirana, and Las Flores (of Victoria) with me. The other fourth of the municipality of Santa Rita was turned over to the parish of Morazán.

I worked only half-time with this apostolic team. They all agreed that I should continue to visit the ANACH co-ops in the departments of Yoro and Colón. In a red Toyota jeep that I always used, I would go out to the Lower Aguan Project in Colón almost every month, visiting on the way some of the Indian tribes, or some of the six new agro-forestry co-ops of the ANACH that we were forming in the villages of Jocón, or some of the twenty subsections of the ANACH in the municipalities of Arenal and Olanchito. Ruben Erazo and I were promoting ANACH co-ops in the municipalities of Sonaguera, Elixir, Savá, Tocoa, and Trujillo in Colón.

Some months I would leave Yoro in the other direction to visit the ANACH co-ops in the municipalities of Morazán, Negrito, Santa Rita, and a small area of Progreso. Sometimes I went on to San Pedro Sula and Tegucigalpa to continue my retreats for the worker, campesino, and Christian Democratic political leaders.

My favorite project at this time was with the ANACH co-op of the Indian tribe of Subirana. From time to time I visited all the nineteen tribes and had two full-time promoters working for the tribes with me: Lucas Cárcamo of Yoro, who knows practically all the Indians of all the tribes, was paid by CARITAS of the Yoro parish, and Adán Palma (a Delegate of the Word from the town of Victoria) was activist of the ANACH for the nineteen tribes. As I mentioned before, many of the chiefs were the worst enemies of their tribes, because they would sell themselves out both to the Ladino landowners who were taking away their lands and to the

Nationalist political bosses of Yoro. That is why I wound up working more with the five tribes who had good chiefs. Besides the Subirana tribe, with the chief Porfirio Zelaya of the tribe of Las Vegas de Tepemechín in the mountains above the town of Las Vegas (of Victoria), we had cooperative projects to fence in a part of their lands for collective farming and to open a small co-op store. (Afterward I will tell of the persecutions and sufferings of this good man Porfirio.)

I worked with the chief Paco Alvarado and the agro-forestry co-op of the tribe of Santa Marta (of Yorito), which collected resin, collectively planted beans, and opened the only co-op store that still continues to operate to the present day, in the house that the tribe built in the village of Santa Marta. Paco Alvarado is a very small Indian who speaks so quietly that when he wants to talk in a meeting there is a hush of absolute silence so that they can hear him. He is small, humble, and extremely poor, but he has five wives in different houses, maintains five families, and is a great chief.

Out in the mountains near La Lima of Olanchito, I worked a lot with two tribes: the tribe of Zapotal, with its old but very active chief, Gumercindo Cruz, who is one of the few Indians alive in Yoro who can still speak their native Jicaque language, and the tribe of Agua Caliente de Guardarrama, with its young chief, Israel Matute, who is a Delegate of the Word of God. We started agro-forestry co-ops with both of them because COHDEFOR promised to open a road for them to take wood and resin out to Jocón. But after a year of being deceived with such unfulfilled promises, the co-ops folded up, and we concentrated on fighting by means of ANACH for the recovery of their tribal lands.

Around this time, the former director of INA, Horacio Maya Posas (the Nationalist lawyer from Olanchito), with some other members of his party, wanted to control the Indian tribes for political purposes and also to get the Indians away from the ANACH and the fight for their tribal lands. Posas's group organized the Indian Institute of Honduras with the idea that they would get plenty of funds for this from the national budget of the Honduran government and from the international Indian institutes. But the Indian Institute of Honduras was so obviously corrupt, managing so shadily the money that the tribes received for lumber concessions, that the military government never made the mistake of giving them government money (which most surely never would have benefited the tribes). Through the Indian Institute, the Nationalist Party got control of more than half of the nineteen chiefs in Yoro through promises and gifts. But some of the chiefs were honest and not for sale.

The chief I liked most was the courageous Juan Estrada of the tribe of Subirana. He has been thrown in jail and threatened with death several times by the Ladino cattlemen for his loyalty to me and to the ANACH in the fight to recover their tribal lands. He still has not sold himself out, but neither has he been able to recover their lands. This will be one of the first recoveries of the revolution when the Honduran people take over power.

For the agro-forestry co-op of the tribe of Subirana I obtained as a gift from a U.S. foundation a small sawmill, and to power it, I bought for five hundred dollars in Progreso an old Ford farm tractor with a power takeoff to connect a belt from the motor to the saw. From COHDEFOR we got permission for the co-op to cut the pine trees from the forests that belonged to the tribe, and a U.S. Peace Corps volunteer came to live in Subirana to help with this project of the tribe. Several of the young men of the tribe learned to run the tractor and the saw, and I have never seen the Indians so proud as when the Ladinos came to them to buy the sawed pine boards, or when three or four of the Indians, mounted on the tractor, drove down the main street of the town of Subirana with all the Ladinos watching them.

The project lasted about two years, until the saw and the tractor were broken and no one could fix them (and I was by then living in the parish of Tocoa, Colón). The tribal co-op always continued with the resin project and with small collective farming projects, but to tell the truth, they have bettered their standard of living hardly at all; it is still one of extreme poverty, hunger, and sickness. I get angry just remembering the misery in which these Indian brothers and sisters of ours have to live because of the unjust capitalist system. I hereby call on all those who love Christ in the poor to join us in one of the revolutionary political-military organizations of Honduras to fight without respite to change this system of institutionalized sin!

Although the new Agrarian Reform Law came out with the great hope of incorporating the masses of campesinos into agricultural production (the new president, General Melgar Castro, promised to give land to 120,000 campesino families during the next two years), the reality is that the agrarian reform completely bogged down and practically came to a standstill in 1975 under the new military administration. With the Decree Number 8 of 1972, more campesinos received land (collectively, in organized groups of the ANACH, UNC, or FECORAH) in two years then in all the ten previous years of "agrarian reform," and the seven years following the new law of 1975. Under the new administration, INA put hundreds of obstacles and legal delays in the way of the requests for land by the campesino organizations. The ANACH and I, at this time, were futilely trying to move INA to remeasure the lands of the nineteen Indian tribes of Yoro, since we only received promises.

Melgar Castro was very populist with his promises; he visited all kinds of massive events all over the country. He even started a new system that was very good for incorporating all the different strata of people in the government. He formed a *Consejo de Estado* or Council of State (like the socialist countries have), where all the principal political parties, professional organizations, organizations of students, workers, campesinos, women, cattlemen, industrialists, and businessmen all had their delegates. In the Council of State were discussed the new laws that the military government wanted to promulgate. This experience of public debate, quite representative of all the people, was very positive during the year that the Council of State lasted.

However, after a few months the worker and campesino organizations finally realized that this was just another demagogic trick to calm them, to put them to sleep, letting them talk and talk in debates with the bourgeoisie in the Council of State, but never solving any of their problems. It was obvious that the agrarian reform had come to a standstill; INA promoted only the big projects that had already been started under Rigoberto Sandoval.

The ANACH and the UNC in April of 1975 started the recovery of lands again in different parts of the country, but now the army immediately evicted them with extreme brutality, burning down their champas, beating up the men and even some of the women, and throwing the leaders in jail. It didn't help the situation any that the ANACH and the UNC were always fighting among themselves, sometimes over the same land. Never would they be able to unify their efforts as long as Reyes Rodriguez was president of the ANACH.

On June 25, 1975, the UNC alone, without any agreement with the ANACH, but with the backing of the CGT (the Central Confederation of Workers) and the Christian Democratic Party, made a "hunger march" toward Tegucigalpa with all its campesino groups from all over the country, in protest against the lack of agrarian reform. About five hundred of them, including women and older children, slept in La Fragua and from there took off for the highway to Tegucigalpa. A little beyond San Manuel several truckloads of soldiers arrived to stop them and, by hitting them and capturing their leaders, broke up the march that was coming from the whole northern and western part of the country.

In the department of Olancho, where the UNC, with the help of the Church, had its strongest regional organization, about a thousand campesino men and women marched out of Juticalpa toward Tegucigalpa. Just a few miles down the highway, the army broke up the march by firing in the air and taking a lot of prisoners. Meanwhile, back in the city of Juticalpa, a platoon of soldiers, behind some teachers and a whole class of grade-school children, rushed into the Campesino Training Center Santa Clara 18 de Febrero (which the diocese of Olancho through Bishop Nicholas D'Antonio had recently sold to the UNC for their regional headquarters) and started shooting at all the occupants. They killed four and captured about twenty, including the cooks. Lincoln Coleman, one of the top leaders of the UNC and a fine Delegate of the Word, was among the four unarmed campesinos murdered there in cold blood by the soldiers.

A couple of hours later, an American Franciscan priest from Wisconsin, Jerome Cypher, innocently drove into Juticalpa from his parish in Culmí to repair his car. The soldiers picked him up and threw him in jail in Juticalpa with the campesino prisoners of the UNC. Father Cypher did not even know what the UNC was, nor any other Honduran popular organization; he was not involved in any of this. The priest that the secret police were looking for was Michel Pitón, a Frenchman who was tall and fair, like Cypher, and who used to help the UNC in their training courses.

The other priest that the DIN had had on their list from a few years back and were also looking for this day was the pastor of Catacamas, Olancho, the Colombian Ivan Betancourt. A few years previously, he also used to help in the UNC courses, but then went to Canada for a year of specialized theological studies on marriage. When he returned to Olancho he no longer was involved with the campesino organizations but dedicated himself to giving "marriage encounters." Well, Ivan on this June 25 was coming in his car from Tegucigalpa toward Juticalpa with his future sister-in-law, who had just arrived in Honduras from Colombia to visit him, and with a university student from Tegucigalpa, Ruth García. Witnesses in a village along the highway saw two cars of the FUSEP (police) chasing Ivan's car at top speed. Afterwards the car was found without its occupants.

During this "hunger march" of the UNC I was in the town of Yoro, where the UNC did not exist, and afterward I went to visit the ANACH co-ops in Victoria, San Antonio, and Sulaco. All of these now had land and their own tractors for plowing. The struggle to get a part of the ejidal (municipality) lands of Sulaco, which the wife of a powerful landowner-politician had fenced in, had been very hard, and INA still had not measured and turned over all the land of the ANACH co-op of San Antonio.

About a week after the massacre against the UNC in Olancho, we thought that everything would be calmed down in Tegucigalpa. So the activist of the ANACH, Marcelino Padilla, two leaders of the San Antonio co-op, and I went from Sulaco in my Toyota jeep through the mountains of Marale to Talanga and Tegucigalpa to demand from the director of INA that the rest of their land be handed over to the San Antonio co-op. At the entrance to Tegucigalpa, however, there was a roadblock of soldiers searching all the cars and their occupants. On finding the pistol that the activist Marcelino always carried, and on seeing that my identification card listed my profession as "priest," they arrested us. Two soldiers took us in my car to Casamata, the central headquarters of the FUSEP in Tegucigalpa, where the four of us were locked up for questioning.

After a few hours, we were called one by one for fingerprinting and separate interrogation. The officer who was questioning me had a folder with the dossier of Padre Guadalupe and had studied all my antecedents with the FUSEP (Police Security Force). During my interrogation he was suddenly called to the telephone and returned saying that I could now leave, that I was free. They returned my personal belongings and the keys to my car, and I left Casamata a little sad about being prisoner for such a short time.

At Centro Loyola I saw Steve Gross, who told me that some university student friends had seen me enter Casamata as a prisoner. They were there taking food to some Christian Democratic student leaders who had been captured in the big roundup on June 25. They let Father Bill Barbieri, who was in charge of Centro Loyola, know, and he called the archbishop, who in turn called the minister of the interior to find out why I was a prisoner. When the military government learned that I was a prisoner without any clear implication in the march of the UNC, they immediately ordered my release, because they did not want any more problems with the Church and the popular organizations after the *massacre* in Olancho.

After several weeks of demonstrations of indignation against the armed forces by the popular organizations, by the hierarchy of the Church, and by the embassies of the U.S. and Colombia because of the massacre of the campesinos in the Center Santa Clara in Juticalpa and the disappearance of the two priests (the American and the Colombian), the two young women, and nine campesino prisoners, President Melgar Castro named an investigating commission that included our Jesuit, Valentín Menéndez, as the bishops' representative. Since the protests, not only in Honduras, but internationally, were increasing, General Melgar ordered the capture of those that the investigating commission found to be clearly implicated: the two rich landowners of Juticalpa, Eduardo Bahr (also owner of a big lumber company) and Mel Zelaya. On Zelaya's cattle ranch, "Los Horcones," were finally found the thirteen dead bodies at the bottom of a deep well that had been dynamited to cover it over. They also put in prison the commander of the military delegation in Juticalpa, Maj. Enrique Chinchilla, and several other officers and soldiers who directly took part in the *torturing* and *killing* of Ivan Betancourt and the two young women, and of Father Cypher and the nine UNC leaders who had been prisoners in the jail at Juticalpa.

To finish the story of these people: They were judged and sentenced to 30 years in prison. In the Central Penitentiary in Tegucigalpa the rich murderers, Mel Zelaya and Eduardo Bahr, had special cells with all the modern comforts and with permission to leave the penitentiary at times to enjoy themselves at night in Tegucigalpa and to go to Olancho with their guards to look after their big business enterprises. Five years later, in 1980, all these murderers of "Los Horcones" were set free from prison by the insulting pardon granted to practically all the prisoners in Honduras by the newly formed National Constituent Assembly.

Since 1974 the bishops on several different occasions had accused the PDCH (the Christian Democratic Party) of utilizing the works and the centers of the Church to promote their party. It is true that almost all the directors and professors of the training centers, of CARITAS, and of the Radio Schools of many of the parishes and dioceses were militants of the PDCH. These were the most dynamic Christians in all these parishes and dioceses. But now, after the massacre of "Los Horcones" and the accusations of the big cattlemen and military men, and even President Melgar Castro, that "the Church was promoting the PDCH and the UNC, using the works of the Church for subversive activities," the Bishops' Conference sent out an order to all the parishes in the country to immediately fire all militant members of the PDCH. The Church, it said, would no longer participate in *Accion Cultural Popular de Honduras* (the Radio Schools) or in CONCORDE (National Coordinating Committee for Development), dominated by militants of the PDCH.

This order of the bishops included accusations that these militants of the PDCH were "false Christians" who have instrumentalized the works of the Church and of the Catholic religion for their own political ends. This caused a lot of resentment among these men and women, who really were (in general) among the best Christians in Honduras, committed to the service of the poor. A few of us priests were not in agreement with this order and did not obey it. I, personally, made more effort than ever to become friends with these militants of the PDCH in the different parts of the country and to offer them spiritual retreats.

From that time in 1975 until today it is very notable how the Catholic hierarchy, the majority of the priests and also the laymen in Honduras retreated from any social commitment and became nonpolitical and very anticommunist. For example, following the lead of their bishop, who became one of the spiritualistic charismatics, many Canadian priests of the departments of Choluteca and Valle drew back from the line of liberation theology and of helping the popular organizations. Although they had read, they no longer believed, the magnificent book of Bishop Proano of Ecuador, *Evangelization, Conscientization, and Politicization*. This book shows that there is no true evangelization without conscientization that comes from analyzing the unjust, sinful reality that we have to change, and without politization of the Catholic masses so that they will enter revolutionary political organizations to help change this unjust society. Our "charismatic group" of progressive priests from different parts of the country, however, became even more strongly committed to seek changes in the Church and in the country. We continued to meet every two months, and we exchanged written material, reflections on liberation theology that we were using in the BCCs of our different parishes. Naturally, we priests did not always agree with one another, but we respected each other's ideas and commitment.

Our team of four Jesuits in the parish of Yoro was very good, and I was happy. We were extending the frontiers of the liberating kind of evangelization, "the good news of the liberation of the poor." With an activist of the ANACH I organized the first subsections and co-ops of the ANACH in several villages of the municipality of Yoro. The best of these groups was the co-op of the village of San Juan, which was the first campesino group in this municipality to get land from INA. I had lent them money to fence in about 170 acres of ejidal land before they got INA to come out from San Pedro Sula to Yoro to give it to them.

But our fine team only lasted six months. I really missed Chema Tojeira and Juan Fidalgo, when they went to Progreso to take charge of Radio Progreso. Father Jerry Tolle, the director of the radio, became the pastor of the parish of Progreso. Joe Fisher became the pastor of Sulaco, separating it again from the parish of Yoro, but the region of Subirana remained with the Yoro parish and the region of San Isidro with the Morazán parish. Charlie Prendergast returned to be pastor of Yoro again, with Bob Voss as assistant, and I went with Fernando Bandeira to start the parish of Tocoa, Colón.

In my opinion the parish of Yoro was, and still is, very important as the frontier of our mission. There is practically no agrarian reform or campesino organization in this territory, but only the almost feudal life of exploitation of the Indians and of the other poor campesinos. In five years our fine team would have transformed this whole mountainous area into a place full of campesino organizations seeking their liberation. Tojeira and Fidalgo were very good, and I hated to lose them as part of our team in Yoro. They did a great job with Radio Progreso, but I still maintain that the formation of Christian revolutionary campesinos in the mountains of Yoro is more important for the liberation of Honduras.

Since Bishop Brufau of the diocese of San Pedro Sula, which includes the departments of Cortés, Atlántida, Colón, Gracias a Dios, and the Bahía Islands, had agreed with the Society of Jesus that we would little by little take over the whole department of Colón, and since Father Fernando Bandeira arrived in June of 1975 from Spain to work on the mission, and since I already knew most of Colón after a year of visiting and promoting the ANACH co-ops there, our superior, Wade, arranged with the bishop to form the new parish of Tocoa and separate from the parish of Trujillo the whole municipality of Tocoa and the part of the municipality of Trujillo that was in the Lower Aguan Project of agrarian reform. Our superior named Fernando as pastor of the new parish (as of August 1, 1975) and me as half-time assistant, with permission to continue working half-time with the co-ops throughout the departments of Yoro and Colón and with retreats.

The plan was that a new priest, Jesús Sariego, would come from Spain in December to the parish of Tocoa to form a team of three Jesuits there, while Valentín Menéndez would replace Tom Halloran as pastor of Sonaguera with another new Spanish priest, "Chico" Ocaña, as assistant. It was Valentín, Fernando, and I who had had the idea of forming a single apostolic zone with the same pastoral plan for the two neighboring parishes of Sonaguera and Tocoa. The zone covered the whole big agrarian reform project of the lower Aguan Valley with its eighty agro-industrial cooperatives of campesinos besides the EACs of nine banana farms in Isletas and the huge project of CORFINO (the Forest Industry Corporation of Olancho), with its sawmills and a paper pulp factory in Bonito Oriental, and its renovation of Puerto Castilla.

After the massacre of "Los Horcones" and the retreat of the frightened bishops from their social commitment to the poor, the Bishops' Conference replaced Valentín Menéndez as director of the National Pastoral Office with a Canadian priest. With that, Valentín was free to go to Sonaguera, and it was he who enjoyed the confidence of Bishop Brufaú to such an extent that he allowed me to work in his diocese under the promised control of Valentín and Fernando. Fernando ("Nando") Bandeira had been a close friend of mine ever since we went around with each other for a month in the Sulaco parish before he returned to Spain after his Third Probation in Colombia. We were developing an excellent team of five Jesuits who would form a Christian ferment in the big development projects in the Lower Aguan Valley.

I thought we were going to face a big obstacle for this kind of work in the four Spanish Daughters of Charity nuns (who still wore their habits and veils) that Bishop Brufau sent to form part of our team, two for each parish. But Nando did a fine job incorporating them little by little, together with the Delegates of the Word in the parish, by means of courses of liberating, evangelical conscientization. After a year they were right on our wavelength and worked well with our team.

Nando invited a married couple from Spain who wanted to be lay missionaries, Antonio and Rita Blanco, to come to Tocoa to be part of our team. They built their own little house in the village of Salamá, right next to our parish training center, and became very Honduran, sharing the life and struggles of the campesinos.

I had a great friend, the Spanish Sister Marina, whom I met in Colombia during my Third Probation in 1964, when she was working with her congregation of the Slaves of Christ the King in the Jesuit retreat house in La Ceja. Afterward she worked for many years in a poor slum of Caracas, Venezuela. In 1974, fifteen of these Slaves of Christ the King in Venezuela obtained permission for a year's experiment of living two-by-two in apartments in the slums, like the poor, without using their religious habits. When the year was up, their superior ordered them to return to live in their convents with their habits and veils again; they refused and, instead, looked for other jobs, forming an association among themselves. I called them "the Liberated Sisters of Christ the King"; later on, more "Slaves" joined these "Liberated Sisters."

Marina and I kept up a periodic correspondence during these later years, and in early 1975 she came to Honduras to go around with me for two weeks in the regions of Subirana and Las Flores to see if she would like to work with us in Honduras. She returned to her work in Venezuela, but now she was filled with the desire to live and work with the poor campesinos in Honduras. When we were forming our team for the Tocoa parish, Nando agreed to invite Marina to join us. She left her work and her sisters in Venezuela, like a true "Liberated" sister, and came alone to live with a poor family in the San Isidro complex, which is made up of the village and three connected co-op colonies, about two miles from Tocoa. Once a year she goes back to Venezuela for the annual meeting of her companions, "the Liberated Sisters of Christ the King."

Marina is still living in a tiny room in the house of this campesino family, where a cot, a table, and a chair scarcely fit. She goes to the river with the campesino women to take her bath and wash her clothes. In my opinion she is the model of a modern, liberating missionary; she is one of the holiest and finest persons that I know, self-sacrificing and friendly. She was an excellent addition to our apostolic team in Colón.

Marina helped me develop my ideas about the future of the Church and religious life, and I include here the first part of a document I wrote and distributed to all my religious friends in Honduras and the United States in 1978.

THE FUTURE OF THE CHURCH AND RELIGIOUS LIFE

What are the most efficacious means for forming the Kingdom of God on earth?

Toward what are the priestly and the religious life evolving?

How do you form basic Christian communities that are liberating communities?

1. The Spirit of God-Jesus is in everyone and, by his actual grace influencing their decisions, is directing the dialectical evolution of the world toward the Parousia, the second coming of Christ, the Omega Point (when the whole universe will be united in Christ), which will be the definitive Kingdom of God. This is the plan of God revealed in the Bible. No movement, political party, or religion (including the Catholic church, the priesthood, and the religious congregations), and no socioeconomic system is an end in itself, but are simply means toward the end of constructing the Kingdom of God in this world. This Kingdom of God will be paradise, the perfect society of brothers and sisters, all equal, sharing everything they have in love. To reach this goal will require the continual perfecting of all men and women and their socioeconomic systems or ways of living in society, that is, it will require the continual twofold revolution: the cultural revolution and the socioeconomic revolution.

2. Analyzing, with the help of marxist science, the present stage of the history of the dialectical evolution of the world

toward the Kingdom of God, the perfect fraternal society, many of us have come to the conclusion that the Spirit of God is moving humanity to change the present capitalist and imperialist system of society, with its private ownership of the means of production and with its exploitation of one human being by another and of the third world by the "first world" with its bourgeois-individualistic-selfish mentality, for a socialist society with social property, eliminating the social classes, and instilling a social mentality of sharing all the riches and all the decisions among all men and women. We do not pretend that this new socialist society will be the Kingdom of God, but rather that it is a necessary means or step toward that end.

3. The principal means for advancing the Kingdom of God, with the necessary socialist cultural revolution and socialist socioeconomic revolution, are not the Church and the religious congregations, but (a) the revolutionary socialist political parties, and (b) popular pressure organizations of the masses, like labor unions, civil rights groups, and so on. The Catholic church, even though it is not the principal instrument, is a necessary means for this twofold permanent revolution, and it is the instrument that God-Jesus himself organized to be the ferment and the visible sign (model) of the new perfect fraternal society and of the new humanity, that is, of the Kingdom of God. That was exactly the role of the first Christians in their basic Christian communities (BCCs). But in these latest centuries the Catholic church and the religious congregations have been neither a model nor a ferment of the evolutionary movement of the Spirit of Jesus toward socialism (the double revolution), but rather, in general, have been a conservative, contrary force.

4. The role of the Church, especially in its base, in the basic Christian communities (BCCs), is to be ferment in the masses (not the masses itself, as it is in Latin America and as many want it to be in the United States and in Europe); its role is to be the model of the new humanity and of the New Society within every human community, especially (for the twofold revolution) as Christian cells within the revolutionary political parties and within the popular mass organiza-

tions (not forming "Christian" parties or "Christian" labor unions). The BCCs should be a revolutionary and critical force within these movements, always having in mind that the twofold revolution is continual until the Parousia. The difference, then, between a Christian revolutionary and any other honest revolutionary is that the Christian is one who should understand God's plan for this world, where the evolution of the world is going, and should recognize and respect the Spirit of God in all men and women. Also he or she should be living in his or her BCC as a model of the New Society. Therefore, generally speaking, one cannot be a Christian individually, but only as an active member of a BCC-model-ferment of the double revolution. But it is clear that we Christians are not the principal promoters of God's Kingdom in this world; nonetheless, we are extremely necessary, like leaven in the bread dough. It is also clear that if we really preach to the poor *this* "good news of the Kingdom of God," the capitalist oppressors will be against us and will no longer belong to our Church. The Church will be identified with the oppressed in their struggle for liberation. The great error of the hierarchy of the Church and the clergy up to now has been to try to be with everyone, with the rich and with the poor, with the oppressors and with the oppressed. But under the present world circumstances, with the class struggle, not to take a clear class option for the poor and oppressed is to be with the status quo.

5. Thus, the principal role of the priest in the plan of God is to be promoter and orientor of these liberating BCCs, and then minister of their sacraments (liturgical signs of their commitment to form a model society of brothers and sisters). The priest should be the most revolutionary, in order to be the stimulus for the rest of the Christians in the BCC. But really, one only learns to be a liberator and revolutionary in the praxis, in the practice. So the priest has to really belong to one or more BCCs. The people in these BCCs will then become his most intimate friends, brothers and sisters. The priest should live *with* and *as* the BCC (share with the families, not just with other celibates), really be part of a neighborhood community, completely incarnated with the

common people, like Jesus was, like the first Christians, like Saint Paul, sharing with them whatever there is of possessions, of problems, of struggles, of dangers. *The priest cannot encourage others to get into the revolutionary struggle, and keep himself hidden.* He has to be the first one to join a revolutionary political party and a popular mass organization demanding their rights. He should be the first one to go to jail or to die for the sake of justice, like Jesus. He should not separate himself from ordinary people, living in a priest's rectory or religious house, being administrator of the Church's wealth, having economic power and privileges. The priest of the future, in general, will work *with* and *as* the poor in order to earn his daily bread and to help economically his BCC. Or if there is a shortage of priests, as in Latin America, and they have to work full-time in the apostolate of many BCCs, they could receive a small salary from the BCCs they are serving.

It is good for priests to form regional priest teams, to get together periodically in order to encourage and challenge one another and to orient each other by common prayer, study, and pastoral planning. These priests can live together or separately but within the boundaries of their own Basic Christian Community. The bishop should be the animator and orientor of these regional priest teams. He too should have his residence living *with* and *as* a BCC of the poor class. The BCC should have the final word on who is to be their priest. And there is no evangelical reason why there cannot be married priests or why the Church in the future should not give permission for this.

6. Religious life in congregations or communities organized apart from the ordinary Christians, the lay people, started about five hundred years after Christ for historic reasons that have now completely changed. Christ did not organize any religious congregation apart from the BCC. During the first three hundred years of the Catholic church, when it was a minority, persecuted by the authorities, and was really ferment in the masses of humanity, and not the masses itself, all Christians lived the "religious life" of sharing their possessions in their BCC, in imitation of Christ. The Church was demanding, exclusive. Those who did not

live up to their commitment had to repent and carry out huge penances, or else they were excommunicated. But after the Emperor Constantine, when the Catholic church became the state religion of the Roman Empire and the masses became Catholics, and the bishops and priests became feudal lords, great landlords, and authorities with temporal power, the Church became corrupt. It was then that the Holy Spirit inspired many men and women to separate themselves from this corrupt Catholic world and form their BCC apart in religious congregations of celibates, at first apart in the desert, and afterward within the world but apart in their monasteries and convents with cloister, under the obedience to a religious superior.

But now in recent centuries we notice a movement of the Spirit of Jesus evolving the religious life toward a greater incorporation in the world. Religious are getting rid of their distinctive habits, their protections, and their privileges. Now that the world is pluralistic again with the separation of church and state, and the Church in many parts is being persecuted for defending justice, and now that the modern theology, because of the practical experience of some theologians in the liberation movements, is coming to understand the role of the Church in the modern world as a minority ferment in the masses, preferably of the poor and oppressed, now we can foresee the tendency of the religious life to become fully incorporated into the BCC. I can see the possibility of the BCCs becoming the religious orders, congregations, societies of the future church.

There will always be a place and a need, however, for a few Christians in each BCC who want to go further in their imitation of Christ, dedicating themselves completely to the double socialist revolution and the formation of God's Kingdom, like Jesus: (a) without being tied down to a family of their own (celibate "for the sake of the Kingdom of God"), and (b) choosing to identify themselves with the most poor and oppressed, living *with* and *as* them in order to help them in their struggle for liberation (Christian poverty "for the sake of the Kingdom of God"). These will form the "vanguard" among the Christians. The religious life will once again be as it was for the first Christians, the community life of all the Christians in their BCCs, striving for their own "perfection" and the cultural, socioeconomic perfection in the whole world. This war was, is, and will be, the true Christian revolution.

7. How can one go about putting all this into practice? How could a parish form a pastoral plan to start this liberating process of radically changing the Church, the priestly and the religious life? This, of course, requires a radical change in the mentality and theology of the pastoral agents: the bishops, priests, religious, and laity. In order to achieve this great change, it seems best not to start from above and try to change the hierarchy of the Church, but to use Christ's strategy of forming in the base, among the lay people, some models of the New Church made up of many revolutionary BCCs, and of the new priest and new religion. To explain how in practice the BCC can be formed so that it will be revolutionary and liberating, let us use as an example of this pastoral process a parish in a poor workers' neighborhood of a large U.S. city.... [And I went on in detail about how this could be done.]

When we arrived in Tocoa August 1, 1975, Nando and I rented for ten dollars a month a tiny, poor house without light or water, in which our two canvas cots just barely fit with a table in between. We made our own breakfast there, but for lunch and supper (when we were not out in a village or co-op) we ate with the family of Don Damaso and Doña Celia, who was eighty years old but still a magnificent cook, paying her fifty cents a meal. The priests in Tocoa still eat at Doña Celia's.

When another Jesuit came to visit us in Tocoa, we would open a small folding cot and stick it partly under the table so it would fit in the house. Obviously, Jesús Sariego would not be able to live there with us when he joined us in December; therefore, Nando fixed up the sacristy of the old wooden church in Tocoa, amplifying it into four little rooms, one as office and three as dormitories. When Jesús came, Nando went to live with him in the sacristy-rectory. I continued to rent our little house in Tocoa, leaving the fourth room of the rectory free for visitors (of which there were at least two or three every month).

When Jesús joined the team, we divided the parish into five sectors; Jesús with the two Daughters of Charity took the two sectors on the left side of the big Aguan River that divides the parish and the department of Colón just about in half. Nando, with Antonio and Rita, took the two sectors of Salamá and Bonito Oriental, besides the town of Tocoa with its four thousand inhabitants on the right side of the river. Marina and I had the sector of Zamora, from Tocoa towards Savá. Most of the co-ops of this sector belonged to the ANACH. I only had one sector because I spent half my time in the department of Yoro with the ANACH co-ops, or in different parts of the country giving retreats. I still went around in the red Toyota jeep that I called "the jeep of the ANACH," because I almost always had some activist of the ANACH along with me. Nando and Jesus got around on big dirt-road motorcycles that they bought.

19. Exploitation of the Campesino Movement

Our apostolic zone of the two parishes of Sonaguera and Tocoa was very interesting for me. Besides the EAC of Isletas, with its nine banana farms, and the construction projects of CORFINO around Bonito Oriental for the paper pulp factory, most of the land of the two parishes that was in the valley on both sides of the Aguan River was divided into lots of about 500 hectares (about 1200 acres), one lot for each of the eighty campesino agro-industrial co-ops of the Lower Aguan Project of INA. The main part of the project would be African palm plantations and, on a minor scale, citrus trees, principally grapefruit.

I explained earlier that this whole valley once belonged to the Trujillo Railroad Company, part of the United Fruit Company but that their tens of thousands of acres of banana farms in this area were destroyed by the Panama disease and the lands abandoned and turned back to the state around 1935. When Rigoberto Sandoval was director of INA, his foreign experts designed the big Lower Aguan Project. Around 1968 Sandoval started transactions for a gigantic loan from IDB of $50 million for this project. Agrarian reform cooperatives would plant 25,000 hectares (about 60,000 acres) of African palm trees, with a contract to sell all the oil that the fruit of the palm trees produced to the Standard Fruit Company, and another 5,000 hectares (about 12,000 acres) of citrus trees with an assured market in Germany. Sandoval already had the model for these co-ops in the famous Guanchías Cooperative near Progreso, which he had promoted with Efraín Díaz Galeas, the perennial president of Sandoval's campesino organization, FECORAH.

In 1970 INA started making the million-dollar installations in Sinaloa, ten miles north of Tocoa, which would be the central offices, modern living quarters, workshops, and so on, of this big project. At the same time INA started helping some landowners in nearby villages to plant some experimental plots of African palm trees. It was not until 1972 that INA had the money from the first stage of the loan to start planting the African palm in some of the newly formed agro-industrial co-ops near Sinaloa, like the Salamá Limited, the San Isidro Limited, and the Nortena Limited. Some of these first co-ops were organized by the INA promoters with campesinos who lived in the villages around Tocoa, but almost 80 percent of the campesinos that make up the present-day eighty cooperatives of the project were brought there by INA from other parts of the country.

This Lower Aguan Project is called the biggest and most important project of "agrarian reform" in Honduras. Nevertheless, it really is not "agrarian reform," but "colonization." In the first place, all the lands of the project are state or national lands; they were not confiscated from any big landowners. The project does not help change, but rather protects, the unjust possession of the land in Honduras. Second, the so-called beneficiaries of this project are principally campesinos brought in from other parts of the country to colonize the underpopulated department of Colón.

This project, on the contrary, has been the escape valve to avoid true agrarian reform in other parts of the country. In so many cases, when the groups organized in the ANACH, and a few of those of the UNC too, have used a lot of pressure and have "recovered" idle fields of big landowners in other parts of the country, INA has finally solved the problem by sending in soldiers to evict these groups from the recovered lands. They are then sent to the Lower Aguan Valley instead of touching the big, illegal, unproductive landowners of Choluteca, Copán, Santa Bárbara, Yoro, Olancho, and so on.

Another objective that INA had in transferring these groups of the ANACH and of the UNC to the Lower Aguan Project was to undo them. Generally a few of their members were sent to fill in several other FECORAH co-ops there, or else the group was pressured to leave the ANACH or the UNC and join FECO-RAH. That is why the authorities and promoters of INA and the activists of FECORAH were so angry with me when, at the end of 1974, I started visiting with Rubén Erazo the co-ops of Colón that had campesinos who formerly belonged to the ANACH and started to form some of them into co-ops affiliated with the National Co-op Plan of the ANACH.

The director of INA, the head of the project, and Efraín Díaz of FECORAH, in all their plans in 1975, still assumed that all the co-ops of the Lower Aguan Valley belonged to FECORAH. Efraín Díaz, the president, Benjamín Garmendia, the vice-president, all the other members of the executive committee, and all the activists of FECORAH received salaries directly from INA and did exactly what the INA authorities asked of them. Before Rubén, the ANACH had never had an activist in Colón, and the UNC still does not have one. All the co-ops of the project were automatically affiliated with FECORAH, at least on paper, even though most of them had never paid the two-hundred-dollar entrance fee.

In August of 1975, when Nando and I moved into Tocoa, I was daily going around with Rubén visiting little by little almost all of the eighty co-ops of the project, and some of them were affiliating themselves with the ANACH. This was ruining the plans of INA, of FECORAH, and of the military government to easily control all the campesinos of the big project. The authorities and the promoters of INA, plus the leaders and activists of FECORAH, started a real war to destroy the ANACH in Colón. They bought off several of the presidents of our ANACH co-ops by giving them salaries as activists of FECORAH. They held up the transactions for loans and other services for the co-ops if they did not go to the bank or to INA with an activist of FECORAH. Under these and other pressures, four or five of our co-ops left us and joined FECORAH.

But, indeed, this gave us our principal argument why the co-ops should belong to the ANACH: to have an independent organization, directed by the campesinos, that can demand from the government their rights—and not an organization of the government as an instrument for the domination and control of docile campesinos. One of our first victories by the ANACH co-ops in Colón was to resist the pressure of INA to buy Allis Chalmers or David Brown tractors from an agency in San Pedro Sula, which gave a commission for each tractor to the subdirector of INA, and to the administration of FECORAH. All our co-ops and the EAC of Isletas bought Massey Ferguson farm tractors and implements at lower prices.

At the end of 1975, this conflict between the ANACH and FECORAH in Colón became critical, because they were beginning the second stage of the loan. All of the forty co-ops destined for the African palm project, including many of those of the ANACH, were to start transplanting the little trees from the seed plots of INA in Sinaloa. The leaders of FECORAH, in the name of all the co-ops (without even discussing it with us of the ANACH or with their own campesinos), accepted the day salary of $1.50 and very low wages for contractual work, like making the holes, planting, chopping the weeds with machetes, and so on. Almost all the campesinos of all these co-ops protested and demanded better pay. In response, INA sent an officer of the Honduran Army to be the new head of the whole project. He brought a platoon of soldiers with him to Sinaloa, and a whole new batch of INA promoters, who were secret agents of army G–2 (intelligence service).

Now, finally, many campesinos of the co-ops understood what we were telling them about the importance of having a campesino organization independent from the government. The FECORAH co-ops, under the threats of the officer, accepted the wages that the bank and INA stipulated for the African palm work. Only about six months later did the ANACH co-ops, which were almost all in the sector from Tocoa to Sava, have their turn to transplant the palm trees into their fields. These fields had been cleared of stumps, leveled by bulldozers, plowed by tractors of INA at tremendous cost to the co-ops. They had to pay for this preparation with their bank loans at the annual interest rate of 11 percent. (I will explain more about this exploitation of the campesinos later on.)

When the first co-op of the ANACH, the Occidental Limited, just on the outskirts of Tocoa, was supposed to make the holes for the transplanting at those low wages, they went on strike. I believe this was the first strike of campesinos and of a campesino cooperative, which theoretically is owner of its own land and production, in the history of Honduras. They simply said that they were not going to make holes for such low wages, and besides, they preferred to plant corn. You should have seen the anger of the officer, not only with the co-op, but with Rubén and with me! He ordered the capture of the whole administrative council of the co-op, and personally went to call an assembly of the fifty or so members of the co-op to threaten them. These Indians from the department of Copán, the same ones that the big landowners of Sonaguera had forced to flee from the village of Juan Lazaro, convinced the officer that he should raise the contract wages for making a hundred holes. This was a victory for all the co-ops of the project.

A few months later the ANACH co-op the Chiripa Limited also went on strike when they had to make holes for transplanting the grapefruit trees in land that was full of rocks and very hard to dig. They also, after threats from the major and many discussions, got INA to raise the pay for each hole in rocky soil. This was at the end of 1976 and we then had twenty co-ops of the ANACH organized under one sectional (regional) leadership. All these co-ops and even a few of FECORAH threatened to go on strike to back up the demands of the Chiripa Limited.

Around this same time our "section" of the twenty ANACH co-ops in Colón threatened to go on strike to back up the fight of the INA employees to have their SITRAINA labor union, which had been very dynamic in denouncing the corruption of the INA authorities. FECORAH, of course, backed up the officer and the newly named director of INA, when they fired or transferred to other parts of the country all the leaders of SITRAINA in Tegucigalpa and in the regional offices of INA, including that of Sinaloa. When new leaders were elected, they too were fired or transferred. The authorities of INA promoted, instead, the formation of a pseudo-labor union, the Association of Nonunionized Employees of INA, to represent all the workers of INA in labor affairs with the authorities. In this way, SITRAINA was completely destroyed, along with all internal opposition to the militarization of INA.

The National Agrarian Institute (INA) became an instrument, then, not for changing the unjust agrarian structures (as the first article of the Agrarian Reform Law proclaims), but for controlling the campesino organizations, which had now become big and powerful. From 1976 to the present date, more than half of all the promoters, accountants, and agronomists of INA have been secret agents of DIN (secret police) or of G–2 (army secret intelligence service). Also, ever since 1976 we have been aware that many of the leaders of the worker, campesino, student, and professional organizations are also secret police agents.

I read and then spread among the labor leaders the information from the books of the former agents of the CIA. These books say that the policy of the United States in Latin America is not to openly destroy the leftist parties, labor unions, or other popular organizations led by leftists, but to let them develop a bit (without allowing them to become too strong) in order to infiltrate secret agents in them. Thus the CIA can learn their ideology, all their strategic and tactical plans, and all the leftist leaders they have, so as to have a good secret file on each one. In this way it will be easy to control them and eliminate them when it becomes necessary.

Of all the countries of Central America, only Honduras and Costa Rica have carried out this plan of the CIA right to the letter. Nicaragua, under Somoza, and El Salvador and Guatemala still today under right-wing military fascists, have not been able to control their lust for open, bloody repression of everything and everyone that smells leftist. That is why the leftist organizations in these latter two countries learned a long time ago the necessity for working clandestinely with a strict system of security against police infiltration.

As I said before, the Honduran governments have been obedient lackeys of the U.S. State Department. This is not only with regard to the leftists, but also in economic policy (favoring the U.S. transnational companies), in the anticommunist military policy of CONDECA, in the populist reformism of the Alliance for Progress (favoring the U.S.-helped "free and democratic" labor movement, cooperativism, agrarian reform, and so on). That is why, up to now, the revolutionary movement in Honduras has not acquired the force that it has in the two most openly repressive countries in Central America.

The military authorities of Colón were quite upset by my influence as a priest on the campesinos of all the co-ops in the project. But what most upset them was a pronouncement that was approved in a meeting of the Colón "section" of the ANACH and signed by the administrative councils of all the twenty ANACH co-ops in the Lower Aguan Project. It demanded of INA a greater respect for our organization of the ANACH, which "they were obviously trying to destroy by many unjust tactics." It demanded of the officer a greater respect for the humble campesinos of all the cooperatives, who "are treated, or rather, mistreated, by him as if he were the owner of all the co-ops, or as if the campesinos were soldiers under his command." We distributed this pronouncement on mimeographed sheets to all the co-ops, and it came out in all the newspapers and over the radio.

The officer called Rubén in and tol him that I was the author of this pronouncement, and that he was going to expel me from the department of Colón. Rubén explained to him that Padre Guadalupe was merely an adviser of the ANACH because of his cooperative experience, and that the pronouncement was an agreement of all the co-ops of the ANACH and not Padre Guadalupe's idea. It is true that I was always in every important meeting of the ANACH in Colón, and I always gave my opinion and directed a short study period in the meetings.

Rubén Erazo is a true campesino and a true leader. How he used to sacrifice himself for the cause of the Honduran campesinos! I really admire him and appreciate his friendship! We used to talk together for hours and hours about everything under the sun. What we most wanted to do, besides making the ANACH strong in Colón so that the co-ops would have an independent voice in the project, was to raise the political consciousness of the campesinos so that they would realize that they were victims of tremendous exploitation, even in the co-ops and with agrarian reform.

Rubén always said that instead of co-ops, it would be better that this big Lower Aguan Project were either state-owned or privately-owned and the campesinos wage-earning workers with their labor union and collectively-bargained contract. Then they could fight for higher salaries, vacation with pay, severance pay when they quit, and so on. In this way, they would have more class consciousness; they would understand the class struggle. In co-ops, which theoretically were owners of their land and of the agro-industry and its profits, the members actually had none of these advantages of salaried workers.

I used to tell him back in 1976 that it was better that the campesinos had their agro-industrial co-ops to learn self-governing socialism. Only now, living in free Nicaragua on its way toward socialism, can I see clearly that under a capitalist government, Rubén was completely right. The co-ops were instruments for co-opting the campesinos into producing always for the transnational companies. They were more enslaved and exploited than the salaried workers. It also happens that, when the co-ops are really producing and making money, like some of those of FECO-RAH, the campesino members forget about the revolutionary struggle to change the unjust capitalist system. They consider themselves as small business owners, participating well and getting personal profit from the capitalist system.

Now at last in 1981 I am also convinced that collective, self-governing co-ops under socialism should not be owners of their land, nor of all the products they produce. These have to be socialized, they cannot be private property; they should belong to all the people, and the state must be in charge of their use for the common good under a national plan. *Such state ownership, however, demands a direct and strong representation of the farmers and workers in the state government, in their local communities, and their own production task forces. All the people must be vigilant to keep the state from falling into the hands of self-serving functionaries and bureaucrats.* The state must remain for, by and of the people.

Production co-ops are really forms of private enterprise (by a group) with the same danger of selfishly seeking the good of just the co-op members and being in competition with other businesses. They became just like capitalist enterprises, instead of seeking the common good of the country, or at least of the region.

The Agro-industrial Cooperative Guanchías Limited, of Santa Rita, Yoro, is a striking example of this capitalist-like cooperative selfishness. I knew the original members of this co-op when they were barefoot campesinos affiliated with the ANACH and fighting to get some land to plant their milpas. This co-op now has about 180 members in Guanchías where they have three rich banana farms, a big hog-raising project, and a factory producing concentrated food for animals. They have about three hundred salaried workers, whom the co-op will not allow to organize themselves into a labor union to obtain the benefits of the Honduran labor laws. This same Guanchías Cooperative has a branch in the Lower Aguan Project with another eighty members, with 4000 hectares (about 9500 acres) of land, 600 hectares of which is in

African palm, plus a thousand head of cattle or more. Meanwhile, some other co-ops of the same project, that are close to Sonaguera, still have not any permanent project or loan from the bank, and not even one cow for their families. Rubén was certainly right.

Nevertheless, I still maintain that the co-ops, like religion, do not have to be "opium for the people"; they can be instruments for the revolution. It all depends on having a revolutionary vanguard in the co-op to lead them down the revolutionary road. The economic power of the co-ops could be an important factor in the revolution. We must politicize the co-ops, helping the campesinos exercise their rights, duties, and power for the development and government of their nation.

Rubén and I gave talks to all the ANACH co-ops, and I also gave some to a few of those of FECORAH that invited me, about the exploitation of the campesinos in the Lower Aguan Project. I would start by talking about the Honduran reality: about the "sin" that is the capitalist system of exploitation of the worker class by the bourgeois class, and about the "sin" on the international level of imperialism, which takes to the United States most of the riches of the Latin-American countries by means of its loans and its transnational companies.

I explained to them that the international loans from the United States had two objectives: first, to make the poor countries dependent on the United States and then, forced by this, to make them back up U.S. foreign policy; and second, of course, for the lucrative profits from the interest on the loans. The bishops of Latin America said in one of their documents that for each dollar that the U.S. government or banks lend to Latin America, two dollars return to the U.S. in interest on the loans and in the purchase of technical help, machinery, petroleum, and other material that the loan contracts always require be bought in the United States.

As a specific example of this, I explained how IDB (the Inter-American Development Bank), having predominantly U.S. capital, was lending to Honduras $100 million just for the Lower Aguan Project. The co-ops will have thirty years to pay this back out of their production. Each co-op in the African palm project signed a loan contract at the annual interest rate of 11 percent with the Honduran government's National Development Bank to finance all the operations, from the clearing of the stumps from the land until five years later when the African palm trees produce fruit to be sold. I explained that the biggest part of the loan that the co-ops were going to repay will be used to pay the high salaries of the employees and advisors of INA and of the bank during these thirty years. We all knew of the case of the three members of a Chilean family who were advisers of Major Arita— an engineer, his wife, and his brother. The three of them together earned $5,000 a month for very little work, while the co-op campesinos planting the palm trees all day long under the tropical sun earned about $75 a month.

We asked the campesinos why they were planting African palm. Do the hungry Honduran campesinos eat this fruit of the palm tree? Who wants this fruit? Well, the nut that grows in clusters on these palm trees contains an oil that can be squeezed out in an extracting plant after being cooked. From this oil many products can be made, principally vegetable oil for cooking and margarine. Both of the U.S. banana companies in Honduras have factories for making vegetable oil and margarine from the oil of the African palm nut: the Tela has the "Clover Brand" factory near San Pedro Sula and the Standard has the "Blanquita" in La Ceiba. The Tela Railroad Company has about 4500 acres of African palm in full production in San Alejo near the port of Tela, but the Standard has very few palm plantations and has been trying to get this basic material for their Blanquita factory.

What could be a better product of agrarian reform than what the Standard Fruit Company needs? thought the unpatriotic Honduran technocrats. Instead of facing the problems of getting more land from the state of Honduras to make their own plantations of African palm, and instead of having to deal with the labor problems with the workers on these plantations, the Standard (and the U.S. embassy "advisers" to the Honduran government) convinced the Honduran government to plant African palm in a big agrarian reform project. They should do this in their national lands in Colón with cooperatives of campesinos and then sell all the oil produced to the Blanquita.

We asked the co-op members who the real beneficiaries are of agrarian reform in Honduras. It is the gringos. They have the biggest business in the world lending us the money for agrarian reform. With this money we buy machinery, petroleum, and many other things from them. When the co-ops finally are producing the fruit of the palm tree, who will have the biggest part of the profit from its final product, the margarine? The gringos of the U.S. Standard Fruit Company.

This is not only the case in the Lower Aguan Project, but also in the Guaymas Project of INA near Progreso, where the EACs and the co-ops are now planting about 8500 acres of African palm to sell the oil to the Tela's Clover Brand factory. Most of the profits also go to the gringos from the marketing in the United States of sugar from the big sugar cane campesino co-ops in Guanchías and San Manuel, from the bananas of the EACs in Isletas and of the co-ops in Guanchías, and also from the cattle project of the co-ops of Puerto Arturo, near the port of Tela, to mention only a few of the "agrarian reform" projects in northern Honduras. While these agrarian reform products go to the United States, Honduras often has to buy from the United States corn, beans, and rice for the daily consumption of the Honduran population.

This African palm project is the worst deceit and exploitation of the campesinos of all these projects of agrarian reform that the U.S. advisers and bankers want. In consultation with some economists of the University of Honduras who were friends of mine, we calculated the following: for each dollar of profit that the final product of the African palm, the margarine and vegetable oil, will give, five cents will go to the campesino cooperative "owners of the land and the palm trees"; thirty cents will go to the owners of the oil extracting plants, which will be INA (the government); ten cents will go to the truck owners and other intermediaries; and fifty-five cents will go to the U.S. owners of the Blanquita margarine plant in La Ceiba (the Standard Fruit Company).

In explaining all this to the campesinos of the co-ops of the Lower Aguan Project (ever since 1976), Rubén and I taught them that they had to insist that at least the oil extracting plants should belong to them in order to give them a little bit more of the profits from their work. But to be owners of the plants the co-ops of the ANACH and of FECORAH will have to come to an agreement and unite themselves in some way. Little by little the campesinos of the co-ops of Colón were forming their class consciousness by means of these struggles for economic betterment. I insisted with them that the imperialist transnational companies and the capitalist-landowning-military Honduran oligarchy would always exploit and dominate the campesinos, even though they were owners of lands and extracting plants, until the campesino-worker class took over all the power in the country and changed the whole capitalist system for a socialist society that would not be dependent on the United States.

I have not described yet how these agrarian reform co-ops are composed, nor how their members live in the department of Colón. Each co-op receives more or less 500 hectares (about 1200 acres) of land (except the Guanchías Limited, which has 4000 hectares in Colón), and should have one hundred campesino members. In reality only the first co-ops, which are already producing fruit from the palm trees, have more than fifty members. Only half of the eighty co-ops are in the African palm or citrus fruit projects, and these have already received provisional titles to their lands. In 1981 the other half are still waiting for the promised sugar cane and cattle raising projects, are just planting milpas collectively in part of their land, and are the poorest of all the co-ops, as poor as they were before coming to the Lower Aguan Project—or maybe even worse.

Even though, before, they did not have a sure place to plant their milpas, or the mountain soil where they lived was no good for corn, at least they had their home, chickens, pigs, and their relatives and friends who helped them. But leaving all this, believing the promises of INA promoters who told them to go to Colón and receive the best lands in Honduras, was difficult and sad. The first groups of families transported from other parts of the country to Colón were incorporated into new co-ops that did not even have champas and lived on food received from AID that INA distributed. Since they were not accustomed to the great heat and humidity of the Aguan Valley, many of them became ill. There was a lot of malaria, and the parasites and amoebas killed the children with dysentery.

Since the campesinos naturally have the mentality of artisans, extremely individualistic, and since most of them had never worked in a co-op or for any big company, they in no way liked working collectively under a work coordinator or having to go to work six days a week with no permission to do other things, as they used to. It is not surprising that more than half of all those thousands of campesino families that INA brought out to Colón from all parts of the country have looked for a way to go back to their original villages, abandoning the co-ops, disillusioned.

The bad propaganda against the Lower Aguan Project that these families made when they returned to their places of origin made it that much harder for INA to convince other campesinos to go to Colón. Many co-ops in the project still only have twenty, or even fewer, members. Until the palm and the citrus trees are in production, the co-op members hardly subsist, as before coming to Colón. But when the co-ops are producing fruit, they can then raise their daily wages and organize other services with the income from the sale of the fruit, although 70 percent of the income goes to the bank to start paying the huge debt each co-op has.

Nevertheless, not everything is negative in the project. African palm and citrus trees are very good plants for the Lower Aguan Valley. Practically every year there are big floods along the Aguan River that always destroy other crops, like corn, bananas, or plantain, but that do not tumble or even damage these trees, once they are fairly big. Nor is there much of a problem with diseases or insect plagues.

Looking ahead to the triumph of the Honduran socialist revolution, this project will be nationalized and leave big profits for the benefit of the people. Besides all this, another good aspect of the project is how the campesinos are being prepared for the self-management of this future socialist agro-industry of the Lower Aguan Valley.

The type of cooperativism promoted in this project is also very good. Everything is done collectively by the members themselves, who thus learn to be responsible. Although it does not exist between one co-op and the next, nevertheless, within each cooperative there definitely is a fine spirit of equality and of sharing their things and helping one another in any necessity. These are very Christian and very socialist virtues. All the possessions and products of the co-op are in common, but the profit is distributed according to the amount of work each one does.

Almost all the co-ops are using the system of the EACs of sharing responsibilities among many of the members by means of committees. This system I adapted to the co-ops of the ANACH and afterward taught to all the INA promoters of the Lower Aguan Project, when a former friend worked on campesino promotion for INA in Colón.

Later on, I learned that this "friend" was a secret agent of the DIN. When I was trying to get him to make a retreat, it is a good thing that in our conversations I only spoke about the ideology of the Christian Democrats. He thought that I had this ideology; he was sounding me out. In 1976 it was he who helped the army storm the offices of the EAC of Isletas. They threw all seven members of the administrative committee in jail in Trujillo, Colón, and accused them of being communists and of misusing the funds of the EAC. As a reward (and so that the campesinos of the EAC of Isletas would not kill him in Colón for his betrayal) INA promoted him to director of campesino promotion in Tegucigalpa.

Efraín Pavón, Porfirio Hernández, and the rest of my friends who founded the EAC spent two years in the prison of Trujillo without any trial or proof against them. Meanwhile, Rafael Sanchez with a group of "opportunists" had sold themselves out to Col. Gustavo Álvarez Martínez, the military head of the whole region of La Ceiba, who had militarized the EAC. These men were fraudulently elected as the new leaders of the EAC of Isletas.

When Sánchez collected proof, a year later, that COHBANA (the government's Honduran Banana Corporation) was cheating the EAC, he, too, was victim of a coup and thrown into the prison of Trujillo, likewise accused of misusing funds of the EAC. The military head of La Ceiba (I believe it was Colonel Bueso Rosa then) named as the new administrative committee of the EAC a group of workers who were secret agents of the DIN. Sánchez was released from prison in 1980 and two weeks later was gunned down on the streets of La Ceiba. *"Sic transit gloria mundi!"* ("So goes the glory of this world!") (Later on I will explain how the multimillion-dollar EAC of Isletas was practically destroyed in 1980.)

20. Developing a Liberation-Oriented Church

Our fine parish team of Tocoa and our zonal team with Sonaguera made a good plan for forming "liberating" basic Christian communities (BCC). I prefix the word "liberating" to the BCC, because there are some BCCs that are alienating: those of the Catholic charismatic movement, the catecumenate movement in Tegucigalpa, and, in general, wherever there is not a priest or some other religious leader with the liberation mentality orienting them. The BCC can end up like some religious groups with great, joyful brotherhood among themselves ("the saved") but who do not get involved in the struggle to form the Kingdom of God in this world.

To form our "liberating" BCCs, preferably within the co-ops and the EACs of Isletas, I wanted to use the San Miguelito method that I had always employed in the parishes of Progreso and Sulaco. But a tremendous Spanish Jesuit, Jesús Bengoaechea, was visiting us every month because some members of our team wanted him to teach us the method of forming liberating BCCs used by the team of Jesuits in the parish of Aguilares in El Salvador (where Rutilio Grande was pastor when he was murdered). We all agreed to use this Aguilares method, although my concern was that the Honduran campesinos of the cooperatives were very different from the pious, religious campesinos of the mountains of El Salvador.

This method was to stay in a village or in a colony of a co-op for about ten days to have a "holy mission," but not like the traditional ones. The themes for each night, when the adults and youth came together after work, were the plan of God for the salvation or liberation of this world. These themes were not preached, but introduced in the form of the Celebration of the Word of God with the Bible study. This was done in small groups with questions followed by a plenary session to hear the answers of each group.

In this way the people became accustomed to discussion in small groups; the plan was to continue doing this after the "mission" once a week in one of their homes, and then on Sunday to bring all the groups of a village together for the plenary session in the Celebration of the Word. In a village or co-op there usually continued two or three of these Bible study groups, using themes and Bible texts with questions that our zonal team prepared each month with the coordinators of the Delegates of the Word, using the *method of see, judge, and act.*

In a village or co-op where there were not enough Delegates or catechists, in the closing mass of the "mission" the community would name some. Afterward, our team gave many training courses for all the Delegates and catechists in our parish training centers in Salama (near Tocoa) and in Sonaguera. I did not help so much in these courses, because I was only half-time in the parish, but I always gave the "missions" in my sector with Marina and then continued helping the new BCCs.

This "mission" method of Aguilares was generally successful in our villages in the mountains, where there are traditionalist campesinos. It had less success in the subsequent formation of a BCC in the co-ops and villages in the valley, where the campesinos now had many other ways to entertain themselves besides meeting for Bible study. Up to today in the EAC of Isletas, the Sonaguera team has not been able to form a single BCC. In the co-ops that were formed almost by force with families from different parts of the country and, thus, without a "natural community," we have formed very few BCCs. In some communities where we finished the "mission" with four Bible study groups, there now remains only one, and in some places none.

The results appear to be almost the same as with the San Miguelito method with which we started the BCC in the Progreso parish in 1965. The big advantage of the San Miguelito method is that it starts with the Family of God course of basic Christian initiation. This course is a synthesis or global vision of the doctrine of Christ in the light of liberation theology in fifteen dialogue sessions and is directed by a priest or nun. It helps to do this before you launch these novices to interpret the Bible in their BCC according to their traditional understanding and prejudices.

The liberating BCCs of our apostolic zone of Tocoa and Sonaguera progressed a lot in those five years, in spite of much opposition and the criticism that we were "communists," and were "changing the customs of our religion." We were quite upset when Valentín Menéndez was named provincial of León in Spain. All the Jesuits of our team signed a letter to Father General Arrupe complaining that it was not following the spirit of our thirty-second General Congregation to take a Jesuit away from his work with the poor in the third world to work in the first world or to reassign a Jesuit who is part of an apostolic team without even consulting the team. However, Valentín left and another fine Spanish Jesuit, Carlos Solano, came to Sonaguera to replace Valentín as pastor and entered easily into our zonal team.

Since I worked half-time in Colón, I always spent two weeks there each month for our team meetings, for the monthly meeting of Delegates and catechists of my sector of Zamora, for the "missions" and the follow-up visits to the BCC groups, and for masses and sacraments in the fifteen villages and co-ops of my sector. During these two weeks each month, I continued visiting and promoting with Rubén Erazo the co-ops of the ANACH in Colón. The other half of the month I would pass through La Ceiba, either to go to Progreso, San Pedro Sula, and Tegucigalpa or to go over the "Culebra" ("Snake") Highway to Olanchito, Jocón, Yoro, Sulaco, and so forth.

Besides visiting the co-ops and the new groups of the ANACH with the activists of the different municipalities, I worked a lot organizing and giving the Spiritual Exercises of Saint Ignatius (adapted and reinterpreted through the liberation theology, as I have already explained) to labor union leaders, Christian Democratic politicians, campesino leaders of the ANACH and, more and more, of the UNC and the UNCAH (the new National Union of Authentic Campesinos). The UNCAH was born when a good group of the most revolutionary leaders of the UNC, principally from around Progreso and Tela, walked out of the National Congress of the UNC in protest because it was being manipulated by militants of the Christian Democratic Party.

The UNCAH held its constituent assembly in our Training

Center La Fragua in Progreso, and my friends who had made retreats with me, Chema Gómez and Adán Quintano, were elected to the first executive committee. Miguel Gutiérrez of the village of Mealer, in Progreso parish, was the first president of the UNCAH. The president of the UNC, Marcial Euceda, is also from Mealer. All these leaders were formerly Delegates of the Word.

From the beginning of 1977, I started spending at least a week each month in the Progreso area because the ANACH was losing many of its organized subsections in Guaymas to the new EAC that INA had promoted there since 1975, and in Guanchías to FECORAH. The ANACH at this time was very much weakened and inactive; Reyes Rodríguez and his people were in the executive committee, and almost all the activists were subordinated to the will of the military authorities of the government in general, and of INA in particular.

I, and other honest campesino leaders in the ANACH, decided not to abandon this organization and its eighty thousand campesinos to this corrupt gang, or to AIFLD (U.S.-controlled), or to the sold-out, unpatriotic "free and democratic" labor leaders of the FESITRANH and the CTH. We doubled our efforts to form new, intermediate, local leaders who, later on, would win control of the ANACH and, one day, of the FESITRANH and the CTH also. We did not agree with the dividing of the campesino movement by the revolutionaries who left the ANACH to form the EAC and who left the UNC to form the UNCAH, instead of working from the bottom, in the local groups, to change the ANACH and the UNC into really revolutionary organizations. These are the two organizations that move the masses of campesinos in Honduras. For our plan of winning control of the ANACH within a few years, the Progreso area was essential because it was (as I have said) traditionally the most revolutionary area in the country.

For this same reason it was important that the new liberation-oriented Church should also be present in the Progreso area more than in any other part of the country, as a ferment and a light within the popular organizations. It was sad to see, however, that some staff members of the parish of Progreso, together with the bishops and many priests in the country, ever since the massacre of "Los Horcones" in June of 1975 and the arrest of Father Steve Gross in Progreso, shied away from major social commitments with the popular organizations. Some priests of the parish were principally sacramentalists.

However, Chema Tojeira in Radio Progreso continued to have contact with the popular organizations, especially with the labor unions. The Delegates of the Word continued celebrating in the villages because a good Spanish Jesuit, Angel de Horna, worked with them, but those who were now leaders of co-ops or EAC, no longer functioned as Delegates.

In 1978 two very good American Jesuits from the California Province arrived, Jack Donald and Bob Grimaldi. They had worked in Jalapa, Mexico, and went to live with and as the poor in Urraco Pueblo in the parish of Progreso, visiting from there the villages of the whole Guaymas region on bicycles. We became close friends. They were great missionaries, sharing the life of the campesinos of Guaymas.

The Catholic church in Latin America has taken "the preferential option for the poor," said the bishops in their Documents of Puebla (Mexico) in 1979. However, some of my American Jesuit brothers are an example of how most bishops and priests interpret this "option for the poor": loving them, serving them, spending their time and money for them with housing projects, Radio Schools, health clinics, and so on. They try to alleviate their miserable poverty, helping a few of them to overcome their poverty by means of a good high school education that will assure them a good-paying job. My hope is that they would also enter into conflict with the *exploiting system* that produces so many poor people. At times they fearlessly denounce the injustices against some poor persons, but they do not attack the root cause of these injustices and of the poverty. They are reformists, developmentalists.

They say they take the option for the poor, but they want to be with all the Catholics, with the poor and with the rich, with the oppressed but without breaking off with the oppressors. They seek union, they say. Christ came to save everyone. We should not get involved in politics or in the class struggle. We should promote peace between the workers and the owners—labor unions, sure, but class struggle, no. A Christian can never approve of violence, they say. It seems to me that all this is using our religion as an ideology, as opium for the people, to impede them from rising up in rebellion to take over the power, change the capitalist system of private ownership of the means of production, and liberate the poor from exploitation and, finally, from poverty. I think these bishops and priests often have good will, but are unconsciously hurting the people, holding back their liberation. However, it is wonderful to see the gradual awakening and metamorphosis taking place in some bishops, priests, and sisters who are working with the poor throughout the world.

As I said, I started to spend at least a week each month in the Progreso area. I had my little "house of prayer" in the village of Camalote near Progreso and, with the ANACH activist, was visiting all the subsections of the area. Almost all of them had obtained at least a little land that became collective production co-ops. We started co-op stores in a number of them. The aim was that they would not leave the ANACH, that those of Guanchías would not pass over to FECORAH, or those of Guaymas to the EAC. Many of our co-ops had already done so, and the activists of the EAC in Guaymas were especially dynamic. The principal leader of them was my good friend, Fausto Orellana Luna, one of my former coordinators of the Delegates of the Word of the Progreso parish and one of the founders of the Las Mercedes Co-op of Toyos. He had also been a member of the national executive committee of the ANACH, until he and other "leftists" were practically expelled from the ANACH in the Convention of 1974 by the politics of Reyes Rodríguez.

Before, in Guaymas, all the campesinos of all the villages were united in the ANACH, but now I found them divided almost in half between the groups that had left the ANACH to become EACs and the co-ops that continued with the ANACH. Naturally, this division served the interests of the enemies of the campesinos. In 1977, INA, whose promoters always tried to change the ANACH co-ops into EACs, (the same as they did to FECORAH), convinced the EAC that the whole region of Guaymas, 12,000 acres won by the ANACH after great battles, should become a big project of African palm trees. The ANACH opposed this idea, and we insisted that basic food crops are the big need of the Hondurans.

Nevertheless INA insisted, and planted a huge seed plot of African palm. At the same time they started leveling and plowing some of the lands of the EAC for transplanting the seedlings. With this, some more of our co-ops left the ANACH and became EACs, because some of their leaders were bought off by giving them jobs working in the seed plot for INA at two dollars a day. At this same time, all the campesinos of Guaymas had just lost most of their corn crop from floods and insect plagues. Finally, in a big assembly, all the twenty co-ops of the ANACH in Guaymas decided to enter the African palm project, and they formed a regional executive committee to represent all these ANACH co-ops, with Francisco "Chico" Gómez as president.

I quietly went alone one day to visit the whole setup that the Tela Railroad Company has in San Alejo, near the port of Tela, with 4500 acres of beautiful African palm plantations and a big oil extracting plant. After all this was shown and explained to me, I asked the person in the central office who did me this favor if it was true that the Tela was going to have a part in administrating the palm project of INA in Guaymas, as it was rumored. As a matter of fact, many times recently engineers from San Alejo had been seen with authorities of INA inspecting the lands of Guaymas, and we knew that the EAC had already agreed that the Tela should supervise the Guaymas Project instead of INA, because of the inefficiency and corruption that INA had shown in the Lower Aguan Project. This person told me that the rumors were true and showed me a big portfolio with all the studies and the project already drawn up by the engineers of the Tela.

For more than an hour I read the project and made notes. I thanked the person and went to inform Chico Gómez. A few days later, in an emergency assembly of the ANACH co-ops of Guaymas, I informed the group that AID (U.S. government), which was going to give the multimillion dollar loan for the Guaymas "agrarian reform" project for 10,000 acres of African palm, insisted to the Honduran government that they would not give it if the project and the money were not completely administered by the Tela Railroad Company, because they did not want another project administered by INA with stealing and inefficiency, as in Colón. Besides buying all the production and administering the whole project, the Tela would supervise with their own field bosses the whole palm tree production process, which the co-ops and EAC would carry out. The campesino organizations would have their representatives, however, in all the decision-making bodies of the project.

The campesinos immediately understood that they would be working for the Tela, even though it was through their own co-ops or EACs, but without the right to have a labor union and other worker rights under the Honduran labor laws. Worst of all was the plan of the Tela to do the plantation work with machinery, as in San Alejo; thus, they would need only five hundred men (members of co-ops and EACs) for the 10,000 acres, instead of the two thousand campesinos who were already in the co-ops of the ANACH and in the EAC. Fifteen hundred campesino families would have to leave the Guaymas area (without doubt to go to the Lower Aguan Project).

Naturally, the campesinos became very angry over this news, and several of the EACs even returned to the ANACH. They were furious with the EAC leaders who were ready to sell out their organizations to the Tela Railroad Company, to give Guaymas back to the Tela after so many years of struggle by the ANACH to get these lands away from the Tela.

I wrote a report on this whole plan of United States domination, of AID, of the Tela Railroad Company, and of their unpatriotic, bought-off Honduran friends, that was publicized first by Radio Progreso and then the newspapers. That was the last that was ever heard about this plan. AID gave the loan, INA is administering the project, and at present all of Guaymas is in African palm plantations. The Regional Agro-industrial Cooperative of the ANACH of Guaymas Limited (CARAGUAL) and the Associative Agro-industry of Campesinos of the Area of Guaymas (EACA) have signed mutual collaboration agreements. About half of the Guaymas campesinos are with each organization, but they are united now in the plan to get an oil extracting plant for Guaymas that will belong to them, not to INA or the Tela. Of course, they had to accept the contract to sell all the oil produced to the Clover Brand (the Tela), which will make the North Americans the principal beneficiaries of the campesinos' years of struggle for agrarian reform in Guaymas.

The ANACH in these years was developing a new Co-op Plan.

Those of us who knew the Lower Aguan Project, where each co-op is its own legal entity and has its own provisional land title, insisted that the ANACH National Co-op Plan should be transformed into a federation of agricultural co-ops, so that each co-op could have its own legal personage and land title. Céleo Gonzáles and other labor leaders insisted on the ANACH staying a single legal entity, for as an agrarian labor union with a Co-op Plan, the co-ops would always depend on the ANACH. But in fact, many co-ops of the ANACH changed over to FECORAH precisely to become individual legal entities which was required for receiving a large loan from the banks.

To resolve this, Antonio Julín Méndez, the president of the National Co-op Plan, came to an agreement with AIFLD and presented an alternative that he had seen in Guatemala: regional co-ops of the ANACH with legal personage, made up of many small local co-ops in the villages of a region. The lands of these local co-ops would be part of the big regional co-op, which would make big projects planned for the whole region, with machinery, offices, warehouses, and so on in common. This system has many advantages and was adopted by the General Assembly of the ANACH Co-op Plan in 1977. The first regional agricultural cooperative of the ANACH (CARAL) was in the department of Atlántida, with offices in Tela, and was quite successful. Another successful one was formed in the department of El Paraíso. I helped form those of Guaymas (CARAGUAL) and of Colón (CARACOL). Only the local ANACH co-ops of the Lower Aguan Project are their own legal entities.

In 1977 a new political party was formed in Honduras called the Revolutionary Party of Honduras. The initiator of this was my friend, Aristides Mejía, who worked for many years with AIFLD and the FESITRANH in labor education and lately with the OIT (the International Work Organization) in Costa Rica. There he became involved with international Social Democratic leaders who wanted to start a party with their progressive, neocapitalist ideology in Honduras. The OIT assigned him to Honduras, and Mejía won the interest of his labor leader friends of the ORIT line for his project. The ORIT is the Interamerican Regional Organization of the OIT, completely dominated and manipulated by the AFL-CIO and AIFLD of the U.S., and to which the CTH and the ANACH are affiliated. These bureau-cratic labor leaders, Victor Artiles, Céleo Gonzáles, Reyes Rodríguez, and company, won over several of the former cabinet ministers of the first populist government of General López Arellano to start this new party with them. They invited me and many other friends of the CTH to the first assembly to decide on the constitution, the name, and the ideological line of the new political party.

Mejía spoke about how the Socialist International and the Social Democratic parties of all the Latin American countries would help us with our new party, which would fight for the benefit of the worker-campesino class and would give many of the leadership positions in the party to worker and campesino leaders. The activists of the ANACH and of the FESITRANH agreed to be the principal activists of "their own" new party.

In the discussion about the name of the new party, I suggested first "Socialist Party" (PASO had not come out into the light of day yet). Mejía wanted to call it the "Social Democratic Party." I told them that we already had four political movements in Honduras along this same neocapitalist line: the Christian Democratic Party, PINU (Party of Unity and Innovation), ALIPO (the progressive movement in the Liberal Party), and the Renovating Nationalist Youth movement in the National Party. What we need in Honduras, I said, is a revolutionary party. Mejia then said why not call it the "Revolutionary Party of Honduras" (PRH). Almost everyone liked this name, and so that was it. After this first meeting, however, I did not stay active in this party, which I saw as reformist rather than revolutionary in character.

21. Some Last Battles for Justice

I believe it was in this year of 1977 that the newly formed "sectional" office of the ANACH was opened in Progreso, which covered both the Guanchías and the Guaymas regions. We decided to have a weekly ANACH radio program over our Jesuit Radio Progreso. Father Chema Tojeira, the director, gladly gave us a free half hour every Saturday at 6:00 P.M. Our program was called "Campesinos Marching Ahead" and was under the direction of the ANACH activists. I always gave a recorded ten-minute talk on the social doctrine of the Church, selecting the parts of the Church documents, like those of Medellín, that condemn capitalism, "institutionalized violence," "economic neocolonialism," the "situation of sin" in Latin America, and so on.

After about five months I decided that it was not effective to be expressing my ideas over the radio anymore, because I already had too many enemies criticizing me and looking for ways to ruin me. One of the new activists of the ANACH for the Progreso section, Saul Socrates Coello, made the program plenty revolutionary. He was a rural teacher (without finishing high school) in the village of El 4 de Marzo near Progreso, where he lived, taught school, planted his milpa, and helped the ANACH a great deal as an activist.

As I said, more and more opposition was building to my activities from all authorities and bourgeoisie in northern Honduras. My name was appearing frequently in the newspapers in these years. One of the things that most upset them was my role at the National Convention of the ANACH in September of each year. Since 1965 the Executive Committee of the ANACH had invited me to open their conventions with an invocation to God, which always came out over the radio and in the newspapers. My "prayers" of 1976 and 1977 prompted much criticism in the newspapers by the bourgeoisie and congratulations in person from the workers. Translations of these two prayers follow:

1976: Our dear Father-God, we want to start off this convention of the campesinos of the ANACH invoking your name. You made the land and the other natural resources of our Honduras for the benefit of all the Hondurans. Well look, Lord, at the kind of society that human beings have formed, in which a minority that is stronger has grabbed up, as owners, the best lands and other sources of production and riches, using the mass of workers and campesinos as their hired hands, like modern slaves. And thus, this minority in Honduras live well, while the big mass of workers and campesinos live in misery.

You, oh Father, sent your Son, Jesus Christ, to this world precisely to change this situation, this kind of unjust, sinful society. As it says in the Gospel of Saint Luke, Jesus came and continues to work in this world "for the liberation of the oppressed." Well, Lord, here you have the principal leaders of the oppressed campesinos organized in the ANACH. Inspire them by your Holy Spirit to take seriously, these campesino delegates to the convention, their historic responsibility to fight for the complete liberation of the oppressed of Honduras and of Honduras itself, fighting to form a new Honduran society without social classes, without some being privileged and others being marginated, without this exploitation of one human being by another, where we will all live as equals, sharing equally in the riches, like brothers and sisters, as you taught us through your Son, Jesus Christ. Amen.

1977: Our Lord Jesus Christ, you came to this world making yourself one of the poor, oppressed class of your time. While being God, you became a poor campesino. Well look, Lord, at how our Honduran campesino brothers and sisters are not only exploited economically, despised socially, used politically, and marginated culturally, but also how ideologically they are taught to conform with small conquests of land and help, to seek for partial liberations. They remain satisfied with having more and more participation in this unjust, exploiting capitalist society. Most of the campesinos lack your spirit of total liberation.

Therefore, our prayer is for you to send your Spirit of Love to these campesinos of the ANACH and to all the poor campesinos and workers, so that they will have more class consciousness, be more conscious that only they, united and organized, can make the revolution and change this sinful capitalist society for a new, more just, more egalitarian, more fraternal, socialist society. We ask that the Honduran campesinos who have given their lives in these battles for justice, following your example, will be an inspiration to the rest of the campesinos, so that they will never conform until we achieve this new society we seek. Amen.

The president of the republic, General Melgar Castro, had persuaded Rigoberto Sandoval to return to Honduras at the beginning of 1976 as director of INA, to satisfy the continual demands of the campesino organizations, to stop their land "recoveries," and to make a show of moving the process of agrarian reform forward. But it was only a "show," demagoguery. The military government did not want to touch the big landowners (since they too were big landowners now), and Sandoval left the country again before the year was out. He did not have the backing of the government or of the armed forces for agrarian reform.

INA continued the big projects already under way, but distributed very little land to the hundreds of campesino groups demanding it. From 1977 to today, INA and the armed forces have been brutally repressing the campesinos who try to "recover" lands. ("Recovering" lands is to the campesino movement what the strike is to the labor movement.) For example, the campesino leagues of the UNC in the whole region of Negrito and Morazán, Yoro, have attempted several times each year to recover lands that they know to be national lands fenced in illegally. Rich cattlemen might have legal title to 2000 acres and have fenced in 4000 acres. The UNC, together with the ANACH groups in the region, have invaded the lands of the Funes ten times with up to five hundred families. Ten times the soldiers have come to violently evict them, burning down the champas they made, and ten times their leaders have been thrown in jail.

All these UNC leaders of Negrito and Morazán are good friends of mine. I know them well because they made spiritual retreats with me during the years 1976 to 1979. In these years I stopped giving retreats to the labor union and ANACH leaders who had the stamp of AIFLD on them. I chose the more revolutionary worker and campesino leaders, even though they still had the mentality of Christian Democrats like most of the leaders of the UNC. I tried to give the revolutionary kind of Spiritual Exercises to all the former Delegates of the Word who were leaders of the ANACH, the UNC, and the UNCAH, and to a few of FECORAH in the departments of Yoro, Colón, Atlántida, and Santa Bárbara. My idea was to help them become Christian revolutionaries.

In 1978 and 1979 a system of following up the retreats with study circles was really functioning well. I was giving a retreat about every other month in some part of the country to campesino and worker leaders or to leaders of the Christian Democratic Party. I also had several retreats with campesino women of the FEMUC (Federation of Campesino Women, united to the UNC) from Santa Bárbara, Olancho, and other parts of the country.

Looking back now over my twenty years of work with the campesinos, I would say that these retreats and study circles were the best help that I have given them. It was "revolutionary evangelization"; it was giving "the good news to the poor" about their liberation, but not only out of the Bible. Without the help of the Marxist-Leninist science on how to analyze reality and how to transform this sinful reality, our preaching of "love of the poor," "seeking justice," "liberation of the oppressed," would just be words, just demagoguery; it would be neither an efficacious love of the poor nor an efficacious seeking of justice.

I was so radical in my convictions from 1976 on, my metamorphosis was so complete, that I can well understand the lack of comprehension about my work from many of the Jesuits in Honduras (not to mention the great opposition of all the bishops). I was told by my superior not to give any more interviews to reporters. My friends, who did not always agree with me, were a consolation; but my real consolation was and is Jesus Christ. The more opposition I ran into all around me—from the bishops, from some of the Jesuits, and from the military and civil bourgeoisie—the more I dedicated myself to communion with the Spirit of Jesus in me. More and more hours at night I spent in solitary study and meditation in my "prayer champas."

Besides my champa in Camalote, where I lived when I was in the Progreso area each month, since 1977 I had been living in a little champa in Zamora, one of my villages in the Tocoa parish. Instead of living in the poor neighborhood of the town of Tocoa and going out every day to my villages and co-ops, our parish team finally gave me permission to live out in my sector of the parish and come in to Tocoa from Colón to be with them for lunch and meetings about twice a week.

I had a great desire to live more and more with and as the poor campesinos, like Christ. Therefore, I got this poor, unoccupied house at the entrance to Zamora, which was loaned to me gratis by the owner. I ate with the family of the Delegate of the Word there for fifty cents a meal. Making the change to living in Zamora was the last sign I needed to detach myself from the use of a car for my work. My pretext always had been that I spent half my time traveling all over the country, which was true. Nevertheless, it became obvious to me that I could not live like the campesinos of Zamora and be the only one in the village who had a car.

I turned my Toyota jeep over to the superior in Progreso, and he gave me permission to buy a motorcycle to go around like the ANACH activists and like the other Jesuits of Tocoa and Sonaguera. By chance, I found a good secondhand Honda 125 dirt bike for only $750, and since 1977 my only vehicle has been the motorcycle. To go from Tocoa to Progreso took me at least six hours. On a long trip like that, I used to get off and walk around awhile every hour; otherwise my back and my bad knee would bother me. In this way I have really traveled a lot, and without any accident (so far!).

I continued visiting the Jicaque Indian tribes in the department of Yoro, with the help of Lucas Cárcamo of CARITAS in Yoro and of Adán Palma as activist of the ANACH. When Sandoval returned as director of INA in 1976, I convinced Reyes Rodríguez and the others of the executive committee of the

ANACH that we should start a big campaign to recover the lands of the nineteen tribes. We took almost all the nineteen tribal chiefs to Tegucigalpa to talk to Sandoval, but neither I, nor Reyes Rodríguez, nor all the chiefs together could convince Sandoval to take an interest in getting back the Indian lands in Yoro. He was only interested in his big, agro-industrial agrarian reform projects, especially those of African palm and of sugar cane.

In 1977 my promoters, Lucas and Adán, and I gave a three-day course in the parish training center in Yoro for all the chiefs and assistant chiefs of the nineteen tribes. We encouraged them all to continue in the ANACH in order to keep its backing and that of all the CTH in their struggle to recover their lands. We left them with the task of consulting with their tribes about the formation of a federation or union of all the Indian tribes of Honduras under the ANACH. We also went around to each of the tribes to promote this idea of a national federation of the tribes.

In August of 1977, together with the ANACH, we called a meeting of all these chiefs and assistant chiefs for the first assembly of Indian tribes in our Center La Fragua in Progreso. All the tribes agreed to organize, not a federation, but the CONA-TRINH-ANACH (National Committee of Indian Tribes of Honduras, under the ANACH) with seven chiefs as an executive board. It was agreed to convoke another assembly within a few months, after visiting and inviting the tribe of Jicaques of the Montaña de la Flor in the department of Francisco Morazán, the Payas in Olancho, the unorganized Lencas in Lempira, and the Miskitos and Sumos in the department of Gracias a Dios.

This second assembly, however, was never realized; the opposition against us was too fierce. We finally gathered copies of all the nineteen land titles that Padre Subirana had acquired for the tribes in 1864, and with the executive board of CONATRINH-ANACH, we made dozens of visits to the offices of INA in Tegucigalpa and San Pedro Sula. At the beginning of 1978, INA reluctantly remeasured the lands of the two tribes of Subirana and Tablón to see exactly where their boundaries were.

Nevertheless, when the co-op of the tribe of Subirana wanted to plow five acres of flat land for a collective cornfield, clearly within their remeasured boundaries, a cattleman of Subirana had the chief, Juan Estrada, thrown in jail. When INA announced that the next title to remeasure was that of the tribe of Las Vegas of Tepemechín, there were so many threats by the cattlemen of the town of Las Vegas against the chief, Porfirio Zelaya, that he had to go away and hide out for a couple of months. Meanwhile, a gang of hired gunmen arrived when the cooperative of this tribe was picking the corn on their collective milpa and, by shooting at them, ran the Indians off and wounded one woman. The gang stole the picked corn and cut the fence wire so that the cattle would enter to eat the rest. There were many complaints made to the civil and military authorities, but since all of them were friends of the cattlemen and against the remeasuring of the Indian lands, nothing was ever done.

The Ladino coffee growers of Yorito, who have their plantations on the lands of the tribe of Santa Marta, threatened the chief, Paco Alvarado, many times. They got the promise of INA that, instead of INA remeasuring the Indian lands, they would be given property titles to their coffee plantations. When Father Bob Voss, the pastor of Yoro, was in the town of Subirana for a mass during this same period, a gunman, hired to kill me, arrived at the church and thought that it was I saying mass. When he asked the nuns, they told him it was Roberto, not Guadalupe.

Around this same time, the corrupt Honduran Indian Institute got some money to buy off several of the tribal chiefs. The chiefs were brought to a course in Tegucigalpa and used to form a Federation of the Indian Tribes of Honduras, for the purpose of destroying the CONATRINH-ANACH and ending the fight for remeasuring the Indian lands. The plan succeeded, for INA was now afraid, and had orders to stop upsetting the big cattle and coffee men of Yoro who had fenced in tribal lands. (I repeat: One of the first conquests of the victorious Honduran revolution is going to be the recovery of the lands of the nineteen Yoro Indian tribes. It is a waste of time and of blood to try to recover them before then.)

In 1978 the Nationalist Party made a secret alliance with a group of high officers of the army who wanted the opportunity to stick their hands in the funds of the ministries and autonomous bodies of the government. Since General Melgar had now become a rich landowner, he had to give others their chance. Besides, in spite of his part in the massacre of "Los Horcones,"

Melgar was considered by the landowners and industrialists to be too easy on the leftists. In August of that year the Armed Forces Supreme Council, by voting among themselves, made another unbloody coup d'état and replaced Melgar as president of the republic with Gen. Policarpo Paz García.

"Polo" Paz, called "Bolo" Paz (a *bolo* is a drinker in Honduras) by those who knew him well, had been a kind of hero in the war with El Salvador, and also a good friend of all the U.S. ambassadors who have been in Honduras. It was he who made the alliance with the Nationalist Party to control the government and the armed forces, and to use strong measures to repress whatever is leftist in the country. Since he continued as head of the armed forces also, one of his first acts was to retire from the army about forty high-ranking officers who were progressive and considered dangerous, including the popular former director of INA, Col. Mario Maldonado.

Paz replaced many of the military officers and civilians in high posts in the government with an even higher percentage of other military officers as cabinet ministers and directors of state institutions, like Hondutel (telecommunications), the National Railroad, INA, and so on. The new president then ordered the formation of regional development councils under the direction of the colonels in command of the military regions, in order to consolidate the armed forces' control over every development project in all the municipalities of the country. *To help in the militarization of Honduras,* the United States tremendously increased its military aid (with more multimillion-dollar loans for arms, tanks, planes, rockets, officer training in the Canal Zone in Panama, more U.S. military advisers in Honduras, and so on). They did so in order to form the strongest and most modern armed forces in Central America, unconditionally committed to following U.S. policy, to protect Honduras and Central America from the "communist, terrorist infiltration." The officers of "the third stage of the armed forces' government" promised to maintain Honduras as an "oasis of peace, surrounded by countries in civil war caused by subversive communists in Nicaragua, El Salvador, and Guatemala." They also promised to put Honduras back on the democratic road with elections in 1980.

Here is an example of how the military officers were going to keep this "peace." At the very beginning of this new government there was an assault by the army on the offices of SUTRASFCO (the union of the Standard Fruit Company workers) in La Ceiba. My friend, the dynamic president of SUTRASFCO, Napoleón Acevedo, and other leaders were captured and imprisoned, while the soldiers helped some workers of an anticommunist, patronal "Democratic Front" break the lock and take possession of the union headquarters. The SUTRASFCO leaders in Coyoles Central (of Olanchito), who were all friends of mine, were beaten up, thrown in jail, and later on fired from the Standard for being "communists." Even today, SUTRASFCO is in the hands of leaders chosen and controlled by the Standard and by the military colonel in La Ceiba.

At the same time that this new governmental coup was being carried out in 1978 by the army officers, many of the best leaders of the ANACH were planning another coup: for the next National Convention, with elections for their executive committee in September. I took part in many meetings with these more progressive leaders who wanted to get rid of Reyes Rodriguez. I went around a lot with them to explain to almost all the subsections in the whole northern part of Honduras the necessity for getting Reyes out of office. Of course, Reyes and his people went all over the country trying to assure his re-election.

The progressive leaders of the ANACH advised me not to go to the convention this year, because it was sure to be ugly. Besides, Reyes and his people knew that I was going around talking against them and so, of course, I was not invited. But to describe what happened, I will insert here a copy of the public letter I wrote after the convention, which we distributed to almost all the subsections of the ANACH in the country and to many other popular organizations. It also came out over the radio and in the newspapers.

A CALL TO ALL THE HONEST CAMPESINOS
OF THE ANACH—OCTOBER 1978

After fourteen years of struggling side by side with you in the ANACH with all my heart, this year for the first time I did not go to the National Convention of the ANACH to ask for God's blessing, because I knew that there was going

to be more foul play than ever. Before the convention, I
heard that some of the delegates to the convention were being influenced by agents paid with money from AIFLD,
from the U.S. embassy, and from the CIA (the U.S. spy
agency). I also imagined that the army would intervene to
assure the victory of the candidate that the U.S. embassy
wanted, just as they did in Isletas and in SUTRASFCO. Because of this same fear, I suppose, at the last moment Julín
refused to be a candidate for the presidency. And now,
those of us of the ANACH who are not in agreement with
the legality of this convention and back up the Committee
for the Defense of the ANACHA fear that some of the leaders of this comittee may be thrown in jail.

I have investigated, and many of the delegates of the convention assure me that the election was fraudulent, because
more than a hundred of the votes received were from persons, including women, who were not legal delegates.

I not only can't bless this dirty work and gangsterism
(typical of some U.S. labor unions), but it is my duty to denounce it and ask all of you honest comrades of the
ANACH to form a solid mass behind the Committee for the
Defense of the ANACH that was formed by the 180 delegates who walked out of the convention in protest over the
election of Reyes.

A document of resolutions of the Committee for the Defense of the ANACH is circulating through all the subsections of the ANACH, which condemns Reyes Rodríguez and
the executive committee and national directive council of the
ANACH. It backs up the Committee for the Defense of the
ANACH in their demand to the Labor Ministry to declare
the elections of the convention illegal. It also demands that a
new convention be called before December 1 to legally and
democratically elect the leaders of the ANACH. If this new
convention is not convoked before December 1, 1978, all the
subsections that sign the document will withdraw, as a solid
block, from the ANACH and, in order not to divide up
more the campesino-worker movement, will join one of the

other existing campesino organizations—but not FECORAH, which is a governmental organization.

I make, then, this call to all the honest members of the ANACH to get your subsections to sign these resolutions right away, in solidarity with those who are trying to eliminate the corruption in our organization. The argument they use, that we who are against the perpetuation of Reyes and his people are communists, is false, and is the same one that the big landowners and capitalists accuse us of. This argument no longer fools the campesinos. Remember, friends, our struggle is the same as Christ's, for the liberation of the oppressed. It is not the ANACH that is the main thing, but the liberation of the Honduran campesinos.

With affection and solidarity,
(signed) Padre Guadalupe

You can just imagine how furious they were with me for this letter, and how they attacked me by every means. Reyes Rodríguez and his followers, Artiles of the CTH and his Labor buddies, the North Americans of the embassy and of AIFLD, the bought-off military officers of the government, the bishops and many of the Jesuits and other priests of the Honduran Church, some of these people wanted to throw me out of the country, or throw me in jail. I knew there would be this reaction against me, but I decided that if my influence with the masses of campesinos in the ANACH was worthwhile for something, it was now my duty to use it to help save the ANACH, even if it cost me my life.

Although I suffered a lot, at the same time I felt a great consolation—first of all because the Spirit of Jesus in me assured me that I had done well out of love for the campesinos and also because of the solidarity and congratulations I received from many of the progressive and honest people in the country.

The 180 dissident delegates who walked out of the convention (leaving it without a quorum for a legal election), headed by Antonio Julín Méndez, incorporated me automatically in their Committee for the Defense of the ANACH. I went around with them again to explain to all the subsections what had really happened in the convention, and we obtained the signatures of hundreds of subsections to support the resolutions of our Committee, which had Julín Méndez as president.

I like the way Julín lived. Several times I went to see him where he lives with his family, renting a poor shack in a slum section of San Pedro Sula. But I was worried about the way Julín was now the favorite of AIFLD or the way he put the headquarters of the Co-op Plan (of which he was still president) in the offices of AIFLD when Reyes did not want him around the ANACH headquarters in San Pedro Sula.

So the ANACH was divided into two bands. Reyes and his people really hated me now, and in the newspapers they publicly blamed me for the division in the ANACH. The executive committee of the ANACH published a pronouncement accusing me of being a traitor to the ANACH, a foreign priest mixed up in politics, which is against the constitution of the republic, and so on.

Well, to end this story the Committee for the Defense of the ANACH, which had the best campesino revolutionaries as activists all over the country, went on adding more and more subsections to its movement, but they never got the extraordinary convention that they demanded. They decided not to leave the ANACH, but to work at raising the consciousness of the members all over the country to have them ready for the next election in the ordinary convention of 1980.

In my exile in Nicaragua I rejoiced in September of 1980 when I heard the result of the election in the ANACH convention. In spite of the hundreds of tricks used by Reyes and his people before and during the convention, when they saw that AIFLD, the labor union bureaucracy under Victor Artiles, and the overwhelming majority of the delegates to the convention were all with Julín, Reyes' group walked out of the convention, and later on formed a new campesino organization, ALCONH. Nevertheless, much more than the needed, quorum remained to elect Julín Méndez president of the ANACH, all friends of mine to the national directive council and Rubén Erazo (of Colón) and Chico Gómez (of Guaymas) to the seven-person national executive committee. It was worth sacrificing myself to help this massive campesino organization be more liberating!

At the end of 1978 and the beginning of 1979, in spite of

being more spied upon and threatened than ever, I not only continued my various work, with the parish apostolate of Tocoa, retreats, study circles on socialism, the co-ops in Colón and Yoro, and the Committee for the Defense of the ANACH, but I also had some very interesting new projects. One of them was helping in the organization of the Bakers Co-op El Faro of Progreso with the former workers of Hawit's Bakery. Previously, they had tried to form a labor union, gone on strike, took over the bakery building, been evicted and thrown in jail by the FUSEP (police), and then fired by Hawit.

With loans from me and from other friends in Progreso, they built a big, open tin-roofed shed and a big brick oven, and without any machinery and overcoming hundreds of difficulties and obstacles, they started producing bigger and cheaper loaves of bread than the commercial bakeries. After a few weeks of a kind of war against the co-op, all the other bakeries in northern Honduras, which had shortly before raised the price of a small loaf to six cents (of lempira), finally had to lower it again to match the five cents of El Faro. Opposition continued, and even threats of death against them, but these wonderful young workers went on. Today the bakers' co-op El Faro has its own building, machinery, and a thriving business.

Another idea that for a long time I had wanted to try was the organization of justice and peace commissions in all the parishes, and afterward, regional and national commissions. Through these groups the progressive Christians in all the parishes in the country would have an instrument for their social activity, to seek social justice. I got the idea while talking to a Crusader sister who used to work with me in Progreso, and who is now part of the Commission for Justice and Peace in Guatemala, which denounces the horrible persecution and repression of the popular leaders there.

But the special light that the Holy Spirit gave me was that the Church should not make the denunciations and use political pressure against the violations of human rights all by itself (as it does in Guatemala, El Salvador, and in practically all countries), but rather the Church should always be "the ferment or leaven in the masses," should be inserted within the popular organizations of the masses. One way to do this could be through the

Church's regional justice and peace commissions forming part of a regional committee for the defense of human rights. Along with all the popular organizations of the region, it would be the organism for denouncing and trying to remedy the injustices and violations of human rights.

For a long time I was also trying to think of a way that the Church could serve, as a neutral force, in the unification of the popular organizations, which are so divided because of ideologies and personalities. The campesinos now have seven different national organizations (ANACH, UNC, UNCAH, FECORAH, EAC, FRENACAIN, ALCONH) fighting among themselves. The same is true of the labor union federations (CTH, CGT, FSI, CUS, Interunion Committee of San Pedro Sula, etc.), with the teachers' organizations (COPEMH, COLPROSUMAH, PRICPMAH, SINEPUDERH, Union Magisterial), with the high school students (FESE, FED, CLES, BRUS), with the university students (FRU, FUR, FUUD, FES), with community development committees (Patronatos FENAPACOMH, FECOPANH, FEPAIN, etc.), with political parties and movements (PLH, PNH, PDCH, PINU, PASO, PCH, PCMLH, PRH, FMLH, URP, MUP, FPH, etc.).

Talking this over with my friends who were leaders of many of these organizations, they all admitted that there was a lot of sectarianism among them, which made it really difficult to unite the popular forces but that such unity was urgently necessary. They all wanted the Church to attempt it around the defense of human rights, which is something that all the popular organizations want. They know that if one group invites all the organizations to come together for some cause, only those of the same ideology show up, but they would all answer a call from the Church. Also, everyone recognized that there was more and more repression against the popular organizations in Honduras, and that only by uniting could they defend themselves.

The biggest problem that I saw was not the organizations, but how to get the parishes to form the justice and peace commissions (JPC). I would have to start in the parishes where I had priest friends who would take an interest in this. The most important regions to organize were Tegucigalpa and San Pedro Sula together with Progreso. Progreso is where the principal forces of the popular organizations are concentrated. I decided to start in Progreso by forming the first JPC with my good Jesuit friend Jack Donald, who lived in Urraco Pueblo but was assistant pastor of the whole parish of Progreso. Jack had the delicate task of getting permission from the parish team of priests to form the parish JPC and to include me as a member. After a meeting with the parish team, Jack told me they had given him permission, and we launched ourselves into the work.

The plan was to form the parish JPC of Progreso, which would take the initiative and invite all the popular organizations of San Pedro Sula, La Lima, and Progreso to a big assembly in our Center La Fragua to organize the Committee for the Defense of Human Rights (CODDERHH), Region of San Pedro Sula, approve some bylaws, and elect a board of directors. In January of 1979 we easily formed the parish JPC with Jack, me, and five capable laypersons who were in agreement with us. We met twice a month to study the Church documents about the JPC (which is an official organization of the institutional Church) and the different international human rights declarations and also to plan the big assembly. José Orellana and I did a lot of work elaborating some bylaws of CODDERHH to serve as a base of discussion in the assembly.

Before the assembly we made a list of 146 different popular organizations of San Pedro Sula, La Lima, and Progreso (the same ones I mentioned above plus many others of women, of cooperatives, of associations of street salesmen, of photographers, of newsmen, of some lawyers and other progressive professional persons, etc.). We wanted CODDERHH to be a classist organization, which would defend the rights of the poor, of the worker-campesino class; therefore, we were not going to invite the organizations of their oppressors, of the bourgeois class. (We were glad that the Nationalist Party did not send a representative.) I spent two weeks going around with Jack or some other member of our JPC to visit the leaders of each one of the 146 organizations, plus about twenty individual professional friends, to explain the idea of CODDERHH and invite them to the assembly.

The day of the assembly, February 11, 1979, it rained all day long, and I was sad, thinking that no one would come from La Lima and San Pedro Sula. However, official representatives of sixty organizations arrived (many others joined later), and we held the assembly, with everyone enthusiastic about organizing CODDERHH—Region of San Pedro Sula. We divided into small groups to study and change the proposed bylaws, and then, in a general session, they were modified and approved. In the election for the board of directors, the assembly wanted me to be president, but I told them that that would hurt CODDERHH, because I had so many enemies. Dagoberto Padilla, the president of SITRACOAGS (the labor union of Echeverry's Sula Banana Company in Guanchías) became the magnificent first president of CODDERHH.

I accepted the vice-presidency. Eight work commissions were also formed: for education, for publicity, for finances, for investigation, for international relations, for legal help, and so forth.

The board of directors and the work commissions met every two weeks, and we started investigating and denouncing injustices and violations of human rights. When the newspapers told about the organization of CODDERHH under the initiative of the JPC of the Progreso parish, some of the Jesuits in Progreso denied that they had given Jack permission to do it and told him that we could not have a JPC of the parish. Jack suggested that we simply change the name to "Christians for Justice" and continue on with the work. This we did, starting with plans to organize CODDERHH in the capital.

Meanwhile, my fellow Jesuits of our team in Colón were completely in agreement with organizing a regional JPC and a regional CODDERHH in Colón. They insisted, however, on the necessity of getting permission from Bishop Brufaú of our diocese. It was decided that I should present the whole project at the next diocesan clergy meeting, which was held with the bishop each month. I made a mimeographed pamphlet with the history of the justice and peace commissions (JPC) in the Church, with quotations from the popes, from Vatican II, and from the Medellín documents. I also explained the need that each Christian community had of an instrument in their parish for seeking social justice and denouncing violations of human rights in their village or neighborhood. I said that it was not the Church's role to make political pressure for justice all by itself, for this would cause a lot of problems for the Church, and besides, the Church should not be a political force like another party or pressure organization. (This was the part that Bishop Brufaú liked.) The bishop and the priests finally agreed that I could help any of the parishes in the diocese of San Pedro Sula that wanted to organize a JPC and COD-DERHH.

The pastors of Choloma, La Masica, and Jutiapa were friends of mine and wanted to start a JPC in their parishes, but it would be first in Colón and then in Tegucigalpa, I told them. In Colón it was easy to organize a JPC, with four members from the parish of Tocoa and four from Sonaguera, and afterward CODDERHH —Region of Colón, with representatives of about thirty popular organizations in a fine assembly in the grade school of Tocoa. However, there were so many secret security agents in the organizations in Colón, and so much militarization of INA, of the EAC of Isletas, and of the co-ops, that many of these organizations were afraid to allow their representatives to continue to take part. A small but dynamic group of us continued, and we made several public denunciations of violations of human rights in the Lower Aguan Valley.

The organization of CODDERHH in Tegucigalpa was the most important, but the most difficult to establish. I could not be there much and I knew of no progressive pastor in all of Tegucigalpa who would want a JPC in his parish that would be the Church group to invite the organizations for CODDERHH. I started visiting my old friends in the capital who had made retreats with me and formed with them, not a JPC, but "Christians for Justice," as in Progreso. So many of them were known as militants of the Christian Democratic Party that I wound up meeting instead with some young ex-seminarians and ex-members of Christian youth groups who now were very revolutionary university students. With them we formed the "Christians for Justice" of Tegucigalpa, which would be the Christian organization present in CODDERHH.

The other difficulty in Tegucigalpa, much worse than in San Pedro Sula, was the sectarianism of the top leaders of the ideologically different leftist political parties and movements. They all lived in Tegucigalpa and at that time had no dialogue among themselves. The principal obstacle to uniting the popular organizations there was the rivalry between the "gordos" ("fat ones" of the pro-Soviet Communist Party of Honduras) and the "flacos" ("thin ones" of the pro-China Communist Marxist-Leninist Party). Between them they had much influence in many of the popular organizations, and they fought against one another like enemies—more than they did against the bourgeoisie.

I had friends in all the different groups and went around visiting them a lot for two months to convince them that we would not allow any of the groups to dominate CODDERHH. I managed to have several preliminary meetings in Centro Loyola with the top leaders of the main progressive, ideological groups in Tegucigalpa: the "gordos," the "flacos," the Christian Democrats, those of PASO (the Socialist Party), and the Liberals. These meetings were held to plan the assembly and to come to an agreement on names for the board of directors of CODDERHH —Region of Tegucigalpa, which they would then support at the assembly.

I stayed two weeks in Tegucigalpa with Jack Donald visiting, explaining, and inviting all the popular organizations (about ninety of them) to the assembly on October 9, 1979, in the University Social Center. About fifty organizations (including all the political parties and movements except the Nationalists) sent their official representatives, and CODDERHH—Region of Tegucigalpa was formed with the lawyer of PASO, Cesar Murillo Selva, as president. Good work commissions were formed with many capable people from the university.

The board of directors of CODDERHH—Region of San Pedro Sula, who ran the assembly, left the new Tegucigalpa board of directors in charge of linking CODDERHH with all the international human rights organizations. But without anyone continuously encouraging these people so that the different groups would work together, this Tegucigalpa branch of CODDERHH has had limited success up to this time. Since I was expelled from the country just a month after this regional branch was formed, I could not help them work together. Only in 1981, out of the

necessity of defending their lives against so much repression going on now in Honduras, have the leftist groups reached some
kind of unity in the FPH (the Honduran Patriotic Front). COD-
DERHH would have helped them a lot, if only they had made it
function.

22. Jail, Exile, and Protests

To explain now about my expulsion from the country, we have to go back to March of 1979. I was in my champa in Zamora, Colón, listening by chance, or by the providence of God, to the news on Radio Progreso (which is hard to get in Colón). I heard an interview with Father Jaime Cadabón, a Jesuit of the parish of Progreso, telling how he had been captured by the FUSEP the day before. He said that Radio Progreso had broadcast, as usual, the coming visits of the priests to the villages and that Padre Jaime was going to have mass in Virtiente on such a day. Virtiente is a village up in the mountains one hour on horseback from Agua Blanca Sur. Three soldiers of the FUSEP interrupted his mass to take him away as a prisoner, but the people of the village insisted that he finish the mass first. Then all of them came down to Agua Blanca Sur along with Jaime and the soldiers.

Jaime was furious with the FUSEP sergeant in Agua Blanca Sur, who had sent soldiers to pick up Padre James (Jaime) Guadalupe Carney because the DIN was looking for him all over the country. Having heard over the radio that Padre Jaime would have mass in Virtiente, the DIN thought that this was Padre Guadalupe and ordered his capture. Jaime Cadabón could not convince the sergeant that he was not Padre Guadalupe, who is a tall gringo, while he is a short, chubby Spaniard. When they took him to Progreso, the DIN realized their mistake and asked Jaime to forgive them.

From this news interview I learned that the DIN and the FUSEP were looking for me all over the country with orders to arrest me. If I had committed some crime, why didn't they speak to the bishop or to my Jesuit superior, as they should? I decided to go right on with my work, but I packed a little bag to have a change of clothes and other things ready if I was going to jail. It seems that the capture of Jaime instead of me made the DIN look so ridiculous that it made them change their plans, for the

FUSEP knew I was in Colón and did not call me in. Instead, a week later I received a telegram from the head of the Immigration Office in San Pedro Sula ordering me to report there immediately with all my documents. Since I was a naturalized Honduran, what would the Immigration Office, which is for foreigners, have to do with me? Nevertheless, I went with a lawyer friend of mine from San Pedro Sula, and the regional head of Immigration told me they were merely making a check of their files on all naturalized Hondurans. With new photos, fingerprints, and photostatic copies of all my documents, they made a new folder on me and sent me home.

In Progreso, Ray Pease, the pastor, told me that for several days before Jaime was picked up, DIN agents had been showing a photo of me to the people who came to mass, asking them if they had seen me around there. From my friends in the ANACH I learned that Reyes Rodríguez was arranging directly with President Paz García for my expulsion from the country. But it certainly was not only the executive committee of the ANACH who wanted me expelled. It was the entire oligarchy of the country, especially the American embassy and the labor leader bureaucrats who had sold out to AIFLD and the CIA, because I denounced them all publicly.

I went on with all my activities, with CODDERHH, with the Committee for the Defense of the ANACH, with retreats, and so on, and for a few weeks no one bothered me. I thought that the crisis of my expulsion had passed because they had found that all my documents were in order and could not expel a Honduran without a legal trial. In April we had a three-day meeting in the parish training center in Trujillo for all the priests and nuns of Colón. On the first night, one of the Daughters of Charity at Trujillo told me that early that morning a DIN agent had come to their convent asking for me, and that she had told him that I was at the training center for a three-day meeting. With that, my Jesuit companions were worried that they might be planning to capture me again.

The next day I got up at 5:00 A.M. with the idea of catching a bus out of Trujillo to hide out in Yoro, but when I got to the bus station I recognized a secret agent of DIN from Tocoa seated there, and he saw me too. I immediately returned to the parish

training center and told my companions that I wanted to get out
of there to hide out somewhere, while they found out what the
authorities wanted with me. We recalled the famous plan, revealed in Bolivia, that the CIA taught to the military leaders of
all the Latin American countries for controlling the progressive
Church. They did it by expelling the revolutionary priests from a
country, not by judicial process according to the law, but by capturing them and quietly deporting them, leaving the bishops afterward to face an accomplished fact.

I knew that if the government expelled me from Honduras
again, the bishops would not do anything; they would be glad.
Of course, the American ambassador would not help me, as he
did in 1968, since he was one of those demanding my expulsion.
That is why I decided to hide out somewhere and fight my case
as I could from inside Honduras, instead of from some other
country, where I could not influence anything in Honduras. I
thought of going to some village in the mountains to live quietly
there with some campesino friends, but my companions all
thought it would be better to go to our Bishop Brufaú and hide
out in his house to force him to investigate my case. He was the
only one who could demand an explanation from the government;
the authorities would not listen to the Jesuits, but they were still
afraid of the bishops.

We asked one of the sisters to drive out of the training center
to investigate whether there were soldiers stopping the cars leaving Trujillo, to see if someone would be able to drive me to San
Pedro Sula. She returned with the news that not only were there
two roadblocks with soldiers checking all the cars (except hers),
but that when she returned she saw three DIN agents by the
house next to the fenced-in Center. She went out again to go
around the block and returned to inform everyone in the parish
center that we were surrounded by soldiers, who would probably
enter at any moment to try to capture Lupe.

They had no sooner hidden me away in a locked closet when
an army lieutenant and an immigration officer entered the training center and asked for me. They were told that I had left early
that morning and asked why they were looking for me. The immigration officer said that they had to talk to Padre Guadalupe
in the Immigration Office in Trujillo and that they should send

me word to report there as soon as possible. Then they left.

But we saw that the half-hidden soldiers surrounding the block did not leave. The officers undoubtedly did not believe I had left and might suddenly enter to search the center. We made a plan with the nuns. Six of them would fill the Toyota jeep and I would lie down in back covered with burlap sacks under the feet of four of them. In another car behind would go another person alone, and if we all got past the roadblocks okay, about twenty miles outside Trujillo I would change cars and go with the other companion to San Pedro Sula while the nuns returned to Trujillo.

In this way we managed to get out of the center and past the soldiers surrounding the block. With the sisters singing and me very quiet and well covered, the sister who was driving shouted to the soldiers at the first roadblock (without stopping) that they were going to a village and would soon return. We did the same thing at the second checkpoint without any problem, but then we saw them stop the second car. We waited for a long while farther down the road, until, to everybody's relief, the other car appeared. About twenty miles farther on, I changed cars and went on to San Pedro Sula. The sisters returned to Trujillo. My companion informed us that the soldiers had merely checked his driver's license and let him pass.

We stayed on the old highway on the lefthand side of the Aguan River, so we would not pass through Tocoa, where, we learned later, the FUSEP had been looking for me since the previous day. Neither did we pass through Sonaguera, but made a detour through the back roads of the Isletas banana farms to come out on the new highway to La Ceiba.

We had a moment of panic on leaving the farms and approaching this new highway when we saw two soldiers stopping and looking into all the cars, but then we realized that they always did this so that people could not take bunches of bananas from the farms without authorization. After looking into our car, they let us pass without any problem but asked us to take one of them to the next village down the road. "Certainly," I said and even held his rifle for him while the young soldier got into the car alongside me. Since 5:00 o'clock that morning I had really enjoyed this adventure.

The next danger was to get across the only bridge over the Cangrejal River into La Ceiba and onto the only highway to Progreso and San Pedro Sula. We stopped two blocks before the bridge, and my companion went on foot. He was frightened when he saw that there were soldiers checking all the cars crossing the bridge. We supposed that the FUSEP of Trujillo had talked by radio to La Ceiba and other places to look for me when they found out I was not in Trujillo. I decided to wade across the river, which was very shallow at that time of year, and meet my companion in the parish rectory in La Ceiba. As I was crossing the river in my underwear about three blocks from the bridge, I saw our car driving safely across. We waited in the parish rectory until nightfall so as not to pass through La Ceiba, Tela, and Progreso during daylight, when many people would recognize me.

We were approaching San Pedro Sula about 9:00 P.M., without further incident, when we saw that up ahead soldiers were stopping and checking all the cars entering the city. We immediately got off the highway onto a dirt road that wound through a slum neighborhood. Finally we came out near the center of the city close to the Cathedral parish rectory where the bishop lived.

Even before entering San Pedro Sula, we noticed a red glow lighting up the whole sky over the city and a huge cloud of smoke going up on the opposite side of the city. We were told later that workers on strike had set fire to the big Bemis-Handal textile factory, and for fear that other labor unions would send workers from La Lima and Progreso to help these of San Pedro Sula, the FUSEP was checking all the cars that entered the city.

We finally got into the rectory to see Bishop Brufaú. I told him that the soldiers had surrounded the parish training center in Trujillo and were trying to capture and expel me from the country without a trial. I explained that my fellow Jesuits and I wanted him to hide me in his house while he found out from the authorities what charges they had against me. He was so taken by surprise that he could hardly talk. But at last he telephoned to arrange for me to stay hidden away in the rectory of one of the parishes in a suburb of San Pedro Sula. He personally took me there and promised to come to talk to me the next day after he had found out something.

I remained hidden in that rectory without seeing the bishop

for five days. The news reports over the radio those days told about the Bemis-Handal fire and the brutal repression against any kind of demonstrations to support the workers of the Bemis, most of whom had been thrown in jail. When these workers took over the installations of the factory during the strike, they were surrounded by hundreds of soldiers of the FUSEP and of the army. The union declared that if the military forces tried to evict them, they would burn down the factory. The famous repressive Col. Gustavo Álvarez Martinez, military commander of northern Honduras at that time and the head of the FUSEP, gave orders to the troops to break down the cyclone fence and enter shooting. Three of the workers were killed, and during the confusion someone started a fire in a storeroom that contained drums of gasoline. The factory was burnt to ashes.

The six leaders of the labor union, who were sentenced to long terms in jail, insisted that they had not done it; nor had they given orders to anyone to start the fire. They said that an infiltrated agent of the DIN had done it. The transnational Bemis-Handal Company was not unhappy about the fire; they mysteriously collected millions of dollars in insurance money for a factory with textile machinery so old that it was not worth that much.

On the second day in my hideout I was listening to Radio Progreso when it suddenly went off the air and did not return. The other radio stations afterward reported how the FUSEP burst into the station to close down Radio Progreso, because the government had suspended the Jesuits' permission for the radio frequency. It took our superior, the director of the radio, Chema Tojeira, and Bishop Brufaú about six months of transactions and haggling with the military government to get their frequency permission and start broadcasting again, but now they could transmit only on long wave and under the direction of Bishop Brufaú. The government forbade Father Ángel de Horna to talk over the radio and would not allow any more criticisms of the government or the "subversive" protest music.

The superior and many of the Jesuits put the blame on me for the reputation of being communists and for the persecution against the Jesuits in Honduras. The open campaign against the Jesuits in El Salvador during these years, with the right-wing landowners and industrialists threatening to kill them all if they did not leave the country, made our position in Honduras more precarious. Therefore, many of the Jesuits, with the superior and Bishops Santos and Brufaú, wanted to get me out of the country. But now that the government was committing the injustice of trying to deport a Honduran priest from the country without any trial to legally condemn him, they had to defend me.

While I was hiding in this parish rectory, my good friend Jack Donald crossed the Ulúa River from Urraco Pueblo in a small dugout boat and walked into San Pedro Sula to visit me and tell me about these things. Another good friend of mine, Padre Chema Tojeira, the director of Radio Progreso, also came to visit me and tell me that my case had nothing to do with the closing down of the radio. Rather, for over a year the rich people of Progreso and San Pedro Sula, and probably some American companies, had been asking the military government to close it down because the microphones of Radio Progreso were always at the disposition of the labor movement to denounce the injustices of the owners and bosses.

When the bishop finally did come to see me, it was only to tell me that I should not go out of the house, because they were still hunting for me. He had not been able to get an interview with Col. Gustavo Álvarez Martinez, the military commander of the region, but he had one scheduled for the following day. Three days later Ray Pease, the pastor of Progreso, came to tell me that Bishop Brufaú had talked to the colonel, who demanded that he hand Padre Guadalupe over immediately to the Immigration Office. The bishop went immediately to Progreso to decide on something with the Jesuits. It was decided that the bishop, our superior, Pease, and I would all go together to talk to Colonel Álvarez and to the head of Immigration.

Two days later we all went to the office of the colonel in the military zone of San Pedro Sula. In a short meeting, without even inviting the bishop to sit down, Álvarez said that I had to report the following day to the head of the Immigration Office with all my documents—nothing more. If they were all in order, they would not expel me from the country as long as the bishop could control my activities so that I would not involve myself any more in political affairs. I was to stick strictly to the work of the Church.

The next day I went with Ray Pease to see the head of the Immigration Office in San Pedro Sula. He merely checked over my documents as a naturalized Honduran citizen and warned me in the same way as Colonel Álvarez had.

This was in May of 1979, and I returned to continue as before with all my activities. I believe it was in June that the two provincials arrived in Honduras, mine from Missouri, and César Jerez of Central America. They came to arrange for the incorporation of the Yoro-Colon Mission and all of Honduras into the Central American Province. Up to then it had included Guatemala, El Salvador, Nicaragua, Costa Rica, and Panama, but not Honduras. Besides that, they had come to talk individually with most of the Jesuits of the mission about my case—whether or not I should continue working in Honduras.

Finally, each of the provincials spoke with me, too, before deciding my case. When Leo Weber told me I should not continue speaking against capitalism, I answered him that it seemed to me, then, that he did not know the social doctrine of the Church, which condemns capitalism. With that, I figured my days as a Jesuit were numbered. But no, both of them, Leo and César, are fine, holy men. Leo said that he did not want to move me out of Honduras when many of the Jesuits, including the Provincial Jerez (who understands liberation theology much better than I) wanted me to go on with my social apostolate. Besides, he told me, John Willmering was going to be named superior of the mission in July, and he agreed that I stay on.

It is hard for North Americans to understand, much less appreciate my continual condemnation of capitalism. This is because few North Americans have personally experienced the cruel, oppressive, "19th century" capitalism of the third world, where workers live in economic slavery, where the rich landowners often value the campesinos as only cheap arms and legs, necessary inconveniences for production and profit.

It is also hard for North Americans to listen when I attack "yankee imperialism" but most North Americans seldom see the faces of the men, women, and children in the third world who are cruelly exploited by the multinational corporations. These giant organizations look for cheap land, cheap resources, cheap help. They want a stable environment (most often enforced by fascist military dictatorships) where safety regulations are few or nonexistent, where consumer products (medicines, pesticides, etc.) are tested without accountability for human and environmental consequences. And always enforcing this capitalistic and imperialistic exploitation is power, the economic, political, and especially military power of the United States, one of the strongest nations in history.

This crisis that I had with some of the Jesuits trying to expel me from Honduras was much harder for me than when the government of Honduras tried to do it. But no, I should try to understand these sincere holy men, as I ask them to try to understand me. Also this is just the dialectical class struggle within the Church. By means of these conflicts the Holy Spirit can, perhaps, make the institutional Church change and be a little more Christian, a little more saving and liberating, a little more on the side of the poor and oppressed.

As for me, these crises always make me more detached from everything in this world that is not part of the revolution for the liberation of the oppressed and the formation of the Kingdom of God on earth. My vocation as a Jesuit, as a priest, and as an approved member of the Catholic church is all secondary to my vocation to help Christ in the liberating revolution. During these crises I abandon myself entirely into the hands of my Father-God with complete confidence that he is using me as his instrument for the salvation of the world. During these crises I feel more united to Christ than ever; I feel, almost physically, his Spirit guiding me, giving me strength, and consoling me. How I thank and love Jesus and his Spirit that our Father gives me!

After reading this last paragraph you will understand when I say that 1979 was a year first of great expectation, and then of tremendous joy for me because of the triumph of the Sandinista revolution on July 19. From August of 1978 when the guerrilla squad sensationally took the National Palace of Managua and held all the congressmen hostage until Somoza freed the tortured Sandinista prisoners, including Tomás Borge and Daniel Ortega, I never missed the exciting broadcasts of the clandestine Radio Sandino. Every day over shortwave I followed step by step the advances and reverses of the armed insurrection of the people of Nicaragua under the leadership of the guerrilla army of the

Sandinista National Liberation Front (FSLN). I felt myself so identified with them, their fight for liberation was so thrilling, I had so many Honduran friends helping them, that I can say that July 19 was the most jubilant day of my life up to then. All my revolutionary friends sang and shouted with me: "If Nicaragua won (their liberation), El Salvador will win, then Guatemala, and then Honduras too will win!"

The most interesting part of it for the Christian revolutionaries of the whole world was how the masses of Catholics in general, and even to some extent the hierarchy of the Church in Nicaragua, for the first time in the history of modern revolutions, played a decisive role in the victory. Even though it was very late, just a few months before the triumph when thousands of good Catholics, including some priests, were already fighting with the guerrillas, for the first time a National Bishops' Conference published a pastoral letter justifying the rising up of the people in arms against an unjust government.

The Church teaches that a people can take up arms in a general insurrection when the four conditions of traditional moral theology for a just war are fulfilled: (1) When there is a situation of insupportable injustice or oppression, or as the bishops said in Medellín, quoting Pope Paul VI in *"Populorum Progressio"*: "Revolutionary insurrection can be legitimate in the case of evident and prolonged tyranny that gravely violates the fundamental rights of the human person and dangerously hurts the common good of the country, whether it proceeds from a single person or from evidently unjust structures." (2) When all the other nonviolent methods have been tried without success. (3) When the war will not produce worse injustices than the existing ones. (4) When there is probability of succeeding.

The Bishops' Conference said in their letter that all these conditions were present in Nicaragua in 1979. And we Christian revolutionaries of all Latin America affirm that all these conditions are present in El Salvador, Guatemala, Honduras, and in Haiti, Jamaica, Colombia, Peru, Chile, Paraguay, Bolivia, Brazil, and in all the countries of Latin America and of the Caribbean that are under the insupportable tyranny of imperialism.

One of the final points of my metamorphosis as a revolutionary was to understand that in Latin America it is the duty of all true Christians to sooner or later enter into and help as they can the armed revolution. If they really want the liberation of the oppressed, at least some priests should enter into the armed struggle as guerrilla fighters in order to give testimony to this Christian duty. How can an apostle of Christ encourage others to risk their lives in armed battle and stay at home, or go to the battlefront but without arms to help in battle? If love for the poor demands that a Christian sometimes has to fight in order to promote their liberation or to defend them, the priest, who is supposed to be the most exemplary Christian, should give an example of this kind of Christian love also.

I, at last, understood that in Latin America all the nonviolent methods for changing the unjust capitalist structures had been spent. As long as United States imperialism existed, there would be only one way to achieve the socialist revolution that we want— the guerrilla war of the armed masses united under a well-organized revolutionary vanguard. I understood that all true Christians had to be revolutionaries and help in this armed struggle for liberation: the priests, brothers, and nuns more than anyone.

In the actual process of making the revolution, the Nicaraguan Christians solved the theoretical problems of whether a Christian can be a Marxist and can fight in a civil war. If being a Christian demands being a revolutionary and a socialist, and to be a revolutionary and a socialist one has to use the Marxist-Leninist science of analysis and transformation of the world, then a Christian needs to understand Marxism. Once you study Marxism-Leninism, you lose your fear of this phantom with which the capitalist propaganda has filled us since we were children. Fighting side by side with the Marxists in the armed revolution for the liberation of the oppressed, Christians become Marxists, and Marxists become Christians (although often not members of the Church). This is the experience of Nicaragua.

I am sure that if a good Christian in the United States or in any other country would understand the analysis that Karl Marx makes of the capitalist system in his classic book *Capital*, showing scientifically that *the essence of the system is selfishness*, the alienation of human beings, and the exploitation of one human being by another, he or she would have to recognize that the captialist system is sinful and would have to do all he or she could to change this economic-social-political system. Since the very essence of the system is sinful, instills selfishness, we cannot just reform the system, we have to change it for another system, a type of socialism that seeks equality and brotherhood without social classes.

For July 31, the feast of Saint Ignatius of Loyola, Father General Pedro Arrupe came to Progreso with the two provincials to make the formal incorporation of the Mission of Honduras into the Central American Province. All of us who belonged to the Missouri Province or any other province of the United States or Spain had the choice of returning to work in the United States or in Spain or applying to the Central American Province, but just for work in Honduras. It was beautiful to see that not a single missionary wanted to leave Honduras.

On this same occasion Father John Willmering, who had been working in the parish of Morazán, was named the new superior of the Honduran Mission. Padre Alvaro Arguello and other Nicaraguan Jesuits who had come to Progreso for the occasion spoke to us about the beauty of the Sandinista revolution. Father Arrupe went back with them to Nicaragua the next day to see it with his own eyes and to talk to the Jesuits there about becoming united, for some of them were with the revolution and some were against it. His goal of unity was not achieved then or even today, two years later.

With Willmering as superior I felt freer to work with the ANACH and to spend time in Tegucigalpa organizing the Christians for Justice and CODDERHH (the human rights committee); after organizing CODDERHH in Progreso and being hidden by the bishop, I had been forbidden by my former superior to go to Tegucigalpa to organize CODDERHH. With the triumph of the revolution in Nicaragua and the enthusiasm of the revolutionary Jesuits there, and knowing that our Central American provincial was very good, I now felt much more support for my activities in Honduras.

I was spending a lot of time outside the Tocoa parish giving retreats and having the monthly follow-up meetings with campesino leaders for the study circles on the documents of the Christians for Socialism, and so on. In September I was in Tegucigalpa promoting CODDERHH, when I learned from the newspapers of a police action that was denounced by the Basic Christian Communities of Zamora and of other villages of our parish of Tocoa. The police agents of the FUSEP had broken open the door of my little house in Zamora at midnight on September 20, looking for me. Why would they look for me at midnight? The campesinos were terrified and thought that I would never return to Zamora. They were even afraid to meet for the Celebration of the Word of God.

When I rode into Zamora on my motorcycle a few days later, fixed the door of my little house, and went on with my customary activities, the campesinos got up their courage again to continue the struggle for their liberation. Nando and many of the leaders of the co-ops had demanded an explanation from the head of the FUSEP in Tocoa, but he simply denied that the FUSEP had anything to do with it, saying that it had to be thieves who broke into my house. However, several of my neighbors in Zamora, when they heard the powerful blows on the door of my house that night, had gotten up and recognized some of the FUSEP agents. Nevertheless, I was not afraid to continue to sleep alone in that little house. At any rate, I told the people, for me it would be the greatest of privileges if God would let me be killed on account of my activities for the formation of his Kingdom here in Honduras.

I have already told how we organized CODDERHH—Region of Tegucigalpa in a big assembly of the popular organizations in October. Our next region to organize was going to be La Ceiba, then Choluteca. But that is as far as I was to go in my work for the defense of human rights in Honduras; instead, my own were seriously violated on November 17.

I had just arrived on my motorcycle at our Center La Fragua about 7:00 A.M., coming from Camalote where I always stayed when I was around Progreso, when a DIN agent pulled up in a car with the head of the Immigration Office in Progreso to ask for me. He told me I had to bring all my personal documents and go with them to the San Pedro Sula Immigration Office right away. They said it was just to check over my papers because one was missing, and then they, personally, would bring me right back before noon.

I told them that I had just recently had all my papers checked, and therefore I would not go. They said that their chief in San Pedro Sula had to talk to me, but that we could go to the Immigration Office in Progreso and he could come here to see me. I said I would be there at 8:00 A.M., but with a lawyer. They accepted that and left. Sensing that this could be the day of my expulsion from the country, I packed a small bag, looked for a lawyer friend, Hector García and with my Jesuit brother Padre Ángel de Horna along as a witness, we went in Hector's car to the Immigration Office.

There the same agents told me that their chief could not come to Progreso, so I should let them see all my personal documents. After I handed them over, they told me I would have to go alone with them to San Pedro Sula. When my lawyer said that they could not force me to go like that, as a prisoner, without a written order from the judge, they answered by calling two soldiers from the FUSEP command post just down the block. The Immigration agent told them to put the handcuffs on me behind my back real tight, to punish me for not collaborating with them. This they did.

Then, after telling Padre Ángel and Hector not to follow, they put me into their car with them and took off for San Pedro Sula at full speed, leaving Ángel, Hector, and my handbag in the car in Progreso. We did not go to the Immigration Office, but to the main command post of the FUSEP on Third Avenue in San Pedro Sula, where they took all my belongings out of my pockets and the belt off my pants. They noted my name in their register, finally took off the handcuffs, and put me into one of the four cells of the small jail they have on the first floor.

All these cells were full of men. Mine had twelve prisoners and not enough room for all of us to lie down at the same time on the cement floor, which was completely filthy with cigarette butts, ashes, orange peels, and even vomit. Most of my cell companions were drunks, or drug addicts, or petty thieves whom the FUSEP had picked up in the last days.

During my hours in this pigpen, from 9:00 A.M. to 3:00 P.M., they kept taking some prisoners out and sticking others in. They literally threw in a young drunk whose clothes were completely drenched from the sobering shower they had given him. This got half the cell wet. The poor fellow took off all his clothes and lay down to sleep completely naked. Then they put three other young fellows in with us, who began to fight. Two of them wanted to kill the youngest one. They beat him quite a lot, until the rest of the prisoners pulled them off.

Relatives sent food to three of the prisoners, but the rest of us got nothing to eat; in these jails the government does not provide anything. I really felt sorry for these poor Honduran companions who were really just victims of the capitalist system, which often leaves the majority of the people in a frightening state of material, spiritual, and cultural poverty in the third world.

At noon we could hear from down the hall the radio of the soldiers announcing the latest news flash: "Padre Guadalupe captured and disappeared; Jesuits and bishops demand an explanation." It happened that Ángel, after my capture in Progreso, immediately told our superior, John Willmering, who went to San Pedro Sula to tell Bishop Brufaú. At about 10:00 A.M. they both went to see the head of the Immigration Office, who directly lied to them, saying that Padre Guadalupe was already on a plane flying to Miami, deported by decree of the military government.

Willmering telephoned our provincial in Saint Louis and then called Father Tom Halloran, who worked in the Jesuit Gesu parish in Miami, Florida. (Before that he had worked for many years with us in Honduras.) John asked Tom to go to the airport to meet me coming in on the morning SAHSA flight. An hour later Tom called Willmering to tell him that SAHSA arrived in Miami without me or any sign of me. With that, Willmering called Archbishop Santos in Tegucigalpa to investigate the "disappearance" of Lupe. That whole day of November 17, and the next day also, the radio was announcing my "disappearance."

About three o'clock in the afternoon the same two agents called me out of the cell, put the handcuffs very tightly on my wrists behind my back again, and took me in a DIN car to the Villeda Morales Airport of San Pedro Sula. In a private office of Immigration they locked me in a small broom closet. About 6:00 P.M. I started kicking on the door, and when they opened it I told them I had to urinate. The DIN agent took off the handcuffs and led me to the private bathroom for the Immigration employees. My hands were swollen and aching after over three hours of being handcuffed. On this trip to the bathroom, an employee of Immigration recognized me and later opened the door of my closet-prison to give me a sandwich and a small carton of milk that he had bought. I thanked him very much.

Then the Immigration officer opened my closet to read to me the decree of the military government, signed by President Policarpo Paz García, canceling my Honduran citizenship. They were going to put me on a plane that was leaving in a few minutes, deporting me to the United States. He said that I should not try anything or speak to anyone.

We got on the plane, which was of TAN airlines, when all the other passengers were already seated. When I was seated, he handed me an envelope with my belongings and a photocopy of the decree he had read to me, and he got off the plane. When we were in the air, I asked the woman in the next seat where this plane was going. She said to Miami, and asked me if I was the Padre Guadalupe who had disappeared. I told her yes.

In this way I became friends with several of these bourgeois Honduran passengers who were going to Miami. But the thought came to me that I would certainly prefer to remain in that pigsty police jail with the poor prisoners than with these well-to-do passengers on a plane to Miami.

I read slowly the Decree Number 360 of the ruling military junta, dated (notice well) March 19, 1979, whereas this was November 17:

> To resolve the solicitude presented to the Executive Power by the Ministry of Government and Justice, dated January 23 of this year, to obtain the cancelation of Decree Number 2142 of the Head of State of September 27, 1973, which granted the Letter of Naturalization to Mr. James Francis Carney, a single, male, adult, priest of North-American nationality. The Ministry of Government and Justice, through investigations of the Immigration Office, states as a fact that Mr. James Francis Carney, known as Padre Guadalupe, not only imparts Catholic doctrine, but he also dedicates himself to the propagation of dissociating doctrines and ideas which hurt the organized government of the country. This Ministry has in its hands a pamphlet entitled "A Call to All the

Honest Campesinos of the ANACH" of October 1978,
signed by Padre Guadalupe, in which he also hurts the U.S.
government and its embassy accredited in our country.
    CONSIDERING: that a foreigner is a naturalized Hondu-
ran when he receives the Letter of Naturalization; that the
Honduran nationality is lost by the cancelation of the Letter
of Naturalization; that all Hondurans are obliged to defend
the country, respect its authorities, and contribute to the
moral and material growth of the nation and of its public
order and security, which has not been fulfilled by Mr.
James Francis Carney. And CONSIDERING: that it is a
faculty of the Executive Power to grant and to cancel Letters
of Naturalization according to the Law and the Constitution
of the Republic. THEREFORE: The Governing Military
Junta, in use of its faculties and applying Articles 21 (No. 2),
23, and 201 (Nos. 3a, 34, and 45) of the Constitution of the
Republic, Article 2 of the Reformed Code of Administrative
Procedures, and Article 81 (No. 2) of the Law of Population
and Immigration Policy, DECREES: the CANCELATION of
Decree Number 2142 of the Head of State, dated September
27, 1973, which granted the Letter of Naturalization to Mr.
James Francis Carney, known as Padre Guadalupe, and
therefore the cancelation of his Letter of Naturalization.
This decree is to be transcribed in the Ministry of Foreign
Relations for its lawful effects. TO BE PROMULGATED.
POLICARPO PAZ GARCIA, Ministry of Government and
Justice,
    (signed) José Cristobal Díaz García.

On the airplane I was thinking that, since I had relinquished
my U.S. nationality to become a nationalized Honduran, and
now I had lost my Honduran nationality, legally I was a man
without a country. I wonder what they will do with me in Miami,
I thought. I hope they send me back to Honduras!
    When we reached Miami it was around 11:00 P.M. The au-
thorities there had already talked to Father Tom Halloran and
had decided to hand me over to the Jesuits of Gesu parish, who
would answer for me until the following Tuesday, when I had to
present myself at the Immigration Office in Miami. They called

up Gesu, and Tom came to the airport for me with the pastor of Gesu, a former theology teacher of mine at Saint Mary's, Father Edwards. So my exile in the States actually turned out to be a bourgeois vacation. Since I had been deported with just the clothes on my back, Tom lent me some money to buy everything I needed, and the Missouri Province later paid him back. Tom could not have been nicer to me.

What concerned me about Gesu was that the self-exiled, counterrevolutionary Cubans, and especially the most bourgeois among them, took this as their preferred parish. Besides this parish, the Jesuits in Miami had the famous Belén College (high school), which had been transferred from Havana together with many of its old Jesuit teachers of the Antilles Province. I had to be very careful how I talked around these Jesuit counterrevolutionaries and their disciples in Miami.

When I arrived for my date with the immigration authorities in Miami, who was the officer in charge of handling my case but the relative of a Jesuit friend who had worked about a year with us in Honduras. Well, he bent over backward to help me. He telephoned Washington and asked them to look for my name in the national files of Americans who had renounced their citizenship. While we were waiting for the answer, he took me out to a restaurant for lunch.

From Washington they called to say that they did not find my name in the files but would continue investigating my case. Meanwhile, I was given written permission to be in the United States for ninety days without any documents and was told that most probably they would give me a passport as an American citizen again, because I wanted to return to work in some country of Central America as soon as possible.

I tried in vain a number of times to call Honduras and also the provincial of Central America, Padre César Jerez, in El Salvador and Nicaragua. I talked with our new Missouri Provincial, Father David Fleming, and he gave me permission to work in any part of Central America, if Padre Jerez accepted me. How happy I was a few days later when I finally got through to Jerez in Nicaragua and he told me that he gladly accepted me! I told him I would prefer to work in El Salvador or in Guatemala with the poor campesinos or Indians who were already involved in the liberation struggle, but if I could not go there, then to Free Nicaragua. He promised to write to me in Saint Louis with my assignment. I told him I might as well take a month to visit my family (as we did every three years) and also take advantage of my stay in Saint Louis to make eight days of the Spiritual Exercises, individually directed by Father John Kavanaugh, who was the Missouri Province coordinator of the social apostolate.

I have copies of some letters I wrote to the Jesuits in Honduras while I was in the States, parts of which I include here because they show a deepened love and gratitude toward the Jesuits. On November 22, 1979, I wrote from Miami:

> Dear brother Jesuits in Honduras,
> You can imagine with what sorrow I say good-bye to you by means of this letter. But I have confidence that the separation will be of short duration. As the refrain says, "Separation makes the heart grow fonder." And thinking about all of you fellow missionaries of Honduras, I am filled with admiration and fondness, but also with shame for not having shown you more of my fondness and admiration in the past. I sincerely thank each one of you for your friendship, for your solidarity with me in my persecutions, and for your patience with me and with my idiosyncrasies. May God permit me to return to live and work with you all again in my beloved Honduras in a not too distant future!
> Your brother,
> Lupe

On December 22 I wrote from Saint Louis:

> My dear brother Jesuits of Yoro and Colón,
> I feel very humble and unworthy, and very grateful for the many magnificent demonstrations of solidarity and affection from so many people and popular organizations of Honduras, but principally for the friendship of you, my dear brother Jesuits. I am appreciating more and more how wonderful is this brotherhood we have, called the Society of Jesus. Also here in the U.S. I have received such affection and understanding from the Jesuits that it has left me con-

fused. I just finished my retreat here in Jesuit Hall of Saint Louis University, during which I meditated on Luke 15 and felt just like the prodigal son who returned to visit his brother Jesuits in the States after so long an absence, and instead of being criticized and questioned about this lack of contact, I was embraced and feasted. God treats me as a little child. I made an individually directed retreat under John Kavanaugh with great profit, and felt myself very united spiritually to all of you there in Yoro and Colón. May Jesus' Spirit guide you always!

Just today I received a letter from the provincial, César Jerez, with my assignment. He told me that the bishop of Estelí in Nicaragua has been asking for a team of Jesuits to help out in his diocese. Three or four of us Jesuits will take over the parish of Ocotal in February with Padre Agustín Torranzo, a Spanish Jesuit who worked in Estelí during the Sandinista war of liberation, as pastor. Till then, we will be living at the Colegio Centroamerica in Managua. This sounds very interesting and I am enthused. I also have a great desire to help the campesinos in El Salvador in this historic time there. Most of all, however, I want to return to work in Honduras as soon as possible. I hope you continue to help me recover my Honduran citizenship! I hope they take my case to the Supreme Court of Honduras and to the Interamerican Court of Human Rights in Costa Rica.

December 26 I will go back to Miami, where I hope to receive a provisional U.S. passport and, with a tourist visa from the Nicaraguan consulate, fly to Managua before the New Year. I talked on the phone to the official in Washington who decided my case, and he told me that, as far as they are concerned, I never lost my U.S. citizenship, even though U.S. law clearly states that if you become a naturalized citizen of another country, you automatically lose your U.S. citizenship. But the present policy is that if a religious nationalized himself in another country for religious reasons of a missionary vocation, he has double nationality and does not lose his U.S. citizenship. They are going to give me a letter stating all of this, because I don't want to hurt my chances for recovering my Honduran citizenship by accepting American citizenship, if it is interpreted as renouncing my Honduran citizenship. On the contrary, I asked them here in the U.S. to give me a document as a man without a country, or as a political exile; but they said they couldn't because I never lost my U.S. citizenship and they considered me an American. This would be true even if I recover my Honduran citizenship, which is what I want.

Your brother, Guadalupe

As soon as it came out over the radio in Honduras that I had been captured and expelled from the country, there were protests and public demonstrations by the Christian communities and the clergy and by practically all the popular organizations of the country. Every day for more than a month the newspapers and radio publicized some of the denunciations and protests. Friends in Honduras kept sending me the newspaper clippings, and Padre Jesús Sariego of our parish team of Tocoa sent me a big scrapbook he had made with over two hundred of these clippings about my case. This was just a part of all that was published in Honduras and in the international press. I also have clippings from the United States, Spain, Germany, Mexico, and elsewhere.

Padre Ángel de Horna sent me a list of the organized groups that managed to get their protests published in the Honduran newspapers. There are forty-seven of the Church and fifty-three of different other popular mass organizations on his list. Besides this, hundreds of other groups and individuals sent letters, telegrams, and pronouncements to the radio stations, or to the Jesuits and to the bishops. Ángel wrote me that few times in the history of Honduras have there been so many protests over a case of injustice, and not only pronouncements, but also mass rallies and even the taking over of churches and other buildings.

As examples of the Church pronouncements, besides those of many basic Christian communities, I have copies of those of the Jesuits of Honduras and of Central America; of the Honduran Bishops' Conference demanding, not my repatriation, but only my legal right to defend myself; of the bishop and clergy of the diocese of Copán; of the archbishop and clergy of Tegucigalpa, promising to take my case to court; of the clergy of Choluteca, of CONFERH (the religious of Honduras); of CLAR (the religious of Latin America); of the parish of Santa Rosa de Copán with a thousand signatures; and of the parishes of Sonaguera and Tocoa with two thousand signatures, after big demostrations with out-door masses in Sonaguera and Tocoa. All of these were demand-ing my return and denouncing the illegality of canceling my Letter of Naturalization without a judicial trial, as required by the consti-tution of the republic and the Universal Declaration of Human Rights of the United Nations Organization. Also, the Christians of Santa Bárbara sent me a cassette with a song they wrote about my case, called "Basta Ya" ("Enough Now").

As examples of those denunciations of the popular organiza-tions, besides those of SITRATERCO and of many other indi-vidual labor unions and co-ops, I have copies of those of COPEMH, COLPROSUMAH, ANACH, UNC, FUNACAMH, EAC, FESITRANH, CTH, CGT, FEUH, FESE, FMLH, MUP, PCH, PDCH, PASO, Honduran Patriotic Front, Christians for Justice, CODDERHH, and others. My favorite protest is from the Indians of the tribes of Yoro that I include here:

> From Subirana, Yoro, November 28, 1979:
> Meeting together in Subirana, we representative members of the Tribes of Subirana, Tablón, Mataderos, Las Vegas de Tepemechín, and Santa Marta, asked ourselves why it would be that Padre Guadalupe was expelled from here? We are not in agreement with this. Padre Guadalupe is the only one who has our confidence and has backed us up in everything, and we need him.

Valentín Castro signed it in the name of the five chiefs present, none of whom can write or even sign his name. I kept a copy of the letter I wrote as an answer to the tribes on December 22 from Saint Louis:

> Dear Indian brothers of the tribes of Yoro,
> With what joy I read the pronouncement of the tribes of Subirana, Tablon, Mataderos, Las Vegas, and Santa Marta demanding my return to Honduras! I thank you all very much! So many organizations have issued their protests against the injustice of taking away my Honduran citizen-

ship; but to tell the truth, of all of them the one that impressed me most was from you, the Indians, whom I love so much, and who up to now have been as though asleep, suffering in silence the injustices done against you.

That is why I wanted to write to all the nineteen tribes of Yoro to tell you not to wait any more for the Ladinos to come to help you, neither those of the government, nor of the Indian Institute. You yourselves have to be organized independently; if you want, you can use the Federation of Tribes, or the National Committee of Indian Tribes of Honduras (CONATRINH), but all the tribes should be in only one organization and avoid any division in the future. And then afterward, you should directly join FUNACAMH, which is the United National Front of Campesinos of Honduras, made up of the ANACH (the dissident part under Camilo Padilla), UNC, and UNCAH. You know you are part of the exploited and oppressed campesino class in Honduras who with the unionized workers should form a single solid block for the liberation of yourselves and of all Honduras. Christ came "for the liberation of the oppressed," as he himself said in Luke 4:18.

When there is a government in Honduras more favorable to the popular struggle, I hope to return to work with you again. But don't be afraid of organizing yourselves to demand your human rights. You are sons of God and brothers of Jesus Christ and, for being so poor, are especially loved by Christ. You must never betray Christ by sinning, nor betray your fellow Indians by selling yourselves to the Ladinos or big landowners, as some of the Indians have already done.

> Your brother,
> Padre Guadalupe

Five extraordinary things about my case caught the attention of the international press: First was the declaration, signed by the bishop and clergy of the diocese of Copán, that all those who had anything to do with my violent capture and expulsion, those who planned it and those who carried it out, were *ipso facto* excommunicated, according to the canon law of the Church. Since 95 percent of the people in Honduras are Catholics, this caused interminable discussions in the newspapers and radio programs until January 1, 1980, when Archbishop Santos celebrated the customary New Year's mass for the government in the Basilica of Suyapa. He appeared in a photo in the newspapers giving a big embrace, or "kiss of peace," to Gen. Policarpo Paz García, who had signed the cancelation of my citizenship.

Second was the taking over of the Cathedral of Tegucigalpa by young university members of the Christians for Justice, of the FEUH, FRU, and BRUS (of PASO), who used a loudspeaker in the tower to inform the people in the big plaza about the injustice of my expulsion. A commission of priests and the rector of the university dialogued with them after a few days, but they said they would not leave or open the cathedral until the government allowed me to return to Honduras. At last, FUSEP forced the door of the cathedral and entered with rifles to capture the occupants and take them away as prisoners.

Third, a few days later, a group of the FPH (the Honduran Patriotic Front) took over the Cathedral of San Pedro Sula demanding my return. And once again after a few days the FUSEP broke into the cathedral by force to take the peaceful occupants to jail.

Fourth, two weeks later the big parish church of Progreso was also taken, but in this way: The FPH held a big demonstration in the park in front of the church in Progreso on December 10 to celebrate the anniversary of the declaration of the United Nations about human rights. After the speeches demanding my return to the country and the release of the worker and campesino leaders in jail, the crowd was invited to a "mass of commitment to human rights" in the church. When the mass was over and the people left, twenty-three leaders of popular mass organizations with the Christians for Justice of Progreso took over the church and locked themselves in. Father Jack Donald, founder of CODDERHH with me, accompanied them to demand my return. After two days with much publicity in the mass media, when they figured their objective of public protest had been accomplished, they left the church before the FUSEP came to take them away prisoners.

Fifth, early in the morning on December 11 about thirty lead-

ers of high school and university student organizations peacefully took over the offices of the United Nations in Tegucigalpa.
They did so in solidarity with the occupants of the church in
Progreso and in protest to the United Nations for the violation of
human rights in Honduras in the cases of Padre Guadalupe and
of a number of worker and campesino leaders who were prisoners. After giving several interviews to international reporters to
get the desired publicity, they left the building at nightfall.

CODDERHH—Region of Tegucigalpa and FPH, with the help
of the lawyer Mauricio Villeda Bermúdez (the son of the former
president of Honduras) volunteered to help the Jesuits and the
archbishop take my case to the Supreme Court of Justice to prove
the unconstitutionality of the military government's procedure
against me. They also presented my case to the Interamerican
Commission of Human Rights of the OAS in Washington to start
the process for taking it to the Interamerican Court of Human
Rights in Costa Rica, which has my Honduran friend, Carlos
Roberto Reyna, as one of its seven judges. Our superior, John
Willmering, went to talk to Archbishop Santos to see if he would
back up the offer of Mauricio to represent the Church before the
Supreme Court, since the archbishop and clergy of Tegucigalpa
had publicly declared their intention of fighting the legality of my
case in the courts. But instead, the archbishop was glad that I was
out of Honduras and forbade Willmering to take my case to the
courts.

Nevertheless, on January 12, 1980, at their own expense, three
lawyer friends of mine came from Tegucigalpa to Managua to
see me, Mauricio Villeda, Cesar Murillo Selva (the president of
CODDERHH of Tegucigalpa), and Eduardo Martell (of PASO).
They wanted me to give them power of attorney to legally represent me, all three together or each one apart, in order to take my
case to the Supreme Court on their own initiative. With the help
of a Nicaraguan lawyer, I gladly signed legal documents to that
effect and gave them copies of all the documents I had. Some
Jesuits from Honduras had brought me the decree of my Letter
of Naturalization, my sworn renunciation of U.S. citizenship, and
the illegal Decree Number 360 canceling my Honduran citizenship. They also took back to Honduras with them the following
public letter, which PASO (the Socialist Party of Honduras)

printed up on a big, attractive poster to distribute and hang up
all over the country:

OPEN LETTER TO THE POPULAR FORCES
OF HONDURAS—January 13, 1980

After my unjust and illegal capture and deportation and
the cancellation of my Letter of Naturalization as a Honduran, I was amazed at the reaction on my behalf by all the
popular forces in Honduras. I have received clippings of
just about everything that has come out in the newspapers
about my case. I am writing this open letter to all of you because I could never write individual letters to the thousands
of friends who have shown their solidarity with me. This is
to sincerely thank from the bottom of my heart all the popular organizations of workers, campesinos, Indians, Delegates of the Word, teachers, students, women, Christian
communities, journalists, political parties and movements,
and also many professional persons and humble people who
on their own account showed their solidarity and their protest.

All of this has deeply moved me and has increased even
more my love for the Honduran people and my commitment to Christ and to you all to give all my energies and
even my life for the liberation of the oppressed of Honduras. I encourage all of you to unite yourselves for the
sake of this liberation, forgetting for now your ideological
differences. How happy I was to hear of the union of the
three most liberating campesino organizations in the United
Front, FUNACAMH! Would that all the popular forces
unite themselves in the FPH, the Honduran Patriotic Front,
and in CODDERHH, the Committee for the Defense of Human Rights! "We have to radically change the unjust economic-social structures of our countries," as several popes
and the Latin American bishops have said. The oligarchy
who have grabbed for themselves the power and the riches
in Honduras, exploiting the masses of workers for their own
benefit, are naturally opposed to these changes.

I am in Nicaragua now working in a rural parish with

poor campesinos and learning how to make these economic-social changes we want by the mobilization of all the people, the glorious Sandinista people. All the honest campesinos, workers, women, students, and professional persons are being organized to take part in the "popular power of the people" in Nicaragua.

Three Honduran lawyer friends of mine came to offer me their services to try to nullify the Decree Number 360 of the military government canceling my Letter of Naturalization. I hope that all of you will continue to back me up in the efforts to recover my Honduran citizenship. *I am a Honduran* —right down to the bottom of my being. No governmental decree can take away my desire to be a Honduran and to love Honduras and its people as my true homeland. I am sure that, with the help of God, I will return to accompany you in the great struggle for our liberation.

> Your fellow countryman and brother,
> (signed) Padre Guadalupe

I don't know all that happened, but the fact is that my lawyers did not get to submit my case to the Supreme Court before the lapse of time stipulated by law. But they and many others thought that I was sure to be included in the indult of general amnesty for prisoners that the Liberals promised to decree if they won control of the National Constituent Congress in the election for congressmen on April 20, 1980. The election was to start the process of returning to constitutional government after seventeen years of military dictatorship.

Under strict orders of the U.S. State Department, who called Policarpo Paz to Washington to tell him so, the cleanest election in the memory of the Honduran people was carried out. The Liberal Party won the majority in the Congress that was to make a new constitution for the republic and a new election law.

When the indult decree of amnesty came out and the jail doors were opened for almost all the prisoners, including the military and rich landowner murderers of "Los Horcones," Olancho, and also the union leaders of the Bemis-Handal, and the five guerrilla revolutionaries of the PRTC (Revolutionary Workers Party of

Central America) who were accused of having kidnapped the general manager of Texaco, everyone thought that I would receive a special amnesty also. But I did not.

The ANACH and many Liberal congressmen were going to make the motion in Congress, presenting about thirty thousand signatures of Hondurans requesting that Congress decree an amnesty for me to return to the country. It was the priests and nuns of our "charismatic group" who got the signatures of Christians in their parishes through the Delegates of the Word, and all the activists of the Committee for the Defense of the ANACH, under Julín Méndez, got signatures in the subsections of the ANACH controlled by them and in other worker and campesino organizations.

Julín, elected to the National Constituent Congress for PINU, along with other ANACH leaders, got an interview with President Paz García to ask for his approval of my amnesty to return to the country. He told them that it was a decision of the Supreme Council of the Armed Forces that Guadalupe would never be allowed to return. I also suspect that Archbishop Santos did not want the congressmen to grant me amnesty. So I remained in exile. At least I now know that I cannot hope to work legally in the Church apostolate in Honduras. But there are other ways that a priest can help in the struggle for the liberation of his people. I will talk about this at the end.

23. To Be a Christian Is to Be a Revolutionary

My stay in Nicaragua has been very profitable! I was part of the parish team of four Jesuits in Ocotal, Nueva Segovia, for a year, but I lived alone in a poor, dirt-floor champa in Mozonte. This is one of the little towns of the parish with about a thousand inhabitants, which is the center of a municipality with fifteen villages that I took care of. I was also named pastor of San Fernando, another small town and municipality with ten villages, which is an established parish by itself. I had to buy a motorcycle in Managua for this work. Since the two parishes of Ocotal and San Fernando reach to the border with Honduras, our people were in continual danger from incursions of the cruel ex-soldiers of Somoza, known as "contras." Thousands of them were in camps just across the border in Honduras, where they had fled in the last days of the popular insurrection of the Nicaraguan people. From there, with secret backing and arms from Honduran army officers and from the U.S. CIA and military advisers in Honduras, they sneak into Nicaragua in armed bands to steal cattle and money and to kill, preferably the campesino leaders of the Sandinista popular organizations in the villages near the border, many of whom are Delegates of the Word of God. This is the counterrevolution backed by the U.S. State Department.

In March of 1981 our good bishop of the diocese of Estelí, Rubén López Ardón, needed a priest for the very isolated and poor parish of San Juan de Limay of the department of Estelí. I offered to go because there were four of us in the Ocotal parish. At last my Ocotal team and the provincial gave me permission, and here I am living in another poor champa in the town of Limay, as I finish writing this book. The town of Limay has about four thousand inhabitants and is a municipality with thirty-five small villages that I visit, a few on my motorcycle and the rest on foot or horseback. I am alone in this parish with two American religious who are good Christian revolutionaries, Nancy Donovan of the Maryknoll sisters and Suzanne Deliee of the Mercy sisters of Connecticut. We form a good team with the lay leaders of the parish council and with many good, Christian revolutionary Delegates of the Word, most of whom also belong to the Sandinista militia.

On the one hand, then, I have been quite happy in Nicaragua, living this wonderful experience of the revolutionary process directly with some of the poorest campesinos in Nicaragua. (Both Mozonte and Limay have the reputation of being very poor areas.) But on the other hand, I have been very restless here in Nicaragua, not with the pastoral work of the Church, but because there is no longer any persecution here. There is no need to denounce and fight against injustices here. The whole organized population, the government, the police, the FSLN, are all doing this. I was used to fighting against repressive authorities and other dangerous enemies paid by the rich in Honduras; here in Nicaragua there are no repressive authorities, and the wealthy no longer control things.

In Honduras I had to teach secretly about the sin of capitalism and imperialism; here the government, the radio, the schools, all teach this liberating doctrine. In Honduras I had to encourage and help the poor to organize themselves in spite of the repression; here in Sandinista Nicaragua the government encourages and helps the masses to belong to the popular organizations. In Honduras the popular organizations (barely allowed to exist) have to take over streets and buildings, go on strikes, and so on to make the government finally listen to them; here the government listens and even obeys the Consejo de Estado (the State Council, like a Congress for passing laws) formed by representatives of all the popular organizations. In Honduras the power is in the hands of a small oligarchy of rich landowners, businessmen, and military officers who obey the U.S. embassy and the U.S. transnational companies; here there is "popular power of the people," and the former oligarchy and the gringos no longer run things. This is why they are crying, and lying about what is happening in Nicaragua, and making counterrevolutionary conspiracies.

I could write another book about this wonderful, popular, Sandinista, revolutionary process and about the intimate relationship between Sandinism, as it is lived today in Nicaragua, and Christianity. The bishops of Nicaragua, a few months after the triumph in their famous pastoral letter of November 17, 1979, titled "The Christian Commitment for a New Nicaragua," said that this revolution is original and different because the Christians and the Church are promoting it. Read carefully what they said in this same official document with regard to socialism and with regard to the class struggle:

If socialism means, as it should mean, giving pre-eminence to the interests of the majority of the Nicaraguans and following the model of a nationally planned economy with progressively more participation of all the people, we have no reason to object. A social project that guarantees the common destiny of the riches and resources of the country and permits that the quality of human life advances upon the base of satisfying the fundamental needs of all, seems very just to us. If socialism implies a continual lessening of injustice and of the traditional inequalities between city and rural life, between the remuneration for intellectual and for manual work; if it means the participation of the worker in the product of his work, thus overcoming his economic alienation, there is nothing in Christianity that implies a contradiction with this process.... With regard to the conflict between the social classes, we think that one thing is the dynamic reality of the class struggle that leads to a just transformation of structures, and a completely different thing is class hatred that directs itself against persons and radically contradicts the Christian duty of being ruled by love. [Page 8]

Here in Nicaragua I miss the dangerous struggle for the liberation of the oppressed in Honduras. I even had time to write this book during the last year, starting in my little shack in Mozonte, especially during my nights of solitary prayer, and finishing it now in my little shack in Limay, writing this by the light of a candle. Maybe God wanted my exile for this. I would certainly never have had time to write this during my continuous struggles in Honduras.

When I spoke to the provincial, Father Jerez, by telephone from the States in 1979 before coming to Nicaragua, I told him that I preferred to work either in El Salvador or in Guatemala where the revolutionary struggle is red-hot. In 1980, when I read about the murders of two priests in the department of

Quiché in Guatemala, leaving the Catholic Indians of two parishes without priests, I wrote to Father Jerez asking him to send me with another Jesuit to replace the priest-soldiers killed in action in Quiché. But shortly after, the bishop of Quiché pulled all his priests and nuns out of the diocese in protest for the repression and persecution of the Church by the government's armed forces.

I really liked the declaration of the CUC, the Committee of Campesino Unity, of the department of Quiché, one of the most dynamic organizations of Guatemala. They said that they did not want any priests to come to Quiché for now because, if they identified themselves with the campesinos and Indians in their struggle, they would be immediately murdered by government agents, and if they did not identify themselves with the cause of the people, the CUC would run them out of Quiché.

It is known that CELAM (the Latin American Bishops' Conference) under the archconservative, anticommunist bishop of Colombia, López Trujillo, has plans to neutralize the progressive priests and religious in all of Central America who favor revolution, especially in Nicaragua, El Salvador, Guatemala, and Honduras. The CUC knows of the agreement that CELAM has with the fascist military government of Guatemala to send a new bishop and conservative priests to Quiché not only to preach against communism but also to promote the "opium" of seeking salvation just in the next world while resigning oneself to the sufferings of this world.

CELAM is looking for this same kind of bishop and priests for Olancho in Honduras. There is talk about anticommunist Polish missionaries. CELAM is at present filling the minds of the Nicaraguan bishops with fear of the phantom of communism, and along with the bishops, some priests, nuns, and laypeople, in courses they are sponsoring in Nicaragua. Bishop López Trujillo and his well-selected helpers are trying to condemn and counteract the theology of liberation. But they will not be able to, because there is a new Church in Latin America, the Church born of the people, of the Catholic people struggling for their liberation. This is perfectly exemplified by the declaration of the Catholic campesinos of the CUC in Quiché, Guatemala.

In both of the parishes where I have lived in Nicaragua you can hear perfectly the two most influential radio stations of Honduras, Radio America and HRN. Every morning I hear the news reports and am up to date on the principal events taking place in my homeland of Honduras. I was glad to hear of the unification of the ANACH, UNC, UNCAH, and FECORAH in FUNA-CAMH (the United National Front of Honduran Campesinos)—and of the tremendous strike of ten thousand campesinos of all the co-ops of the Lower Aguan Project, backed by all of FUNA-CAMH.

The strike was to demand that the African palm oil extracting plants belong to the campesino co-ops of the ANACH and FECORAH, who are producing the palm nut in Colón, not to the corporation that the government formed with some rich private businessmen. The campesinos achieved their demand after striking for many weeks. This was what Rubén Erazo and I had been promoting in Colón for a number of years.

But also every day I get filled with sorrow and anger to hear of the brutal repression, torture, and murder of more and more leaders of the popular organizations by the police, or by paramilitary squads who are secretly under the police. How sad I was to hear the stupid election campaign in 1980 and 1981, spending so much energy and so many millions of lempiras for a process that is another huge deception of the poor masses of Honduras. The people love the carnival atmosphere of elections and blindly go to give their votes for one of the four legal parties, all of which are of the bourgeoisie who exploit them, and all of which are subservient to the gringos. Maybe experiencing once again this deception, the working masses at last will realize that by elections like these they will never win their liberation. The poor masses of El Salvador finally took up arms after two deceitful and fraudulent elections in recent years. The same thing happened in Guatemala. In Colombia 60 percent of the people no longer waste time going to vote.

One of the things that angers me most, especially over HRN radio, is hearing the continual campaign of lies during the last two years about the revolutionary process in Nicaragua: that there are no ex-soldiers of Somoza organized in armed bands along the border in Honduras who cross over into Nicaragua to steal and kill; that there is no longer freedom of expression in Nicaragua; that there is persecution of the Church; that the

Cuban Marxists control the country and are brainwashing the Nicaraguans, and so on, and so on. One commentator refers each day to the "Sandinista communists who have a totalitarian dictatorship worse than that of Somoza, directed by Cubans with Soviet money."

But this counterrevolutionary campaign of lies does not originate in Honduras; it comes from certain transnational news agencies, which belong to the richest capitalists-imperialists of the United States and Europe. These false ideas about Nicaragua are not only spread in Honduras, but in all the capitalist countries of the world. That is why the people of the United States, for example, know almost nothing of the truth about the very Christian Nicaraguan revolution. In general, they picture it as just one more socialist country dominated by the Soviets. As a result, they allow the U.S. government to cut off all economic help, including a loan to buy wheat in the United States, which has always been Nicaragua's principal source of wheat.

Talk about brainwashing: the people of the United States, a big percentage of whom are university graduates, are saturated with anticommunist propaganda from these transnational news agencies of the United States, especially television. They allow their present government to directly intervene again and again in the countries of the third world, with arms and military "advisers" for the most repressive and even genocidal governments. These governments use the weapons against their own poor masses of people, as in El Salvador, Guatemala, Honduras, Chile, Argentina, Paraguay, Uruguay, and so on, in Latin America alone, not to mention those regimes of the same kind in Africa, the Middle East, and Asia.

The U.S. military "advisers" in El Salvador are right now actually directing the armed forces of the genocidal Christian Democratic–military coalition government against the masses of Salvadoran people in rebellion. I read all about the system that the military officers of Latin America learn in the courses they receive in the U.S. military schools in Panama and in the United States. This system permits a small group of U.S. military experts, as "advisers," to really direct the operations of the whole army and of all the security and intelligence forces of the country that asks for their help. The saddest part for me is that the top Honduran military officers are those who have most completely sold themselves out to the gringos, and more than in any other country of Central America, they obey all the "suggestions" they receive from the U.S. embassy. How sad it was to hear of the sudden signing of the peace treaty between Honduras and El Salvador after eleven years of unfruitful negotiations, simply because of the sudden need to open diplomatic relations and the border between the two countries so the Honduran Army could help exterminate the guerrilla forces of the people of El Salvador that are close to the border!

What an example the humble revolutionary masses of Nicaragua, El Salvador, and Guatemala are giving to the humble masses of Honduras! My brothers, fellow Hondurans, wake up!

On December 23, 1982, I used Radio Venceremos, the hidden radio of the Salvadoran Revolutionaries, to speak to the Honduran people. I deplored the current, blatant United States militarization and occupation of Honduras. I described the new police state being set in place in Honduras. I called upon all Christian soldiers (Honduran, Salvadoran, Guatemalan) to refuse obedience to officers ordering the repressive killing and genocide of their own people. Some excerpts follow:

> My dear people of Honduras:
> I am taking advantage of the solidarity that there is between the oppressed Salvadoran and Honduran peoples to send my greetings by way of Radio Venceremos. I also send some thoughtful reflections to the entire honorable people of Honduras on the occasion of it being three years since my unjust and illegal explusion from Honduras, and on the occasion of the approaching great feast of the birth of our Savior, Jesus Christ. He came into this world "for the liberation of the oppressed," as it says in the gospel of St. Luke (Chapter 4, verse 18).
> Some Hondurans may ask, "Liberation from what?" For one thing, brothers and sisters, does it not bring you pain and make your blood boil, as happens with me, to witness how our country of Honduras, today more than ever before, is being sold away to serve the interests of the rich of the United States? Yes, the present leaders of government and the armed forces of Honduras are selling out their country. Honduras now is a country surrendered and completely su-

pervised: It is under the control of the Department of State
of the United States. The armed forces are directly under
the direction now of the "military advisers" of North America and their helpers. It is the same as with the armed forces
of El Salvador. I, for one, cannot be quiet! A true Christian
cannot be quiet when he sees such terrible injustices!

I want to congratulate our Honduran bishops, for their
recent forthright pastoral letter, through which the entire
episcopal conference denounced the ever-increasing, terrible
repressions in Honduras, by way of torture, kidnappings,
disappearances and assassinations by the military, and denounced the systematic violation of human rights and constitutional rights of Honduran citizens. A special note of
thanks is owed to the bishops for having denounced the formation of the civil defense committees, whose function it is
to help the repressive security forces to uncover the so-called
"subversives." By the antiterrorist law and the militarization
of the country, as if the National Congress had decreed a
state of siege, the ruling government of Honduras is following to the letter the fascist "Doctrine of National Security."
This is what the bishops in their statements to the country-
at-large have so wisely condemned. All of this the rulers try
to hide behind the hypocritical facade of a liberal, democratic government.

I call upon all my brothers in the military, rank and file as
well as officers, not only those of the army but also those of
FUSEP in Honduras, as well as those in Guatemala and El
Salvador, those who are Christians and who love their country, to bear in mind the power of God and his Commandments. As the martyred Archbishop Oscar Arnulfo Romero
said: "A soldier has the moral obligation to obey God before
obeying the order of an officer who wants to kill innocent
people."

How can a Christian soldier justify the torture and killing
of brother campesinos, including women and children, who
seek freedom and nothing more? How can a pilot, who is a
Christian, bomb a defenseless village of people who are his
own compatriots? I, for one, do not understand such a
thing! This is terrorism! Oh yes! These are horrible sins! A

truly patriotic soldier or officer should rather use his arms to throw out the gringos from his country for the sake of freedom for his country. A patriotic officer should have a sense of shame at seeing the army obey and serve gringos as if it were the point of a spear held against the people of Central America, people who want to be free rather than servile, who seek to make their country independent and sovereign.

Let us all pray: That God be our help in attaining peace! That the North Americans leave us in peace! That the high government officials of Honduras stop selling out their country! Oh, that the spirit of Jesus, Liberator, Savior, be born in the heart of each Honduran this Christmas!

Padre Guadalupe

Not long ago, in June of 1981, I had the opportunity to visit Cuba. I could say many good things about free Cuba and its revolutionary process. But Cuba is very different from Nicaragua. In the first place, it is not, and never was, as poor and underdeveloped as Nicaragua. On the other hand, the Catholic church in Cuba is much more underdeveloped than in Nicaragua, where the Church changed after Vatican II and Medellín and, in general has been with the poor, promoting the revolutionary process. The Cuban Church, both before and after the revolution has, in general, been with the bourgeoisie. Very few of its priests have lived with the poor. It was and, sad to say, still is, mostly pre–Vatican II, pre-Medellín. Most of the priests and lay Catholics do not know about the theology of liberation.

Many of the upper classes, the bourgeoisie, were anti-Batista and helped overthrow his regime, but after the triumph in Cuba they became counterrevolutionaries (the same as the anti-Somoza bourgeoisie in Nicaragua). Hundreds of thousands of these "Catholics" chose to escape from socialist Cuba, because they selfishly wanted the same privileges as before. This included most of the priests and religious. Many of these "bourgeois" priests, both inside and outside of Cuba, helped the counterrevolution try to overthrow Fidel Castro.

In the attempted invasion in 1961 on the beaches of Girón by the Cuban counterrevolutionaries (who came from the Nicaragua of Somoza with the direct help of the U.S. government and air force under John F. Kennedy), there were several of these priests. Very few priests have remained in Cuba; most of the ones who did remain are old, as are most of their parishioners. At the masses I attended in Cuba there were mostly elderly people, who clearly did not want to change their traditional style of Catholicism.

There is no persecution of the Church today in Cuba. It is a shame that the Catholics in Cuba (with a few very good exceptions) have not incorporated themselves into the human, socialistic, revolutionary process there. The youth of Cuba are with the revolution. They are socialists and, therefore, do not feel at home in the Catholic church there. In Central America, however, there are enough revolutionary, liberation theology priests to make the Church attractive to the youth.

We Christian revolutionaries believe that the construction of true socialism has not been fully completed any place in the world; not in the Soviet Union, not China, not Cuba. Thus, we Christian revolutionaries in Central America are not going to establish a Socialist government copying the Soviet model, nor any other model, but we will create a pure Central American model, and in Honduras, a pure Honduran model. These models will be completely impregnated with true Christianity that seeks the total liberation of men and women.

We Christian Revolutionaries of Central America believe that the basis of the new Christian Socialist system will be a spirit of equality and brotherhood, rather than seeking personal gain. This search for personal gain, inculcated continuously by propaganda, education, and structures of capitalism is a main cause of the injustices which we suffer at every level of life. The strongest, the most unscrupulous go ahead in the world. Meanwhile, the weakest and the workers are used by the owners as servants, or as a means of production. In the same way, the strongest countries, with the same selfish mentality exploit the poor countries. The nations often act like animals, the strongest eat up the weakest.

Under the capitalist system in which we live today (including Russia which has the same mentality, really), life is a struggle. My country is against other countries; my business is in competition with other businesses to see how much I can get. Even the worker has to be in competition with the other workers to see if he or she can get ahead. This is the so-called free enterprise system, free competition, free market, the consumer society. Well, this is what I call materialism. This system foments selfishness and injustices, hatred, and class warfare.

All this is contrary to what Christ taught us. Love your neighbor as yourself. If we are all brothers and sisters, men and women, white and black, professional people and illiterate people, Catholics and Communists, how can I accept that some have privileges and others none? How can we follow a system that demands that its members live only for themselves? Each one in opposition to others? Each one fighting to see what he or she can get?

We Christian Socialists want to help liberate people from this consuming drive for personal gain and to build a Christian Socialist society with structures that will not encourage self-seeking at the expense of the common good. The great means of production will belong to the entire community of people for the sake of all in order to redistribute the resources equally among the citizens. At the same time, there will always be private property for personal use, like family homes and family means of production without any exploitation of workers. Each one will work for the common good according to the individual's ability and receive an adequate wage for his or her work.

I could say that these two years in exile from Honduras have been for me like a long spiritual retreat, in which I am looking for the will of God for this revolutionary who has finished his metamorphosis.

Since "the task of every revolutionary is to make the revolution," the only question for me is: how? in what capacity? with which organization? I have the deep desire (which I am convinced comes from the Spirit of Jesus) to completely join the Honduran guerrillas. All of us Hondurans who are truly Christian should do so. Since I am now a Christian revolutionary, I now clearly understand that there is only one road that leads to the liberation of the oppressed in capitalist Honduras: the revolutionary war of the people. I am not less a Christian, nor less a priest, by also being a revolutionary. I am more Christian than ever; I can more truly love my neighbor, especially the poor. Now I can love them efficaciously, and really help in their liberation and salvation.

We Christian-Marxists who believe in God fight side by side in Central America with the Marxists who do not believe in God in order to form together the new socialist society of brothers and sisters, which will be pluralistic, not totalitarian, that is, which will respect the beliefs of everyone. A Marxist is never dogmatic, but is dialectical. A Christian does not dogmatically condemn anyone, but respects the beliefs of others. A dogmatic, anticommunist Christian is not a real Christian; and a dogmatic, anti-Christian marxist is not a real marxist.

I will have to give up being a Jesuit for a time, until the triumph, because the present laws of the Society of Jesus do not permit a Jesuit to be a guerrilla fighter. It pains me to have to do it, but I want to be honest and not hurt the Jesuits by joining the guerrillas as a disobedient fugitive from the Society, forcing them to expel me. My Catholic priesthood no one can take away from me; nor will I ever renounce it.

Ninety percent of the guerrilla fighters in Central America are Catholics and need the presence of a priest not only for the sacraments, but to help them reflect evangelically about what is going on. If the armies of the capitalist bourgeoisie can have their chaplains, with much more right the people's army of liberation should have its priest chaplains. At any rate, I have to be with my people in their struggle for liberation.

To finish my book, now that I have finished my metamorphosis, I invite all Christians who read this to get rid of any unfair and un-Christian prejudices you have against armed revolution, socialism, Marxism, and communism. I would hope that this book has helped you get rid of any mental blocks that you might have because of capitalist propaganda and a false, bourgeois version of Christianity that has been put into our heads since childhood. There is no contradiction whatsoever between being a Christian and a priest, and being a Marxist revolutionary.

Some Christian revolutionaries want to distinguish between "socialism," "Marxism," and "communism." Since there are so many types of socialism, a Christian can easily be a "socialist." Christians can also call themselves Marxists, while always explaining that though they accept and use this scientific analysis of society and method for transforming society, they do not accept the philosophical atheistic world vision of Marxism. Some want to reserve the use of the word communism to describe the totalitarian type of socialist society that has existed especially under the repressive regime of Stalin in Russia, which, of course, no Christian would want. But the regime of Stalin was neither socialist, nor Marxist-Leninist, nor communist.

We in the modern age will have to learn what real communism could be—a really Christian society, the Kingdom of God, which I have often described in this book. The socialism that we want is a necessary step toward this Christian communism. In the twentieth century there is no "third way" between being a Christian and being a revolutionary. To be a Christian is to be a revolutionary. If you are not a revolutionary, you are not a Christian!

Ad Majorem Dei Gloriam!—For the greater glory of God!

Epilogue: What Happened to Padre Guadalupe

The following epilogue is the result of a full year of investigation by the members of Padre Guadalupe's family. This investigation took the family to Honduras several times. We visited jungle villages, spent hours questioning cautious, tight-lipped military and embassy officials, spoke over Honduran radio and television appealing for information. We interviewed guerrilla prisoners, Church authorities, and human rights activists. We spent days studying Honduran newspaper accounts and spoke with hundreds of journalists and media people who were covering Honduras.

In the United States, the investigation took the family to Washington, D.C., several times. We continually wrote letters and made phone calls to the White House, Congress, the State Department, and the Intelligence Committee, and sought information under the Freedom of Information Act.

It would take another whole book to relate the frustrations and challenges of this family investigation. We have continually come up against two "cover-ups" of the truth: one by the Honduran military, one by the U.S. State Department, military, and CIA. We do not even have a body. Nor is there an effort to give us a body.

We share here the story of Padre Guadalupe's fate as we now see it. We promise to continue our investigation until all the truth is known with certainty.

*   *   *

His friends in the little Nicaraguan border villages never asked Lupe where he was going, but everyone knew. He had never hidden his intention of returning to Honduras. About July 17,

1983, he crossed the Rio Coco and was once again on his beloved Honduran soil.

Guadalupe was traveling with a group of ninety-six Hondurans of the Revolutionary Party of Central American Workers—Honduras (PRDC–H). Since Lupe had always been a chaplain to Honduran workers and campesinos, it was no surprise to find him as a chaplain and spiritual adviser to this group. They carried guns but had no trucks, no tanks, no planes, no supply lines, and very limited fighting experience, which, if any, consisted of battles against the CIA-directed Contras who were terrorizing and attacking Nicaraguan villages from Honduran bases. The group was hardly an army (or maybe *a very poor people's army);* but they did not have in mind the winning of a rich man's war but helping in a poor man's revolution. The group's mission was to help the poor campesinos and workers of Honduras fight for land and social justice. An exiled Honduran priest said Lupe was so touched that he cried when he was assured that he could accompany the group to Honduras. A Jesuit friend gave him a blanket for the cold mountain nights.

The Honduran side of the Rio Coco is triple-canopied jungle, dense, swampy, mountainous, jungle terrain, unmapped, untamed, and unpopulated. The small band had to hack their way through the jungle for eight or nine days before establishing their base camp at Congolón, high in the Codillera Entre Rios, where peaks reached 9,200 feet. The date was now July 26.

The military intelligence of Honduras and the United States were immediately aware of the camp at Congolón. By August 4, a special Honduran counterinsurgency task force was headquartered at Nueva Palestina, the only village in that jungle area. The following day, August 5, a special United States counterinsurgency force (one hundred and fifty paratroopers of the Southern Command) parachuted into the territory. Soon the small revolutionary group was cut off from food and civilian help, and was being hunted relentlessly in the heavy jungle.

All we know about Padre Guadalupe during this time comes from his captured companions, interviewed later by family members. Several prisoners spoke of sleepless nights spent talking with Padre Lupe about their families, their religion, and their dreams for Honduras. They also said he would "retire by himself to pray privately." After a month of living in the jungle, the prisoners said Padre Guadalupe was weak and tired but that "Lupe had no room in his head to give up, to quit. He never even mentioned the possibility."

The first "battle," reported by the Honduran military, took place on August 28. Some newspaper reports state that up to fifteen hundred Honduran troops were hunting for the revolutionaries assisted by U.S. advisers, intelligence, and helicopters. Three revolutionaries were reported killed in this battle.

On September 3, a second battle took place, with "mop-up" exercises on September 4. It is at this time that our family believes that Padre Lupe and Dr. Reyes Mata, the leader, were captured. We do not know the details of the September 4 battle, except that the Honduran Army reported that ten revolutionaries were killed. But we do know from General Gustavo Álvarez Martinez's letter that Padre Lupe's wooden chalice, his holy oils, his sacramental stole, his communion cloths, and his catechism material were "recovered" by a Honduran soldier on September 4.

The capture of Padre Guadalupe and Dr. Reyes Mata did not immediately reach the press. What did reach the press was the helicopter ride of General Álvarez to Olancho to take charge of the counterinsurgency operation. Our family's suspicion is that this arrogant, Argentinian-trained general flew to Nueva Palestina to oversee the interrogation of his long-time personal enemy. Padre Guadalupe had accused Alvarez of violating human rights and being "on the take" from the U.S. fruit companies before Lupe's expulsion from Honduras.

The prisoners were not held at the army tent camp in Nueva Palestina for long. The only prison for the revolutionaries was a rectangular pit dug in the ground behind the army tents. (Our family spotted this pit during our investigation; the Honduran helicopter flew us over the spot by mistake.)

Alvarez acted quickly; on September 5 peasant workers at the secret CIA-directed military base at El Aguacate reported four helicopters arriving with Álvarez and his prisoners. Since no one (reporters, congresspeople, etc.) can visit this secret base from which the Contra bombing of Nicaragua takes place, this CIA base was a perfect place for secret interrogations, tortures, and executions. The prisoners were interrogated "efficiently" on September 5 and 6. Using this information, remnants of the revolutionary group were located for battles on September 7, 9, 10, and 11.

By this time the press was becoming suspicious. U.S. reporters were beginning to ask questions about U.S. military participation in the battles, U.S. helicopters transporting Honduran soldiers, U.S. planes flying reconnaissance, U.S. intelligence debriefing prisoners. Honduran newspapers also started to print some news. *El Heraldo* reported that Dr. Reyes Mata was captured on Saturday, September 10, "by Honduran troops with U.S. advisers." *El Heraldo* also said that the story was confirmed by the families of soldiers living in Juticalpa near the CIA base at El Aguacate. Word was starting to leak out about the prisoners at El Aguacate. It is not surprising that there was and is some confusion about battle dates, places, and prisoners; the Honduran and U.S. military, the Honduran government, and the U.S. State Department control all information very carefully in Honduras.

But the truth will out. By September 14–15, the Honduran press was full of news concerning the prisoners. We believe it was at this time, if not sooner, that the decision was made by the top Honduran military, with the knowledge and compliance of its U.S. "advisers," to eliminate Padre Guadalupe and Dr. Reyes Mata. Their imprisonment could no longer remain hidden.

We do not know the exact details of what happened to Guadalupe. Perhaps he did starve to death in prison (thus the rumor of starvation). The Honduran peasants say "Lupe would only starve to death if he were confined within four walls." Perhaps he was just allowed to die for lack of medical care. Perhaps he was tortured to the point of death, the interrogators using up his last remaining strength and it was this that gave rise to the rumor that "he died of exhaustion." Since we have not yet received Lupe's body, perhaps he is still in an underground prison somewhere. We will continue our investigation until we know the complete truth.

We include here a report brought to our family by the Christian Human Rights Organization of Honduras. The captured companions of Padre Guadalupe, who were one source for this report, have since been killed.

October 1983
DENOUNCEMENT BY THE CHRISTIAN HUMAN RIGHTS COMMISSION OF HONDURAS—CCRIDEHH

Military Advisers of the North American CIA torture in hidden-away Honduran Prisons and Carry on Repression of the People.

1. One hundred and thirty-four CIA agents (officially working in Honduras as employees of the North American embassy, AID, and as advisers) are carrying out acts of repression against the Honduran people and are helping and directing the Somacista group, Democratic Force of Nicaragua (FDN).

2. One of the main areas where these agents work is on the Honduran-Nicaraguan border, known as the banks of the Patuca River in the department of Olancho. The main headquarters of the XII Battalion of the Honduran army is the base at El Aguacate. The campesino people in the area have seen these North Americans when they lead the task forces of the Honduran army and of the Somacista group, both in their attacks against Nicaragua as well as in the counterinsurgency exercises, which they have been carrying out since August.

3. These North Americans* participated directly in the tortures and interrogations that ended with the cowardly assassination of the priest James Carney (Padre Guadalupe), also of other revolutionary leaders. These acts took place in the middle of September in two hidden basements that they were using at El Aguacate, where the FDN also watch over the weapons and ammunitions donated by the CIA.

4. These data and much more are the object of a major investigation. They show the executive and foul role that the Honduran army permits the CIA and other military troops that occupy Honduras to play.

5. We also denounce that the rural areas of Honduras have been converted into regions of terror, because of the actual maneuvers of the Big Pines II. Recently in the area of the Lower Aguan, not quite fifteen kilometers from the regional center of the military encampments (CREM), three campesino leaders were assassinated (two of them were Delegates of the Word of God) by part of a task force directed by the Green Berets. The campesinos who were assassinated and their other companions were resisting their displacement that the army was causing, in order to use land that belonged to the campesinos for the construction of the installations of the military base of the CREM.

6. We call upon all the Christians of the world to intensify their strug-

---

*We have removed the names of the two CIA agents and a Honduran military officer for the sake of our investigation, but they have been submitted to the House Intelligence Committee of the U.S. Congress.

gle against war and against the military intervention that the United States is carrying on in Honduras and in other Central American countries.

Juticalpa, Olancho, Honduras.
Christian Human Rights Commission of Honduras (CCRIDEHH)

Predictably, on September 16 the Honduran military denied to all news media the existence of prisoners at El Aguacate. Two days later, the Honduran military released its first, final, and official position regarding the disappearance of Padre Guadalupe. *They said that they knew nothing.* However, they said that a prisoner, during interrogation, speculated that Padre Guadalupe *probably starved to death in the jungle.* To this day, all Honduran and United States government agencies give this "official" position. Officially therefore, Padre Guadalupe has become one of *los desaparecidos* (the disappeared).*

We conclude Lupe's story with what might well be his last words. It seems that in El Aguacate prison a Honduran soldier lent Lupe his Bible. In the margins of this Bible, Lupe wrote some messages. This Bible was given to our family with Lupe's wooden chalice, stole, communion cloths, and catechism.

In the Old Testament section of the Bible in the Book of Jeremiah is the story of Jeremiah being held prisoner in the bottom of a cistern in his own country's military base. His crime was challenging the conscience of his people. Here Lupe wrote *"hombres sufridos porque hablaron la verdad"* ("Men are suffering because they spoke the truth"). Certainly he was telling us where he was being held, what was being done to him, and how he lived and suffered for the truth.

Joseph and Eileen Connolly
Family Members of Padre Guadalupe

---

*For a more detailed investigative report on the fate of Padre Guadalupe see George Black and Anne Nelson "Mysterious Death of Fr. Carney" *The Nation,* August 4–11, 1984.

Acknowledgments

The family of Padre Guadalupe Carney thanks the members of the United States, Honduras, and international press for their help and kindness during our investigation, especially during our trips to Honduras. We owe special thanks to Don Marsh, Ian MacBryde, and Chris Michelswirth of ABC Television, Channel 2, St. Louis, for their trip to Honduras to cover the initial stages of our investigation. Reporter Bob Adams of the *St. Louis Post Dispatch* was an inspiration during this investigative period.

We thank Colin Cameron and David Jessel from the British Broadcasting Corporation (BBC) "Heart of the Matter" series, for their two documentaries covering our second trip to Honduras as well as our investigative efforts in Washington, D.C. Two investigative reporters, George Black and Anne Nelson, were extremely helpful during this second period.

Our report given in the epilogue is a summary of our family investigation. In thanking the media for their interest in the disappearance of Padre Guadalupe, we in no way imply that we represent their thinking. We have come to have a deep respect for the sacred trust held by these men and women of the media who have as their profession both to seek and tell the truth.

Glossary

ACPH	Honduran Popular Cultural Action
AFL-CIO	American Federation of Labor-Congress of Industrial Organizations
AID	Agency for International Development
AIFLD	American Institute for Free Labor Development
ALCONH	New campesino organization formed by those who walked out on a corrupt ANACH convention
ALIPO	Progressive movement in the Liberal Party
Alliance for Progress	Organization created by President John F. Kennedy to enact social reforms in Latin America
ANACH	National Association of Honduran Campesinos
ANDEP	National Association of Delegates of the Word
an apostolate	a particular evangelical work
Apostleship of Prayer	An organization headed by the Jesuit General, dedicated to spreading devotion to the Sacred Heart of Jesus and to praying for the intentions of all its members
Association for Human Promotion	An agency which organized all types of co-ops and gave loans and technical help

barrios	neighborhoods
BCC	Basic Christian Community—"a church born from the people"
BID	Bank of Interamerican Development (same as IDB)
Big Pines II	Open-ended amalgam of U.S. Military "exercises" including training, airfield costruction and joint maneuvers with the Honduran Military from August, 1983 to March, 1984
Blessed Sacrament	The Body of Christ under the appearance of bread
CARACOL	Regional Agricultural Cooperative of the ANACH of Colon
CARAGUAL	Regional Agricultural Cooperative of the ANACH in Guaymas
CARAL	Regional Agricultural Cooperative of the ANACH of Atlantida
CARITAS	A self-supporting philanthropic group who follow guidelines of secular institutes and work with the poor and oppressed
CASIL	Agricultural Cooperative of San Isidro Limited
campesinos	peasants
Caballeros de Christo Rey	Movement which tried to incorporate more men into the active life of the Church
catechists	Lay teachers of Christian Doctrine
Celadores	Group within the Apostleship of Prayer

CELAM	Latin American Bishops Conference
CESA	Center for Agricultural Services
CGT	Central Confederation of Workers
champa	Shack with dirt floor, roof of palm leaves, and walls of sticks either tied with vines or of mud plastered on a network of sticks tied together
CIA	Central Intelligence Agency (U.S.)
CIAS	Center for Investigation and Social Action of the Jesuits in Colombia
CIOSL	International Confederation of Free Labor Organizations
CLAR	Religious of Latin America
CLES	High school student organization
CODDERHH	Committee for the Defense of Human Rights in Honduras
COHBANA	Honduran Banana Corporation
COHDEFOR	Honduran Corporation for Forest Development
COLPROSUMAH	A teachers organization
CONCORDE	National Coordinating Committee for Development
CONDECA	An anti-Communist organization
CONATRINH	National Committee of the Indian Tribes of Honduras

COPEMH	A teachers organization
CONFERH	Religious of Honduras
CORFINO	The Forest Industry Corporation of Olancho
Consejo de Estado	In Nicaragua the State Council for passing laws
coyote	wolf—in Honduras a middleman who bought crops at a very low price by paying in advance to the producers before the harvest
CREM	Center for Regional Military Instruction
CTH	Confederation of Workers of Honduras
CUC	Committee of Campesino Unity in Guatemala
Cursillos de Christiandad	A short course of basic Christianity which has for its goal converting nominal Catholics into active Christians
CUS	A labor union federation
Delegates of the Word	Lay leaders of the Church in small communities
DESAL	Institute of the Catholic University in Chile
DIN	(Same as DNI) Department of National Investigation—the secret police
EAC	Associative Agro-Industry of Campesinos
EACA	Associative Agro-Industry of Campesinos of the area of Guaymas

ejidal	township
FANAL	Largest campesino organization in Colombia
FAO	United Nations Organization for Cultural Development
FASH	Authentic Federation of Labor Unions of Honduras
FBI	Federal Bureau of Investigation (U.S.)
FECESITLIH	Central Federation of Free Workers Unions of Honduras
FECOAGROH	Federation of Agricultural Cooperatives of Honduras
FECORAH	Federation of Agrarian Reform Cooperatives of Honduras
FECOPANH	A community development committee
FED	An organization of high school students
FEMUC	Federation of Campesino Women, united to the UNC
FENACH	National Federation of Honduran Campesinos
FENAGH	National Federation of Cattlemen
FENAPOCOMH	A community development committee
FENTCH	National Federation of Farm Workers
FEPAIN	A community development committee
FES	University student organization

FESE	Federation of Secondary Education Students
FESISUR	Federation of Labor Unions of the South
FESITRANH	Trade Union Federation of National Workers of Honduras
FEUH	Federation of university students of Honduras
First Probation	First week of the Jesuit novitiate, getting to know the novitiate and its rules and making a retreat to see if one is serious about his vocation
FMLH	A political movement
FPH	A political movement
FRENACAIN	Campesino national organization
FSLN	The Sandinistas in Nicaragua
FRU	University Front for Reform
FUNACAMH	United National Front of Campesinos of Honduras
FUR	University Revolutionary Front
FUUD	United Democratic University Front, a right wing organization
FUSEP	Public Security Force (police in Honduras)
G-2	Army secret intelligence service
IDB	(same as BID) Bank of Interamerican Development

INA	National Agrarian Institute
ITT	International Telephone and Telegraph, a multinational corporation
JPC	Justice and Peace Commission
juniorate	In Jesuit seminary basically the first two years of university studies, following the novitiate
Legion of Mary	Worldwide organization of lay Catholics, under the patronage of the Blessed Virgin Mary, who participate in every aspect of the lay apostolate except taking care of material needs which is the function of the St. Vincent de Paul Society
Liberation Theology	That theology based on the gospel teaching of Jesus who taught and exemplified God's special concern for the poor, who opposed the exploitation of the weak by the powerful, and who spoke of a liberating God. This theology draws parallels between the biblical experience of total liberation and contemporary experiences of third world people struggling against the modern oppressor system
Licentiate in Theology	Theological Degree received by Jesuits after completing four years of theology, the equivalent of a master's degree in a secular university
Lower Aguan Valley Project	Begun in 1968 with a loan from IDB whereby agrarian reform cooperatives would plant sixty thousand acres of African palm trees with a contract to sell all the oils from the fruit of these trees to Standard Fruit Company, and another twelve thou-

sand acres of citrus fruit trees with an assured market in Germany

machete

a large knife

Mancha Brava

"The Angry Mob," a paramilitary force backed by the Nationalist Party and the army

Medillin Conference

A conference of Latin American bishops held in Medillin, Colombia, in 1968 which reaffirmed that God wants the liberation of the oppressed, thus giving impetus to the liberation theology of Latin America

milpa

corn

Minor Orders

The four ecclesiastically instituted grades leading to the major orders of subdeacon, deacon, and the priesthood. They are the order of porter or doorkeeper, lector or reader, exorcist, and acolyte.

MISEREOR

Organization of German bishops

monitores

Campesinos who know how to read and help other campesinos put into practice what the teachers in the radio schools tell them to do

MUP

A political movement

NDB

National Development Bank

novitiate

First two years of Jesuit spiritual training in the seminary after which vows are taken

OBEC

Organization of Banana Exporting Companies

OIT

International Labor Organization

ONIS	Organized group of progressive priests in Peru
OPEC	Organization of Petroleum Exporting Countries
ORIT	Interamerican Regional Organization of the OIT
PASO	Socialist Party of Honduras
PCH	Communist Party of Honduras
PDCH	Christian Democratic Party of Honduras
PCMLH	Marxist-Leninist Communist Party of Honduras
philosophate	In Jesuit seminary it follows the juniorate and consists of three years of further study with a heavy concentration on philosophy
PINU	Innovation and Unity Party
PRH	Revolutionary Party of Honduras
PRICPMAH	A teachers organization
PROCCARA	Program for Campesino Formation in Agrarian Reform
PRTC	Revolutionary Workers Party of Central America
Radio Schools	Classes given to campesinos via the Church-owned radio station in Honduras
regency	That part of Jesuit training which consists of three years of teaching after completing the philosophate

SAHSA	Airline which services Honduras
SAL	Organized group of progressive priests in Colombia
S.J.	Society of Jesus (Jesuits), a Catholic order of Religious founded by St. Ignatius of Loyola in 1538
SJC	St. John's College, located in Belize
SITRACOAGS	Labor union of Sula Banana Company in Guanchias
SITRAINA	Labor union of INA employees who were dynamic in denouncing corrupt INA authorities
SITRATERCO	Syndicate of Workers at Hard Labor of the Tela R.R.
SINEPUDERH	A teachers organization
SLUH	St. Louis University High School
Spiritual Exercises of St. Ignatius	Written by St. Ignatius, founder of the Jesuits, they are the basic experiences which form a Jesuit
Standard Fruit Company	One of the largest multinational corporations in Honduras, a subsidiary of Castle and Cooke
SUTRASFCO	Labor union of the Banana Farms of Standard Fruit
TAN	An airline servicing Honduras
Tela R.R. Company	Honduran name for United Brands, a subsidiary of United Fruit Company

theologate	Three years of study in theology before ordination to the priesthood, and one year following
Third Probation	Final year of Jesuit formation after ordination, usually after a year or two of experience, after which final vows can be taken (frequently called Tertianship)
UAW	United Auto Workers
UFW	United Farm Workers
ultreya	Meeting of members of the "Cursillos" to reinforce their commitment
UNC	National Union of Campesinos
UNCAH	New National Union of Authentic Campesinos
United Brands	Tela R.R. in Honduras, a subsidiary of United Fruit Company
United Fruit Company	One of the largest multinational corporations, owns United Brands (Tela R.R. in Honduras)
U. of D.	University of Detroit
URP	Peoples Revolutionary Union
USO	United Service Organization, established during World War II for U.S. servicemen— "a home away from home"
UTC	Union of Workers of Colombia
wolves	(same as coyotes) middlemen who exploit the campesinos

Index

FASH (Authentic Federation of Labor Unions of Honduras), 196
Fate of Father Guadalupe, 442–447
Favors, superstitions about, 141
FECESITLIH (Federation of Free Labor Unions of Central Honduras), 191; retreat with, 294
FECOAGROH, 214
FECORAH (Federation of Agrarian Reform Cooperatives of Honduras), 214–216, 233; and ANACH, 264; Lower Aguan Valley project and, 360; salaries accepted by, 361
FEMUC (Federation of Campesino Women, UNC), 385
FENACH, 134, 148; U.S. embassy and, 188, 189
FENAGH (National Federation of Cattlemen), 277
FENTCH (National Federation of Farm Workers), 196
FESISUR (Federation of Labor Unions of the South), 196
FESITRANH (Federation of Labor Unions of Northern Honduras), 189, 191, 192, 194; and ANACH document, 304; 1967 International Workers' Day rally, 224; retreat for, 294
Fidalgo, Juan, 348
First Holy Communion, 4
First International Meeting of Christians for Socialism, 306
First Probation week, 73, 75–76
Fisher, Father John, 125, 126, 196
Fisher, Father Joseph, 73–74, 79, 223, 236–237, 250; defense of Father Guadalupe by, 296; and Indian co-ops, 298; and Radio Progreso, 240; and Sulaco mission, 348
Five-Year Development Plan, 333
Food: in barrios, 180; prices of, 182
Football scholarship, 14
Ford factory, Detroit, 56–57, 62–63
Forest Park, Saint Louis, 13
Forestry co-ops, 274–277
Fort Benning, Georgia, 23
Fort Chaffee, Arkansas, 33–34
Fortín, Luis Bográn, 212–213
Fontainbleau, France, 45

Foucauld, Charles de, 92, 93–95, 110, 152
4-F classification, 16
FPH (Honduran Patriotic Front), 400; protest of expulsion, 424
France in World War II, 32–41
Franciscan sisters, 171–172, 204, 263
Francis Xavier, Saint, 84
Freire, Paulo, 203
FUNACAMH, 426
FUSEP: and Cadabón, Father, 401; and Radio Progreso, 406; at Zamora champa, 413
Fusz Memorial, 89
"The Future of the Church and Religious Life," 351–356

Gale, Oscar, 189, 251
Galeas, Efraín Díaz, 192, 194–196, 232, 233, 235, 360
Gandhi, Mahatma, 92, 95–96; doubt in, 310
Garaudy, Roger, 303
Garcia Birichiche Farm, 329
García, Juan Manuel, 268
Garcia, Policarpo Paz, 389, 424
García, Ruth, 344
Garméndia, Benjamín, 233, 360
General strike, September, 1968, 243–252
German prisoners of war, 43–44
G.I. Bill, 50
Girardi, Julio, 303, 311
God: abandonment to, 93; arguments against existence of, 32; knowledge of, 8; proofs of, 74–75; requests to, 8–9
Gold resources, 184
Golf, 108; caddy job, 5
Gómez, Chema, 375
Gómez, Francisco, 378, 394
Gonzales, Céleo, 189, 194, 218, 219, 304, 380, 381; in 1968 general strike, 243
Grace, actual, 92
Grace and the Human Condition (Segundo), 290
Grande, Father Rutilio, 372
Grandparents, 3
Grimaldi, Father Bob, 376
Gross, Father Steve, 162, 269, 321, 344; and Centro Loyola, 345

USO, 45–46
UTC (Union of Workers of
Colombia), 151

V-1, V-2 rockets, 37–38
Valencia, Bishop, 150
Valenta, Jack, 73
Vallejo, Roberto, 240
Van Vleet, Father Paul, 103, 165; at
Yoro Mission, 107
Vatican, visit to, 47–48
Vatican Council II, 236, 237
Vekemans, Father Roger, 199–200
Venereal disease, Army information
on, 28–29
Villartoro, David Fúnes, 264
Villegas, Elías, 214–215
Virgin Mary, 9
Virgin of Guadalupe: choosing name
of, 128; requests to, 116
Vocation, crisis of, 64–68
Voss, Father Bob, 316, 388; at Yoro,
338, 348
Voullaime, René, 94
Vows: delay of, 176–177; final vows,
236; first vows, taking of,
83–84

Wade, Father Jarrell Patricio,
202–204, 240, 242, 315
Wainwright, Juan Pablo, 187
War with El Salvador, 9, 253–272
Waters, Father John, 263
Weber, Father Leo, 316–317, 408
Whelan, Marty, 73
Willmering, Father John, 412, 415, 425
Wood production, 183–184
Woods, Charlie, 97, 100–101, 102;
assignment of, 121
World War II, 23–49

Xicaque Indians. *See* Jicaque Indians

Yorito parish, 273–277
Yoro mission, 103–104; assignment
to, 107; 1961 trip to, 116–120;
1962 assignment to, 130–131; in
1975, 338–348; popularity with
youth, 144; popular religion at
136–140

Zamora champa, 386; FUSEP, 413
Zapotal Indians, 340
Zelaya, Lorenzo, 188
Zelaya, Mel, 346
Zelaya, Porfirio, 340